C000284013

# Psychology
## Study and Revision Guide

Jean-Marc Lawton
Eleanor Willard

Every effort has been made to trace all copyright holders, but if any have been inadvertently overlooked, the Publishers will be pleased to make the necessary arrangements at the first opportunity.

Although every effort has been made to ensure that website addresses are correct at time of going to press, Hodder Education cannot be held responsible for the content of any website mentioned in this book. It is sometimes possible to find a relocated web page by typing in the address of the home page for a website in the URL window of your browser.

Hachette UK's policy is to use papers that are natural, renewable and recyclable products and made from wood grown in well-managed forests and other controlled sources. The logging and manufacturing processes are expected to conform to the environmental regulations of the country of origin.

Orders: please contact Hachette UK Distribution, Hely Hutchinson Centre, Milton Road, Didcot, Oxfordshire, OX11 7HH. Telephone: +44 (0)1235 827827. Email education@hachette.co.uk. Lines are open from 9 a.m. to 5 p.m., Monday to Friday.  You can also order through our website: www.hoddereducation.com

ISBN: 9781510449534

© Jean-Marc Lawton and Eleanor Willard 2019

First published in 2019 by

Hodder Education,

An Hachette UK Company

Carmelite House

50 Victoria Embankment

London EC4Y 0DZ

www.hoddereducation.com

Impression number  10 9 8 7 6 5 4 3 2

Year       2023 2022

All rights reserved. Apart from any use permitted under UK copyright law, no part of this publication may be reproduced or transmitted in any form or by any means, electronic or mechanical, including photocopying and recording, or held within any information storage and retrieval system, without permission in writing from the publisher or under licence from the Copyright Licensing Agency Limited. Further details of such licences (for reprographic reproduction) may be obtained from the Copyright Licensing Agency Limited, www.cla.co.uk

Cover photo © nosha – stock.adobe.com

Typeset in Goudy Oldstyle Std 10/12 pts by Aptara Inc.

Printed and bound by CPI Group (UK) Ltd, Croydon, CR0 4YY

A catalogue record for this title is available from the British Library.

# Contents

# How to use this study and revision guide

Welcome to the *Psychology for the IB Diploma Study and Revision Guide*. This book will help you plan your revision and work through it in a methodical way. The guide follows the Psychology syllabus topic by topic, with revision and exam practice questions to help you check your understanding.

You can keep track of your revision by ticking off each topic heading in the book. Tick each box when you have:

■ revised and understood a topic

■ used the exam-type questions.

Use this book as the cornerstone of your revision. Don't hesitate to write in it and personalize your notes. Use a highlighter to identify areas that need further work. You may find it helpful to add your own notes as you work through each topic. Good luck!

## ■ Features to help you succeed

**Expert tip**

These tips give advice that will help boost your final grade and identify typical mistakes that students make and explain how you can avoid them.

**EXAM-TYPE QUESTIONS**

Practice exam questions are provided. Use them to consolidate your revision and practise your exam skills.

**Key terms**

The definitions of essential key terms are provided. These are words that you can be expected to define in exams.

**■ STRENGTHEN YOUR LEARNING**

This feature consists of comprehension-style exercises that can be found at the end of each section. The idea of this feature is to reinforce your knowledge and understanding of the topics featured and to help prepare you to attempt some exam-style questions.

To answer the questions, use the information contained within the study and review guide, but you could use any other relevant psychology books available to you as well.

## Getting to know the exam

| Exam paper | Duration | Format | Topics | Weighting | Total marks |
|---|---|---|---|---|---|
| Paper 1 (SL) | 2 hours | Section A: three short-answer questions<br>Section B: essay from a choice of three topics | Section A: core approaches to psychology<br>Section B: biological, cognitive and sociocultural approaches to behaviour | 50% | 49<br>Section A: 27<br>Section B: 22 |
| Paper 2 (SL) | 1 hour | One question from a choice of three on one option | Option topics | 25% | 22 |
| Paper 1 (HL) | 2 hours | Section A: three short-answer questions<br>Section B: essay from a choice of three topics. One, two or all of the essays will reference the additional HL topic | Section A: core approaches to psychology<br>Section B: biological, cognitive and sociocultural approaches to behaviour | 40% | 49<br>Section A: 27<br>Section B: 22 |
| Paper 2 (HL) | 2 hours | Two questions: one from a choice of three on each of two options | Two options | 20% | 44 |
| Paper 3 (HL) | 1 hour | Three short-answer questions | A list of six static questions on approaches to research | 20% | 24 |

# Command terms and question types

In the 'Strengthen your learning' feature, comprehension-style exercises are provided to help reinforce your knowledge and understanding of the topics featured and to help prepare you to attempt some exam-style questions.

In order to successfully answer the questions, you need to understand the different sorts of questions contained, as these inform what kind of an answer is required. Understanding the command terms will help you answer the questions.

■ **Outline** – the command word 'outline' means to describe a specific element of knowledge. For example, the question '*Outline research methods used to study the biological approach*' would require a description of the different types of research method used by psychologists to study the biological approach. For instance:

> The biological approach is studied through the use of laboratory experiments, where variables are strictly controlled and tested to establish cause and effect relationships.
>
> Scanning methods are also used to monitor brain activity, especially in specific brain areas and for specific behaviours, while the brains of dead people are scrutinized through post-mortem examinations. Because of practical and ethical restrictions on examining live human brains, animal studies are often used, in the belief that there is a continuation from animal to human physiology. When studying rare or unique behaviours, case studies are often used.

It should be noted that 'outline' type questions do not require any analysis or evaluation – for instance, that it is not always possible to generalize from animal to human physiology.

■ **Explain** – the command word 'explain' means to show your understanding. This therefore requires more than just a description of something, but a deeper level of answer that gives reasons as to why something should be so. For instance, for the question '*Explain the biological approach in terms of genetics*':

> The biological approach sees behaviour as being influenced by genetics through the hereditary transmission of genes from parents to a child. Such genes code behaviour either directly (such as the transmission of genetic abnormalities), or indirectly through the interaction of genes with environmental experience. The process of evolution is genetically transmitted via natural selection and genes can also exert an influence over biochemistry and neural functioning.

■ **Summarize** what research studies have suggested about... – this type of question gets you to focus on research studies, but what is not required is a description of such studies in terms of their hypotheses, procedure, etc. Instead, what is needed is a focus upon the conclusions drawn from the results of such studies. This should be done in your own words to show your understanding. For instance, for the question '*Summarize what research studies have suggested about the biological approach*':

> Benedetti (2007) illustrated the use of laboratory experiments in assessing the biological approach, by showing that light therapy had a positive physiological effect in reducing depression in the majority of patients.
>
> Meanwhile, D'Esposito et al. (1995) highlighted the use of scanning techniques in assessing the biological approach, by demonstrating that the prefrontal cortex is involved in working memory, as the brain area was activated when verbal and spatial tasks were performed together, but not independently of each other.

The contribution of post-mortems to the biological approach was demonstrated by Reeves & Plum (1969), who reported that an obese female had no functioning ventromedial hypothalamus. This suggests that the ventromedial hypothalamus brain area is important in regulating eating around a healthy body weight.

The reliance of the biological approach on animal studies is shown by Coleman (1973), who, using genetically modified mice, demonstrated the role of the hormone leptin in the control of eating behaviour.

Scoville & Milner (1957) showed the value of case studies to the biological approach, by reporting on the unusual case of HM, who had damage to his hippocampus that resulted in long-term memory loss. This indicates the important role of biology in the creation of long-term memories.

- ■ **What other evaluative points** (including practical applications and issues and debates) can be made about... – this type of question requires an appraisal of a topic subject, for instance, a theory, model or explanation, in terms of strengths and weaknesses, that is not based on research evidence. Again this should be written in your own words to show your understanding of the points being made. For instance, for the question *'What other evaluative points (including practical applications and issues and debates) can be made about the biological approach?'*:

The biological approach to explaining mind and behaviour has strengths, such as the fact that it generally uses scientific methods that produce objective, unbiased results, which can be repeated to check for accuracy, allowing the establishment of cause and effect relationships. Another strength is that the biological approach can be combined with the cognitive approach to identify which physiological systems and brain structures are involved in different mental processes. The biological approach also has positive practical applications, such as the production of effective drug treatments. Antipsychotic drugs that affect dopamine levels have been seen to reduce schizophrenic symptoms in many patients.

The biological approach does have its weaknesses though, such as the fact that it doesn't consider how learning experiences help to shape behaviour. There are also aspects of mind that seem non-physical, which the biological approach cannot explain, like memories.

The biological approach can also be seen to use both nomothetic methods of study, such as experiments, where research is carried upon groups of participants and generalized to target populations, and idiographic methods of study, such as case studies, where research is carried out upon and only relates to specific individuals.

- ■ **Questions that refer to specific research studies** will require more than just a summary of the conclusions drawn. The named study will need to be *outlined* in terms of its aims, procedure and findings, *analysed* in terms of its conclusions and *evaluated* in terms of its strengths and weaknesses. For instance, for the question *'For Wernicke's classic (1864) study into aphasia, in your own words, state the aims, procedure, results, conclusions and evaluative points'*:

The aim of Wernicke's study was to identify the specific brain area that allows humans to understand language. The study was a case study performed on one man, after his death, who had normal hearing and speaking abilities, but couldn't comprehend speech.

The post-mortem inspection of his brain revealed that a specific brain area, the rear parietal/temporal region of the left hemisphere of his brain (next to the auditory cortex), was damaged.

It was concluded that this brain area, which became known as Wernicke's area, was responsible for comprehending speech and words.

Consistent findings were found when patients with similar brain damage were examined, which suggests the results are reliable.

Using the 'Strengthen your learning' exercises should help you to construct higher quality answers when you come to attempt exam-type questions. The 'Strengthen your learning' exercises are designed, though, to be attempted before you have a go at the exam-style questions.

# Biological approach

## Introduction

Revised

The **biological approach** sees the mind and behaviour as products of our physiology, with several forms of physiology exerting an influence: **neural structures** (including the brain and nervous system), **the process of evolution**, **genetics** and **biochemistry**. These can be seen to exert individual influences, as well as combining with each other to exert a collective influence.

> ### Key terms
>
> **The biological approach** – the idea that mind and behaviour are products of an individual's physiology.
>
> **Neural structures** – nerve cells within the brain that exert an influence upon behaviour.
>
> **The process of evolution** – the process by which behaviours become more widespread in a population through natural selection due to their adaptive survival value.
>
> **Genetics** – inherited physiological material that influences development and behaviour.
>
> **Biochemistry** – the influence of chemical processes within the body upon behaviour.

The biological approach is based upon several assumptions and uses specific forms of research, which have associated ethical considerations to take into account.

## Assumptions

Revised

| Biological influence | Description |
|---|---|
| *Neural structures* | Specific brain areas and the action of the nervous system are used to explain mind and behaviour. |
| *Genetics* | Aspects of mind and behaviour are seen to be inherited by genetic transmission. |
| *Process of evolution* | Mind and behaviour are shaped over time through natural selection to increase survival and reproduction chances. |
| *Biochemistry* | Hormones and neurotransmitters are seen to exert direct and indirect influences upon mind and behaviour. |

## Research methods

Revised

Laboratory-based experiments are used to establish causality, as well as scanning methods, like fMRI scans, to measure specific brain activity. Post-mortems of deceased people's brains are also used to examine brain function. There is also a large reliance on animal experimentation, as a continuation from animal to human physiology is assumed. Case studies are performed to study individual instances of behaviours.

Research raises ethical issues of experimentation upon animals, as well as gaining informed consent from mentally disordered individuals.

## Research

- **Benedetti (2007)** found that daily sessions of light therapy reduced two-thirds of patients' depression inventory scores by 50 per cent, illustrating the value of laboratory experiments in researching behaviour.

- **D'Esposito *et al.* (1995)** used fMRI scans to find the prefrontal cortex was activated when verbal and spatial tasks were performed simultaneously, but not separately, suggesting the brain area is involved in working memory.

- **Reeves & Plum (1969)** found, using a post-mortem, that the ventromedial hypothalamus of an obese female was destroyed, suggesting the brain area is associated with obesity.

- **Scoville & Milner (1957)** conducted a case study of HM, finding that the hippocampus brain area was involved in creating long-term memories.

- **Coleman (1973)** used genetically modified mice to find leptin is involved in the regulation of eating, demonstrating the value of animal experimentation for understanding human behaviour.

## Positive evaluation

- The approach generally produces scientific, objective findings that permit causality and replication to check validity.

- The biological and cognitive approaches are combined into cognitive neuroscience to identify the biological basis of mental processes.

## Negative evaluation

- The approach neglects the role of environmental learning experiences upon behaviour.

- The approach cannot explain non-physical elements of the mind, like the reconstruction of memories, as these are not stored as physical representations.

## Practical application

- The approach has led to many effective drug therapies, such as the use of antipsychotic drugs to treat schizophrenia.

## Issues and debates

- Methods used are generally *nomothetic*, as research is conducted across groups of individuals and findings are generalized to whole populations. Case studies are more *idiographic*, as findings relate to one specific instance.

---

### ■ STRENGTHEN YOUR LEARNING

1 Explain the biological approach in terms of:
   a  neural structures,
   b  genetics,
   c  the process of evolution,
   d  biochemistry.

2 Outline research methods used to study the biological approach.

3 Summarize what research studies have suggested about the biological approach.

4 What other evaluative points (including practical applications and issues and debates) can be made about the biological approach?

---

### Expert tip

Ensure you understand the main principle on which the biological approach is formed – that mind and body are products of our physiology – but that also you can provide some detail about this in terms of the different types of biological influence, namely: neural structures, genetics, the process of evolution and biochemistry. You should be able to explain the individual influence of each of these.

# Techniques used to study the brain

Magnetic resonance imaging (MRI) and **functional magnetic resonance imaging** (fMRI) are scanning techniques that use magnetic fields and radio waves. With MRI, this is used to create detailed images of the brain, while fMRI looks at blood flow in the brain to detect areas of activity, associated with specific behaviours.

**Computerized axial tomography** (CAT) scans provide a still picture of the physiology of the brain using X-rays. Images are merged to form a 3D picture of the brain.

**Positron emission tomography** (PET) scanning shows which brain areas are involved in specific behaviours by creating dynamic images of levels of radioactivity in the brain (after injecting radioactive fluorodeoxyglucose into the bloodstream).

**Electroencephalography** (EEG) gives an overall picture of activity within the brain. Electrodes attached to the scalp record electrical events in the brain to monitor specific behaviours by comparing different levels of electrical signal.

## Research

- **Szycik et al. (2017)** used fMRI scanning to find no differences between the brain activation patterns of violent and non-violent computer game players when viewing emotionally sensitive pictures, suggesting desensitization to violence does not occur at the neuronal level.

- **Wei et al. (2015)** reviewed CAT scans of 5,507 depressive patients, finding a relationship between right-hemisphere strokes and depression, but not between left-hemisphere strokes and depression. This suggests post-stroke depression results more from right-hemisphere than left-hemisphere brain damage.

- **Azari et al. (2001)** used PET scans to find that religious participants, when reciting psalms, activated brain circuits permitting meditative states, which did not occur in non-religious participants, demonstrating the role of the brain in religious experience.

- **Aspinall et al. (2015)** found different levels of brain arousal associated with people walking around different environments of Edinburgh, suggesting brain activation is influenced by environmental input.

## Positive evaluation

- Due to the availability of equipment and relatively cheap cost, CAT scans allow large numbers of brains to be scanned, making results more valid.

- As PET scans are dynamic, they allow brain activation changes associated with specific behaviours to be detected.

- fMRI scans give great amounts of detail, as they provide moving pictures, therefore informing about patterns of activation and localization of function.

- EEG usage has been useful in studying the different stages of sleep, and being non-invasive carries minimal risks of harm.

## Negative evaluation

- **Stelzer et al. (2014)** highlighted issues with the way fMRI data is analysed, leading to publication of false results, illustrating that apparently objective measures can still be problematic.

- As CAT scans take static pictures, they can identify structural damage in individual brains, but cannot localize activity in typical brains.

- The tight space involved in MRI/fMRI scanning can be uncomfortable, causing distress, which with fMRI scans can produce unreliable readings.

- PET scans are relatively expensive, limiting their usage, and as radiation is involved, they incur health risks.

### Key terms

**Magnetic resonance imaging** – scanning technique that uses magnetic fields and radio waves to create detailed brain images.

**Functional magnetic resonance imaging** – scanning technique that uses magnetic fields, radio waves and blood flow to detect areas of activity within specific brain structures.

**Computerized axial tomography** – scanning technique that uses X-rays to create static three-dimensional images of the brain.

**Positron emission tomography** – scanning technique involving the injection of radioactive material to create dynamic brain images.

**Electroencephalography** – scanning technique that uses electrodes attached to the scalp to monitor electrical activity within the brain.

## ■ Practical application

■ Scanning techniques have identified specific brain areas associated with mental disorders, allowing therapies to be more targeted.

## ■ Issues and debates

■ There are ethical considerations with scanning usage. Patients need to be aware of procedures and risks to be able to give fully informed consent.

> ■ **STRENGTHEN YOUR LEARNING**
>
> 1 Outline techniques to study the brain.
> 2 Summarize what research studies have suggested about techniques used to study the brain.
> 3 Assess techniques used to study the brain in terms of their strengths and weaknesses (including practical applications and relevant issues and debates).

> **Expert tip**
>
> As well as knowing what the individual techniques for studying the brain are, and how they work, it is also a good idea to know what the similarities and differences between the various techniques are so that you can demonstrate a high level of understanding by making comparisons of them.

# Localization

Revised ☐

The brain has two hemispheres connected by the corpus callosum, a bundle of nerve fibres that allow the hemispheres to communicate. **Localization** concerns in which part of the brain specific functions occur.

# Hemispheric lateralization

Revised ☐

**Hemispheric lateralization** concerns the distinction between functions of the right and left hemispheres.

Most brains are *contralateral*, the right hemisphere dealing with the left side of the body and vice versa. For example, information in an individual's right visual field is processed by their left hemisphere. When a function is dealt with by one hemisphere, it is *lateralized*, with the division of functions between the two hemispheres known as hemispheric lateralization:

■ *Left hemisphere* – for most people, language processing occurs in the left hemisphere. A stroke on the left side of the brain therefore affects speech. The left hemisphere also focuses on detail in visual information.

■ *Right hemisphere* – recognizing emotions in others occurs in the right hemisphere, as does dealing with spatial information (knowing where things are in relationship to each other in the visual field). The right hemisphere also processes overall patterns in visual information.

> **Key terms**
>
> **Localization** – the identification of behaviours to the specific brain areas in which they are carried out.
>
> **Hemispheric lateralization** – the tendency for neural functions and cognitive processes to be specialized to one specific hemisphere of the brain.

## ■ Research

■ **Dundas *et al.* (2015)** found faces are processed predominately in the right hemisphere, suggesting face recognition is lateralized.

■ **Collins & Mohr (2013)** found the brain becomes less lateralized with age, the non-dominant hemisphere supporting the superior hemisphere for any given task, which suggests age should be considered when assessing lateralization.

## ■ Positive evaluation

Split-brain patients gave psychologists a method to assess lateralization, though the degree to which findings from the brains of epileptics are generalizable to the general population is questionable.

## ■ Negative evaluation

■ Not all brain areas have been mapped out in terms of their functions, so the degree to which lateralization occurs is not known.

## KEY CLASSIC STUDY

### 'HEMISPHERE DECONNECTION AND UNITY IN CONSCIOUS AWARENESS'

**Sperry (1968)**

#### Aim

- To assess lateralization in split-brain patients.

#### Procedure

- Stimuli were presented to the separate visual fields of epileptic patients who had had their corpus callosum severed (to reduce their fits) to assess lateralization of function. (This would not be possible in non-split-brain individuals, as their two hemispheres can communicate.)

#### Findings

- Words presented to the right visual field could be read aloud.
- Words presented to the left visual field could be understood (by pointing to an object corresponding to the word), but could not be said aloud.
- Objects held in the right hand could be named, but not those in the left hand.

#### Conclusion

- Language is localized predominantly in the left hemisphere.

#### Evaluation

- Subsequent research found that, although visual perception is split between hemispheres, overall perception is not, as the 'split' is only temporary.

### ■ Practical application

- Research into lateralization has led to effective methods of developing functional recovery of the brain after trauma, like brain stimulation.

### ■ Issues and debates

- Lateralization of function takes a reductionist view of brain function, with specific functions seen as occurring in separate brain areas. The holistic theory of brain function sees functions, like memory, as occurring throughout the brain.

#### ■ STRENGTHEN YOUR LEARNING

1. Explain what is meant by localization of the brain.
2. Explain localization in terms of hemispheric lateralization.
3. For Sperry's classic 1968 study into hemispheric brain disconnection, in your own words, state the aims, procedure, results, conclusions and evaluative points.
4. What have research studies suggested about hemispheric lateralization?
5. What other evaluative points, including practical applications and relevant issues and debates, can be made about lateralization of function?

#### Expert tip

In order to write top-level answers to exam questions on localization and hemispheric lateralization, it is necessary to display a deep level of knowledge and understanding of specific functions, such as the processing of language. Similarly, displaying a deep level of knowledge of Sperry's split-brain studies, as a method of assessing lateralization, would be a good idea.

## Motor centres

Revised ▢

**Motor centres** are brain areas concerned with movement, controlled from the *motor cortex*, located in the *parietal lobe*. The *primary motor cortex* sends information to the muscles via the brain stem and spinal cord. This brain area is important for complex movements and non-basic actions, like coughing and crying. The spinal cord and brain coordinate movements, while the *premotor cortex* helps plan movements and the *prefrontal cortex* stores sensory information prior to a movement and assesses the probability of outcomes of movements.

#### Key term

**Motor centres** – the influence of the primary motor cortex brain area upon control of movement.

# Somatosensory centre

Revised

The **somatosensory** brain area focuses upon sensory information. It is located next to and works with the motor cortex in the parietal lobe to permit movement around one's environment. Touch is perceived in the somatosensory cortex, with processing of some body areas, like the face, involving larger parts of this brain area than others.

# Visual centres

Revised

The *primary visual cortex*, located in the occipital lobe, is the main **visual centre**, with visual information conveyed along two pathways, one in each hemisphere. One pathway contains components of the visual field and the other the location of the components within the visual field.

# Auditory centres

Revised

The **auditory centre**, located in the temporal lobe, processes sounds. The *primary auditory cortex* receives information from both ears via two pathways, one in each hemisphere, which transmit information about what a sound is and where it is located.

> **Key terms**
>
> **Somatosensory centre** – the influence of the somatosensory cortex brain area upon the perception of touch.
>
> **Visual centres** – the influence of the visual cortices brain areas upon the perception of vision.
>
> **Auditory centres** – the influence of the auditory cortices brain areas upon the perception of hearing.

## Research

- **Kawai et al. (2015)** found rats could execute previously learned skills when their motor cortex was lesioned, but they could not learn new skills, which suggests the motor cortex is necessary for learning new motor skills.

- **Hu (2016)** found the somatosensory centre was sensitive to pain in amputated limbs that were no longer present, illustrating the brain area's role in perceiving sensations.

- **Overgaard (2011)** reported on 'blindsight', a phenomenon where someone feels something is in their visual field, but they have no sight of it. This illustrates how visual processing in the brain uses two visual pathways from the eyes.

- **Hyde et al. (2009)** found changes in the structure of the auditory centre and the motor cortex in six-year-old children who had practised on musical instruments for 15 months, compared to a control group who had not learned to play. This illustrates the role of the auditory and motor cortices in processing music.

## Positive evaluation

- There is a wealth of research evidence to support the existence in the brain of different centres for specific activities.

## Negative evaluation

- Several brain areas are often activated when processing an activity, which suggests that the idea of specific brain areas for specific behaviours is simplistic.

## Practical application

- Paralysed people can regain movement through microchips inserted into their motor cortex. Thoughts of movement activate neurons around the microchip, signalling a computer to alert electrodes placed on the body to activate muscles needed to execute desired movements.

## Issues and debates

- Much research into locating specific brain centres, where lesions are created to identify function, has been performed on animals, creating issues of generalization to humans, whose physiology is often radically different.

# Language centres

**Broca's area**, located in the left temporal lobe, is responsible for production of speech, while **Wernicke's area**, close to the auditory cortex, is important for understanding language and accessing words. Other brain areas are involved too, depending on the function required and the modality of the language, e.g. sound, written, spoken, etc.

### ▣ Broca's area

The function of Broca's area is speech production. The area is situated in the frontal lobe, next to the temporal lobe, in the dominant hemisphere (96 per cent of right-handers and about 75 per cent of left-handers have the left hemisphere as their dominant hemisphere for language).

### ▣ Wernicke's area

The function of Wernicke's area is understanding language – most specifically, speech. The area is close to the auditory cortex and is found where the temporal and parietal lobes meet in the dominant hemisphere for language (usually the left hemisphere). It is linked to Broca's area through a bundle of connecting neurons called the arcuate fasciculus. Wernicke's area is found in deaf people who use sign language, which indicates that it serves for more than just speech.

> **Key terms**
>
> **Broca's area** – a specific brain area within the frontal lobe associated with speech production.
>
> **Wernicke's area** – a specific brain area close to the auditory cortex associated with understanding language and speech.

## KEY CLASSIC STUDY

### 'APHASIC SYMPTOM COMPLEX'

**Wernicke (1874)**

#### Aim

- ▣ To locate the brain area responsible for understanding language.

#### Procedure

- ▣ Wernicke examined the brain of a man (after his death) who could hear and speak, but not understand language.

#### Findings

- ▣ Damage was found in the rear parietal/temporal region of the patient's left hemisphere, close to the auditory cortex.

#### Conclusions

- ▣ The brain area (now called Wernicke's area) is important for understanding speech and accessing words.

#### Evaluation

- ▣ Examination of similar patients showed damage to the same brain area, suggesting the findings to be reliable.

### ▣ Research

- ▣ **Broca (1861)** performed a post-mortem on a man called LeBorgne, who could only say the word 'Tan', finding damage to his left temporal lobe, which suggests the brain area (now known as Broca's area) is responsible for speech production.

- ▣ **Mesulam (2015)** studied 72 aphasic patients, finding damage in Wernicke's and Broca's areas, the dorsal premotor cortex and underlying axonal pathways, casting doubt on Wernicke's area being solely responsible for language comprehension.

### ▣ Positive evaluation

- ▣ Studying patients with specific forms of language damage has helped identify brain areas involved in the production and comprehension of language.

### ■ Negative evaluation

■ An MRI scan on LeBorgne's brain showed damage to additional areas, suggesting language production is not confined solely to Broca's area.

■ Research into language centres often involves case studies of abnormal patients, making generalization to non-abnormal populations difficult.

### ■ Practical application

■ The provision of enriched learning environments has facilitated recovery of language abilities in those with damage to language centres, especially in children, whose brains are more plastic.

### ■ Issues and debates

■ The fact that damage to specific language centres can be overcome with rehabilitation suggests a role for both nature, in terms of biologically determined brain structures, and nurture, in terms of environmental learning experiences, supporting the interactionist point of view.

---

**■ STRENGTHEN YOUR LEARNING**

1  Explain localization in terms of the functions of the following brain areas: somatosensory centre, visual centre, auditory centre, Broca's area and Wernicke's area.

2  Summarize what research studies have suggested about the above brain areas.

3  What other evaluative points, including practical applications and relevant issues and debates, can be made about these brain areas?

4  For Wernicke's classic (1874) study into aphasia, in your own words, state the aims, procedure, results, conclusions and evaluative points.

---

**Expert tip**

The centres of the brain, such as the motor and language centres, are very factually based, so evaluation of this topic area will mainly centre on research studies that illustrate the specific roles of the various centres, such as **Hu (2016)**, which illustrates the somatosensory centre's role in perceiving sensations.

# Neuroplasticity

Revised ▢

Most people with brain damage make some recovery and sometimes the brain can adapt and find another way to complete a function. Level of recovery depends on the type and severity of trauma.

**Neuroplasticity** is the brain's ability to replace a function lost by anatomical damage. Cell bodies cannot be replaced, but sometimes axons can. There are three main anatomical ways that the brain can replace axon function.

1  *Increased brain stimulation* – if the undamaged hemisphere is stimulated, recovery from a stroke can improve.

2  *Axon sprouting* – damage to an axon results in lost connections to adjoining neurons, but their neighbouring neurons can grow extra connections to compensate. This can replace function if the damaged axon and the replacements perform similarly.

3  *Denervation supersensitivity* – axons that perform similarly to damaged ones can become aroused to a higher level to compensate.

**Key term**

**Neuroplasticity** – the ability of the nervous system, especially the brain, to adapt to the environment and replace function following damage.

# Functional recovery of the brain after trauma

Revised ▢

Rehabilitation can help the brain compensate for loss of function, by an individual learning how to use their working faculties and functions to compensate for those lost to injury. Several factors affect **functional recovery**:

1  *Perseverance* – sometimes a function may appear lost, but it is because an individual is not 'trying' hard enough. Perseverance can eventually restore some function.

**Key term**

**Functional recovery** – the ability of the brain to compensate for loss of function through rehabilitation.

2 *Physical exhaustion, stress and alcohol* – recovering function can be exhausting and stress and alcohol consumption can affect the ability to use recovered functions.

3 *Age* – recovering function can become more difficult with age.

4 *Gender* – women appear more able to recover from trauma as their function is not as lateralized (concentrated in one hemisphere).

## Research

- **Danelli *et al.* (2013)** found that a boy who had most of his left hemisphere removed due to a tumour had resulting language ability difficulties, which after six years of rehabilitation were overcome. This suggests his right hemisphere 'relearned' his lost language abilities, illustrating the neuroplasticity of the brain.

- **Takatsuru *et al.* (2009)** found function could be regained following strokes through brain stimulation of the non-damaged hemisphere, demonstrating how non-damaged brain areas can compensate for function in damaged areas.

- **De la Plata *et al.* (2008)** found that individuals over 40 recovered less function following brain trauma than younger individuals, indicating age to be a factor in neuroplasticity.

## Positive evaluation

- Research has shown that much brain development occurs in adolescence. This, plus the recovery of function in adult stroke patients, suggests neuroplasticity is not limited to childhood.

- The success of rehabilitation programmes from brain injury is strong evidence for the neuroplasticity of the brain.

## Negative evaluation

- Assessing the level of recovery after trauma is difficult, as there is usually no record of the level of functioning prior to trauma.

- Age, perseverance and gender are recognized as important factors, but the mechanisms by which they exert an influence upon the chances of neuroplasticity are not fully understood.

## Practical application

- Research into neuroplasticity has led to the formation of effective rehabilitation programmes for those losing function due to brain damage.

## Issues and debates

- The concept of neuroplasticity does not suffer from gender bias, as it is recognized that females have greater neuroplasticity in functional recovery than males.

---

### ■ STRENGTHEN YOUR LEARNING

1 Explain what is meant by neuroplasticity.
2 Outline the three main anatomical ways that the brain can replace axon function.
3 Explain what is meant by functional recovery of the brain after trauma.
4 Outline factors that affect recovery of the brain.
5 What have research studies suggested about neuroplasticity and functional recovery of the brain?
6 What other evaluative points, including practical applications and relevant issues and debates, can be made about neuroplasticity and functional recovery?

### Expert tip

Do not regard plasticity and functional recovery as separate things. Instead, you should be able to explain how plasticity concerns the brain's ability to replace a function lost by anatomical damage and then use your knowledge of functional recovery to explain the different ways in which this can occur.

# Neurotransmitters and their effect on behaviour

Brain signals are communicated by synaptic transmission. A **synapse** is a 'gap' between neurons, across which nerve signals are transported chemically by **neurotransmitters** to be taken up by an adjacent neuron. The reaction to neurotransmitters is not universal and depends upon how the signal is responded to by the receiving neuron in terms of the neuron's *action potential* (which is dependent on how a neurotransmitter affects the flow of ions through the neuron). The effect of signals can be *excitatory*, making it more likely for a neuron to fire and carry on the signal, or *inhibitory*, making it less likely for a neuron to fire and thus stop the signal.

## Serotonin

**Serotonin** is a neurotransmitter involved in emotion, motor, cognitive and basic autonomic behaviour too. The arousal level of the nervous system is mediated by serotonin and it helps coordinate behaviours.

## Dopamine

High levels of the neurotransmitter **dopamine** are associated with schizophrenia by prompting thought-process disorders through increasing activity in brain neurons. Dopamine is also associated with reward-motivated behaviour through low levels in the substantia nigra brain area.

### ■ Research

- **Cherek (1996)** found that drugs that decreased serotonin levels in ten men lowered their aggression levels within five hours, illustrating the relationship between serotonin and aggression.

- **Bailer et al. (2005)** used fMRI scans to find heightened levels of serotonin in anorexics' brains, especially those with high anxiety levels, which suggests serotonin's effect upon emotion can act as a trigger for anorexia nervosa.

- **Davis et al. (1991)** found that high levels of dopamine in the mesolimbic dopamine brain system are associated with positive symptoms of schizophrenia, like hallucinations, while high levels in the mesocortical dopamine system are associated with negative symptoms, like thought-process disorders, illustrating the influence of dopamine upon schizophrenia.

- **Dani & Biasi (2001)** found that nicotine acts upon dopaminergic brain systems that reinforce the pleasant effects of smoking, leading to smoking addiction, illustrating the association of dopamine with reward-motivated behaviour.

### ■ Positive evaluation

- The fact that serotonin has a broad effect on aggression across many species suggests it is an evolutionary adaptation linked to increased survival chances.

- Drug therapies based on modifying neurotransmitter levels in the brain have proven effective in addressing a range of abnormal conditions, like depression, schizophrenia and obsessive-compulsive disorder.

### ■ Negative evaluation

- Although dopamine is associated with schizophrenia, there is much evidence to suggest that abnormal levels of the neurotransmitter are not the only explanation for the disorder. Many other biological and psychological factors seem to be involved too.

---

**Key terms**

**Synapse** – the small gap between one neuron and another across which nerve impulses are carried by neurotransmitters.

**Neurotransmitters** – biochemicals found within the brain involved in transmitting messages between neurons.

**Serotonin** – a neurotransmitter that mediates the arousal levels of the nervous system and helps coordinate behaviour.

**Dopamine** – a neurotransmitter associated with reward-motivated behaviour and schizophrenia.

■ Using biochemistry alone to explain complex human behaviours is rather simplistic. It is unlikely that any single behaviour can be explained by reference to one single neurotransmitter, and such explanations are therefore incomplete.

## ■ Practical application

■ Selective serotonin reuptake inhibitors (SSRIs) are serotonin-based drugs that have proven effective in reducing symptoms in depressive patients.

## ■ Issues and debates

■ As the effect of neurotransmitters on behaviour appears to be influenced by genetics and the process of evolution, it indicates a biological basis to their actions that is more a product of nature than nurture.

> **Expert tip**
>
> Exam questions on neurotransmitters are not likely to require focus on a particular neurotransmitter. However, in order to provide a high level of descriptive detail, and a solid platform on which to base evaluation, it would be a good idea to have a comprehensive knowledge of how specific neurotransmitters, such as dopamine and serotonin, affect behaviour.

> **■ STRENGTHEN YOUR LEARNING**
>
> 1 Explain how neurotransmitters affect behaviour, including the role of dopamine and serotonin.
> 2 Summarize what research studies have suggested about how neurotransmitters affect behaviour.
> 3 What other evaluative points, including practical applications and relevant issues and debates, can be made about how neurotransmitters affect behaviour?

# Hormones and behaviour

Revised ☐

**Hormones** are chemicals transported in bodily fluids, which affect many behaviours and are secreted by the endocrine system, a collection of glands within the body. The pituitary gland, located near the hypothalamus, is the 'master gland', due to its central role in hormone production.

> **Key term**
> **Hormones** – chemical messengers released from glands throughout the body.

# Oxytocin

Revised ☐

**Oxytocin** is a polypeptide hormone produced in the hypothalamus that controls key aspects of the reproductive system. Its action is greater in females, where it works in tandem with oestrogen, and facilitates childbirth by stimulating contractions as well as 'letting down' milk for breastfeeding. It is released during physical interactions, like sex and hugging, to facilitate intimacy and bonding. It also affects female social behaviour, like mate selection, 'nesting', monogamy and the nurturing of children.

> **Key term**
> **Oxytocin** – a hormone associated with maternal behaviours and attachment formation and maintenance.

## ■ Research

■ **Campbell (2008)** found oxytocin increased maternal behaviour in female rats, even when not pregnant, demonstrating the effect of oxytocin on reproductive behaviour.

■ **White-Traut (2009)** found oxytocin levels in saliva were highest immediately before breastfeeding, decreased at initiation of feeding and rose again 30 minutes before feeding, illustrating oxytocin's importance in breastfeeding.

## ■ Positive evaluation

■ Oxytocin may be able to help explain autism, due to its role in facilitating empathy (experiencing the emotions of others). People with autism have low levels of oxytocin, which may relate to their lack of empathy for others' feelings.

## ■ Negative evaluation

■ Much research into the effects of oxytocin is done on animals, creating problems of generalization to humans.

## KEY CLASSIC STUDY

### 'EFFECTS OF MDMA AND INTRANASAL OXYTOCIN ON SOCIAL AND EMOTIONAL PROCESSING'

Kirkpatrick *et al.* (2014)

### Aim

■ To assess the immediate effects of MDMA (ecstasy) and oxytocin.

### Procedure

■ Sixty-five participants were administered either MDMA, oxytocin or a placebo.

■ Measures of emotion recognition, sociability and physiology were taken.

### Results

■ MDMA created feelings of euphoria, while oxytocin raised feelings of sociability and enhanced recognition of sad facial expressions.

### Conclusions

■ MDMA and oxytocin increase similar feelings of sociability and favourable perception of others.

### Evaluation

■ The use of a control group allows the effect of the independent variable (MDMA/oxytocin or not) on the dependent variable (level of sociability) to be seen; however, as many extraneous variables were not controlled for, causality cannot be established.

■ There is an ethical consideration in administering a potentially harmful substance to some participants.

## ■ Practical application

■ Oxytocin is often given to women during the final stages of labour to decrease blood loss and thus increase chances of successful childbirth.

## ■ Issues and debates

■ It is simplistic to think of oxytocin as a 'female' hormone, as it exerts influences on male behaviours too, such as in experiencing orgasm.

# Testosterone

Revised

**Testosterone** is an androgen, a male hormone (though found in lower levels in females). Testosterone is linked to aggression, though more so in animal species and generally in humans by aggressive reactions to social provocation. Testosterone is also associated with masculinization of the brain and male-type behaviours like competitiveness.

## ■ Research

■ **Deady (2006)** found that women with high testosterone levels had low levels of reproductive ambition and maternal feelings, which suggests female maternal feelings are affected by testosterone.

■ **Wu & Shah (2011)** used genetically modified mice to find that testosterone coordinates the display of male territorial and sexual behaviours, illustrating its role in masculinization.

## ■ Positive evaluation

■ The fact that high levels of testosterone in females generally lead to male-type behaviours supports the idea of testosterone being a 'male' hormone.

■ Much research into testosterone is laboratory-based, permitting replication to check the validity of results.

### Key term

**Testosterone** – an androgen (male) hormone generally found in higher levels in males, which is associated with masculinization of the brain and heightened levels of aggression.

**KEY CLASSIC STUDY**

## 'PRENATAL ANDROGEN EFFECTS ON PSYCHOLOGICAL ORIENTATION'
Beltz *et al*. (2011)

### Aim
- To assess the effect of testosterone on career choice.

### Procedure
- Forty-six women with congenital adrenal hyperplasia (CAH), which involves exposure to high levels of testosterone in the womb, were compared with 31 of their brothers, 27 males with CAH and 21 unaffected sisters.
- Career choice was labelled person-centred or non-person-centred.

### Results
- Females with CAH chose non-person-centred careers, as did males with and without CAH, while non-CAH females chose person-centred careers.

### Conclusions
- Exposure to high levels of testosterone in the womb affects psychological orientation.

### Evaluation
- Many other factors that were not considered also affect career choice, such as personality, academic history, etc., lowering the validity of the findings.

## Negative evaluation
- Testosterone stimulates aggressive feelings, but other factors have greater influence over whether aggression actually occurs. For example, social learning theory better explains if aggressive feelings lead to actual aggression.
- The effects of testosterone are problematic to assess, as it is difficult to isolate testosterone from other biochemical influences in real-life scenarios.

## Practical application
- Male animals, such as horses, are often castrated in order to lower testosterone levels and make them more docile and easier to handle.

## Issues and debates
- Research into testosterone is somewhat gender-biased, as females are difficult to test, because of fluctuations in testosterone levels related to their menstrual cycles.

# Adrenaline

Revised ☐

**Adrenaline** is a part of the flight-or-fight response. The hypothalamus recognizes a threat, like a predator, and signals the adrenal glands near the kidneys to release adrenaline into the bloodstream, prompting physical changes, such as increased blood flow and faster breathing to help the body temporarily deal with the threat, such as by moving faster. Adrenaline is thus associated with behaviours involving arousal, like aggression and sexual attraction.

> **Key term**
>
> **Adrenaline** – a hormone that plays an important role in the flight-or-fight response, which is associated with arousal behaviours, such as aggression and sexual attraction.

## Research
- **Zuckerman (1983)** found high levels of adrenaline in sensation-seekers, people who like stimulating environments that heighten arousal. This suggests adrenaline is linked to personality.

■ **McKinney (2015)** found that as adrenaline levels in participants increased, so did the level of attraction to a member of the opposite sex, which suggests that adrenaline heightens sexual arousal.

## Positive evaluation

■ As adrenaline is a physical substance, levels of it produced in response to stimulation can be measured objectively, allowing statistical analysis of results.

## Negative evaluation

■ Evidence concerning adrenaline is often correlational and so does not show causality.

■ Adrenaline often works in conjunction with testosterone and so its individual action is difficult to assess in real-life situations.

## Practical application

■ Relationship counsellors restimulate attraction in relationships by heightening adrenaline levels, and thus sexual arousal, through participation in physical activities.

## Issues and debates

■ Focusing on single effects of adrenaline, rather than on collective effects in conjunction with other biochemicals, forms a reductionist rather than holistic approach.

---

**■ STRENGTHEN YOUR LEARNING**

1  What is the endocrine system?

2  Explain the role of oxytocin, testosterone and adrenaline on behaviour.

3  Summarize what research studies have suggested about the role of oxytocin, testosterone and adrenaline on behaviour.

4  For Beltz et al.'s (2011) study into prenatal androgen effects, in your own words, state the aims, procedure, results, conclusions and evaluative points.

5  What other evaluative points, including practical applications and relevant issues and debates, can be made about oxytocin, testosterone and adrenaline on the role of behaviour?

---

**Expert tip**

Many students only use research evidence as a source of evaluative material. However, better students will also use other forms of evaluation in order to build a sophisticated commentary about a topic when answering exam questions. For example, relevant practical applications and issues and debates could be included as part of an evaluation of hormones and behaviour.

# Pheromones and behaviour

Revised ☐

**Pheromones** are ectohormones, as they are released outside the body, such as in sweat, which act as a method of communication to other individuals in the environment. It is thought that humans might detect pheromones through the vomeronasal organ in the nose, which connects up to the hypothalamus.

*Releaser pheromones* trigger immediate behavioural effects, like sexual attraction. *Primer pheromones* set up behaviours more slowly, like synchronizing menstruation in females. *Signaller pheromones* convey information, like genetic odour. *Modulator pheromones* alter behaviour, like making individuals more relaxed.

In humans, pheromones are associated mainly with reproductive behaviour, such as in motivating sexual activity and synchronizing menstruation in females.

---

Key term

**Pheromones** – chemical substances released into the external environment to produce a behavioural effect on other individuals.

KEY CLASSIC STUDY

## 'OLFACTORY INFLUENCES ON THE HUMAN MENSTRUAL CYCLE'

**Russell *et al.* (1980)**

### Aim

■ To assess the effects of pheromones on menstruation.

### Procedure

■ Underarm perspiration (from a donor female) and alcohol was rubbed on the top lips of one group of women, with just alcohol rubbed on the control group's upper lips, daily for five months.

■ Timings of menstrual cycles were compared with that of the donor woman.

### Results

■ Females receiving the donor's pheromones became more synchronized with her menstrual cycle, which did not occur with the control group.

### Conclusion

■ Menstrual synchrony can occur from nasally received pheromones.

### Evaluation

■ As the effect of pheromones is unconscious, demand characteristics cannot have occurred, increasing the validity of findings.

■ The study is supported by research on women living in close proximity, suggesting results to be reliable.

## ■ Research

■ **Verhaeghe *et al.* (2013)** reviewed research into the effects of pheromones, finding that exposure to the male hormone androstadienone increased attractiveness in mates, improved mood, heightened focus and increased sexual arousal and desire, which suggests that pheromones do elicit a number of behavioural effects in humans.

■ **Huoviala & Rantala (2013)** found that administering androstadienone to 40 male participants increased cooperative behaviour in decision-making tasks, which suggests that pheromones can affect male behaviour.

## ■ Positive evaluation

■ Pheromones eliciting an influence upon menstrual cycles makes sense from an evolutionary perspective, as synchronized menstruation would have a survival value in allowing females to get pregnant and give birth at the same time and so be able to suckle each other's babies.

■ Although many studies suggest pheromones do not influence human behaviour, such effects may be more difficult to detect in humans as the effects are subtle and do not create simple stereotyped behaviours, as in insects.

## ■ Negative evaluation

■ It may be that humans are not behaviourally affected by pheromones. The vomeronasal organ is present in foetuses, but withers before birth and so may not detect pheromones.

■ Studies that suggest pheromones synchronize female menstruation have been thrown into doubt by findings being statistically explicable by chance factors; as menstrual cycles occur over 28 days, a degree of overlap of cycles should be expected.

## ■ Practical application

■ Pills containing the male pheromone androstadienone are claimed to increase female sex drive, especially females who are ovulating, so are taken to seduce females.

## ■ Issues and debates

■ There are ethical issues of informed consent with using pheromones to unconsciously influence behaviour, such as using androstadienone to seduce females.

---

**■ STRENGTHEN YOUR LEARNING**

1  Explain how pheromones affect behaviour.

2  Summarize what research studies have suggested about how pheromones affect behaviour.

3  For Russell *et al.*'s (1980) study into olfactory influences on the human menstrual cycle, in your own words, state the aims, procedure, results, conclusions and evaluative points.

4  What other evaluative points, including practical applications and relevant issues and debates, can be made about how pheromones affect behaviour?

---

**Expert tip**

A useful point to stress when writing about pheromones and behaviour is their evolutionary significance, as this would convey a good understanding of a possible reason for their existence. Specific examples could then be given, such as pheromones eliciting an influence upon menstrual cycles, to illustrate your comprehension of this point.

# Genetics and behaviour

Revised ☐

Each person has a **genotype**, a **genetic** code that sets potentials for abilities. Genes interact with environmental factors to produce a person's **phenotype**: the amount of their genetic potentials for abilities that they actually realize. The means by which genes affect development is called *genetic expression*. Genes only affect behaviour when they are 'switched on' by environmental triggers and the effects of this can be both physiological and psychological. Single genes do not generally 'cause' a behaviour on their own; instead a number of genes tend to exert small individual influences to produce an overall cumulative influence on a behaviour.

Aggression is thought to be genetically influenced, through certain genes influencing testosterone levels by having an effect on how the hormone is metabolized in the body. This is also seen to be true for serotonin, dopamine and adrenaline. Genes also affect the brain, especially the frontal lobe, by determining the extent to which receptors are able to process testosterone in neurons located here, leading to reduced control and thus heightened aggression in response to aggressive environmental cues.

The monoamine oxidase A (MAOA) gene is associated with aggression. It expresses itself through affecting levels of neurotransmitters. MAOA is an enzyme (under control of the gene) that breaks down neurotransmitters in the brain. People with a low activity form of the gene often have higher levels of aggression.

**Key terms**

**Genotype** – the genetic make-up of an individual.

**Genetics** – the inherited characteristics of an individual.

**Phenotype** – the characteristics shown by an individual that occur from an interaction of their genes and environmental experience.

# Study methods

Revised ☐

Various study methods, such as twin studies, adoption studies and gene mapping studies, are conducted to assess the contribution of genetics to behaviour:

■ *Twin studies* – monozygotic (MZ) twins are 100 per cent genetically similar, while dizygotic (DZ) twins are only 50 per cent genetically similar. Therefore, if an ability is more common among MZ than DZ twins, it suggests that ability has an inherited component to it.

■ *Adoption studies* – adopted children share genes with their biological parents, but they do not share their environment with them (as they have not grown up with them); and they share environment with their adoptive parents, but not genes. Therefore, if an ability is more similar to that of biological parents than adoptive parents, it suggests the ability has an inherited component.

■ *Gene mapping* – if individuals with high levels of a specific ability share genes that individuals without high levels of that ability do not have, it suggests those genes are associated with expression of that ability.

## KEY CLASSIC STUDY

## 'ABNORMAL BEHAVIOUR ASSOCIATED WITH A POINT MUTATION IN THE STRUCTURAL GENE FOR MONOAMINE OXIDASE A'

**Brunner *et al.* (1993)**

### Aim

■ To assess the influence of the MAOA gene on aggression.

### Procedure

■ A case study was conducted on a Dutch family whose members demonstrated high levels of aggressive behaviour.

■ Levels of monoamine were measured from urine samples.

### Results

■ Five males of the family had high urine levels of monoamines due to possessing a shortened version of the MAOA gene (which only males can possess), the effect of which was to produce low levels of the MAOA gene and therefore not absorb monoamines and remove them from the body.

■ The males also exhibited heightened levels of aggression, manifested as rape, arson and violence, when threatened, angry or frustrated.

### Conclusions

■ A link is suggested between genes, biochemistry and aggression.

### Evaluation

■ The study was a case study of one family, presenting problems of generalization to the wider population.

■ The findings do not explain why some males with the shortened MAOA gene do not exhibit heightened aggression.

## ■ Research

■ **Moffitt (1992)** performed a longitudinal study from birth on 442 New Zealand males, to find that those with the shortened version of the MAOA gene who had suffered abuse as children were nine times more likely to indulge in anti-social behaviour, including aggression. This suggests the gene needs a particular environmental trigger to express itself in a manner that leads to aggression.

■ **Cases *et al.* (1995)** studied mice genetically engineered to have low MAOA levels, to find they had abnormal levels of serotonin and heightened aggression as adults, which supports human studies that indicate aggression occurring due to the influence of the MAOA gene.

■ **Crisp *et al.* (1985)** found for anorexia nervosa a concordance rate of 55 per cent between MZ twins, but only 7 per cent between DZ twins, suggesting a genetic component to the disorder.

## ■ Positive evaluation

■ The diathesis-stress model can explain why only some males with the shortened form of the MAOA gene (and one-third of men have it) exhibit heightened aggression. The gene predisposes such men to aggression (diathesis), but aggression only occurs with the presence of certain environmental triggers (stress).

■ The introduction of DNA testing has presented psychologists with an effective means of identifying specific genes associated with particular behaviours.

## ■ Negative evaluation

■ Behaviours, such as aggression, cannot generally be solely explained by genetics. If genetics was the sole cause, then concordance rates between MZ twins for a given behaviour would be 100 per cent. As they are not, it indicates environment plays a role too.

■ As the shortened version of the MAOA gene only occurs in men, it cannot explain aggression in females. Nor can it explain aggression in men who do not possess the shortened version.

■ There are many other non-biological theories of aggression that have a wealth of research support, such as de-individuation, where individuals in a crowd lose the usual controls over their behaviour. This suggests psychological causes to aggression rather than biological ones, such as through genetic influences.

## ■ Practical application

■ DNA testing presents a means of identifying those who may possess, due to their possession of certain genes, undesirable behaviours like aggression, with the possibility of genetic modification to reduce the chances of such behaviour occurring. This would present ethical considerations though, such as the threat of aborting unborn babies, as they may have the genetic potential for such undesirable behaviours.

## ■ Issues and debates

■ If a behaviour resulted solely from the influence of genes, it would support an argument for nature via genetic determinism. As this generally isn't so, it supports more the idea of interactionism: where nature, through biological factors, and nurture, through environmental factors, interact to collectively produce the behaviour.

---

**■ STRENGTHEN YOUR LEARNING**

1 Outline the role of genetics on behaviour, with especial focus upon aggression.
2 Explain the study methods that are used to assess the contributions of genetics to behaviour.
3 Summarize what research studies have suggested about the role of genetics on behaviour.
4 For Brunner *et al.*'s (1993) study into the MAOA gene and aggression, in your own words, state the aims, procedure, results, conclusions and evaluative points.
5 What other evaluative points, including practical applications and relevant issues and debates, can be made about genetics and behaviour?

---

**Expert tip**

When answering questions on genetics and behaviour, credit can be earned by explaining the rationale behind how twin adoption and gene mapping studies work in terms of deciding the extent to which behaviour is innate or learned from environmental interactions.

# Evolutionary explanations for behaviour

Revised ☐

**Evolutionary explanations** see behaviours as genetically transmitted, with behaviours that have a survival value allowing individuals who possess those behaviours to survive to sexual maturity, reproduce and pass on the behaviours to their offspring. Thus over time these behaviours become more widespread in a population. This process is called natural selection.

For example, males and females are seen as evolving different sexual strategies to maximize their chances of reproductive success. Males are never certain of paternity and produce lots of sperm; therefore, their best strategy is to have sex with as many females as possible. Females are always certain of maternity and produce relatively few eggs, so their best strategy is to select genetically fit, resource-rich males and encourage them to remain in monogamous pair bonds so that they and their children will be well cared for.

Another example is anxiety, which has a survival value, as anxious people will be more wary of putting themselves in danger. Even abnormal anxiety disorders

---

**Key term**

**Evolutionary explanations –** interpretations that see behaviours that incur a survival value as being acted upon by natural selection to become more widespread within a population.

like OCD may have a survival value, as in prehistoric times it would have been sensible to be fearful of things that had a risk of infection. OCD may, therefore, be an evolutionary 'hangover'.

KEY CONTEMPORARY STUDY

## 'AVERAGENESS OR SYMMETRY: WHICH IS MORE IMPORTANT FOR FACIAL ATTRACTIVENESS?'

Komori *et al.* (2009)

### Aim

- To assess whether facial symmetry, as an indicator of genetic fitness, predicts attractiveness.

### Procedure

- Komori *et al.* asked 114 participants to rate the attractiveness of 96 facial photographs, which were also assessed on 72 features, as to how far they deviated from the gender average and from the opposite side of the face.

### Results

- Increased facial symmetry correlated with increased attractiveness in male images.

### Conclusions

- Facial symmetry in males is attractive, as strong genes are required to produce bodily symmetry and so facial symmetry indicates genetic fitness.

### Evaluation

- Signs of fertility in females, such as youthfulness and full breasts, are more attractive to males as indicators of reproductive fitness than facial symmetry.

- Facial symmetry only relates to initial attraction and other factors would be more important in formation of relationships, like ability to provide resources.

## Research

- **Marks & Nesse (1984)** reported that lacking concern for others risks exclusion from social groups, and as many OCD sufferers have concern for others' welfare, this risk is reduced, suggesting the condition has an evolutionary value.

- **Buss (1989)** found, using participants from 37 cultures, that males prefer young, physically attractive females, while females prefer resource-rich, ambitious, industrious males, supporting evolutionary explanations of gender differences in attractiveness.

## Positive evaluation

- There is a common-sense value to behaviours that increase survival chances becoming more widespread through natural selection and many behaviours can be explained in this way.

## Negative evaluation

- Evolutionary explanations cannot explain heterosexual couples who decide to remain childless.

## Practical application

- Evolutionary explanations of mental disorders may help clinicians gain a better understanding, which could lead to effective therapies.

## Issues and debates

- The evolutionary explanation of relationships is not gender-biased, as it offers a plausible account of male and female differences in reproductive strategies.

■ **STRENGTHEN YOUR LEARNING**

1  Outline evolutionary explanations of behaviour, including explanations of reproductive strategies and anxiety.

2  Explain the study methods that are used to assess the contributions of genetics to behaviour.

3  Summarize what research studies have suggested about evolutionary explanations for behaviour.

4  For Komori *et al.*'s (2009) study into symmetry and facial attractiveness, in your own words, state the aims, procedure, results, conclusions and evaluative points.

5  What other evaluative points, including practical applications and relevant issues and debates, can be made about evolutionary explanations for behaviour?

**Expert tip**

A common mistake when evaluating evolutionary theory is to say that a limitation is that the theory cannot be empirically tested. However, this is not strictly true; predictions can be made about how behaviour should be if evolutionary theory is true and then these predictions can be examined to see if they are true or not.

# The role of animal research in understanding human behaviour

Revised ☐

Animals are used as participants when there are practical or ethical reasons for not using human participants, with such research often functioning as a starting point for subsequent human research. Animal physiology is seen as similar enough to humans, albeit in an often simpler way, that findings from **animal research** are generalizable to humans. Also, as the developmental cycle of rodents (who comprise 95 per cent of animal research participants) takes less time than that of humans, it allows research to occur in a much quicker time.

**Key term**

**Animal research** – experimentations carried out on non-human animals, in the belief that findings are generalizable to humans.

## ▨ Research

■ **Harlow (1959)** found that baby monkeys raised in isolation preferred contact with a soft-towelling mother providing no food than a wire mother providing food, refuting the theory that attachments occur with those that feed babies.

■ **Pitman (1989)** reviewed evidence to show that animal studies explained how the compulsive behaviours of obsessive-compulsives were reinforced, supporting the use of such studies to explain human behaviour. However, **Andrews-McClymont et al. (2013)** found animal studies could not explain the hoarding behaviour often shown in OCD, lowering support for animal research.

■ **Hodgkin & Huxley (1952)** found it possible to insert electrodes on to the neurons of giant squid to study action potentials, which is not possible with humans (due to the relative size of axons), illustrating how research is sometimes only possible with animals.

■ **Clapcote et al. (2007)** used genetically modified mice to induce schizophrenic symptoms, demonstrating genetic influences upon the disorder. Such research would not be ethically permissible with humans, nor could it occur in such a short time period.

## ▨ Positive evaluation

■ Studies like those of **Savage-Rumbaugh et al. (1986)** on language usage in apes have arguably led to increased awareness of animal consciousness and greater consideration of ethical concerns.

■ Animal studies generally permit tightly controlled conditions, permitting causality to be established and replication to occur to assess validity of findings.

## ▨ Negative evaluation

■ Animal physiology does not always work as in humans. The drug thalidomide, tested on rodents in the 1950s, appeared safe, but when given to humans produced severe physical defects in babies.

■ Humans have complex cognitive abilities, so the findings from studies of animals with simple cognitive abilities do not relate to humans, and using animals with more complex cognitive abilities, like primates, are often considered to be unethical.

## ■ Practical application

■ Animal testing has led to the introduction of many effective psychotherapeutic drugs that have produced a better quality of life for human sufferers.

## ■ Issues and debates

■ Animal research attracts criticism for the ethical concerns raised; indeed, many animal experiments performed in the past would not be permissible now. Some argue, though, that animal testing that benefits humans, like drug testing, should be allowed.

■ Ethical guidelines for experimentation upon animals differ from those of humans, concentrating more on their physical rather than psychological welfare. Some researchers, though, see animals, especially those with higher levels of cognition, as having consciousness and being deserving therefore of the same ethical considerations as humans. Studies of animals in the wild are seen as permissible if they do not lower the reproductive fitness of participants.

> ### Expert tip
>
> When discussing the debate over whether the results of animal experimentation can be generalized to humans, it is sensible to examine both sides of the argument by presenting relevant studies. For example, **Pitman's (1989)** study could be used to show how animal studies explain how OCD behaviours are reinforced in humans, while **Andrews-McClymont et al.'s (2013)** study could be used to show how this may not be so.

---

### ■ STRENGTHEN YOUR LEARNING

1  Explain why animal research is used to understand human behaviour.

2  Summarize what research studies have suggested about the role of animal research in understanding human behaviour.

3  What other evaluative points, including practical applications and relevant issues and debates, can be made about the role of animal research in understanding human behaviour?

---

# Can animal research provide insight into human behaviour?

Revised ■

Some see **biological continuation** from animals to humans, permitting generalization of findings, while others see animals as qualitatively different, creating **extrapolation**. A key argument is that humans are more complex and therefore animal experimentation provides little insight.

**Comparative psychology** compares animals, from insects to primates, to humans, with such comparisons seen as useful through causation, survival value, evolution and ontogeny.

> ### Key terms
>
> **Biological continuation** – the perception that generalizations can be made between simpler and more complex forms of life.
>
> **Extrapolation** – when findings of animal research are used to help explain human behaviour.
>
> **Comparative psychology** – a branch of psychology that compares different forms of life to understand the origins and development of behaviour.

| Type of comparison | Similarity of comparison |
|---|---|
| Causation | Animal behaviour is planned and motivated and so comparable with humans. |
| Survival value | Animal and human behaviour are motivated by their ability to enhance chances of survival and so are comparable. |
| Evolution | Animal and human sexual behaviour are motivated by their ability to maximize reproductive opportunities and so are comparable. |
| Ontogeny | Maturation of behaviour in animals and humans occurs similarly, though quicker in many animals, allowing comparison and research to be conducted more rapidly. |

**KEY CLASSIC STUDY**

## 'THE APE AND THE CHILD: A STUDY OF ENVIRONMENTAL INFLUENCE UPON EARLY BEHAVIOUR'

### Kellogg & Kellogg (1933)

### Aim

- To assess whether a chimpanzee could be taught language alongside a human.

### Procedure

- A case study was performed where ten-month-old human Donald and eight-month-old chimp Gua were raised together in the researchers' home.
- Language abilities of human and chimp were assessed.

### Results

- After one year, Gua outperformed Donald in comprehension tests, responding to 20 command words to Donald's 3.
- Donald spontaneously developed the ability to form spoken words. Gua could only make chimpanzee sounds.
- After nine months, the study was stopped as Donald was making chimpanzee sounds to communicate with Gua.

### Conclusions

- Although direct comparison of humans with chimpanzees is problematic, there is some continuity between species.
- Although similar, humans and chimpanzees display qualitative differences.

### Evaluation

- The fact that Donald was ten months old and Gua eight months old when the study began may have acted as a confounding variable. The study should have been performed with neonate humans and chimps so that learning experiences were identical.
- As this was a case study, it is arguable how representative it is and thus presents generalization problems.

## ■ Research

- **Lycett & Dunbar (2000)** found single men touched their phones more than males in relationships and paid more attention to their phones when the male-to-female ratio in a group was high. This was similar to the lekking strategy of peacocks, when groups of male birds maximize the display of tail feathers to attract females, thus demonstrating how comparing animal and human behaviour can reveal motivations underpinning behaviour.

- **Andics et al. (2014)** found using fMRI scans that dogs and humans were alike in their ability to differentiate between words and non-word sounds. Dog brains have an area that processes human language in a similar way to humans, which suggests that animals can offer insight into complex human behaviours.

## ■ Positive evaluation

- Comparative studies of animals and humans often reveal explanations for behaviour not possible solely from human studies.

- Using comparative studies raises human awareness of the complexity of animal behaviour, which can lead to greater ethical considerations for their treatment.

## ■ Negative evaluation

- There is a danger of researcher bias, where researchers make selective comparisons supporting their research expectation and ignore comparisons that do not.

- There are problems in inferring emotions from animal behaviour. For example, aggression is often inferred from animals' dominance behaviour, but dominance behaviour is not always aggressive in humans and much human aggression is verbal, which would not occur with animals.

## Practical application

- When examining potentially toxic substances, scientists use animals to test for potential effects on humans using neuroinformatics, which incorporates elements of neuroscience, genetics and computer science, to make extrapolation from animal brain data to human brains possible.

## Issues and debates

- Animal studies are reductionist, as they do not consider the complexity of human behaviour that their findings are being extrapolated to.

# Ethical considerations in animal research

Revised

Research that would not be ethical if performed on humans is argued to be permissible, by some, if it potentially benefits humans. However, critics argue for similar **ethical considerations** for animal research, though currently ethical considerations vary across species and are often centred on how humans perceive different species (like more consideration being given to 'cuddly' animals kept as pets) and their level of physiological similarity to humans.

> **Key term**
>
> **Ethical considerations** – moralistic guidelines for the conducting of research.

Bateson's cube is a model that considers three domains:

1 *Quality of research* – research that is of high quality is seen as permissible.

2 *Medical benefit* – research of high medical benefit is seen as permissible.

3 *Degree of suffering* – research incurring low suffering is seen as permissible.

The model describes different research situations that are permissible and not permissible. For instance, a high degree of suffering is never permissible, but a moderate level of suffering is permissible if the quality and medical benefit of research is high.

Another method of assessing the acceptability of animal research is the 3Rs, where research methods should be used that:

1 can *replace* animal testing,

2 *refine* techniques that reduce suffering,

3 *reduce* the number of animals used.

## Research

- **Dawkins (1990)** found that animals suffer when prevented from doing things they naturally want to do, which stresses them. This suggests animal research should be designed using tasks and environments familiar to animals.

- **Hooijmans *et al.* (2010)** report that using systematic reviews of all animal studies done in a particular research area reduces the need for repeating studies for which valid results already exist.

## Positive evaluation

- Testing animals using tasks and environments familiar to them increases the validity of the findings and thus the degree of extrapolation possible to humans.

## Negative evaluation

- With Bateson's cube, different levels of suffering are subjective with no overall agreed definition of them.

- Due to the desire for validity, many researchers are reluctant to use fewer animals in studies, making reduction difficult.

## ■ Practical application

■ Bateson's cube is used to ensure research occurs in ways acceptable to groups with different viewpoints.

## ■ Issues and debates

■ Culture bias is present in animal research, as some cultures see all life as sacred and so do not permit painful animal testing, while others see animals as merely a resource to benefit humans.

---

### ■ STRENGTHEN YOUR LEARNING

1   Present an argument for and against animal research being able to provide insight into human behaviour.
2   Outline the types of comparisons made in studies of comparative psychology.
3   Summarize what research studies have suggested about animal research being able to provide insight into human behaviour.
4   For Kellogg & Kellogg's (1933) study into teaching human language to a chimp, in your own words, state the aims, procedure, results, conclusions and evaluative points.
5   What other evaluative points, including practical applications and relevant issues and debates, can be made about animal research providing insight into human behaviour?
6   Explain ethical considerations of psychological research on animals.
7   Summarize what research studies have suggested about ethical considerations of psychological research on animals.
8   What other evaluative points, including practical applications and relevant issues and debates, can be made about ethical considerations of psychological research on animals?

### Expert tip

A common mistake when addressing ethical considerations in animal research is for students to present a passionate argument for or against one side of the debate. Such answers are often unbalanced. Better answers will present, in an unbiased, detached fashion, both sides of the argument.

---

### EXAM-TYPE QUESTIONS

1   Explain how the function of one or more parts of the brain is determined. (9 marks)
2   Outline one study investigating neuroplasticity. (9 marks)
3   With reference to a study investigating neurotransmitters and their effects on behaviour, outline one strength and one limitation of a research method used in the study. (9 marks)
4   Outline one or more techniques used to study the brain in relation to behaviour. (9 marks)
5   Evaluate techniques used to study the brain in relation to behaviour. (22 marks)
6   Discuss neuroplasticity of the brain. (22 marks)
7   Discuss the limitations of localization as a model of the brain and behaviour. (22 marks)
8   Discuss two or more studies related to neurotransmitters and their effect on behaviour. (22 marks)
9   Explain how pheromones may influence one human behaviour. (9 marks)
10  Outline one study of how hormones affect human behaviour. (9 marks)
11  With reference to a study, outline the ethical considerations of investigating the effects of pheromones and behaviour. (9 marks)
12  Discuss the effects of hormones on human behaviour. (22 marks)
13  Evaluate evidence that pheromones play a role in human behaviour. (22 marks)
14  Explain how genes affect human behaviour. (9 marks)
15  Outline one twin study of genes and behaviour. (9 marks)
16  Outline evolutionary explanations for one human behaviour. (9 marks)
17  Explain ethical considerations in animal research. (9 marks)
18  Evaluate the evidence for links between genes and behaviour. (22 marks)
19  Discuss studies of genetic relatedness. (22 marks)
20  Discuss evolutionary explanations for behaviour. (22 marks)

# 2 Cognitive approach

## Introduction

Revised

**Cognitive psychology** concerns the study of mental structures and processes, comparing the mind to a computer, where information is input and analysed to initiate a response. Cognitive psychology, by assessing how humans process sensory information, seeks to reveal the hidden mental processes that motivate behaviour. The mind basically is seen as an information-processing device.

The cognitive approach links with the biological approach to form *cognitive neuroscience*, which aims to discover the biological basis, in terms of specific brain areas involved, to the mind.

> **Key term**
> **Cognitive psychology** – the scientific study of mental processes.

## Assumptions

Revised

To explain behaviour, cognitive psychology focuses on information processing, which occurs between stimuli and responses. Such processing is seen as influenced by **schemas**, mental representations that individuals have of their world that allow them to organize and interpret information in a pre-set way that fits their world view. Schemas are formed from experience and thus are ever changing as knowledge of the world, whether right or wrong, changes. Individuals therefore perceive the world differently due to differing experiences.

> **Key term**
> **Schemas** – a readiness to interpret sensory information in a pre-set manner.

## Research methods

Revised

The cognitive approach uses a full range of research methods, such as laboratory-based experiments, correlational studies, self-reports, case studies, observations and brain-scanning techniques.

### ■ Research

- **Bruner & Mintern (1955)** found that participants seeing a figure that could be either a letter 'B' or a number '13' perceived it as a 'B' when seen between an 'A' and a 'C', and as a '13' when presented between a '12' and a '14', illustrating the use of laboratory experiments in demonstrating how schema influences perception by people seeing what they expect to see, based on previous experience.

- **Scoville & Milner (1957)** reported on HM, who, as a result of brain surgery, could not create new long-term memories, though his short-term memory was fine, illustrating the use of a case study to show how humans have separate short-term and long-term memory stores.

- **D'Esposito et al. (1995)** used fMRI scans to show that the prefrontal cortex is associated with the workings of the central executive, the controlling system of the working memory model, demonstrating the value of brain-scanning techniques in cognitive psychology.

### ■ Positive evaluation

- Cognitive psychology is superior to behaviourism as it permits understanding of the mental processes occurring between stimuli and responses that motivate behaviour.

- The cognitive approach can be combined with the biological and sociocultural approaches to give a deeper comprehension of behaviour and mind.

### ■ Negative evaluation

- The approach over-focuses on information processing at the expense of how emotional and social factors affect thinking and behaviour.

- Viewing the mind as working like a computer is too simplistic; humans often possess spirituality and levels of creativity not seen in computers.

## Practical application

■ Research by Piaget and Vygotsky on cognitive development led to significant changes in how children are schooled, leading to big advancements in education.

## Issues and debates

■ Aside from the usual ethical issues connected to psychological research, cognitive psychology often studies individuals with brain damage; therefore, care should be taken to ensure harm does not occur, as well as protecting the confidentiality and anonymity of such participants.

---

### ■ STRENGTHEN YOUR LEARNING

1 Explain what is meant by cognitive psychology.
2 Explain what is meant by cognitive neuroscience.
3 Outline the assumptions upon which the cognitive approach is based. Include reference to information processing and schemas in your answer.
4 What type of research methods does the cognitive approach use?
5 Summarize what research studies have suggested about the cognitive approach.
6 What other evaluative points, including practical applications and relevant issues and debates, can be made about the cognitive approach?

---

**Expert tip**

Evaluation of the cognitive approach should focus not just on the level of research support, but also on comparisons with other approaches to draw out the relative strengths and weaknesses of the cognitive approach.

# The multi-store model of memory – Atkinson & Schiffrin (1968)

Revised ☐

## Description

Revised ☐

The **multi-store model** (MSM) explains how sensory information flows through a series of three storage systems. Sensory information initially passes briefly to **sensory memory** (SM), with whichever of the information that is paid attention to transferring temporarily to **short-term memory** (STM). From here, information that is processed sufficiently transfers for more permanent storage to **long-term memory** (LTM). The three stores differ in terms of:

1 *encoding* (how information is represented in storage),
2 *capacity* (how much information can be stored),
3 *duration* (how long information can be stored for).

### ■ Sensory memory

SM is not under conscious control, but is an automatic response to sensory information captured by the sense organs. Information is encoded in its raw sensory form, capacity is enormous, but duration is very limited.

### ■ Short-term memory

STM stores information received from SM and is a temporary store of information currently being paid attention to. Information here is mainly coded acoustically, though other sensory modes are used too. Capacity is limited to between five and nine items, with duration being a maximum of about 30 seconds, which can be extended by rehearsing information in STM.

### ■ Long-term memory

LTM stores information for lengthy periods, which transfers from STM through being processed sufficiently. Information here is coded mainly semantically (by meaning), capacity is potentially unlimited and duration can be for a lifetime.

---

**Key terms**

**Multi-store model** – a cognitive explanation of memory that sees information flowing between a series of storage systems.

**Sensory memory** – a short-duration store that holds impressions of information received by the senses.

**Short-term memory** – a temporary store that holds small amounts of information for brief periods.

**Long-term memory** – a permanent store that holds limitless amounts of information for lengthy periods.

## KEY CLASSIC STUDY

## 'INFLUENCE OF ACOUSTIC AND SEMANTIC SIMILARITIES ON LONG-TERM MEMORY FOR WORD SEQUENCES' BADDELEY (1966)

### Aim
- To assess which forms of encoding dominate in STM and LTM.

### Procedure
- Seventy-five participants were presented with one of four word lists repeated four times:

  ☐ List A – acoustically similar words (sounded the same as each other)

  ☐ List B – acoustically dissimilar words (sounded different from each other)

  ☐ List C – semantically similar words (meant the same as each other)

  ☐ List D – semantically dissimilar words (had different meanings from each other)

- To assess encoding in STM, participants were given a list containing the original words in the wrong order. Their task was to rearrange the words in the correct order.

- To assess encoding in LTM, the procedure was the same, but with a 20-minute interval before recall, during which participants performed another task to prevent rehearsal

### Results
- For STM, participants with List A (acoustically similar) performed the worst, with a recall of 10 per cent. They confused similar-sounding words. Recall for the other lists was between 60 and 80 per cent.

- For LTM, participants with List C (semantically similar) performed the worst, with a recall of 55 per cent. They confused similar-meaning words. Recall for the other lists was between 70 and 85 per cent.

### Conclusions
- For STM, as List A was recalled the worst, it indicates that there is acoustic confusion in STM, suggesting STM is coded mainly acoustically.

- For LTM, since List C was recalled worst, it indicates that there is semantic confusion in LTM, suggesting LTM is coded mainly semantically.

### Evaluation
- The findings make sense, as when you have to remember a shopping list, it is best to repeat it aloud (acoustic rehearsal) while walking to the shops (STM), but when recalling a book you have read, you remember the plot, rather than every single word (LTM).

- The small difference in recall with STM between semantically similar (64 per cent) and semantically dissimilar (71 per cent) lists suggests there is also some semantic coding in STM.

## ■ Research

- **Crowder (1993)** found that SM only retains visual information for a few milliseconds, but for 2–3 seconds for auditory information, which suggests sensory information is encoded into different sensory stores of different durations.

- **Peterson & Peterson (1959)** found participants could recall 90 per cent of nonsense trigrams after 3 seconds, but only 5 per cent after 20 seconds, which suggests STM duration is limited to a maximum of 30 seconds.

- **Jacobs (1887)** found the capacity for recalling increasingly long lists of single-digit numbers or letters was nine for numbers and seven for letters, which indicates the capacity of STM is limited.

■ **Bahrick et al. (1975)** found that participants who had left school in the last 15 years identified 90 per cent of ex-school friends' faces and names from photos, while those who had left 48 years previously identified 80 per cent of names and 70 per cent of faces, indicating that duration for LTM is long-lasting.

## ■ Positive evaluation

■ The model is supported by amnesia cases. Patients either lose their LTM or their STM abilities, but not both, supporting the idea that STM and LTM are separate memory stores.

■ The MSM, as the first cognitive explanation of memory, was influential, inspiring interest and forming the basis for the working memory model, leading to a greater understanding of how memory works.

■ There is considerable research evidence for the existence of separate memory stores of SR, STM and LTM.

## ■ Negative evaluation

■ The main criticism of the MSM is that it is oversimplified. It assumes there are single STM and LTM stores, but research indicates several types of STM, like one for verbal and one for non-verbal sounds, and different types of LTM, like procedural, episodic and semantic memories.

■ MSM describes memory in terms of structure, namely the three memory stores and the processes of attention and verbal rehearsal. However, MSM focuses too much on structure and not enough on processes.

■ The MSM does not consider that memory capacity cannot be measured purely in terms of the amount of information, but rather by the nature of the information to be recalled. Some things are easier to recall, regardless of the amount to be learned.

## ■ Practical application

■ Capacity of STM can be increased through chunking, where the size of the units of information is increased – for example, 19391945 as eight units of information is harder to recall than 1939 and 1945 as two units, denoting the start and finish dates of the Second World War.

## ■ Issues and debates

■ Most research into the MSM uses laboratory experiments and sees human memory as working in the same way for everyone and as such is a nomothetic, as opposed to an idiographic, approach.

---

■ **STRENGTHEN YOUR LEARNING**

1 Draw a diagram showing how the MSM sees information flowing between separate storage systems.

2 Explain what is meant by encoding, capacity and duration.

3 Outline the encoding, capacity and duration of SM, STM and LTM.

4 For Baddeley's (1966) study into encoding in STM and LTM, in your own words, state the aims, procedure, results, conclusions and evaluative points.

5 Summarize what research studies have suggested about the MSM.

6 What other evaluative points, including practical applications and relevant issues and debates, can be made about the MSM?

**Expert tip**

A common mistake when using research studies to evaluate the MSM is to over-describe studies in terms of their procedure. Such detail is largely irrelevant when making evaluative points. Instead, use the findings of such studies to explain whether the model is supported or not.

# The working memory model – Baddeley & Hitch (1974)

Revised ▢

## Description

Revised ▢

The **working memory model** (WMM) is a multi-component explanation of short-term memory. Initially, there were three components: the **central executive**, which oversees two 'slave' systems, the **visuospatial sketchpad** and the **phonological loop**. A third slave system, the **episodic buffer**, was added in 2000 to address shortcomings of the model.

The model focuses on what an individual is 'working on' at a given time (is paying attention to), hence its name, and perceives STM as an active memory store that can hold visual and auditory information simultaneously.

### ▢ Central executive

The central executive (CE) acts as a filter in deciding which sensory information is attended to and then decides which slave systems to allocate it to. The CE has a limited capacity.

### ▢ Visuospatial sketchpad

The visuospatial sketchpad (VSS) is a temporary, limited capacity store for visual and spatial items and the relationships between them. It subdivides into the visual cache, which stores information about form and colour, and the inner scribe, which stores information about spatial relationships of objects in one's environment.

### ▢ Phonological loop

The phonological loop (PL) is a temporary, limited-capacity store for auditory information. It subdivides into the primary acoustic store, which stores words/sounds in the order they were heard, and the articulatory loop, which permits sub-vocal repetition to retain information in the PL.

### ▢ The episodic buffer

The episodic buffer (EB) is a temporary store of integrated information from the CE, PL, VSS and LTM.

### ▢ Research

- **Baddeley (1996)** reported that participants found it difficult to generate lists of random numbers while simultaneously switching between pressing numbers and letters on a keyboard, suggesting the two tasks were competing for CE resources. This supports the idea of the CE being limited in capacity and only being able to cope with one type of information at a time.

- **Gathercole & Baddeley (1993)** found participants had difficulty simultaneously tracking a moving point of light and describing the angles on a hollow letter F, because both tasks involved using the VSS. Other participants had little difficulty in tracking the light and performing a simultaneous verbal task, as they involve using the VSS and the PL, indicating the VSS and PL to be separate slave systems and that the VSS has limited capacity.

- **Klauer & Zhao (2004)** reported more interference between two visual tasks than between a visual and a spatial task, implying the existence of a separate visual cache and inner scribe.

- **Trojani & Grossi (1995)** reported a case study of SC, who had brain damage affecting the functioning of his PL, but not his VSS, suggesting the PL to be a separate system and that components of the WMM are located in different brain areas.

> **Key terms**
>
> **Working memory model** – a cognitive explanation of memory that perceives short-term memory as an active store holding several pieces of information simultaneously.
>
> **Central executive** – component of the WMM that oversees and coordinates the components of working memory.
>
> **Visuospatial sketchpad** – component of the WMM that deals with visual information and the physical relationships of items to each other.
>
> **Phonological loop** – component of the WMM that deals with auditory (sound-based) information.
>
> **Episodic buffer** – component of the WMM that acts as a temporary store of integrated information from the central executive, visuospatial sketchpad, phonological loop and long-term memory.

## KEY CONTEMPORARY STUDY

### 'EXHIBITING THE EFFECTS OF THE EPISODIC BUFFER'
#### Alkhalifa (2009)

#### Aim
- To assess the existence of the episodic buffer.

#### Procedure
- Forty-eight participants saw numbers presented on a screen either as a sequence (i.e. one after another) or in parallel fashion where numbers appeared simultaneously in different parts of the screen. Numbers of sufficient complexity were used to overwhelm the capacity of both the PL and the VSS.
- Participants had to answer problem-solving questions concerning the numbers presented.

#### Results
- Participants presented with sequential numbers got more problem-solving questions correct than those presented with numbers in parallel fashion.

#### Conclusions
- As sequential processing was more effective, it suggests the total capacity of WM is larger than that of the PL and the VSS combined, supporting the existence of the EB (there is a limit to the amount of information that can pass from perception to learning, as parallel processing causes a hindrance to learning).

#### Evaluation
- It might be that the EB provides the storage space and the CE the underlying processing of information that allows separation of accurate recall from false memories and delusions.
- The addition of the EB shows how science works, with the model updated after research like this identified shortcomings with the original version.

---

- **Prabhakaran et al. (2000)** used fMRI scans to find greater right-frontal brain activation for combined verbal and spatial information, but greater posterior activation for non-combined information, providing biological evidence of an EB that allows temporary storage of integrated information.
- **Alkhalifa (2009)** reported on a patient with severely impaired LTM who demonstrated STM capacity of up to 25 prose items, far exceeding the capacity of both the PL and the VSS. This supports the existence of an EB, which holds items in working memory until they are recalled.

## Positive evaluation

- The WMM explains more than the MSM, as, not only does it acknowledge more than one type of STM, it also acknowledges the contribution of other mental processes to memory, like attention, reasoning, reading, comprehension, problem-solving, spatial and visual processing.
- The model explains the execution of everyday tasks; for example, reading, through use of the PL, and navigation around one's environment, through use of the VSS.
- There is a wealth of research evidence to support the existence of separate slave systems whose functions are located in different brain areas.

## Negative evaluation

- Although the existence of the episodic buffer is supported by evidence, it is not clear how the EB combines information from other parts of the model and from LTM.
- The WMM is unable to explain accelerations in processing ability that occurs with practice and over time.

■ Little is known about the workings of the CE, nor its capacity, and as the CE is the controlling component of the model, this weakens overall support for the explanation.

## Practical application

■ Computerized working memory training that uses systematic exercises based on breaking down instructions into steps and frequently repeating them has proven effective in maintaining focus and improving recall in those with working memory impairments.

## Issues and debates

■ As the PL is associated with the evolution of more complex language usage in humans, where increases in short-term memory ability led to being able to remember more complex vocalizations, which led to advanced features of language like grammar, it suggests that language development is under biological control and therefore more a result of nature than of nurture.

> ### ■ STRENGTHEN YOUR LEARNING
> 1 Draw a diagram showing the components of the WMM.
> 2 Name the four main components of the WMM and briefly describe their functions.
> 3 Explain the difference between:
>    a the primary acoustic store and the articulatory loop, and
>    b the visual cache and the inner scribe.
> 4 For Alkhalifa's (2009) study into the episodic buffer, in your own words, state the aims, procedure, results, conclusions and evaluative points.
> 5 Summarize what research studies have suggested about the WMM.
> 6 What other evaluative points, including practical applications and relevant issues and debates, can be made about the WMM?

> ### Expert tip
> A good idea when answering questions on the WMM (and indeed the MSM) is to draw a diagram of the model. This will gain a little amount of credit in itself, but more importantly will serve as a useful plan in helping construct an answer.

# Long-term memory

*Revised* ☐

## Types of long-term memory

*Revised* ☐

Just as with STM, LTM divides into several types, each with a separate function and associated with different brain areas. **Episodic LTM** and **semantic LTM** are declarative types, as they can only be recalled if consciously thought about, while **procedural LTM** is non-declarative, as it can be recalled without conscious thought.

### Episodic LTM

Episodic LTM (ELTM) gives an autobiographical record of personal experiences – for example, when your birthday is – and is influenced by emotions present at the time of encoding, with strength of ELTMs being dependent on degree of processing of information during encoding.

### Semantic LTM

Semantic LTM (SLTM) contains knowledge of things learned, such as that the capital of Mali is Bamako. Generally longer lasting than ELTMs, the strength of SLTMs relates to degree of processing during encoding. SLTMs tend to emerge from ELTMs.

### Procedural LTM

Procedural LTM (PLTM) allows the performance of learned tasks, such as how to surf. As most PLTMs involve motor skills, they take longer to encode than SLTMs and ELTMs.

> ### Key terms
> **Episodic LTM** – a form of LTM for events occurring in an individual's life.
>
> **Semantic LTM** – a form of LTM for meanings, understandings and other concept-based knowledge.
>
> **Procedural LTM** – a form of LTM for the performance of particular types of action.

## Research

- **Tulving (1989)** used radioactive tracing elements to find greater activation in the frontal lobes of the brain during thinking about ELTMs than when thinking about SLTMs, but greater activation in the posterior area of the cortex during thinking about SLTMs than when thinking about ELTMs. This supports the idea of ELTM and SLTM involving different brain areas and thus being separate types of LTM.

- **Vicari et al. (2007)** reported on CL, an eight-year-old girl with brain damage who exhibited deficiencies in ELTM functions, but who still had semantic memories. This suggests that episodic and semantic memories are separate systems using different brain areas.

- **Finke et al. (2012)** reported on PM, a 68-year-old professional cellist who suffered brain damage that affected his ELTM and SLTM, but not his PLTM. He could not recall learning to play the cello, nor explain what a cello was, but his ability to play was unaffected. This suggests PLTM is a separate type of LTM.

## Positive evaluation

- Episodic memory helps individuals to distinguish the difference between real events and imagination/delusions.

- The fact that different forms of brain damage affect different areas of LTM supports the existence of separate types of LTM located in different brain areas.

## Negative evaluation

- It is not fully known which brain areas are involved with PLTM, as examples of individuals with damaged PLTM, but not SLTM and ELTM, are rare.

- The extent to which ELTM and SLTM systems are different is unclear, as although different brain areas are involved, there is overlap between the two systems, with semantic memories often originating in episodic memory.

## Practical application

- Vanderbilt University, USA, built a robot, ISAC, with ELTM, as well as SLTM and PLTM, so it can solve tasks in a more human-like manner by making associations between new tasks and stored experiences to decide which information to put into working memory.

## Issues and debates

- There is a degree of gender bias to research into LTM, as it generally assumes male and female LTM ability to be identical. However, **Herlitz et al. (1997)** found that females have better ELTM abilities, possibly as they have superior verbal ability.

---

### ■ STRENGTHEN YOUR LEARNING

1 Explain what is meant by implicit and explicit LTMs and how this relates to semantic, episodic and procedural LTM.

2 Outline:
  a semantic,
  b episodic,
  c procedural LTM.

3 Summarize what research studies have suggested about types of LTM.

4 What other evaluative points, including practical applications and relevant issues and debates, can be made about types of LTM?

---

### Expert tip

When discussing types of LTM, give an actual example of each type, as this will help demonstrate your understanding of the different types. Presenting examples on their own without any explanation of them would not attract much credit though.

# Gregory's (1970) top-down theory

As sensory data is often incomplete or ambiguous, Gregory saw **perception** as being an ongoing, unconscious search for the best interpretation of sensory data based on previous experience. This involves going beyond data provided by sensory receptors to include processing information at a higher, 'top-down' cognitive level. Perception is therefore indirect, as it is not directly experienced from sensory information (as Gibson believed). The theory explains visual illusions as occurring because expectations based on previous experience are used to interpret incoming sensory information, but sometimes this is prone to error, with false perceptions occurring. For example, we learn, from experience, what objects look like when they are superimposed upon each other, i.e. that an object placed partially in front of another object blocks out aspects of that object from view. We then use this learned information to add a third dimension of depth to flat, two-dimensional images, which results in a misperception – namely, an illusion.

> **Key terms**
>
> **Gregory's top-down theory** – an explanation of perception that involves cognitive processing that goes beyond just sensory input.
>
> **Perception** – an individual's interpretation of sensory data.

## Perceptual schema

**Perceptual schema** sees perception as biased due to previous experiences, cultural factors and emotional and motivational influences. Thus, people see what they want or expect to see, increasing opportunities for errors to occur. Perceptual schema occurs in several ways.

> **Key term**
>
> **Perceptual schema** – the idea that perception is biased due to cultural, motivational and emotional influences.

### Expectation

Expectation involves individuals perceiving what they expect to perceive based on previous experience.

### Emotional influences

Emotional factors form a bias to perceive, or not, certain features of sensory data, like perceptual defence, where emotionally threatening stimuli take longer to perceive.

### Motivational influences

Perception is influenced by motivational factors like hunger, with images of drinks seen as increasingly more attractive as individuals become thirstier. This could have an evolutionary basis, where perception focuses on requirements necessary for survival, like finding water.

### Cultural factors

Cultural factors influence individuals to perceive environmental features in certain ways. People from different cultures may perceive identical sensory data differently because of differing environmental experiences. For example, the Müller-Lyer illusion consists of two lines of equal length, where line A appears longer than line B. However, the illusion is only perceived in cultures where individuals live in a 'carpentered' world of manufactured straight lines, angles and so on. Those from cultures where buildings are made from natural materials do not experience the illusion, as they subconsciously read the third dimension of depth into it from experience.

### Research

- **Brochet *et al.* (2002)** found that expert wine tasters described white wines, altered with a tasteless, odourless dye to look red, in terms descriptive of red wines. This suggests they were overly influenced by the colour, which created an expectation that altered their perception in line with Gregory's theory.

- **Lazarus & McCleary (1951)** found that nonsense syllables presented so rapidly that they were not consciously perceived increased participants' anxiety levels if previously paired with electric shocks, which suggests that emotional factors influence perception unconsciously in line with Gregory's theory.

- **Solley & Haigh (1948)** found that children drew a bigger picture of Santa Claus and his sack of toys as Christmas approached, but afterwards Santa Claus and his sack shrunk, which implies that motivational factors influence perception as suggested by Gregory.

- **Stewart (1973)** found Tongan rural children were less likely to experience the Müller-Lyer illusion than urban children, but the more familiar they became with an environment of straight lines and rectangles, the more prone to the illusion they became, illustrating how cultural factors shape perception through the use of schema, in line with Gregory's theory.

- **Gregory (1970)** found that when participants were presented with a concave (sunken) face, it was perceived as an illusion, appearing as a normal convex face. This suggests that the knowledge of faces being convex, learned from experience of faces, overrides the direct information about the face being concave that is supplied via the senses. This therefore supports Gregory's belief that visual illusions are false perceptions formed from expectations based on previous experience.

## Positive evaluation

- Gregory's theory motivated interest and research that led to greater understanding of perception and generated evidence to support his model.

- It seems logical that interpretations based on previous experience occur when viewing conditions are incomplete or ambiguous. If incomplete features indicated an animal to be a duck or a rabbit, the fact it was on water would suggest that it was a duck.

## Negative evaluation

- Research supporting Gregory generally involves laboratory experiments, where fragmented and briefly presented stimuli are used, which are difficult to perceive directly. Gregory thus underestimates how informative sensory data can be in the real world, where it may be possible to perceive directly.

- People's perceptions, even those from different cultures, are very similar. This would not be true if individual perceptions arose from individual experiences, weakening support for Gregory.

- Gregory's idea that memory is constantly searched to find the best interpretation of incoming sensory data would be time-consuming and inefficient, casting doubt on his theory.

## Practical application

- The use of schema through expectation is used in food frauds, the passing off of inferior foods as superior ones. For example, labelling cheap types of red-coloured fish as expensive red snapper creates expectations that shape diners' perceptions to taste such fish as red snapper.

## Issues and debates

- Gregory's theory sees perception as shaped mainly by learning experiences and thus is more of a result of environmental nurture than biological nature.

---

**■ STRENGTHEN YOUR LEARNING**

1 Explain why Gregory saw perception as a top-down process.
2 What is meant by perceptual schema?
3 Explain how schema affects perception in terms of:
   a expectation,
   b emotional influences,
   c motivational influences,
   d cultural factors.
4 Summarize the extent to which research supports Gregory's idea of schema determining perception.
5 What other evaluative points, including practical applications and relevant issues and debates, can be made about Gregory's theory?

---

**Expert tip**

A sophisticated way of evaluating Gregory's theory (and Gibson's too) is through the use of the nature versus nurture debate. Gregory's theory tends to support the nurture debate (while Gibson's theory supports the nature debate). An explanation of how this is so would attract high-level credit.

# Gibson's (1966) bottom-up theory

Revised

Gibson believed that there was enough information within the **optical array** (the pattern of light reaching the eyes) for perception to occur directly (bottom-up), without higher-level cognitive processing. Individuals' movements and those of surrounding objects within an environment aid this process, which involves innate mechanisms requiring no learning from experience. This permits perception to occur swiftly, allowing individuals to function safely in their environment.

Perception is seen as due to the direct detection of environmental invariances, unchanging aspects of the visual world that possess sufficient sensory data to allow perception of environmental features, like depth, distance and the spatial relationships of objects in relation to each other.

Gibson saw **texture gradients** found in the environment as similar to gradients in the eye, allowing the experience of depth perception. From this, he developed his theory that focuses upon the optical array, texture gradients, **optic flow patterns**, **horizon ratios** and **affordances**.

> **Key terms**
>
> **Gibson's bottom-up theory** – an explanation that sees perception as occurring directly from sensory input without a need for further cognitive processing.
>
> **The optical array** – the structured pattern of light received by the eyes.
>
> **Texture gradients** – surface patterns that provide sensory information about objects.
>
> **Optic flow patterns** – unambiguous sources of information that directly inform perception.
>
> **Horizon ratios** – invariant sensory information concerning the position of objects in relation to the horizon.
>
> **Affordances** – the meaning of objects that permits actions to be carried out upon them.

## The optical array

Revised

The optical array is the structure of patterned light received by the eyes that provides a data source rich enough for direct perception. Movement of the body and eyes continually updates the sensory information being received from the optical array.

## Optic flow patterns

Revised

Optic flow patterns are unambiguous sources of information concerning height, distance and speed that directly inform perception and provide a rich, ever-changing source of information. 'Optic flow' refers to the visual phenomena continually experienced concerning the apparent visual motion that occurs as individuals move around their environment.

## Texture gradients

Revised

Texture gradients are surface patterns providing sensory information about depth, shape, etc. Objects have surfaces with different textures permitting direct perception of distance, depth and spatial awareness. Due to constant movement, the 'flow' of texture gradients conveys a rich source of ever-changing sensory information to an observer.

## Horizon ratios

Revised

Horizon ratios are another type of invariant sensory information permitting direct perception. They concern the position of objects in relation to the horizon. Objects of different sizes at equal distances from an observer present different horizon ratios, which can be calculated by dividing the amount of an object above the horizon by the amount below.

# Affordances

Revised ☐

Affordances involve attaching meaning to sensory information and concern the quality of objects to allow actions to be carried out on them (action possibilities). For instance, a ballet slipper 'affords' dancing. Affordances are therefore what objects mean to observers and are related to psychological state and physical abilities. For a child who cannot walk properly, a mountain is not something to be climbed.

Gibson saw affordances as relaying directly perceivable meaning to objects because evolutionary forces shaped perceptual skills so that learning experiences were not necessary. This rejects Gregory's belief that the meaning of objects is stored in LTM from experience and requires cognitive processing to access.

## ▦ Research

- **Maher & West (1993)** found that observers could recognize animal species from films of them clad in black with lights on their joints, illustrating the wealth of information gained from optic flow patterns that allows perception to occur directly.

- **Frichtel & Lecuyer (2007)** found infants as young as four months could perceive by using texture gradient, from a film of a car driving through scenery. This implies, as stated by Gibson, that the ability is innate, as the participants were too young to have had sufficient learning experiences to gain the ability.

- **Creem-Regehr et al. (2003)** found that restricting participants' viewing conditions did not affect their ability to judge distances using horizon ratio information, suggesting that this form of invariant sensory information is an important component in Gibson's theory of direct perception.

- **Warren (1984)** studied whether participants could judge if staircases portrayed with differently proportioned steps could 'afford' to be climbed; whether they actually could be climbed depended on the length of a participant's legs. It was found that participants were sensitive to the affordance of 'climbability' and, according to Gibson, this was achieved by the invariant properties of the light reflected from the staircases, therefore supporting his concept that affordances do not rely on experience.

## ▦ Positive evaluation

- Gibson's theory, which sees perception occurring without recourse to high-level cognitive processing, can explain how perception occurs so quickly, which Gregory's theory cannot.

- There is a wealth of research evidence supporting the components of Gibson's theory. Indeed, fairly recent evidence even offers some support for the most controversial element of his theory, that of affordances.

- Gibson's notion that perception may have a biological basis has some support. **Logothetis & Pauls (1995)** identified neurons in the brains of monkeys that seem to permit perception of specific objects regardless of their orientation. Further support came from **Rizzolati & Sinigaglia (2008),** who found that the anterior intraparietal brain area is involved in the direct perception of object affordances.

## ▦ Negative evaluation

- Gibson's theory cannot really explain why visual illusions are experienced. He dismissed them as artificial laboratory constructions that were viewed under restrictive conditions, but some illusions occur naturally under normal viewing conditions.

- Gibson's theory is incomplete in not recognizing the influence of environmental learning experiences upon perception. A combination of Gregory's and Gibson's theories might provide the best explanation: Gibson's for ideal viewing conditions and Gregory's for less than ideal conditions where there is not enough information for direct perception.

■ The idea that the optical array provides direct, unlearned information about what objects (affordances) allow individuals to do seems unlikely. Such knowledge is affected by cultural influences, experiences and emotions. For instance, how could an individual directly perceive that a ballet slipper is for dancing?

## ■ Practical application

■ On the approach to junctions and roundabouts, parallel lines are painted on the road surface that are increasingly close together, giving a false impression of speed by affecting optic flow patterns in order to slow drivers down and decrease accidents.

## ■ Issues and debates

■ Gibson's theory can be considered reductionist in the sense that it regards perception as determined by innate factors, thus ignoring the mediating influence of learned environmental experiences.

---

**■ STRENGTHEN YOUR LEARNING**

1 Explain why Gibson saw perception as a bottom-up process.
2 What is the optical array?
3 Outline Gibson's theory in terms of:
   a optic flow patterns,
   b texture gradients,
   c horizon ratios,
   d affordances.
4 Summarize the extent to which research supports Gibson's theory.
5 What other evaluative points, including practical applications and relevant issues and debates, can be made about Gibson's theory?

---

**Expert tip**

Be careful not to dismiss Gibson's idea of affordances too easily (that the ability to attribute meaning to objects is innate and does not require learning). Research like that of **Warren (1984)** actually gives some support to the idea.

# Thinking and decision-making

`Revised` ☐

Thinking and decision-making are related cognitive processes involving the processing of information in order to select from available options. However, humans do not necessarily think in the most rational way and thus do not always make logical decisions.

Individuals in very different situations have similar thought processes in making decisions, which suggests people possess a common set of cognitive processes. It is the limitations of these processes that restrict choice and can lead to illogical decisions.

**Key terms**

**Thinking** – the actions of the conscious mind to interpret, plan and make predictions about the world around us.

**Decision-making** – a cognitive process involving making a choice from available options.

# The information processing approach

`Revised` ☐

The **information processing approach** (IPA) focuses on the thought processes that humans use in making decisions. This is represented in the **adaptive decision-maker framework** and in the **dual process theory**.

## ■ The adaptive decision-maker framework

The adaptive decision-maker framework (ADMF) focuses upon choice in decision-making – for instance, in buying a house – especially with preferential choice problems, where no single option is best in all aspects of choice. Preferential choice problems are solved by acquiring and evaluating information about possible choices. Available options vary according to:

1 their perceived desirability, such as which features of a house and its location are most important,

2 the degree of certainty of their value, for instance, whether the local school is as good as reports say,

3 the willingness of a decision-maker to accept loss on one aspect of a choice in return for gain on another aspect, such as a longer commute in exchange for a rural location.

**Key terms**

**The information processing approach** – an explanation that focuses upon the thought processes involved in decision-making.

**The adaptive decision-maker framework** – an explanation of decision-making that focuses on choice.

**Dual process theory** – an explanation that sees thinking as occurring on a continuum from unconscious to conscious means.

## ▣ Heuristics

**Heuristics** are simpler decision-making processes that involve less cognitive effort by only focusing on some relevant information. This leads to fewer logical decisions, especially when there are a number of important aspects to consider. Several types of heuristics have been identified:

**Key term**

**Heuristics** – the making of decisions by the use of mental short cuts that focus on one aspect of a problem, while ignoring others.

| Type of heuristic | Description |
|---|---|
| *Lexographic strategy* | Selecting the option with best value on what is considered the most important aspect. |
| *Satisficing strategy for decisions* | Choose first option that meets minimum levels on all important aspects. |
| *Majority of confirming decisions* | Consider options in pairs on important aspects – 'winning' option is retained and compared against winning option of another pair until one option is left. |
| *Elimination by aspects* | Reject options not meeting minimum level for most important aspect – repeat for second most important option until one option is left. |

## ▣ Decision task variables

Choice of decision-making strategy is by decision-task variables, like time pressure, where decisions have to be made within a certain time period. Errors in judgement-making can occur through rush-to-judgement (making decisions too quickly) and delay-to-judgement (making decisions too slowly). Choice of decision-making strategy is also affected by the number of choice alternatives – for example, whether a choice has to be made from two options or from ten options.

## ▣ Role of emotions and goals in decision-making

The ADMF focused originally on the accuracy of decision-making and the amount of cognitive effort in decision-making, but it was later extended to include the role of emotion and desired outcomes of a decision.

### ▣ Choice goals framework for decision-making

Several factors are involved in deciding between available choices:

1  *maximizing accuracy of decision-making,*

2  *minimizing cognitive effort,*

3  *minimizing negative emotions while making decisions and afterwards,*

4  *maximizing the ease of justifying a choice to yourself and others.*

The importance of different factors varies with different choice-making situations. With decision-making involving negative emotions, simpler decision-making strategies are often selected that lead to cognitive performance being worsened through decisions taking longer to arrive at and by an increased risk of error in choice occurring.

Negative emotions are aroused when a trade-off is made between two highly valued options – in such situations, individuals often use emotion-focused coping.

### ▣ Coping theory

Individuals respond to negative emotions in one of two ways:

1  *Problem-focused coping* – negative emotions indicate how important a decision is, so focus is on making the best choice to avoid being influenced by negative emotions.

2  *Emotion-focused coping* – focus is on minimizing negative emotions, rather than quality of decision-making; for example, not making a choice, getting someone else to make the choice, avoiding the distressing aspects of a choice, making a choice that is easier to justify, etc.

**Key term**

**Coping theory** – an explanation of how individuals respond to negative emotions when making decisions.

## ■ Dual process model

Part of the IPA, the dual process model (DPM) sees thinking as occurring on a continuum, from System 1, intuitive, mainly unconscious thought, through to System 2, analytic, controllable, conscious thought. System 1 thinking occurs without use of language and gives a feeling of certainty. It permits quick, automatic decision-making that involves little cognitive effort when cognitive energy is simultaneously being used elsewhere, like when paying attention to driving a car and being asked to make a decision about food choices. System 2 thinking is limited by working memory, is rule based, develops with age, uses language in its operation and does not necessarily give feelings of certainty. System 2 thinking involves higher-level information processing activities that require attention and that characterize most decision-making, but System 1 thinking, which occurs below the level of consciousness, is now seen as having an effect upon on System 2 thinking. The correction model argues that initial decisions occur quickly through System 1 thinking, with this decision either being expressed immediately or being confirmed/corrected by System 2 thinking. In this way, System 2 thinking is seen as a check upon System 1 thinking.

Research suggests that System 1 thinking produces better decisions compared to System 2, because unconscious thought organizes information in memory in 'clusters' that relate to a specific choice option, which clearly separate out different choice options.

## ■ Research

- **Payne (1976)** found, when getting participants to make choices between flats to rent based on several important aspects, like price, size and location, when a choice had to be made between two options, participants considered information relating to more aspects than when a decision had to be made between several flats. When choosing between several flats, decision strategies were used that eliminated possible choices as quickly as possible. This illustrates that thought processes concerned with decision-making vary with task complexity.

- **Hancock & Warm (1989)** reported that negative emotions associated with choice decisions damaged cognitive performance, with decisions taking longer to make and more chance of errors in choice occurring. This illustrates the harmful influence that negative emotions can have on decision-making, as stated by the ADMF.

- **Schwartz *et al.* (2002)** found that satisficers are people who select the first option that meets their threshold for acceptability (one that is 'good enough'), not necessarily the best option, and do not experience regret if they later encounter a better option. Maximizers, however, are individuals who consider all options in order to select the best one and are often reluctant to commit to choices due to worries about making the right choice. This suggests that decision-making style is related to individual differences in personality.

- **Dijksterhuis (2004)** found that participants who were given some time to choose between options of flats to rent, but were not allowed to think about the options (by being given distractor tasks), made better decisions than those who had to make immediate decisions or were given time to choose and were allowed to think about options. This supports the idea that unconscious thinking leads to the best decisions, as unconscious thought is an active process that leads to information in memory about choice options being arranged in a more clearly separate and organized fashion.

## ■ Positive evaluation

- More effective decisions are made when a mix of heuristics is used; indeed, the heuristic of 'elimination by aspects' combines features of the 'lexographic strategy' and 'satisficing strategy for decisions' heuristics.

- Research into thinking and decision-making has allowed greater understanding of how cognitive processes work in unison with each other – for example, the role that memory and attention play in thinking and decision-making.

- Models of thinking and decision-making allow psychologists to identify the reasons why humans do not necessarily make the most logical choices when making decisions, which leads to a greater understanding of the decision-making process.

## Negative evaluation

- Knowledge gained about the IPA could be used to exploit thinking and decision-making processes of consumers by the advertising industry, so that people form positive impressions of, and buy, certain products.

- The IPA neglects the role of social influence in thinking and decision-making. Research into minority influence shows that the views of a persistent, committed minority group greatly affect the thinking and decision-making of individuals.

- Much research into thinking and decision-making involves laboratory experiments, the results of which cannot be generalized to real-life situations. For instance, in experiments, participants are told what the important aspects of a decision-making choice are, while in real life, people generate their own important aspects, with different ones for different individuals.

## Practical application

- Many people with anxiety problems are maximizers. Encouraging such individuals to use satisficing strategies when making decisions, where they accept the first acceptable option they encounter, lowers anxiety levels about decision-making.

## Issues and debates

- There is a problem of defining phenomena, like the decision choices people have, in an objectively measureable way. Often such definitions do not exist, or may be so artificial as not to relate to real-life choices.

---

### ■ STRENGTHEN YOUR LEARNING

1 What are thinking and decision-making?
2 Briefly describe, in terms of its main features, the adaptive decision-maker framework.
3 What are heuristics?
4 Explain the following heuristics:
   a lexographic strategy,
   b satisficing strategy for decisions,
   c majority of confirming decisions,
   d elimination by aspects.
5 What is meant by decision task variables?
6 Outline the choice goals framework for decision-making.
7 Outline coping theory in terms of how individuals respond to negative emotions.
8 Outline the dual process model; be sure to include System 1 and System 2 thinking in your answer.
9 Summarize what research evidence has suggested about thinking and decision-making.
10 What other evaluative points, including practical applications and relevant issues and debates, can be made about thinking and decision-making?

---

### Expert tip

Some students struggle with the topic area of thinking and decision-making, as it can be quite theoretical. A good idea, therefore, is to use practical examples. For example, when detailing heuristics, use the example of someone considering several options when buying a house (or similar) to show understanding of the concept.

# Reliability of cognitive processes

Revised ☐

## Reliability of memory

Revised ☐

The accuracy of judgements in court cases depends on the reliability of **eyewitness testimony** (EWT). In 75 per cent of cases where people are found through DNA to have been wrongly convicted, the original guilty verdict was based on unreliable EWT.

### ■ Reconstructive memory

Memories are not accurate versions of events, but instead are reconstructions, influenced by active schemas, ready-made expectations based on previous experiences, moods, existing knowledge, contexts, attitudes and stereotypes. Schemas are used to interpret the world and fill in the gaps in knowledge. With EWT, events are not recalled as they happened, but are reconstructed from schemas active at the time of recall.

Reconstructed memories are influenced by several factors. **Misleading information**, often in the form of misleading questions, can 'suggest' to people that events occurred in a certain way, which is how that event is then recalled. **Post-event information** (misleading information added to an event after it has occurred) can also lead to people having false memories of that event. There is also 'false memory syndrome' (FMS), where traumatic memories, apparently 'recovered' from repression into the unconscious mind, are actually false memories created by suggestion through the questioning of psychotherapists.

> **Key terms**
>
> **Reliability of memory** – the extent to which recall produces consistent results.
>
> **Eyewitness testimony** – the recall of observers, of events previously experienced.
>
> **Reconstructive memory** – the phenomenon by which memories are not accurate versions of events previously experienced, but are built from schemas active at the time of recall.
>
> **Misleading information** – knowledge given that suggests a desired answer.
>
> **Post-event information** – misleading information added to an event after it has occurred.

## KEY CONTEMPORARY STUDY

### 'MAKE MY MEMORY: HOW ADVERTISING CAN CHANGE OUR MEMORIES OF THE PAST'

**Loftus & Pickrell (2003)**

#### Aim
■ To see whether false memories could be created through the use of post-event information.

#### Procedure
■ One hundred and twenty students who had visited Disneyland in childhood were divided into four groups and instructed to evaluate advertising copy, fill out questionnaires and answer questions about a trip to Disneyland.

■ *Group 1* read a fake Disneyland advertisement featuring no cartoon characters.

■ *Group 2* read the fake advertisement featuring no cartoon characters and was exposed to a cardboard figure of Bugs Bunny placed in the interview room.

■ *Group 3* read the fake Disneyland advertisement featuring Bugs Bunny.

■ *Group 4* read the fake advertisement featuring Bugs Bunny and saw the cardboard figure of Bugs Bunny.

#### Results
■ Thirty per cent of participants in Group 3 and 40 per cent of participants in Group 4 remembered or knew they had met Bugs Bunny when visiting Disneyland (impossible, as he is a Warner Brothers character).

■ Those exposed to post-event information were likelier to relate Bugs Bunny to other things at Disneyland not suggested in the advertisement, like seeing Bugs and Mickey Mouse together.

#### Conclusions
■ Use of post-event information can create false memories.

■ Verbal and pictorial suggestions can contribute to false memories.

#### Evaluation
■ The study is superior to Loftus's study of car crashes (see below), as it uses memory of a real-life event rather than something watched on video.

## Research

- **Allport & Postman (1947)** found that participants who saw a picture of a black man and a white man arguing, where the white man had a knife and the black man was unarmed, often recalled the black man as brandishing the knife, as participants often held schemas about black people being aggressive and carrying weapons. This illustrates how memories are reconstructed from schemas active at the time of recall.

- **Bartlett (1932)** found that when a participant was told a Navajo Indian story that made little sense to them and then had to relate the story to another participant and so on, for six or seven participants, the memory of the story got increasingly shorter and changed to fit the participants' cultural backgrounds. This illustrates how memories are reconstructions based on schema, where we remember what we think should have happened based on experience and knowledge rather than what actually happened.

- **Loftus & Palmer (1974)** found that participants' estimates of car speeds viewed on video were affected by which verb they were given in a question asking, 'How fast were the cars going when they contacted/hit/bumped/collided/smashed each other?' This illustrates how misleading information can affect the reliability of EWT.

- **Loftus (1975)** found that 17 per cent of participants who watched a film of a car ride and were asked, 'How fast was the car going when it passed the white barn?', when there was no barn, recalled seeing a barn one week later, supporting the idea that post-event information, where information is added after an event, affects recall.

- **Kaplan & Manicavasagar (2001)** found, from reviewing case studies of FMS, that 'retrieved' memories were false ones induced by therapy, supporting the notion that false memories can be created by suggestion.

## Positive evaluation

- False memories of sexual abuse etc. can have shattering consequences for families involved, highlighting the important role research plays in showing how such claims can be creations of suggestion.

- EWT has impacted on the legal system. In Britain, it is no longer possible to convict on the strength of uncorroborated EWT.

- Understanding the often unreliable nature of memories has led researchers to develop techniques that improve the accuracy of recall, such as the cognitive interview, a technique used by police and military forces to enhance EWT.

## Negative evaluation

- Much EWT research is laboratory-based, where inaccuracies in recall have only minimal consequences, plus real-life events have more emotional impact. **Foster et al. (1994)** demonstrated that EWT was more accurate for real-life crimes than simulations, which suggests that laboratory scenarios do not reflect real-life incidents.

- Participants do not expect researchers to deliberately mislead them, so inaccurate recall is to be expected, as they believe researchers are telling the truth.

- Misleading information only affects unimportant aspects of memory. Memory of important events is not easily distorted. Also information that is obviously misleading does not tend to lead to inaccurate recall.

## Practical application

- Advertisers apply post-event information effects on memory by using nostalgic images to manufacture false positive memories of their products to get consumers to buy them.

## ■ Issues and debates

■ Reconstructive memory illustrates the mind–brain divide debate. Memories appear to be reconstructions, which indicates that memories are not stored in a physical sense, like music is as a download, CD or vinyl record. This suggests that some elements of the 'mind' are non-physical and thus beyond biological explanation.

> ### ■ STRENGTHEN YOUR LEARNING
>
> 1  What is meant by reconstructive memory?
> 2  Explain how reconstructive memory is affected by:
>    a  misleading information,
>    b  post-event information,
>    c  false memory syndrome.
> 3  For Loftus & Pickrell's (2003) study into memories of Bugs Bunny, in your own words, state the aims, procedure, results, conclusions and evaluative points.
> 4  Summarize what research evidence has suggested about reconstructive memory.
> 5  What other evaluative points, including practical applications and relevant issues and debates, can be made about reconstructive memory?

> **Expert tip**
>
> A common mistake when answering questions on the reliability of memory is to over-focus on **Loftus & Palmer's (1974)** study of estimating the speed of cars involved in accidents. A much better example is **Loftus & Pickrell's (2003)** study concerning memories of Bugs Bunny and Disneyland, as it involves a real-life incident experienced by the participants.

# Cognitive biases in decision-making

`Revised` ☐

**Cognitive biases** are illogical, systematic errors in thinking that negatively affect decision-making. There are several cognitive biases:

■ *Framing effects* – how situations are perceived affects how decisions are made. With gambling, if individuals perceive themselves in a position of gain, having won a big bet, they are unlikely to take risks. However, if they perceive a situation of loss, having lost a big bet, they are likely to take risks to recover losses.

■ *Use of information* – certain types of information are favoured:
   ☐ easily available information,
   ☐ easily memorable information,
   ☐ information displaying an individual positively (**self-serving bias**),
   ☐ information supporting an established belief (**confirmation bias**).

■ *Judgement* – information with potential sources of uncertainty are not favoured (as they decrease confidence). Also, once decisions are made, new information inconsistent with the decision is ignored (insufficient anchoring judgement).

## ■ Post-decision evaluation

Decisions are evaluated in ways that protect self-esteem and build confidence and control.

**Fundamental attribution bias** is when favourable outcomes are seen as resulting from actions under personal control and unfavourable ones as outside personal control.

**Illusion of control** is when the understanding of how events occur becomes distorted, like by creating superstitions.

**Hindsight bias** is when outcomes are perceived as predictable, even when there is no evidence for this.

## ■ Research

■ **Marsh & Hanlon (2007)** found that biologists made different observations of salamanders according to different expectations of them they had been given, demonstrating the effect of confirmation bias, even among experts in a field.

> **Key terms**
>
> **Cognitive biases in decision-making** – illogical, systematic errors in thinking that negatively affect decision-making.
>
> **Self-serving bias** – favouring information that shows oneself in a favourable way.
>
> **Confirmation bias** – favouring information that supports an established belief.
>
> **Fundamental attribution bias** – the tendency to see favourable outcomes as resulting from actions under personal control and unfavourable outcomes as being due to factors beyond personal control.
>
> **Illusion of control** – the idea that people's understanding of a situation is illogical in order for them to believe they can influence external events.
>
> **Hindsight bias** – the tendency to perceive an event as having been predictable, even though there was no information for predicting this occurrence.

- **Brandt *et al.* (1975)** found that teachers attributed the success of students to their teaching skills, and the failure of students to the students' poor quality, supporting the self-serving bias, that information displaying individuals in a positive way is favoured.

- **Fluke *et al.* (2010)** found that the main reason for superstitions was to gain control over uncertain situations, supporting the idea of illusion of control, where people believe they can influence external events.

## Positive evaluation

- Examples of cognitive bias can be seen in real life. For example, those who hold paranormal beliefs exhibit illusion of control, which has the effect of reducing anxiety, like believing they can ward off evil forces.

- The existence of cognitive biases is supported by a wealth of research evidence.

## Negative evaluation

- Studies of bias often use artificial laboratory situations that suffer from a lack of ecological validity, producing results not applicable to real life.

- Studies of bias often involve the unethical use of deception, like those used to investigate self-serving bias. Such studies are generally now seen as unjustifiable.

## Practical application

- Bookies' odds do not match the chances of horses winning races, but instead exploit cognitive biases. On the last race of the day, when most punters have lost large sums, odds on favourites are shortened and longer odds are offered on less-fancied horses, as such punters are more likely to make large, risky bets on outsiders.

## Issues and debates

- Conclusions concerning cognitive biases tend to be nomothetic, seeing individuals as affected similarly, when actually there are wide individual differences, linked to personality, in the degree to which cognitive biases affect people.

---

**■ STRENGTHEN YOUR LEARNING**

1 What are cognitive biases?

2 Explain how cognitive biases can influence thinking and decision-making through:

   a framing effects,

   b use of information,

   c judgement.

3 Explain post-decision evaluation in terms of:

   a fundamental attribution bias,

   b illusion of control,

   c hindsight bias.

4 Summarize what research evidence has suggested about cognitive biases.

5 What other evaluative points, including practical applications and relevant issues and debates, can be made about cognitive biases?

---

**Expert tip**

A common mistake when using research studies as evaluation is to then evaluate the studies themselves in terms of their methodology – for instance, that they lack ecological validity (are not true to real life). However, unless this is centred on the question, such as assessing whether cognitive biases exist in decision-making, this would not be very creditworthy.

# Emotion and cognition

## The influence of emotion on cognitive processes

**Emotion** is a state of mind determined by mood, with cognitive factors increasingly seen as important in the experience of emotion.

### Theories of emotion

#### Lazarus's (1982) cognitive appraisal theory

Lazarus saw emotion as arising from an individual's interpretation and explanation of particular events, with two important cognitive aspects of emotion:

1 the nature of cognitive appraisals underlying emotional responses, and

2 the determining preceding conditions of those cognitive appraisals.

Two types of appraisal methods underpin cognitive appraisal:

1 *primary appraisal*, concerning the meaning and significance of an event to an individual, and

2 *secondary appraisal*, concerning an individual's assessment of their ability to cope with the consequences of that event.

Lazarus stresses the importance of cognition, as when we experience an event, thoughts precede physiological arousal and the sensation of emotion (which occur simultaneously). Therefore, some cognitive processing must occur before an individual experiences an emotional response to an event.

#### Emotion and perception

Perception is biased by schema (see page 33), but schemas also affect perception through emotional factors, creating a bias to perceive (or not) certain features of sensory data. Important here is **perceptual defence**, where emotionally threatening stimuli take longer to perceive.

#### Emotion and memory

Memory can also be affected by schema (see page 34), but memory is also affected by emotional factors through **flashbulb memory**, **repression** and contextual emotional effects.

Emotion affects all stages of memory: encoding, storage and retrieval.

Emotionally arousing stimuli can also lead to amnesia where no physical damage to brain structures occurs. This occurs as retrograde amnesia, where memories occurring before a traumatic event are lost, or anterograde amnesia, where new memories cannot be created after experiencing an emotional event.

#### The effects of emotion upon memory as a process

1 *Encoding* – **cue-utilization theory** sees high levels of emotion focusing attention on emotionally arousing elements of an environment, with these elements becoming encoded in memory and not non-emotionally arousing elements.

2 *Storage* – emotional arousal consolidates information in storage, making memories longer lasting. This is not immediate, as the hormonal processes involved in consolidation take time and because emotional experiences incur more elaboration between new information and previously stored information.

3 *Retrieval* – as emotional aspects of events are encoded with sensory aspects, reconstruction of memories is influenced by the degree of emotional similarity between circumstances of encoding and circumstances of retrieval. This occurs through:

---

### Key terms

**Emotion** – a state of mind determined by one's mood.

**Cognitive appraisal theory** – an explanation that sees cognitive processing as occurring before an individual can experience an emotional response to an event.

**Perceptual defence** – the process by which stimuli are not perceived or are distorted due to their threatening or offensive nature.

**Flashbulb memory** – strong, vivid memory of an event with a high emotional impact.

**Repression** – a form of motivated forgetting where emotionally threatening memories are hidden in the unconscious mind to prevent feelings of anxiety.

**Cue-utilization theory** – an explanation that sees high levels of emotion focusing attention on to the emotionally arousing elements of an environment, so that these elements become encoded in memory and not the non-emotionally arousing elements.

☐ the **mood-congruence effect**, concerning the ability of individuals to retrieve information more easily when it has the same emotional content as their current emotional state,

☐ **mood-state dependent retrieval**, concerning the ability of individuals to retrieve information more easily when their emotional state at the time of recall is similar to their emotional state at the time of encoding.

### ■ Flashbulb memory

Important emotional events are stored in a complete manner that contains the circumstances and the emotional reaction, as well as the details. Such events may be shared by many, like a traumatic news event, or be personal, like the birth of a child. People are confident that flashbulb memories are accurate, as they are important to them, but research suggests that such memories are not completely accurate.

### ■ Repression

Repression is a type of motivated forgetting, where traumatic events are 'hidden' in the unconscious mind, but affect conscious behaviour. There is much debate over whether repression exists.

### ■ Emotion and decision-making

Emotions, especially negative ones, can lead to changes in decision-making strategies that impact on the effectiveness of decisions made (see page 46).

## ■ Research

■ **Speisman *et al.* (1964)** found that when shown a film about Aboriginal circumcision, participants experienced the most physiological arousal when the traumatic element of the film was heightened through manipulation of the soundtrack, so that emphasis was focused on the jaggedness of the knife, pain of the boys, etc. This suggests that the cognitive appraisal of what people think about a situation affects the level of arousal experienced, supporting Lazarus's theory.

■ **Hardy & Legge (1968)** found that an acoustic stimulus presented with words flashed momentarily on a screen was detected at higher intensity with emotive than neutral words, supporting the idea of perceptual defence affecting perception.

■ **Bower (1981)** found that participants' recall of word lists, personal experiences recorded in diaries and childhood experiences were related to the mood they were in at the time of recall, supporting the idea that people retrieve information more easily when their emotional state at time of recall is similar to their emotional state at time of encoding.

■ **Hirst *et al.* (2011)** found that accuracy of flashbulb memories to a US terrorist attack was accurate after 10 days, but only 65 per cent so after one year and 60 per cent so after 10 years, with memory best for central facts. This supports flashbulb memory as a phenomenon, but suggests such memories lose accuracy over time.

■ **Holmes (1990)**, in reviewing 60 years of research into repression, found no solid evidence of the phenomenon, weakening support for repression being a valid explanation.

## ■ Positive evaluation

■ Focusing on emotionally threatening aspects of an experience makes evolutionary sense. There is an immediate survival value in doing so and remembering such aspects helps an individual be prepared for similar future situations.

---

**Key terms**

**Mood-congruence effect** – the ability of individuals to retrieve information more easily when it has the same emotional content as their current emotional state.

**Mood-state dependent retrieval** – the ability of individuals to retrieve information more easily when their emotional state at the time of recall is similar to their emotional state at the time of encoding.

- Research suggests that emotions are not innately programmed into brains, but are instead cognitive states generated from sensory information, which supports the idea of emotion being a cognitive process in itself.

## Negative evaluation

- The use of stimuli presented too momentarily for conscious recognition suggests that perceptual defence is a real phenomenon rather than a response bias, where participants are embarrassed to recognize such stimuli or are genuinely unfamiliar with them.

- Flashbulb memories are vulnerable to post-event information, incorrect information added to the event after they have occurred, which suggests that flashbulb memories are not always accurate.

## Practical application

- Emotional stimuli are used to stimulate recall in people with amnesia, as emotional stimuli often serve as retrieval cues to prompt the recall of apparently forgotten information.

## Issues and debates

- Research into emotion brings risks of harm, so studies need to be carefully designed to minimize such risk so that potential harm is no greater than that from everyday experience.

---

**■ STRENGTHEN YOUR LEARNING**

1 Outline Lazarus's cognitive appraisal theory.
2 Explain how emotion affects perception; include the idea of perceptual defence in your answer.
3 Explain how emotion can affect:
  a  encoding of memories,
  b  storage of memories,
  c  retrieval of memories (include in your answer reference to the mood-congruence effect and mood-state dependent retrieval).
4 Explain what is meant by:
  a  flashbulb memory,
  b  repression.
5 Summarize what research evidence has suggested about the influence of emotion on cognitive processes.
6 What other evaluative points, including practical applications and relevant issues and debates, can be made about the influence of emotion on cognitive processes?

---

**Expert tip**

When writing about the influence of emotion on cognitive processes, be careful not to over-focus on theories of emotion themselves. Instead, answers should focus on how emotion affects cognitive processes, such as memory and perception, in order to gain credit.

# Cognitive processing in the digital world

Revised ☐

Psychologists are interested in the effects of **digital technologies** (DTs) on attention, especially the effects of multitasking, like using DTs during lectures, with research suggesting that humans cannot perform several tasks simultaneously, but just switch tasks swiftly, which expends cognitive energy, leading to errors being made. Cognitive psychologists are also interested in the effects of DTs on learning processes and memory.

**Key term**

**Digital technologies** – electronic devices and systems that generate, process and store data.

# The effects of modern technology on cognitive processes

## ■ Positive effects

DTs work best when used by small groups, as group usage stimulates deeper-level analysis of material than individual use. DTs also aid learning more when used in short and focused ways and are especially beneficial to lower-attaining students and those with learning disorders or from disadvantaged backgrounds, as they provide intensive support to aid learning. DTs are most beneficial when used as support for learning, rather than being the sole means of learning, and in certain subjects, like mathematics, where deeper levels of cognitive processing are not necessary. Overall, DTs improve learning if they focus on assisting what is to be learned rather than being a means of learning in themselves.

## ■ Negative effects

DTs are associated with attention deficit hyperactivity disorder (ADHD), internet addiction disorder and decreased cognitive performance, through overloading visual working memory. Also younger individuals, who grow up only knowing DTs, are increasingly unable to use other forms of media, like reading books.

Over-use of computers can overload visual working memory, decreasing cognitive performance. Additionally, digital multitasking, like using laptops in lectures, is associated with lower test scores and constantly recording information on digital devices makes information less likely to enter LTM as individuals are distracted from properly encoding information as it is experienced.

Compared to DTs, writing is a more effective means of storing and organizing information. Writing enhances learning (compared to typing) as it allows the brain to receive feedback from motor actions, creating a more meaningful motor memory. This helps individuals establish connections between reading and writing. It also seems that the longer time it takes to write by hand has a time-related effect on learning.

DTs can create 'shallow thinkers'. Constantly looking information up on the internet and thus not thinking deeply about it leads to weak memories lacking in detail.

## ■ Research

- **Liao (2007)** found that computer teaching produced better test scores, but only when used in small-group rather than individual learning situations, which suggests DTs are effective learning tools when they encourage deeper-level cognitive processing through discussion.

- **Moran *et al.* (2008)** found that using digital videos in teaching boosted test scores, but only when utilized in a focused way for short periods, which suggests that DTs can be effective when used as a means of supporting learning, rather than a means of learning in themselves.

- **Carr (2010)** found that students who used a laptop during a lecture to access internet information related to the lecture did worse in a test on the content of the lecture than those who did not use DTs during the lecture. This suggests that multitasking through the use of DTs has a negative effect on learning by diverting attention.

- **Mueller & Oppenheimer (2014)** found that participants using pen and paper in a lecture to make notes scored equally on a test for facts with participants using a laptop, but outscored the laptop participants for understanding ideas, which suggests typing leads to 'mindless processing'.

> **KEY CONTEMPORARY STUDY**
>
> ## 'GOOGLE EFFECTS ON MEMORY: COGNITIVE CONSEQUENCES OF HAVING INFORMATION AT OUR FINGERTIPS'
>
> Sparrow *et al.* (2011)
>
> ### Aims
>
> ■ To assess whether the internet has become an external memory system.
>
> ■ To assess whether internal encoding of memory is focused more on where information can be found, rather than the information itself.
>
> ### Procedure
>
> ■ Four laboratory experiments were conducted that tested whether participants:
>
>   □ were 'primed' to use a computer when they did not know the answer to a question (by seeing if computer-related words were read more quickly on hard questions than easy ones)
>
>   □ would recall information they believed they could access online later on
>
>   □ would recall where specifically to find information they believed would be available online
>
>   □ would recall where to find information more than the information itself.
>
> ### Results
>
> ■ Computer-related words were read more quickly on hard questions than easy ones.
>
> ■ Information participants believed would not be available online later on was recalled best.
>
> ■ Participants had poor recall of where specifically information was stored online.
>
> ■ Participants recalled where information was stored more than the information itself.
>
> ### Conclusions
>
> ■ When a question is difficult, people are primed to use a computer to find the answer.
>
> ■ When people believe an answer is online, they do not feel the need to encode it in memory, nor do they encode where the information is online.
>
> ■ People do not specifically recall where external memories are located.
>
> ### Evaluation
>
> ■ For many people, computers have become an external source of memory, as they see them as swift sources of vast amounts of information.

## ■ Positive evaluation

■ As positive and negative effects of DTs have now been identified, future research should try and identify ways in which DTs enhance cognitive performance, especially as an aid to learning.

■ As over 50 per cent of individuals store digitally all-important personal information, it seems digital devices are replacing autobiographical memory.

## ■ Negative evaluation

■ Studies of DTs focus on subjects that use them more, like mathematics, and should not be generalized to other subjects, like psychology, where critical thinking is more important.

■ Many schools are rushing into creating digital learning environments, believing it will boost cognitive performance. However, DTs are only effective when used in certain ways and in certain subjects.

## ■ Practical application

■ Combining traditional learning methods with DTs, targeted in an engaging, manner to small groups rather than individuals, is the most effective manner of using DTs to enhance learning.

## ■ Issues and debates

■ Research into the effects of modern technology on cognitive processes has cultural validity, as studies were carried out on a cross-section of cultural groups, allowing clear conclusions to be drawn.

---

### ■ STRENGTHEN YOUR LEARNING

1 In what ways are cognitive psychologists interested in digital technologies?

2 Outline the positive effects of DTs on cognitive processing.

3 Outline the negative effects of DTs on cognitive processing.

4 For Sparrow *et al.*'s (2010) study into Google effects on memory, in your own words, state the aims, procedure, results, conclusions and evaluative points.

5 Summarize what research evidence has suggested about the effects of DTs on cognitive processing.

6 What other evaluative points, including practical applications and relevant issues and debates, can be made about the effects of DTs on cognitive processing?

### Expert tip

Better answers to questions concerning cognitive processing in the digital world will focus on both positive and negative effects in order to give a balanced account, with research evidence used to illustrate such effects.

---

## EXAM-TYPE QUESTIONS

| | |
|---|---|
| 1 Discuss models of memory. | (22 marks) |
| 2 Evaluate one model of memory. | (22 marks) |
| 3 To what extent do findings from one or more psychological studies related to schema theory support the understanding of thinking and decision-making? | (22 marks) |
| 4 Discuss schema theory in relation to two cognitive processes. | (22 marks) |
| 5 Consider what schema theory has informed about thinking and decision-making. | (22 marks) |
| 6 Discuss schema processing in relation to top-down and bottom-up processing. | (22 marks) |
| 7 Outline one study investigating schema theory. | (9 marks) |
| 8 Evaluate one research study of one model of memory. | (9 marks) |
| 9 Explain how schema theory affects perception. | (9 marks) |
| 10 Discuss the reliability of one cognitive process. | (22 marks) |
| 11 Outline reconstructive memory. Evaluate reconstructive memory with reference to studies. | (22 marks) |
| 12 Outline and evaluate the reliability of cognitive processes in relation to biases in thinking and decision-making. | (22 marks) |
| 13 Evaluate the reliability of two cognitive processes. | (22 marks) |
| 14 Outline the reliability of reconstructive memory. | (9 marks) |
| 15 Describe one study relevant to the reliability of cognitive processes. | (9 marks) |
| 16 Evaluate biases in thinking and decision-making by reference to one or more studies. | (9 marks) |
| 17 Discuss the influence of emotion on two cognitive processes. | (22 marks) |
| 18 Evaluate the effect of emotion on memory. | (22 marks) |
| 19 Outline the influence of emotion upon one cognitive process other than memory. Evaluate the influence of emotion upon one cognitive process other than memory with reference to studies. | (22 marks) |
| 20 Discuss what studies have suggested about the influence of emotion on cognitive processes. | (22 marks) |
| 21 Outline one research study of the influence of emotion upon one cognitive process. | (9 marks) |
| 22 Outline the influence of emotion on memory. | (9 marks) |
| 23 Evaluate one or more studies of the influence of emotion upon one cognitive process, other than memory. | (9 marks) |
| 24 Discuss the influence of digital technology on cognitive processes. | (22 marks) |
| 25 Outline and evaluate the positive and negative effects of digital technology on one or more cognitive processes. | (22 marks) |
| 26 Discuss what studies have suggested about cognitive processing in the digital world. | (22 marks) |
| 27 Evaluate the negative effects of digital technology on cognitive processes. | (22 marks) |
| 28 Outline the positive influences of digital technology on one or more cognitive processes. | (9 marks) |
| 29 Discuss one research study on the effect of digital technology on one cognitive process. | (9 marks) |

# 3 Sociocultural approach

## Introduction

Revised

The **sociocultural approach** focuses on the context in which behaviour occurs. For instance, the influence of social groups, such as peers and family, upon behaviour is considered, as are cultural and subcultural influences, because behaviour exhibited is seen as a reflection of those influences.

> **Key term**
>
> **Sociocultural approach** – psychological approach that focuses on the social and environmental contexts in which behaviour occurs.

## Assumptions

Revised

There are three key assumptions of the sociocultural approach:

- Individual behaviour is influenced by the environment we live in.
- Individual behaviour is influenced by a sense of belonging and connectedness to others.
- Each individual constructs their own **self-concept** and **social self**.

> **Key terms**
>
> **Self-concept** – the perception that an individual has of their self, constructed from their interactions with others and their environment.
>
> **Social self** – a perception of self as being influenced through interactions with social groups.

### Environmental influence on an individual

Emphasis is upon cultural attitudes and ideologies, with focus also on environmental influences, such as the media, education, family factors and physical environment (e.g. urban and rural locations), as well as a consideration of the effect of others upon an individual's behaviour.

### Sense of belonging and connectedness

Humans are seen as social, with a need to be involved with others, with much behaviour occurring within groups. Social relationships are important to an individual's sense of well-being, so conformity to group norms in order to be accepted is common.

### Construction of the self-concept and social self

The self is seen to be constructed through interactions with others and by cultural influences that shape how we perceive ourselves. 'Self' can vary between different contexts, such as within different groups and cultural settings.

## Research methods

Revised

As the approach focuses on context, naturalistic observations of behaviour in real-world settings are favoured. Ethnography is also used, where researchers become part of the context to observe more and gain greater understanding. Interviews allow further insight into behaviour, while focus groups allow the effect of others to be assessed. Case studies are additionally used to study individuals in unique circumstances.

### Research

- **Asch (1955)** found that participants would conform to obviously wrong answers in the presence of a group in order to fit in, illustrating the important sociocultural influence that others exert on individual behaviour.
- **Nasser (1986)** found that female Arab students attending London universities had much higher rates of eating disorders than Arab females attending Cairo universities, illustrating the role cultural influences exert upon behaviour.
- **Williams (1981)** reported that children's aggression levels in a remote area of Canada rose after the introduction of television, demonstrating the sociocultural influence of media upon behaviour.

## ■ Positive evaluation

■ Naturalistic observations provide ecologically valid results that reflect behaviour in real-world situations.

■ The approach considers the important influence that others have upon behaviour, rather than looking artificially at individual behaviour in isolation.

## ■ Negative evaluation

■ The approach tends to neglect biological influences upon behaviour.

■ The lack of laboratory-based experiments creates problems in establishing causality and replicating studies to check validity of findings.

## ■ Practical application

■ Family therapy is a treatment for schizophrenia, based on sociocultural assumptions, that sees interactions within families as important in reducing symptoms of the disorder.

## ■ Issues and debates

■ Sociocultural explanations tend not to be culture-biased, as they generally consider the influences that cultural and subcultural factors have upon behaviour.

---

**■ STRENGTHEN YOUR LEARNING**

1 Explain what is meant by the sociocultural approach.
2 Outline the three key assumptions of the sociocultural approach to understanding behaviour.
3 What research methods are used to study the sociocultural approach?
4 Summarize what research evidence has suggested about the sociocultural approach.
5 What other evaluative points, including practical applications and relevant issues and debates, can be made about the sociocultural approach?

---

**Expert tip**

Probably the best way to build some detail into an answer, when explaining the sociocultural approach, is to outline the main assumptions that the approach is formed upon in influencing individual behaviour.

---

# The individual and the group

Revised ☐

## Social identity theory

Revised ☐

**Social identity theory** (SIT) sees self-esteem as central to individual identity, and to feel good about ourselves, we need to feel good about the **in-groups** we identify with, perceive ourselves as having similar characteristics to their members and adopt in-group norms as our own, as well as perceiving ourselves as superior to **out-groups** we do not identify with.

SIT includes the out-group homogeneity effect, where members of out-groups are seen as not only different from in-group members, but as more similar to each other than in-group members.

### ■ Research

■ **Neto (2016)** found that Portuguese children rated other Portuguese people as having more positive and less negative features than people from Brazil and Cape Verde, which suggests in-group favouritism and out-group negativism forms in childhood.

■ **Crandall & Stangor (2005)** found that when participants were told in-group members held a belief, they were more likely to report the belief themselves than those not told this. This supports SIT, where individuals adhere to in-group norms.

---

**Key terms**

**Social identity theory** – an explanation that considers how group membership is an essential part of individual identity.

**In-groups** – social groups that an individual belongs to or identifies with.

**Out-groups** – social groups that an individual does not belong to or identify with.

## KEY CLASSIC STUDY

### 'EXPERIMENTS IN INTERGROUP DISCRIMINATION: THE MINIMAL GROUP PARADIGM'

**Tajfel (1970)**

### Aim

- To see how, and to what extent, group membership is influential in behaviour and attitude change.

### Procedure

Sixty-four schoolboys aged 14–15 years were randomly put into two groups:

- *Experiment one* – participants gave small rewards of money to a pair of boys who were either in-group or out-group members, using a book of matrices that had pairs of numbers that converted into money.

- *Experiment two* – participants selected options from matrices, with three choices:

  - ☐ *maximum joint profit* – giving the largest amount to members of both groups

  - ☐ *maximum in-group profit* – giving the largest amount to an in-group member, regardless of the amount to an out-group member

  - ☐ *maximum difference* – giving the largest possible difference in amounts between an in-group and out-group member.

### Results

- The boys favoured in-group members, allocating them more points.

- When out-group members stood to gain if participants chose a larger number of points, participants sacrificed points to in-group members so that out-group members would not benefit.

### Conclusions

- Favouritism is shown towards in-group members, though discrimination to out-group members is more important than rewarding in-group members.

### Evaluation

- Demand characteristics could occur through the matrices being seen as a game to 'win', and it was this expectation that shaped behaviour.

## Positive evaluation

- Everyday life shows evidence of in-group and out-group behaviour – for instance, between sports team fans.

- SIT has been influential in helping understand how prejudice between different groups arises.

## Negative evaluation

- In-groups can have cliques – groups within groups – that differ from each other, which suggests social behaviour is more complex than SIT believes.

- Research into SIT tends to be laboratory-based and lacking in ecological validity, with results not applicable to real-life situations.

## Practical application

- To break down prejudices between groups, similarities are emphasized between individuals of in-groups and out-groups.

## Issues and debates

- In-group favouritism and out-group negativism can be seen to have an evolutionary survival value and so can be perceived as a result of biological determinism.

■ **STRENGTHEN YOUR LEARNING**

1  Outline SIT, including reference to in-groups and out-groups.

2  For Tajfel's (1970) study into intergroup discrimination, in your own words, state the aims, procedure, results, conclusions and evaluative points.

3  Summarize what research evidence has suggested about SIT.

4  What other evaluative points, including practical applications and relevant issues and debates, can be made about SIT?

**Expert tip**

Take care when writing about social identity theory not to over-focus on **Tajfel's (1970)** experiment into inter-group discrimination in terms of outlining the procedure of the study. More important is to use the findings of the study to assess to what extent group membership is influential in behaviour and attitude change.

# Social cognitive theory

Revised ☐

Social cognitive theory (SCT) incorporates **social learning theory** (SLT) in seeing behaviour as learned by *observation* and *imitation* of others acting as *models*, according to the consequences of their behaviour. This involves **vicarious reinforcement**, as rewards and punishments for behaviour occur to the model, not the person observing the behaviour. Imitation is more likely to occur if a person *identifies* with a model.

SLT considers cognitive aspects of behaviour known as **mediational processes**.

| Mediational processes | Description |
| --- | --- |
| *Attention* | To be imitated, behaviour must be focused on. |
| *Retention* | The behaviour must be retained in memory for future use. |
| *Reproduction* | We must be capable of performing the observed behaviour. |
| *Motivation* | The vicarious reinforcement must be great enough for us to imitate it. |

## ■ Research

■ **Schuetz *et al.* (2017)** found that 8 out of 12 horses that witnessed humans use a feeding apparatus imitated the behaviour, compared to 2 out of 12 that did not witness it, which suggests social learning can occur across species.

■ **Fitneva *et al.* (2013)** found some 4–6-year-olds, with no communication problems, preferred to observe an action demonstrating how to solve a problem than ask a question about how to do it. This suggests social learning is instinctive and under biological control.

## ■ Positive evaluation

■ SLT is a superior explanation of behaviour, as it considers the role of cognitive processes between a stimuli and a response, which behaviourism does not do.

■ SCT combines elements of sociocultural and cognitive explanations, making the theory more valid, as behaviours are rarely focused on one level of explanation.

## ■ Negative evaluation

■ SLT cannot explain how novel behaviours arise without the presence of models demonstrating them.

■ Many behaviours have an inherited, biological component to them that SLT does not consider.

## ■ Practical application

■ Apprentice mud masons in Mali learn building skills by observing and imitating master masons at work, rather than by formal tuition.

**Key terms**

**Social cognitive theory** – an explanation that sees behaviour as learned through observing and imitating others' behaviour due to its consequences.

**Social learning theory** – a social cognitive explanation that sees behaviour as learned from observation and imitation of role models who are seen to be vicariously reinforced.

**Vicarious reinforcement** – the observation of rewards occurring to role models for their behaviour, which increases the chances of the behaviour being imitated by the observer.

**Mediational processes** – cognitive aspects that influence behaviour.

**KEY CLASSIC STUDY**

## 'THE BOBO DOLL EXPERIMENT'

**Bandura *et al.* (1961)**

### Aim
- To assess the role of a model on subsequent behaviour.

### Procedure
- Seventy-two male and female children aged 3–5 years observed either a male or a female adult behaving either aggressively or not to a 'Bobo' doll.
- Participants then played with toys, including a 'Bobo' doll and the number of aggressive acts was recorded.

### Results
- Children who observed aggressive behaviour behaved more aggressively, boys more so than girls.
- There was more imitation of same-sex models.

### Conclusions
- There is a behavioural effect from observing aggressive behaviour, which can occur after a delay following observation.

### Evaluation
- Subsequent studies showed aggression was more likely if the observed behaviour was rewarded, supporting SLT.
- Children, instead of imitating observed behaviour, may have believed the purpose of the doll was to be hit, invalidating the study.
- The study can be considered unethical, as it could be seen to be promoting aggressive behaviour towards others.

## ■ Issues and debates

- SLT suggests behaviour is learned and thus results from nurture rather than nature. Thus there is additionally the suggestion that behaviour results from environmental determinism.

---

**■ STRENGTHEN YOUR LEARNING**

1 Outline social cognitive theory (in terms of SLT). Include reference to imitation, identification and vicarious reinforcement.
2 Outline the mediational processes involved in social learning.
3 For Bandura *et al.*'s (1961) Bobo doll study, in your own words, state the aims, procedure, results, conclusions and evaluative points.
4 Summarize what research evidence has suggested about SLT.
5 What other evaluative points, including practical applications and relevant issues and debates, can be made about SLT?

---

**Expert tip**

A good evaluative point to make about social learning theory is how it favours nurture rather than nature, as the theory stresses the role of environmental learning rather than genetics in developing behaviour.

## Reciprocal determinism

Revised ☐

**Reciprocal determinism** explains how the environment and an individual affect each other. This effect, known as triadic reciprocity, works on three levels: behavioural, cognitive and environmental, with all three levels interlinking to maintain a cycle of behaviour, thought and environment.

An important element of this is **self-efficacy**, which is a cognitive construct that has specific effects on behaviour and environment. For instance, someone with low self-efficacy for gymnastics believes they will perform badly as a gymnast. This raises their anxiety levels, making them unable to cognitively process information necessary to perform adequately and so they perform poorly. This reinforces the idea that they are poor at gymnastics, with their teacher (the environment) taking the viewpoint that they lack gymnastic ability, and the behaviour continues in

---

**Key terms**

**Reciprocal determinism** – the ways in which an individual affects their environment and vice versa.

**Self-efficacy** – situation-specific confidence.

a cycle. Behaviour here started from a thought process, but it could equally start from a bad environmental experience that makes them think they lack ability.

## Research

- **Williams & Williams (2010)** examined data on achievement and attitudes to education, finding a feedback loop between self-efficacy and mathematics achievement in 24 out of 33 countries. This illustrates the relationship between self-efficacy and reciprocal determinism and how reciprocal determinism occurs in education.

- **Wardell et al. (2012)** found that adolescents with positive expectancies about alcohol were likely to drink more and often. If they came to believe that others tended to drink less, they lessened their intake, while if they thought others drank more, they increased their intake, which highlights how making comparisons to others in an environment affects decision-making and how personal behaviour influences how individuals view others' behaviour.

- **Pourrazavi et al. (2014)** found that mobile phone usage in Iran became excessive between dating couples, as one person's increased usage motivated their partner to increase their usage and so on. Subsequent moderation through self-control moderated their partner's usage too, illustrating a good example of reciprocal determinism.

## Positive evaluation

- Reciprocal determinism can explain better than other theories how behaviours are perpetuated and how an individual and their environment can simultaneously affect each other.

- The theory explains how, as physical capabilities decline with age, this can be compensated for by increases in cognitive functioning through advances in knowledge and skills, showing how the more elderly can continue to function adequately.

## Negative evaluation

- There is not a lot of research evidence on reciprocal determinism, as it is difficult to test, requiring examination of three simultaneous elements.

- The theory focuses too much on the situation at the expense of personality traits, which often contribute more to behaviour than is acknowledged.

- Cognitive factors are over-emphasized at the expense of biological factors, which often affect decision-making, regardless of past experience or cognition.

## Practical application

- Teachers give feedback highlighting how success comes from hard work, getting students to believe they have potential, which creates a positive attitude, increasing the chances of future work being of good quality.

## Issues and debates

- The theory can be considered holistic, as it includes a combination of factors, rather than reducing behaviour down to a single explanation.

---

### ■ STRENGTHEN YOUR LEARNING

1 Explain what is meant by reciprocal determinism; include in your answer reference to triadic reciprocity and self-efficacy.

2 Summarize what research evidence has suggested about reciprocal determinism.

3 What other evaluative points, including practical applications and relevant issues and debates, can be made about reciprocal determinism?

---

### Expert tip

Remember when detailing concepts concerning reciprocal determinism, such as triadic reciprocity and self-efficacy, not to just name them, but to also fully explain them in order to demonstrate your understanding of them.

# Conformity

**Conformity** involves yielding to group pressure and is an important feature of SCT, as it explains how present others can change beliefs and behaviour. Conformity generally helps society to function efficiently, but can be harmful when it leads to negative outcomes, like conformity to bullying.

There are three types of conformity:

1 **Compliance** – a weak form of conformity involving public, not private, agreement with a group's beliefs and behaviour, in order to gain acceptance. It only occurs in the presence of the group.

2 **Identification** – a stronger form, involving public and private acceptance of a group's beliefs and behaviour, as group membership has benefits. Only occurs in the presence of the group.

3 **Internalization** – the strongest form, involving public and private acceptance of a group's beliefs and behaviour. Occurs without the presence of the group.

Several situational variables affect conformity: the size of majority influence, amount of agreement within a group, task difficulty, whether responses are made publicly and social norms. Individual factors are gender, mood, personality, age and culture.

> **Key terms**
>
> **Conformity** – yielding to group pressure (majority influence).
>
> **Compliance** – publicly but not privately going along with majority influence to gain approval.
>
> **Identification** – public and private acceptance of majority influence in order to gain group acceptance.
>
> **Internalization** – public and private acceptance of majority influence through adoption of a group's belief system.

## ▇ Research

- **Asch (1955)** found that conformity increased with the size of a majority (up to a maximum point), the level of agreement within a majority and the difficulty of a task, illustrating how situational variables affect conformity.

- **Carli & Eagly (1981)** performed a meta-analysis of conformity studies, finding that women generally conformed more, illustrating how gender affects conformity.

- **Milgram (1961)** found Norwegians conformed more than French participants to obviously wrong answers concerning acoustic tones, demonstrating how culture affects conformity.

- **Tong (2008)** found participants conformed more to wrong mathematical answers given by confederates when in a positive mood, illustrating the effect of mood on conformity.

- **Adorno et al. (1950)** reported that highly conformist people had personality traits of insecurity and unquestioning submission to authority, illustrating the effect of personality on conformity.

- **Pasupathi (1999)** found that conformity, having risen during childhood and adolescence, declines with later age, which illustrates how age affects conformity and that people become more independent with age, requiring less social approval from others.

## ▇ Positive evaluation

- Identification allows individuals to know what behaviours are expected of them in different social contexts, allowing society to function effectively and safely.

- Research showing how increased task difficulty leads to heightened conformity demonstrates how normative social influence (conforming to be accepted) can change to informational social influence (conforming to find the right answer) (see below).

## ■ Negative evaluation

■ Research does not identify why women conform more; perhaps society socializes females to be more compliant, or maybe evolution primes females to be conformist due to their biologically more nurturing and cooperative nature.

■ Studies of conformity are artificial and so lack ecological validity, as they bear little relevance to everyday situations.

## ■ Practical application

■ Compliance helps people with relationships when moving to new locations. By adopting group norms of behaviour, dress, etc. they will be invited into social situations, allowing friendships to form.

## ■ Issues and debates

■ As conformity is affected by situational and individual variables, it shows how external and internal factors interact to produce overall levels of conformity.

---

### ■ STRENGTHEN YOUR LEARNING

1 Define conformity.
2 Outline the three types of conformity: compliance, identification and internalization.
3 Summarize what research evidence has suggested about conformity.
4 What other evaluative points, including practical applications and relevant issues and debates, can be made about conformity?

---

**Expert tip**

Probably the best way to demonstrate factors that affect conformity is by using relevant research studies to do so, such as **Tong's (2008)** study showing the effect of mood on conformity and **Milgram's (1961)** study showing the effect of culture on conformity.

# Explanations for conformity

`Revised ☐`

There are two main explanations for conformity:

■ **Normative social influence (NSI)** – involves a need to belong, through being accepted and avoiding rejection and ridicule. Individuals agree with majorities due to their power to reward and punish and therefore this involves *compliance*, where public, but not private, agreement with a majority occurs.

■ **Informational social influence (ISI)** – involves a need to be correct to bring certainty to life. In novel situations or those with no clear way of behaving, individuals look to others for information on how to behave. This involves *social comparison* with others to see if behaviour matches theirs. ISI involves stronger forms of conformity, like identification and internalization, where public and private agreement with a majority occurs.

---

**Key terms**

**Normative social influence** – a motivational force for approval and acceptance.

**Informational social influence** – a motivational force to look to others for guidance in order to be correct.

---

## ■ Research

■ **Jenness (1932)** found that participants' second individual estimates of sweets in a jar were closer to a group estimate than their first individual estimate. As the number of sweets was difficult to estimate, it supports the existence of ISI, where people look to others for guidance in uncertain situations.

■ **Sherif (1935)** found participants' second individual estimates of how far a light moved converged towards a group norm, suggesting participants internalized others' judgements through ISI.

## ■ Positive evaluation

■ ISI and NSI have an evolutionary survival value. Looking to others for guidance in dangerous situations and group membership could both be beneficial to health.

## ■ Negative evaluation

■ Research like **Jenness (1932)** does not explain why people conform to obviously wrong answers.

## KEY CLASSIC STUDY

### 'OPTIONS AND SOCIAL PRESSURE'

#### Asch (1955)

### Aim

- To assess the extent to which participants would conform to obviously wrong answers.

### Procedure

- A laboratory experiment using an independent groups design.

- One hundred and twenty-three male participants, who answered aloud last or second last among a group of 7–9 confederates, had to say which of three comparison lines matched a stimulus line.

- On 12 of 18 trials, confederates deliberately gave the same wrong answer.

- The number of conforming responses was recorded.

- A control group of 36 males was tested individually on 20 trials.

### Results

- The control group had an error rate of 0.04 per cent (three mistakes in 720 trials).

- On the 12 critical trials, there was 32 per cent conformity to wrong answers.

- Seventy-five per cent of participants conformed to at least one wrong answer (25 per cent never conformed).

- Five per cent conformed to all wrong answers.

### Conclusions

- Conformity to wrong answers occurs to gain acceptance/avoid ridicule.

- There are individual differences in the levels of NSI.

### Evaluation

- The study is unethical; deceit was involved (use of confederates and being told it was a study of visual perception) and it was stressful.

- As overall conformity was 32 per cent, on most occasions people are independent, not conformist.

- Asch's procedure became a paradigm study: the accepted method of investigating conformity.

## Practical application

- Ambiguous tasks are used to draw individuals together when forming cohesive groups, such as in sports teams.

## Issues and debates

- As ISI and NSI have an evolutionary survival value, they can be argued to be biological forces resulting from nature not nurture.

### STRENGTHEN YOUR LEARNING

1 Explain what is meant by normative social influence.
2 Explain what is meant by informational social influence.
3 For Asch's (1955) study into conformity, in your own words, state the aims, procedure, results, conclusions and evaluative points.
4 Summarize what research evidence has suggested about ISI.
5 What other evaluative points, including practical applications and relevant issues and debates, can be made about explanations of conformity?

### Expert tip

A good means of constructing an evaluation of NSI and ISI, rather than just focusing on support from research studies, is to explain their evolutionary relevance in terms of their survival value, as this will attract higher level credit.

# Stereotypes

Stereotyping involves grouping types of individuals together on the incorrect basis that they possess similar qualities – for instance, that all redheads are aggressive. Judgements about individuals are made by reference to **stereotypes** held about them, with stereotyping about in-group members tending to be positive, but negative for out-group members, leading to prejudice and discrimination against out-group members.

Stereotyping has the effect of simplifying the world and the people in it, making it easier to understand and deal with.

> **Key term**
>
> **Stereotypes** – a collection of beliefs or attitudes held towards someone due to their membership of a particular group.

## KEY CONTEMPORARY STUDY

### 'ACCURACY OF NATIONAL STEREOTYPES IN CENTRAL EUROPE: OUT-GROUPS ARE NOT BETTER THAN IN-GROUPS IN CONSIDERING PERSONALITY TRAITS OF REAL PEOPLE'

#### Hřebíčková & Graf (2014)

#### Aim
- To assess the validity of racial stereotypes in Europe.

#### Procedure
- There were 2,241 participants from five European countries who gave data on their perceptions of characteristics relating to members of their own and the four other European countries.
- Personality measurements of 17,377 participants (who were natives of the five European countries) from other studies were collected.
- The two sets of data were assessed for their degree of similarity.

#### Results
- National stereotypes of each country, including participants' own country, existed.
- There were no significant differences in personality characteristics between members of different nationalities.

#### Conclusions
- Different stereotypes exist about different nationalities.
- There is no relationship between stereotypes of different nationalities and individuals' actual personalities.

#### Evaluation
- The use of anonymous questionnaires reduced the chances of socially desirable answers. Participants could honestly express negative stereotypes without fear of social disapproval.

## ■ Research

- **Shih *et al.* (1999)** 'primed' Asian students, so they were aware of stereotypes regarding mathematical ability (that Asians are better than non-Asians, and males are superior to females) and found that Asian women performed better when their ethnic identity was primed than when their gender identity was primed. This illustrates how stereotyping affects behaviour positively and negatively.

- **Steele & Aronson (1995)** found that black students performed worse on a test when they believed it was a test of academic ability rather than a problem-solving exercise. This suggests that stereotyping (in this case, that black people lack academic ability) affects performance so that it matches and thus perpetuates stereotypes.

## ■ Positive evaluation

- There is a wealth of evidence that suggests stereotyping can affect behaviour across a wide range of social groups.

- Stereotyping explains how prejudice and discrimination against other social groups can arise and thus presents possibilities of addressing them by breaking down negative stereotypes.

## Negative evaluation

- Research into stereotyping does not consider other influential factors, like anxiety and negative thinking, which therefore reduces the validity of findings.

- Research into stereotyping generally involves non-experimental methods, presenting problems in establishing causality and replicating studies to check the validity of findings.

## Practical application

- Highlighting positive stereotypes, rather than negative ones, about particular social groups can be used to heighten performance in a wide range of areas.

## Issues and debates

- Stereotyping tends to involve both gender and culture bias, where negative viewpoints of other cultures and the opposite gender are formed and maintained by over-emphasizing examples that support such stereotypes.

---

### ■ STRENGTHEN YOUR LEARNING

1  Explain what is meant by stereotyping.
2  Give one reason for people having stereotypes.
3  For Hřebíčková & Graf's (2014) study into stereotyping, in your own words, state the aims, procedure, results, conclusions and evaluative points.
4  Summarize what research evidence has suggested about stereotyping.
5  What other evaluative points, including practical applications and relevant issues and debates, can be made about stereotyping?

---

**Expert tip**

Ensure when outlining stereotyping that you explain not just what it is, but also what its purpose is in terms of making the world an easier place to comprehend and deal with.

# Cultural origins of behaviour and cognition

Revised ☐

## Culture and its influence on behaviour and cognition

Revised ☐

**Culture** concerns the learned and shared behaviours and beliefs of members of a society, with culture influencing both behaviour and cognition.

Culture has differing levels: deep culture refers to culture at the cognitive level (beliefs, values, thought processes, etc.), while surface culture is shallower and focuses on behaviours, customs, etc. of a culture.

### ■ Culture and day care

Parenting varies cross-culturally, with day care reflecting parenting practices within a culture. At the surface level, differences exist in class sizes and disciplinary practices, while the deep level involves transmission of different values through cultural socialization.

### ■ Culture and mental health

Culture-bound syndromes are culturally specific mental disorders, like Koro, a South East Asian syndrome, where males fear penis retraction leading to death. Such disorders are a cognitive effect of a particular culture and are culturally learned.

---

**Key terms**

**Culture** – identifiable groups of people bound together by attitudes, values, goals and customs.

**Culture and day care** – the types and effects of different cultural forms of non-parental care.

**Culture and mental health** – the types and effects of different forms of culturally specific mental disorders.

## Culture and obedience

Obedience occurs cross-culturally, but the Milgram paradigm, where participants are ordered to administer by a scientist what they believe to be real shocks of increasing intensity, revealed cross-cultural differences in obedience levels. This could be due to cultural differences in the status of scientists and the degree to which people of different cultures are socialized to obey.

## Research

- **Tobin (1987)** found that Japanese educators disliked the small classes of the American pre-school system, as the lack of interaction would stifle social development, while American educators disliked the large classes of the Japanese system, as it limited individual attention from a teacher, illustrating cultural differences in day care.

- **Roldán-Chicano et al. (2017)** found that Susto, a Bolivian culturally bound syndrome of fear of death from fright, continued in Bolivians emigrating to Spain, emphasizing the strength of cognitive constructs in culture-bound syndromes.

- **Blass (1999)** reported that the Milgram paradigm produced obedience levels to the highest shocks possible of 90 per cent in Spain, but only 40 per cent in Australia, illustrating culturally socialized differences in obedience – for example, Australians having a historic disregard for authority.

## Positive evaluation

- Research into cultural differences has led to increased familiarity and understanding of cultural differences, reducing cross-cultural tensions and hostilities.

- Examining behaviours from a cultural perspective reveals if they are genetically or environmentally based. Behaviours found in all cultures are suggested to be genetic in origin, while this differing across cultures would seem to be learned.

## Negative evaluation

- People with an authoritarian personality characterized by high levels of neuroticism and fear of minorities are more likely to be obedient, with cultures that foster such personality characteristics more likely to be obedient, which suggests personality has been neglected as a factor when considering cultural influences on obedience.

- Research conducted in different cultures can use differing methodologies that can explain some of the variation in findings, which suggests cultural differences may sometimes be exaggerated.

## Practical application

- Successful globalization where trade and knowledge is exchanged daily across cultures has occurred due to understanding how and why other cultures think and act.

## Issues and debates

- The fact that cultural differences in behaviour and cognition exist suggests they result from environmental influences of nurture rather than biological influences of nature.

**Key term**

**Culture and obedience** – cross-cultural differences in compliance to authority figures.

■ **STRENGTHEN YOUR LEARNING**

1 Explain what is meant by culture.

2 Explain what is meant by culture having different levels.

3 Explain the relationship between culture and:

 a day care,

 b mental health,

 c obedience.

4 For Hřebíčková & Graf's (2014) study into stereotyping, in your own words, state the aims, procedure, results, conclusions and evaluative points.

5 Summarize what research evidence has suggested about culture and its influence on behaviour and cognition.

6 What other evaluative points, including practical applications and relevant issues and debates, can be made about culture and its influence on behaviour and cognition?

**Expert tip**

Build detail into answers concerning culture and its influence on behaviour and cognition by focusing on individual areas of relevance, such as culture and day care, mental health and obedience. This will also widen the scope for the sorts of research studies you can use as evaluation.

# Cultural dimensions

Revised ☐

**Hofstede (1983)** states that cultures vary in several ways:

1 *Individualism/collectivism* – the extent to which a culture focuses on the needs of the individual or the greater good. Collectivist cultures emphasize social roles more.

2 *Uncertainty avoidance* – the extent to which a culture, and the way in which it operates, maintains stability, such as in emphasizing job security and safe behaviours.

3 *Power/distance* – the extent to which countries are hierarchical, such as how structured society is and how domineering leaders are.

4 *Masculinity/femininity* – cultures that emphasize ambition, competition and money are more masculine, while those that emphasize negotiation, cooperation and harmony are more feminine.

5 *Time orientation* – the extent to which long-term or short-term gain is emphasized. Long-term cultures stress persistence and resilience more, as well as maintaining tradition and dignity; short-term cultures less so.

6 *Indulgence/restraint* – the extent to which cultures desire immediate gratification of needs, with indulgent cultures wishing for swift individual gratification and valuing personal freedom. Cultures of restraint emphasize the needs of society more and putting others before oneself.

**Cultural dimensions** acquired by individuals through **cultural socialization** affect wide-ranging behaviours, like relationships, which in individualistic cultures occur on a voluntary basis, but on a more arranged basis in collectivist cultures.

**Key terms**

**Cultural dimensions** – the ways in which cultures vary.

**Cultural socialization** – cross-cultural differences in the transmission of values, beliefs and norms from one generation to another.

## ■ Research

■ **Kim & Coleman (2015)** found people with a strong individualist perspective were very assertive and those with a strong collectivist perspective very conflict-reluctant, while those with milder individualistic and collectivist perspectives exhibited more integrative styles of assertiveness and conflict-reluctance. This suggests there is variability within cultural dimensions to behaviour.

## ■ Positive evaluation

■ Apart from the uncertainty/avoidance dimension, there is research evidence to support the existence of different cultural dimensions.

■ Cultural dimensions underpin stereotypes of different nationalities in terms of behaviour, beliefs and values.

### KEY CONTEMPORARY STUDY

## 'WAITING FOR THE SECOND TREAT'

Lamm *et al.* (2017)

### Aim

■ To assess the effect of culture on delaying gratification.

### Procedure

■ Participants were 125 German and 76 Cameroonian children, aged four years, who were left alone with desirable food items after being told they could eat the food immediately or wait and get more of it.

### Results

■ Of the Cameroonian children, 69.7 per cent delayed gratification, compared to 28 per cent of German children.

### Conclusions

■ Children from cultures that value long-term gains delay gratification more than those from cultures stressing short-term gain.

■ Parenting styles culturally influence whether children favour long- or short-term gains. German parenting styles teach children to be more rapidly reactive to individual needs than Cameroonian ones.

### Evaluation

■ The use of a standard methodology makes cross-cultural comparisons valid.

■ The study only assesses cultural effects on two dimensions: time orientation and individualism/collectivism.

## ■ Negative evaluation

■ Cultural dimensions are criticized for having little predictive ability.

■ Individual behaviour within cultures varies greatly, suggesting cultural dimensions have little influence.

## ■ Practical application

■ *Interactive conflict resolution* (see page 214) takes into account cultural dimensions, to successfully negotiate resolutions between opposing cultural groups.

## ■ Issues and debates

Cultural dimensions involve emic and etic concepts. Emic research assesses one culture to understand culture-specific behaviour, while the etic approach compares cultures to identify universal behaviours.

---

### ■ STRENGTHEN YOUR LEARNING

1  Outline the various ways in which Hofstede believed culture varied.

2  Explain what is meant by culture having different levels.

3  For Lamm *et al.*'s (2017) study into the effect of culture on delaying gratification, in your own words, state the aims, procedure, results, conclusions and evaluative points.

4  Why did Kim & Coleman (2015) conclude that there is variability within cultural dimensions to behaviour?

5  Summarize what research evidence has suggested about cultural dimensions.

6  What other evaluative points, including practical applications and relevant issues and debates, can be made about cultural dimensions?

---

### Expert tip

A relevant debate to include as part of your evaluation when answering questions on cultural dimensions is that of emic and etic concepts. Be sure, though, to not just describe the concepts, but to focus on how they specifically relate to cultural dimensions in order for such material to be considered creditworthy.

# Cultural influences on individual attitudes, identity and behaviours

Revised

## Enculturation

Revised

**Enculturation** is the process of learning about one's culture. This involves learning cultural social norms, like behaviours, language and values.

### ■ Cultural socialization

Cultural socialization is the process by which the norms, values and behaviours of a culture are transmitted within a cultural grouping. It is how we learn to conduct ourselves within society. Such cultural transmission stems from social learning, with models enacting culturally acceptable behaviours and values to be observed and imitated.

An example is language, with different cultural groupings having different culturally transmitted languages and dialects. This occurs in three different directions

1 *Horizontal transmission* – involves transmission between individuals of the same generation, such as slang used by a certain age group.

2 *Vertical transmission* – involves transmission across generations between related individuals, such as parents teaching which words are acceptable in which situations.

3 *Oblique transmission* – involves transmission between unrelated individuals of different generations, such as language usage taught by teachers in a school.

Cultural transmission ensures that individuals learn appropriate information for different contexts – for example, if children learn to use language in a culturally appropriate way, enculturation is easier.

### ■ Research

■ **Wang & Vallotton (2016)** found American parents used more infant signing (a form of pre-language involving using signs to symbolize objects and actions) involving object signs, while Taiwanese parents used more action signs. This illustrates vertical cultural transmission with different cultures.

■ **Kaya & Oran (2015)** found that Turkish taught to people as a second language had less sociocultural input if taught outside Turkey, the result being that learners were not as aware of subtle features of language compared to those taught inside Turkey. This demonstrates the effects of oblique transmission.

■ **Maes et al. (2006)** found evidence of cultural transmission of smoking behaviour between twins, supporting the idea of horizontal transmission, with vertical transmission also evident, illustrating how different forms of cultural transmission interact in the process of enculturation.

### ■ Positive evaluation

■ Cultural transmission has supporting evidence, with cross-cultural studies distinguishing it from social learning, as the content of the learning is culture-dependent.

■ Cultural transmission allows members of a culture to develop pride in their cultural heritage, which increases the chances of such cultural heritage being protected and transmitted to the next generation.

> **Key term**
>
> **Enculturation** – the process by which an individual learns culturally appropriate behaviour and norms.

## ■ Negative evaluation

■ Cultural transmission is only one element of learning behaviours. Biological and environmental factors also play important roles, so cultural transmission should not be regarded as an explanation on its own.

■ Cultural transmission is becoming less important with globalization occurring, as the increased connectedness of cultures due to modern transport systems and computer-based forms of social media is breaking down the differences between cultures, resulting in them becoming more similar.

## ■ Practical application

■ Cultural transmission occurs with the media. Newspapers, TV, etc. play an important part in teaching culturally acceptable views and behaviour.

## ■ Issues and debates

■ Cultural transmission can be accused of reductionism, as there is a lack of consideration of other diverse factors that contribute to learning, such as genetics and environmental experiences. A more holistic approach that includes all contributing factors would have more explanatory validity.

---

**■ STRENGTHEN YOUR LEARNING**

1 What is meant by:
  a  enculturation,
  b  cultural socialization.
2 Explain what is meant by culture having different levels.
3 Explain how cultural transmission occurs via:
  a  horizontal transmission,
  b  vertical transmission,
  c  oblique transmission.
4 Summarize what research evidence has suggested about cultural transmission.
5 What other evaluative points, including practical applications and relevant issues and debates, can be made about cultural transmission?

---

**Expert tip**

Do not make the mistake of thinking that enculturation and cultural socialization are different concepts. Cultural socialization is part of enculturation and should be explained as such.

# Acculturation

Revised ☐

**Acculturation** is the process by which a person from one culture adopts the behaviour and values of another culture, while still retaining some of their original cultural practices. Generally seen in terms of a minority culture adopting elements of a majority culture, as with immigrants, acculturation though is a two-way process, where those of the majority culture also adopt elements of the minority culture. There are varying stages of acculturation: assimilation, separation, integration and marginalization, with level of acculturation dependent on factors of level of acceptance and level of rejection of a new culture.

**Key term**

**Acculturation** – the process by which an individual learns culturally appropriate behaviour and cultural norms for a new culture.

| Stages of acculturation | Description |
| --- | --- |
| Assimilation | Adopting behaviours and beliefs of a new culture and losing aspects of the original culture. This is acculturation in its fullest form as the new culture becomes all encompassing. |
| Separation | Rejecting cultural change towards a new culture, but retaining the behaviour and beliefs of the original culture. |
| Integration | Retaining some original cultural behaviours and beliefs and adopting some of the new culture's practices. |
| Marginalization | Rejecting behaviour and beliefs of the original and the new culture. |

## KEY CONTEMPORARY STUDY

## 'GETTING THE MOST OUT OF LIVING ABROAD'

Tadmor *et al.* (2012)

### Aim

■ To examine why living in another culture only benefits some.

### Procedure

■ Seventy-eight students who had lived abroad for at least a year were placed into three groups:

  ☐ *bicultural* (embraced elements of the new culture and retained some of the original culture)

  ☐ *separated* (retained their original culture's practices)

  ☐ *assimilated* (adopted the new culture as their own).

■ Tests were given to assess whether living abroad affected the groups equally.

### Results

■ The bicultural group did best on measures of *integrative complexity* (being able to creatively mix different viewpoints) and in the following years created more products and innovative products.

### Conclusions

■ Integration of cultural practices leads to more flexible thinking.

### Evaluation

■ Causality is not shown; it may be that flexible thinkers became more integrative rather than integration leading to more flexibility.

## ■ Research

■ **De Mamani *et al.* (2017)** found that level of symptom severity in schizophrenic patients of minority cultures was not affected by acculturation, but quality of life improved best in integrated individuals, demonstrating how integration can help those with poor mental health.

■ **Serafini *et al.* (2017)** found that Spanish-speaking immigrants who became assimilated and integrated into American culture had higher levels of substance abuse than those who became separated and marginalized, illustrating negative aspects of acculturation.

## ■ Positive evaluation

■ Research into acculturation allows psychologists to understand how acculturation can be achieved in the most effective manner.

## ■ Negative evaluation

■ If individuals spend lots of time with immigrants from their original culture, they initially settle quicker but eventually acculturation stagnates.

## ■ Practical application

■ Acculturation by exposure to language and communication practices of a new culture produces the most rapid transition of cultural practices.

## ■ Issues and debates

■ There is an issue with acculturation regarding making subjective judgements about which cultural behaviours and values are appropriate and desirable. For example, moving from a culture that has a negative view about consuming alcohol to one with a positive view.

---

### ■ STRENGTHEN YOUR LEARNING

1 Explain what is meant by acculturation.
2 Outline the stages of acculturation.
3 For Tadmor *et al.*'s (2012) study into the benefits of living in another culture, in your own words, state the aims, procedure, results, conclusions and evaluative points.
4 Summarize what research evidence has suggested about acculturation.
5 What other evaluative points, including practical applications and relevant issues and debates, can be made about acculturation?

---

**Expert tip**

When outlining the process of acculturation, relevant detail, which will gain higher levels of credit, can be achieved by description of the stages of acculturation, such as assimilation, integration, etc. These can then each be evaluated by reference to specific research studies, such as **De Mamani *et al.*'s (2017)** study that focuses on integration.

# Universalism/relativism

Revised ☐

**Universalism** sees human behaviour and thinking as generalizable globally, while **relativism** sees human behaviour and thinking as culture-dependent and therefore not generalizable globally. Cultural bias can occur where research findings from one cultural group are applied to all cultures. This can occur due to ethnocentrism, where researchers assume that behaviour and thinking in their culture is the norm.

## ■ Cultural relativism

Cultural relativism perceives no global 'rights' and 'wrongs' and that individual behaviour should be viewed in terms of cultural contexts before judgements are made. For example, social norms are culturally relative as what is desirable in one culture may be undesirable elsewhere. Cultural relativism can also be seen in culture-bound syndromes, such as *kayak angst* among Inuit people, where sufferers fear drowning at sea – not found in other cultures, it is a unique product of environmental threats.

## ■ Emic and etic perspectives

Researchers who believe findings from one culture are universal are imposing an **etic** viewpoint, while researchers who believe findings are only applicable to the culture being tested are adopting an **emic** viewpoint. Conducting cross-cultural research brings dangers of an imposed etic through researchers using methods and tools applicable to their own, but not other cultures, so that invalid conclusions are drawn. Replication of studies originally done in western cultures in other cultures has sometimes involved an imposed etic.

## ■ Research

■ **Henrich *et al.* (2010)** compared cross-cultural research into cognitive psychology, finding differences in fields of visual perception, fairness, cooperation, spatial reasoning, categorization and inferential induction, moral reasoning, reasoning styles, self-concepts and related motivations and the heritability of IQ. Much research was conducted on WEIRD participants (white, educated, industrialized, rich, democratic), who are not globally representative. This demonstrates how an imposed etic can create invalid conclusions.

■ **Mead (1935)** reported gender differences between three tribes in Papua New Guinea, which suggested gender roles are socially constructed. After marrying a man with 'traditional' views on gender roles, she dramatically changed her viewpoint to that of gender roles being biological. This illustrates how the researcher's cultural viewpoints affect the conclusions they reach.

---

**Key terms**

**Universalism** – the viewpoint that all humans are the same and that behaviour is generalizable globally.

**Relativism** – the viewpoint that behaviour is culture-dependent and therefore not generalizable across cultures.

---

**Key terms**

**Emic perspective** – when research is conducted within a researcher's own culture with a relativist viewpoint.

**Etic perspective** – when research is conducted outside of a researcher's own culture with a universalist viewpoint.

## ■ Positive evaluation

- Globalization may be lessening cultural differences, so that the danger of an imposed etic occurring is reduced.

- Much current research acknowledges cultural relativism and includes researchers acknowledging their own cultural perspectives, lessening the possibility of an imposed etic occurring.

## ■ Negative evaluation

- The culture that a researcher is from can cause participants of different cultures to react differently, with this being a difficult problem to overcome.

- Another problem that is difficult to overcome is the differing status of science and psychology within different cultures. This can affect how participants behave in studies cross-culturally, again biasing results.

## ■ Practical application

- Recognizing that bias can occur in research, such as an imposed etic, has led to psychologists designing and using much more culture-fair methods of investigation.

## ■ Issues and debates

- Issues of cultural bias also tend to involve gender bias, as cultural viewpoints of gender roles impact the conclusions drawn.

---

**■ STRENGTHEN YOUR LEARNING**

1 Explain what is meant by universalism/relativism.
2 Explain what is meant by cultural relativism.
3 Explain what is meant by emic and etic perspectives.
4 Summarize what research evidence has suggested about emic and etic perspectives.
5 What other evaluative points, including practical applications and relevant issues and debates, can be made about universalism/relativism?

---

**Expert tip**

Instead of perceiving universalism and relativism as separate, unconnected concepts, it is more accurate to describe them as opposite ends of a continuum, with universalism referencing behaviour and thinking as applicable to all cultures, and relativism seeing them as relating to only one specific culture and thus not representative of all cultures.

# Factors underlying cultural change

Revised ☐

Cultures do not remain constant; over time, cultural beliefs and behaviour change. Several factors influence **cultural change**, like **geographical mobility**. Migrants bring different cultural beliefs and behaviours with them, which can impact upon and change the cultural beliefs and behavioural norms of the culture they have migrated to. Therefore, acculturation affects people migrating from one culture to another, but also affects people native to the culture that migrants move to.

The degree of geographical mobility of a population within a culture also has cultural effects, like moving from rural to urban areas, which can affect social networks, such as friendship and family influences, due to increased/decreased amounts of contact with different groups of people. Frequency of geographical mobility also affects how permanent or transient relationships are, which affects

**Key terms**

**Cultural change** – the variations over time of cultural norms, values and behaviours.

**Geographical mobility** – the degree of movement of members of a cultural grouping to other cultural locations.

individuals' level of commitment to each other and has secondary effects, like on mental health, through the level of social support individuals can call on.

Other factors influencing cultural change include education systems, cultural affluence (or lack of it) and modernization.

## Research

- **Efremkin (2016)** reported the historical positive influence that migrants can have in terms of modernization and intellectual exchange upon a culture. This suggests that immigrants can act as agents of social and cultural change.

- **Oishi (2010)** found that in the USA geographical mobility was linked to different friendship styles within areas of high social mobility. This illustrates how geographical mobility can have a sociocultural effect on subgroups in terms of the kinds of interactions and relationships formed.

- **Adams & Plaut (2003)** found that, in Ghana, which has low geographical mobility, smaller numbers of friendships are formed, compared to America, which has greater geographical mobility. When asked, 29 per cent of Ghanaians, compared to only 4 per cent of Americans, thought having many friends was foolish, due to the degree of obligation involved in being a friend, illustrating cultural effects of geographical mobility.

## Positive evaluation

- Research into cultural change has highlighted the beneficial effects migration can have on a culture, which has helped diffuse racial tensions between people of different cultural backgrounds.

- The effects of cultural change through migration are generally more positive than negative.

## Negative evaluation

- Factors that influence cultural change do not exert an influence in isolation and should therefore be considered collectively. For instance, friendship groups are not just influenced by geographical mobility, but also affluence, level of education, etc.

- Friendships are formed for many reasons, not just for social support. Geographical mobility influences in terms of friendship numbers and type. How large this influence is, compared with other influences, like personality type, is difficult to establish.

## Practical application

- Cultures can be seen to have advanced, in terms of operating more efficiently, by incorporating positive cultural elements of those migrating into a culture.

## Issues and debates

- Research into cultural change involves ethical issues of social sensitivity. Care should be taken when designing and conducting research to consider in advance the possible harmful effects such research could have – for instance, in terms of heightening prejudice and harmful discrimination.

■ **STRENGTHEN YOUR LEARNING**

1   Outline factors underlying cultural change.

2   Summarize what research evidence has suggested about cultural change.

3   What other evaluative points, including practical applications and relevant issues and debates, can be made about cultural change?

**Expert tip**

When considering the effects of cultural change through migration, as part of an evaluation of factors affecting cultural change, it should be stressed that evidence tends to see such effects as more positive than negative.

# The influence of globalization on behaviour

Revised ☐

## How globalization influences behaviour

Revised ☐

**Globalization** is the process of interaction and integration of people from different cultures that creates an increasingly interconnected world with reduced cultural differences. Globalization affects beliefs and behaviour in several ways.

### ▨ Nationalism

**Nationalism** is an attitude towards your own and other countries. Individuals can perceive their national identity to be under threat from globalization, through being 'overtaken by foreign ideas'. The response is increased commitment to national identity (one's national in-group) and hostility towards those of other nationalities (one's out-groups), who are perceived as threatening the established way of life through globalization.

However, interdependence on other countries, such as through the imports they provide, means what was foreign becomes familiar, which weakens national boundaries and hostility towards other nationalities, which accelerates globalization.

### ▨ Identity effects

Globalization reduces national identity, as people become used to living within a mixture of cultural influences. This is resisted by some, who see certain cultural influences, like American ones, as dominating and having negative effects. Mobility between cultures leads to increased bicultural relationships, further weakening national identity.

### ▨ Body image and eating disorders

Exposure to other cultures incurs global behavioural effects. For instance, globalization of media influences has resulted in increased levels of anorexia nervosa across cultures, due to thinner body shapes being perceived as more attractive.

### ▨ Research

■ **Sobol *et al.* (2016)** found that, with globalization, Dutch participants preferred to buy Dutch foodstuffs, but global luxury items, showing how globalization affects different areas of behaviour.

■ **Roca & Urmeneta (2013)** found binational marriages in Spain increased from 8,000 in 1996 to 30,000 by 2009, demonstrating the effects of globalization on relationships.

### ▨ Positive evaluation

■ Globalization has had beneficial effects in reducing conflicts between nations.

### ▨ Negative evaluation

■ It is difficult to assess the impact of globalization, as it occurs in conjunction with other influences.

**Key terms**

**Globalization** – the occurrence of trade, cooperation and geographical mobility across cultures.

**Nationalism** – an individual's attitude towards their own and other cultures.

**Globalization and identify effects** – the effect of globalization upon individuals' sense of national identity.

**Globalization and body image** – the effect of globalization upon cultural ideas of desirable body shapes.

**KEY CONTEMPORARY STUDY**

## 'EATING BEHAVIOURS AND ATTITUDES FOLLOWING PROLONGED EXPOSURE TO TELEVISION AMONG ETHNIC FIJIAN ADOLESCENT GIRLS'

Becker *et al.* (2002)

### Aim

- To assess the effect of TV upon body image in a previously TV-free culture.

### Procedure

- An initial group of 17-year-old Fijian participants had their eating attitudes measured before TV was introduced.
- A second group of 22-year-olds had their eating attitudes measured three years after TV was introduced.

### Results

- There was a significant increase in indicators of eating disorders.
- After TV was introduced, anxiety about weight increased and changes occurred in attitudes to weight loss and diet, with the ideal body image slimmer than before.

### Conclusions

- The introduction of TV caused a cultural shift in perception of body image.

### Evaluation

- No clinical diagnosis of eating disorders was made, so it is not known if prevalence of eating disorders was changed by the introduction of TV.
- Different groups were tested before and after the introduction of TV, so results may have been due to individual differences.

## ■ Practical application

- Globalization has allowed medical advancements to be made available across the world, with medicines being transported across countries.

## ■ Issues and debates

- The concept of globalization can be seen as culturally biased, as the assumption of its positive benefits and inevitability is somewhat of a western cultural viewpoint.

---

**■ STRENGTHEN YOUR LEARNING**

1 Explain what is meant by globalization.
2 Explain how the following factors relate to globalization:
   a nationalism,
   b identity effects,
   c body image and eating disorders.
3 For Becker *et al.*'s (2002) study into eating behaviours and attitudes, in your own words, state the aims, procedure, results, conclusions and evaluative points.
4 Summarize what research evidence has suggested about globalization.
5 What other evaluative points, including practical applications and relevant issues and debates, can be made about globalization?

---

**Expert tip**

Detail about how globalization affects beliefs and behaviour can be achieved by reference to nationalism, identity effects and body image and eating disorders. Evaluation of each of these, in terms of their validity, can then be realized by reference to relevant research studies, such as **Becker *et al.*'s (2002)** study that assesses the effects on body image of introducing TV into a culture.

# The effect of the interaction of local and global influences on behaviour

**Globalization of behaviour** (behaviours that are global) and **localization of behaviour** (behaviours specific to the areas they originate from) are opposite ends of a behavioural continuum, with **glocalization** describing behaviours that are global, but adjusted to fit specific local environments – for instance, incorporating foreign words into another culture's language.

## Consumer behaviour

Global brands of consumer goods are best accepted when they adapt to allow cultural identity to be preserved – for example, McDonald's not selling burgers made of beef in India, where cows are regarded as holy. Marketing of global brands also uses adaptation to promote sales, like Guinness advertised in Nigeria as good for virility, an important priority for African men. Hybrid cultures occur from glocalization, like the incorporation of Indian curries in British culture.

## Sport

Glocalization occurs when sports are adapted to suit specific cultural locations. For example, basketball, an American sport, was marketed in China by underplaying the competitive element of the game and stressing its collectivist elements in order to fit Chinese cultural practices. American aspects of cheerleaders and mascots were used, but also Chinese adaptations, like dancing dragons.

## Research

- **Gineikiene & Diamantopoulos (2017)** found that if global consumer goods were marketed so that they were perceived as domestic rather than foreign, people were more likely to buy them, illustrating the power of glocalization upon consumer behaviour.

- **Lim & Park (2013)** found that receptiveness to new types of electrical goods was greater in Americans than South Koreans and this was related to Americans scoring higher on individualism and masculinity, which suggests the level of glocalization is linked to personality factors.

- **Zhou *et al.* (2017)** found Chinese men liked that Chinese cultural elements had been combined with American ones in promoting basketball in China, as it was not seen to threaten Chinese cultural identity. This demonstrates the importance of adapting global behaviours to local considerations in order to gain their acceptance.

## Positive evaluation

- Social identity theory can be used to explain consumer behaviour. Global brands are successful that acknowledge the cultural identity of potential consumers so that they fit with their in-groups.

- It is difficult to conduct laboratory-controlled experiments into glocalization, making causality difficult to establish.

## Negative evaluation

- Sometimes emphasizing the foreignness of a product, rather than adapting it to fit local cultural traditions, makes it most attractive, which indicates that glocalization is not always the most successful strategy in consumer behaviour.

- There are important considerations, other than whether a product is local or global, for whether it is seen as desirable, indicating that it is important not to overemphasize the role of globalization and glocalization in behaviour.

> **Key terms**
>
> **Globalization of behaviour** – behaviours that have become cross-cultural.
>
> **Localization of behaviour** – behaviours that remain specific to the areas they originate from.
>
> **Glocalization** – behaviours that contain elements of globalization and localization.

## ■ Practical application

■ Many sports have been adapted to suit local cultural practices – for example, using foreign dancing girls between overs in Indian cricket matches wearing Indian style dress and demonstrating Indian cultural-style dancing.

## ■ Issues and debates

■ Exploration of the effects of globalization, localization and glocalization upon behaviour uses sociological concepts and methods, illustrating how psychology can be combined with other disciplines in understanding the mind and behaviour.

> ### ■ STRENGTHEN YOUR LEARNING
>
> 1  Outline the effects of globalization on:
>
>    a   consumer behaviour,
>
>    b   sport.
>
> 2  Summarize what research evidence has suggested about the effects of globalization.
>
> 3  What other evaluative points, including practical applications and relevant issues and debates, can be made about the effects of globalization?

> **Expert tip**
>
> When explaining glocalization, and to show your understanding of the concept, it would be a good idea to use real-life examples, such as marketing the American sport of basketball in China by including Chinese cultural elements.

# Methods used to study the influence of globalization on behaviour

Revised ☐

To study globalization, it is necessary to adopt a 'glocalization' of research methodology, where hybrid versions of usual methodologies are used in order to suit the different cultures they are being applied to. This is done by **adaptation of measures**.

> **Key term**
>
> **Adaptation of measures** – the varying of researching methodologies when conducting studies across cultures in order to gain valid results.

## ■ Adaptation of measures

When researching different cultures, methodologies need to be adapted in terms of linguistic, construct validity, cultural response and sample factor considerations.

### ■ Linguistic considerations

Translating questionnaires/tests into different languages has to be done carefully to ensure it is testing the same things cross-culturally. This involves careful scrutiny of translations to ensure versions are identical, including pilot testing translated versions before actual research commences.

### ■ Construct validity considerations

Construct validity concerns the extent to which a test measures what it claims to measure. To ensure construct validity when conducting cross-cultural research, a combination of etic and emic perspectives is often used. This involves researchers familiarizing themselves with cultural norms in the cultures they are studying, so that cultural biases are challenged by what they observe.

### ■ Sampling considerations

To try and ensure representative samples and sampling equivalence across cultures are achieved, it is necessary to include examples of all types of people within different cultures, including their subcultures, in appropriate proportions.

### ■ Cultural response considerations

Cultures and subcultures can demonstrate varying response biases, such as to words used in test questions. Therefore, response biases within cultures need to be considered during analysis of results to ensure appropriate interpretation of findings.

## Research

- **Koopmans *et al.* (2016)** reported that when due care was taken in translating tests from Dutch to English, including conducting pilot studies, the measuring capability of a questionnaire was found to be valid, demonstrating the importance of careful scrutiny when translating tests for use across cultures.

- **Schaffer & Riordan (2003)** reviewed cross-cultural research to find widespread problems with testing variables in the same manner and in finding representative samples across samples, illustrating the difficulties researchers have conducting valid research into globalization.

- **Kim & Kim (2016)** found different patterns of response bias between western and Korean participants that were attributable to cultural differences, demonstrating how responses should be analysed, with cultural considerations in mind.

## Positive evaluation

- Using hybrid methodologies when conducting cross-cultural research has led to more valid findings being realized, leading to a greater understanding of globalization.

## Negative evaluation

- Appropriate adaptation does not always occur, as researchers with a universalist and etic mindset are less likely to think that their research tools need adapting for the culture they are studying.

- Research tool adaptation is a lengthy process that many researchers do not have sufficient time to do thoroughly, leading to invalid findings.

## Practical application

- Nowadays, cross-cultural research often includes researchers taken from the different cultures being assessed in order to diminish bias effects when studying globalization.

## Issues and debates

- Consideration of etic and emic perspectives and their effects upon cross-cultural research is an essential feature of designing effective research methodologies.

---

### ■ STRENGTHEN YOUR LEARNING

1 Explain why adaptations of measures are necessary when studying the influence of globalization on behaviour.

2 Explain the following adaptations of measures:
   a  linguistic considerations,
   b  construct validity considerations,
   c  sampling considerations,
   d  cultural response considerations.

4 Summarize what research evidence has suggested about adaptations of measures.

5 What other evaluative points, including practical applications and relevant issues and debates, can be made about adaptations of measures?

---

### Expert tip

When writing about the glocalization of research methodologies (through adaptation of measures), be careful not to just outline the various hybrid versions, such as linguistic considerations, but to also evaluate them, through research evidence, such as **Koopman *et al.*'s (2016)** study concerning the translation of tests from Dutch to English (unless a question only requires an outline).

## EXAM-TYPE QUESTIONS

1  Outline one study investigating social identity theory.                                                                     (9 marks)

2  With reference to a study investigating social cognitive theory, outline one strength and one limitation
   of a research method used in the study.                                                                         (9 marks)

3  Explain how stereotypes influence behaviour.                                                                                (9 marks)

4  Evaluate research studies related to stereotypes.                                                                           (22 marks)

5  Discuss social identity theory.                                                                                             (22 marks)

6  Evaluate social cognitive theory.                                                                                           (22 marks)

7  Outline one or more studies investigating cultural dimensions.                                                              (9 marks)

8  Outline how culture can affect behaviour.                                                                                   (9 marks)

9  Explain ethical considerations relating to one study of cultural dimensions.                                               (9 marks)

10 With reference to a study investigating the influence of culture on behaviour and cognition, outline
   two strengths of a research method used in the study.                                                           (9 marks)

11 Discuss culture and its influence on behaviour and cognition.                                                               (22 marks)

12 Evaluate research studies of cultural dimensions.                                                                           (22 marks)

13 Discuss one or more aspects of the cultural origins of behaviour and cognition.                                            (22 marks)

14 Explain how enculturation affects cognition and/or behaviour.                                                              (9 marks)

15 Outline one research study relating to acculturation.                                                                       (9 marks)

16 Outline one or more methods used to study the influence of globalization on behaviour.                                     (9 marks)

17 Discuss enculturation.                                                                                                      (22 marks)

18 Evaluate research studies related to acculturation.                                                                         (22 marks)

19 Contrast enculturation and acculturation.                                                                                   (22 marks)

20 Discuss how globalization may influence attitudes, identities and behaviour.                                              (22 marks)

21 Evaluate the effect of the interaction of local and global influences on behaviour.                                        (22 marks)

# Abnormal psychology

## Introduction

Revised

There are four criteria for defining **abnormality**, each with strengths and weaknesses: **deviation from social norms**, **failure to function adequately**, **deviation from ideal mental health** and **statistical infrequency** definitions of abnormality.

## Deviation from social norms definition

Revised

Each society has norms, unwritten rules for acceptable behaviour. Any behaviour varying from these norms is abnormal. The definition draws a line between desirable and undesirable behaviours, labels individuals behaving undesirably as social deviants and allows intervention into their lives to help them.

Norms vary across cultures, situations, ages and gender, so what is acceptable in one context will not be in others. An important consideration is the degree to which social norms are deviated from and how important society perceives those norms.

### ■ Strengths

- Social norms give guidance to people as to how they, and others, should behave in different contexts, allowing a simple evaluation of whether behaviour is 'acceptable' or not.

- The definition allows intervention that protects society from the effects an individual's abnormal behaviour can have on others, as well as helping abnormal individuals who may not be able to help themselves.

### ■ Weaknesses

- Social norms are not real, but are based on the opinions of ruling elites within society rather than majority opinion. Social norms are then used to 'control' those seen as a threat to social order. A true definition of abnormality should be objective and free from subjective opinion. Those who do not conform to social norms may not be abnormal, but merely individualistic or eccentric.

- Social norms are often underpinned by moral standards and vary, as social attitudes change. Therefore, as social norms do not remain constant, they are a poor means of determining abnormality. For example, homosexuality was listed as abnormal on the International Classification of Diseases classification of mental disorders until 1990.

> **Key terms**
>
> **Abnormality** – a psychological or behavioural state leading to impairment of interpersonal functioning and/or distress to others.
>
> **Deviation from social norms definition** – that behaviours violating accepted social rules are abnormal.
>
> **Failure to function adequately definition** – that abnormality concerns an inability to cope with day-to-day living.
>
> **Deviation from ideal mental health definition** – that abnormality concerns a failure to meet the criteria for perfect psychological well-being.
>
> **Statistical infrequency definition** – that statistically rare behaviours are abnormal.

## Failure to function adequately definition

Revised

Individuals are abnormal when their behaviour suggests that they cannot cope with everyday life, such as disrupting the ability to work and conducting interpersonal relationships. The definition focuses on individual suffering, drawing attention to personal experiences associated with mental disorders.

**Rosenhan & Seligman (1989)** suggested seven features of personal dysfunction. The more an individual has, the more they are classed as abnormal.

| Features of personal dysfunction | Description of the feature |
| --- | --- |
| Personal distress | A key feature of abnormality. Includes depression and anxiety disorders. |
| Maladaptive behaviour | Behaviour stopping individuals from attaining life goals, both socially and occupationally. |
| Unpredictability | Displaying unexpected behaviours characterized by loss of control, like attempting suicide after failing a test. |
| Irrationality | Displaying behaviour that cannot be explained in a rational way. |
| Observer discomfort | Displaying behaviour causing discomfort to others. |
| Violation of moral standards | Displaying behaviour violating society's moral standards. |
| Unconventionality | Displaying unconventional behaviours. |

To assess how well individuals cope with everyday life, clinicians use the Global Assessment of Functioning Scale (GAF), rating their level of social, occupational and psychological functioning.

## Strengths

■ The definition allows assessment of the degree of abnormality. With the GAF being scored on a continuous scale, it allows clinicians to see the degree to which individuals are abnormal and thus decide who needs psychiatric help.

■ The definition provides a checklist that individuals can use to assess their level of abnormality and allows judgement by others of whether individuals are functioning properly, as it focuses on observable behaviours.

## Weaknesses

■ Abnormality is not always accompanied by dysfunction. Psychopaths, people with dangerous personality disorders, can cause great harm yet still appear normal.

■ The features of dysfunction are subjective; although GAF measures levels of functioning, it does not consider behaviour from an individual's perspective. What is normal for an eccentric, like wearing extravagant clothes, would be abnormal for an introvert.

# Deviation from ideal mental health definition

Revised ☐

Abnormality is perceived in a similar way to physical health, by looking for an absence of well-being, in mental health. Any deviation from normal is abnormal.

**Jahoda (1958)** described six characteristics individuals should exhibit to be normal. An absence of any of these characteristics indicates abnormality. The more characteristics individuals fail to meet and the further they are away from realizing individual characteristics, the more abnormal they are considered to be.

| Characteristics of ideal mental health | Description of characteristics |
| --- | --- |
| Positive attitude towards oneself | Having self-respect and a positive self-concept. |
| Self-actualization | Experiencing personal growth and development. 'Becoming everything one is capable of becoming.' |
| Autonomy | Being independent, self-reliant and able to make personal decisions. |
| Resisting stress | Having effective coping strategies and being able to cope with everyday anxiety-provoking situations. |
| Accurate perception of reality | Perceiving the world in a non-distorted fashion. Having an objective and realistic view of the world. |
| Environmental mastery | Being competent in all aspects of life and able to meet the demands of any situation. Having the flexibility to adapt to changing life circumstances. |

Like the deviation from social norms and the failure to function adequately definitions, this definition focuses on behaviours and characteristics seen as desirable, rather than undesirable.

## ■ Strengths

■ The definition stresses positive achievements rather than failures and distress, and emphasizes an optimistic approach to mental problems by focusing on what is desirable, not undesirable.

■ The definition allows identification of what is needed to achieve normality, allowing formation of personal goals to work towards and achieve, thus fostering self-growth.

## ■ Weaknesses

■ Most people do not meet all of the ideals all of the time; therefore, according to this definition, most people are abnormal. Thus the criteria may actually be ideals (how individuals would like to be) rather than actualities (how they actually are).

■ Many of the criteria are vague and difficult to measure, making assessment of people's mental health difficult to achieve in any objective manner.

# Statistical infrequency definition

Revised ☐

Behaviours that are statistically rare are abnormal. What is statistically rare depends on normal distribution. Normal distribution curves show what proportions of people share characteristics and behaviours. Most people are on or near the mean for these characteristics and behaviours, with declining amounts either side of the mean. Individuals outside 'the normal distribution', about 5 per cent of a population (two standard deviation points away from the mean), are classified as abnormal.

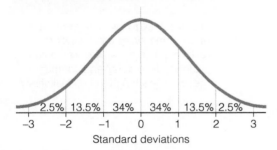

**Figure 4.1** Normal distribution curve

The definition states which behaviours are abnormal but makes no value judgements about them.

## ■ Strengths

■ The definition can be appropriate, as in many situations, statistical criteria can define abnormality – for example, mental retardation is a rare occurrence away from the statistical norm.

■ The definition can be considered objective, as once a 'cut-off point' has been agreed for a characteristic or behaviour, it becomes an impartial way of deciding who is abnormal.

## ■ Weaknesses

■ It is not clear how far behaviour should deviate from the norm to be abnormal. Many disorders, like depression, vary greatly between individuals in terms of severity.

- Some statistically frequent 'normal' behaviours are actually abnormal. About 10 per cent of people will be chronically depressed at some point in their lives, which suggests depression is so common as to not be abnormal under this definition.

## Practical application

- The deviation from ideal mental health and failure to function adequately definitions are used to identify areas of a person's psychosocial functioning that need improvement, with humanistic self-growth methods, such as encounter groups like Alcoholics Anonymous and eating disorder support groups, used to foster self-improvement.

## Issues and debates

- All definitions of abnormality have an element of **cultural relativism** to them. Social norms vary within and across cultures, making it difficult to know when they are being broken and, with diagnosis of abnormality often based on social norms of the majority white population, causing ethnic minorities to be over-represented in the abnormal population. With the failure to function adequately definition, what is considered normal functioning also varies culturally, as is the case with definitions of ideal mental health (for example, autonomy is not seen as desirable in collectivist cultures). Additionally, what is statistically normal varies culturally, making judging people of one culture by the statistical norms of another culture problematic.

> **Key term**
>
> **Cultural relativism** – the idea that definitions of what is 'normal' functioning vary from culture to culture and are equally valid.

---

### ■ STRENGTHEN YOUR LEARNING

1  Describe the following definitions of abnormality:

   a  deviation from social norms,

   b  failure to function adequately (including Rosenhan & Seligman's features of personal dysfunction),

   c  deviation from ideal mental health (including Jahoda's characteristics of ideal mental health),

   d  statistical infrequency.

2  Evaluate each of the above definitions in terms of their strengths and weaknesses.

3  Explain why all definitions of abnormality have an element of cultural relativism to them.

---

> **Expert tip**
>
> The best way to evaluate definitions of abnormality, as there is not really much in the way of research evidence, is to detail and compare their relative strengths and weaknesses.

# Approaches to diagnosis and classification systems

Revised ☐

## The biological approach

Revised ☐

The **biological approach** perceives abnormality similarly to physical ill health, as due to malfunctioning biological processes, especially in the working of the brain. Abnormal conditions are diagnosed from their symptoms, using diagnostic manuals, with each disorder seen as having its own particular pattern of symptoms. There are four types of biological factors causing abnormal conditions.

> **Key term**
>
> **Biological approach** – model of abnormality that perceives mental disorders as illnesses with physical causes.

| Biological factor | Description |
|---|---|
| *Bacterial infections and viruses* | Damage to the brain through infection, e.g. 'paralysis of the insane' where a sexually transmitted bacterium impairs memory, intellect, personality and mood, as well as causing delusions, bizarre behaviour and eventual death. |
| *Brain damage* | Damage to the brain through accidents and degeneration, e.g. Alzheimer's disease, caused by destruction of cells within the nervous system, leading to chronic memory impairment. |
| *Biochemistry* | Abnormal levels of neurotransmitters lead to abnormality, e.g. heightened acetylcholine levels are associated with depression. |
| *Genetic factors* | Genes determine inherited levels of vulnerability, e.g. OCD is highly heritable. |

# The cognitive approach

Revised ☐

In the **cognitive approach**, abnormality is seen as due to distorted and irrational mental processes, which influence emotions and behaviours. Abnormal individuals make inaccurate attributions about their own and others' behaviour that lead to inaccurate expectations and become real through self-fulfilling prophecies. For example, attributing failed relationships to a lack of social skills, so expecting relationships to fail, and then deliberately sabotaging relationships.

**Beck (1963)** saw depression occurring through the cognitive triad, three illogical thought processes that result in irrational, negative feelings, leading to depression.

**Key term**

**Cognitive approach** – model of abnormality that perceives mental disorders as due to negative thoughts and illogical beliefs.

| Component of cognitive triad | Description |
|---|---|
| *The self* | Individuals regard themselves as helpless, worthless and inadequate. |
| *The world* | Obstacles are perceived within the environment that cannot be dealt with. |
| *The future* | Personal worthlessness is seen as hindering improvements. |

# The sociocultural approach

Revised ☐

In the **sociocultural approach**, the social and cultural context in which individuals live determines the stressors they are exposed to and thus the types of disorders they are vulnerable to, with some disorders only occurring in specific cultures (like Koro, a fear of death through retracting genitals, found in South East Asia) or in varying levels in different cultures, like anorexia nervosa.

Overall, the approach considers social norms, roles within social environments, cultural and family background to determine vulnerability to abnormality. Abnormality is thus not perceived as a disease, but as arising from dysfunctional sociocultural systems.

**Key term**

**Sociocultural approach** – model of abnormality that perceives mental disorders as determined by social and cultural environments.

# Classification systems

Revised ☐

Diagnosis of mental disorders uses **classification systems**, based on the idea that certain symptoms can be grouped together as a syndrome (illness) with an underlying cause separate from all other syndromes. There are two main classification systems: the Diagnostic and Statistical Manual of Mental Disorders, 5th edition (DSM-V) and the International Classification of Diseases, 10th revision (ICD-10).

**Key term**

**Classification systems** – the categorizing of mental disorders by reference to their symptoms.

## DSM-V

Used in the USA, DSM-V contains descriptions, symptoms and other criteria to list mental disorders as separate syndromes, as well as other possible syndromes that need further research.

## ICD-10

Created by the World Health Organization and used globally, ICD-10 uses signs and symptoms to classify 11 general categories of mental disorders.

---

### KEY CONTEMPORARY STUDY

### 'TWIN STUDIES ON OBSESSIVE-COMPULSIVE DISORDER: A REVIEW'

**Grootheest *et al.* (2005)**

#### Aim
- To assess the degree to which OCD is an inherited condition.

#### Procedure
- A meta-analysis of 28 twin studies conducted between 1929 and the present day, consisting of 10,034 twin pairs, was assessed for degree of heritability of OCD.

#### Results
- OCD had a heritability level of between 45 and 65 per cent in children and between 27 and 47 per cent in adults.

#### Conclusions
- OCD has a strong genetic basis, especially childhood forms of the disorder.

#### Evaluation
- Many early twin studies used different diagnostic criteria for OCD, lowering the reliability of results.
- As heritability was not 100 per cent, environmental factors must be necessary to 'trigger' the disorder.

---

## Research

- **Boury (2001)** used the Beck Depression Inventory to find that depressives misinterpret facts and experiences in a negative fashion and feel hopeless about the future, giving support to Beck's cognitive explanation.

- **Elliot (2016)** reviewed evidence to find that poverty increases the chances of mental health problems and that abnormal conditions were increased in severity by the stigma and discrimination that having such conditions brought. This supports the idea that dysfunctional sociocultural systems can lead to abnormality.

## Positive evaluation

- The biological and cognitive approaches are combined into cognitive neuroscience to try and identify specific brain areas associated with cognitive elements of mental disorders.

- The success of cognitive behavioural therapies in treating a wide range of mental disorders supports the idea that abnormal conditions can be explained by reference to the cognitive approach.

- The sociocultural approach can explain why the occurrence of mental disorders varies across different contexts, such as between and within cultures, over time and across genders, giving it a degree of face validity.

■ Classification systems contain elements of all approaches to diagnosis, allowing clinicians of differing psychological schools to use and communicate with common diagnostic tools.

## ■ Negative evaluation

■ Many mental disorders do not have distinguishing physiological symptoms, which reduces support for the idea that abnormal conditions are purely a result of malfunctioning physical processes.

■ Cognitive dysfunctions associated with mental disorders may often result from biological factors, like brain damage or abnormal biochemistry, which suggests cognitive elements are more effects of abnormality than causes.

■ Research into the sociocultural approach often uses non-experimental methods, such as self-reports, making cause-and-effect relationships difficult to establish.

■ DSM-V revisions lack research support, with inter-rater reliability for many disorders low. The drugs industry is also accused of having influence over its creation, with many panel members who wrote the revision having ties to the drugs industry.

## ■ Practical application

■ Each approach to diagnosis has associated treatments: drug therapies from the biological approach, cognitive behavioural therapy from the cognitive approach and behavioural therapies from the sociocultural approach. However, eclectic treatments, which combine different therapies, often have greater success than individual treatments, reflecting the multi-causal nature of many mental disorders.

## ■ Issues and debates

■ Each approach to diagnosis can be considered reductionist, as they fail to consider other approaches to the causation of abnormality. A holistic approach that combines elements of all approaches to explain abnormality probably reflects the origins of most mental disorders.

---

**■ STRENGTHEN YOUR LEARNING**

1 Explain how the biological approach views the diagnosis of abnormality.
2 Outline the four types of biological factors that are seen as causing abnormal conditions.
3 Explain how the cognitive approach views the diagnosis of abnormality.
4 Outline the components of the cognitive triad.
5 Explain how the sociocultural approach views the diagnosis of abnormality.
6 Explain what is meant by classification systems; include reference to DSM-V and ICD-10.
7 For Grootheest *et al.*'s (2005) twin study into OCD, in your own words, state the aims, procedure, results, conclusions and evaluative points.
8 Summarize what research evidence has suggested about how psychological approaches view the diagnosis of abnormality.
9 What other evaluative points, including practical applications and relevant issues and debates, can be made about how psychological approaches view the diagnosis of abnormality?

---

**Expert tip**

A useful way of evaluating approaches to abnormality is to compare them against each other in terms of their relative strengths and weaknesses, such as level of research support and effectiveness of treatments based on individual approaches.

# The role of clinical biases in diagnosis

## ■ Placebo effect

The **placebo effect** occurs when patients' mental health improves due to an expectation of recovery, with clinicians wrongly assuming that recovery was due to correct diagnosis and treatment and the theories upon which they were based.

## ■ Medical model

The **medical model**, based on the biological approach, sees the causes of mental health as biological, with treatments based on removing physical symptoms. However, most mental disorders are characterized by non-physical factors that the medical model cannot explain or treat. Clinicians therefore can easily make incorrect diagnoses and prescribe inappropriate treatments.

## ■ Psychoanalytic theory

**Psychoanalytic theory** sees mental disorders as due to unresolved traumas occurring during psychosexual stages of development during childhood. Such traumas are then repressed (hidden) in the unconscious mind, to affect adult conscious behaviour. Treatment is based on giving sufferers insight into the origins of their problems. However, there is little evidence that this is true. Therefore, psychoanalytic clinicians can easily give incorrect diagnoses and treatments.

## ■ Cultural bias

**Cultural bias** concerns the tendency to over-diagnose members of other cultures as suffering from mental disorders due to cultural misperceptions of clinicians.

## ■ Research

- **Goldberg & Huxley (1992)** found that about 50 per cent of cases of depression and anxiety went undiagnosed by British clinicians, including 14 per cent of patients with persistent depression, which suggests under-diagnosis is a common occurrence.

- **Cochrane (1977)** found people of West Indian descent were seven times more likely to be diagnosed as schizophrenic in Britain than in the West Indies, which suggests invalid diagnoses were made due to cultural bias.

- **Kirsch *et al.* (2002)** found that more than half the drug trials for antidepressants sponsored by drug companies in the USA between 1987 and 1989 were insignificant, but not published, which suggests incorrect viewpoints about mental disorders favouring the medical model are being encouraged, which could lead to clinicians making biased diagnoses in favour of such viewpoints.

- **Holmes (1990)** reviewed 60 years of research into repression to find no evidence of the phenomenon, weakening support for the explanation. This suggests that diagnoses of disorders based on the psychoanalytic model are biased and incorrect.

## ■ Positive evaluation

- Clinicians are becoming more aware of their biases in diagnosis, which has reduced the effect of clinical bias, causing expectations that lead towards a placebo effect.

## ■ Negative evaluation

- Most mental health clinicians are white, middle-to-upper class males, which leads to incorrect diagnosis on the basis of cultural bias.

- It is possible that large numbers of ethnic minority people being diagnosed as mentally disordered are not due to misdiagnosis, but due to a greater number of stressors, like poverty and racism.

---

**Key terms**

**Placebo effect** – where improvement in a patient's condition is due to an expectation of improvement rather than any actual therapeutic effect.

**Medical model** – the perception of mental disorders as illnesses with physical causes to be treated with physical therapies.

**Psychoanalytic theory** – the perception of mental disorders as due to unresolved traumas formed during psychosexual stages of childhood development, which become repressed in the unconscious mind, to affect adult conscious behaviour.

**Cultural bias** – the tendency to over-diagnose members of other cultures as suffering from mental disorders.

## ■ Practical application

■ The World Health Organization argues that treatment effectiveness (and the theories they are based on) would be more valid if results of all drug trials were published, not just the ones favouring the medical model.

## ■ Issues and debates

■ Drug companies are seen as influencing clinicians to make incorrect diagnoses favouring the medical model, in order to boost profits. They are accused of sponsoring research and influencing the construction of DSM-V to favour the medical model.

---

■ **STRENGTHEN YOUR LEARNING**

1 Explain how the following affect the role of clinical biases in diagnosis:
   a placebo effect,
   b the medical model,
   c psychoanalytic theory,
   d cultural bias.
2 Summarize what research evidence has suggested about the role of clinical biases in diagnosis.
3 What other evaluative points, including practical applications and relevant issues and debates, can be made about the role of clinical biases in diagnosis?

---

**Expert tip**

When answering questions on clinical biases in diagnosis, instead of focusing on just one form of bias, you should aim to cover several areas of bias, such as cultural bias, the placebo effect, etc. This will give access to a wider range of evaluative material too, allowing a wider ranging, more sophisticated answer to be constructed.

# Reliability and validity of diagnosis

Revised ☐

**Reliability of diagnosis** refers to the consistency of symptom measurement and affects classification and diagnosis in two ways:

| Method of reliability | Description |
|---|---|
| Test–retest reliability | A clinician makes the same consistent diagnosis on separate occasions using the same information. |
| Inter-rater reliability | Several clinicians make identical diagnoses of the same patient, independently of each other. |

Making reliable diagnoses is difficult due to a lack of physical symptoms with mental disorders and also because of comorbidity, where patients simultaneously have two or more mental disorders, creating confusion over which disorder is being diagnosed.

**Validity of diagnosis** refers to how accurate, meaningful and useful a diagnosis is. Validity is assessed in several ways:

| Method of validity | Description |
|---|---|
| Reliability | A valid diagnosis must first be reliable, though reliability itself does not ensure validity. |
| Predictive validity | If diagnosis leads to successful treatment, diagnosis is valid. |
| Descriptive validity | Patients diagnosed with different disorders should be different from each other in terms of classification. |
| Etiological validity | Patients with the same disorder should have the same cause. |
| Convergent validity | For diagnostic measuring tools to be valid, they should correlate with other diagnostic tools known to be valid. |

**Key terms**

**Reliability of diagnosis** – the consistency of diagnosis of symptom measurement.

**Validity of diagnosis** – the accuracy of diagnosis of symptom measurement.

Descriptive validity is reduced by comorbidity, where patients have two or more simultaneous disorders, while predictive validity is difficult to attain, as therapies are often based on clinicians' biased viewpoints as to what constitutes effective treatments.

# Reliability and validity of diagnosis of OCD

Revised ☐

The development of standardized rating scales, like the Yale–Brown Obsessive Compulsive Scale (Y-BOCS), has improved the reliability and validity of diagnosis, though some clinicians doubt whether OCD is a separate disorder, with many sufferers also having comorbid Tourette's syndrome.

## ■ Research

- **Leckman & Chittenden (1990)** found that 50 per cent of Tourette's syndrome patients also had OCD, which suggests that OCD is not a separate disorder.

- **Di Nardo & Barlow (1988)** found that reliability of diagnosis for OCD was 80 per cent, indicating reliability of diagnosis to be high, which was supported by **Foa et al. (1987)**, who found high correlations between clinicians', patients' and independent observers' ratings of OCD features, which suggests good inter-rater reliability.

- **Deacon & Abramowitz (2004)** found, using the Yale–Brown Obsessive Compulsive Scale, regarded as the 'gold standard' measure for OCD, on 100 patients, that there were problems accurately measuring OCD components, which implies measurements of OCD lack some validity.

## ■ Positive evaluation

- OCD has easily observable symptoms that assist in clear diagnosis, thus contributing towards high levels of reliability.

- Compared to other anxiety disorders, the diagnostic reliability of OCD is very high.

## ■ Negative evaluation

- Diagnoses of OCD bring long-term negative effects upon sufferers, yet such diagnoses are made with little evidence of the disorder actually existing as a separate condition.

- The secretive nature of OCD and the lack of specialized psychiatry services for the disorder can make reliability of diagnosis difficult to establish.

## ■ Practical application

- The improved reliability and validity of diagnosis of OCD resulting from classification system updates has seen the prescription of more effective treatments.

## ■ Issues and debates

- One unresolved issue with OCD is whether it is a disorder that some people have or whether it is something that most, if not all, people have, but in differing degrees, with individuals diagnosed as having OCD being those whose symptoms are so severe that they interfere with their ability to cope effectively with everyday life.

# Reliability and validity of diagnosis of anorexia nervosa

Revised

Reliability and validity of diagnosis has improved over time, as diagnostic categories and methods of assessment have been amended. Reliability of diagnosis of patients is problematic, especially as many sufferers are young. Diagnosis of anorexia nervosa (AN) and bulimia nervosa (BN) as separate disorders seems possible, but the idea of AN having separate subtypes is not yet proven.

## ▉ Research

- **Eddy *et al.* (2008)** assessed 216 AN and BN patients weekly for seven years, finding one-third of AN patients switched over to BN (though were likely to relapse back again) and half switched from one subtype of AN to another. BN patients were unlikely to switch to AN. This suggests there is a distinction between AN and BN, but the idea of separate subtypes of AN is not supported.

- **Nicholls *et al.* (2000)** used 81 participants aged 7–16 years to find that ratings of eating disorders between two clinicians (ignorant of each other's ratings) produced a concordance rate of 35 per cent when using ICD-10, 63 per cent when using DSM-V (though 50 per cent of children could not be classified) and 88 per cent when using the Great Ormond Street (GOS) criteria. This suggests that DSM and ICD criteria are of little use in classifying children's eating disorders, but the GOS criteria, specially developed for children, are more reliable.

- **Stice *et al.* (2004)** found that the Eating Disorder Diagnostic Scale displayed reliability, convergent validity and predictive validity in anticipating responses to a prevention programme and future onset of eating disorders. This suggests the scale is reliable and valid.

## ▉ Positive evaluation

- Early indications are that the new DSM-V classification system provides reasonable effective reliability and validity of AN diagnosis and is an improvement on DSM-IV.

- Classification systems have allowed clinicians to explore whether eating disorders are separate syndromes, or are subsets of each other.

## ▉ Negative evaluation

- One criterion for AN diagnosis is body weight being below 85 per cent of that expected. However, 28 per cent of sufferers have body weight above this criterion and this criterion also fails to consider age, gender, ethnicity or frame size and so has low predictive validity in forecasting treatment outcomes.

- The criteria for diagnosing AN do not take into account important factors such as losing weight due to religious fasting, lowering reliability and validity of diagnosis.

## ▉ Practical application

- The fact that classification systems allow reasonably accurate diagnosis of different eating disorders, such as AN and BN, allows clinicians to prescribe more specific treatments to meet patients' needs.

## ■ Issues and debates

■ Criteria for diagnosis of AN are influenced by western sociocultural factors, like the way in which body weight and shape are perceived. For instance, many cultures do not associate thinness with feminine beauty.

---

**■ STRENGTHEN YOUR LEARNING**

1 Explain what the difference is between reliability and validity of diagnosis.

2 What is meant by:
   a test–retest reliability,
   b inter-rater reliability?

3 What is meant by:
   a predictive validity,
   b descriptive validity,
   c ecological validity,
   d convergent validity.

4 Summarize what research evidence has suggested about the reliability and validity of diagnosis of OCD.

5 What other evaluative points, including practical applications and relevant issues and debates, can be made about the reliability and validity of diagnosis of OCD?

6 Summarize what research evidence has suggested about the reliability and validity of diagnosis of anorexia nervosa.

7 What other evaluative points, including practical applications and relevant issues and debates, can be made about the reliability and validity of diagnosis of anorexia nervosa?

---

**Expert tip**

A common mistake students make is to focus on reliability and validity in general terms, rather than on how they relate to diagnosis of specific abnormal conditions. Such answers would gain little credit.

---

# Cultural relativism and ethical considerations in diagnosis

Revised ☐

## ■ Cultural relativism

Cultural relativism concerns the idea that definitions of what is normal functioning vary from culture to culture but have equal validity.

All definitions of abnormality are culturally relative, as no definition applies to everyone, with normal functioning varying between cultures. Therefore, when clinicians from one culture diagnose an individual from another culture, unless they are aware of the individual's cultural background, they may diagnose their culturally normal behaviour as abnormal from their own cultural viewpoint.

**Key term**

**Ethical considerations in diagnosis** – an appraisal of the moral consequences of diagnosing mental disorders.

## ■ Ethical considerations in diagnosis

Diagnosis aims to correctly identify disorders so that appropriate treatment can be given. But there are several ethical consequences of diagnosis. First, diagnosis can be used to discriminate against certain people – for example, using diagnostic criteria to classify homosexuality as a mental disorder, thus justifying the 'treatment' of homosexuals to 'cure' their abnormality. Diagnostic criteria have also been used by some regimes to classify dissidents as abnormal, justifying their incarceration in psychiatric institutions.

Labelling individuals as abnormal puts a stigma on to them that is difficult to remove and that will affect their employment, relationship chances, etc. Labelling also leads to a 'career' as a mental patient, with repeating cycles of hospitalization that leads to institutionalization, where an individual cannot live meaningfully outside of the hospital environment. Hospitalization can incur the ethical issue of harm through the over-use of psychoactive drugs, used as a 'chemical cosh' to control patients. Labelling can even create a self-fulfilling prophecy, where patients 'grow into' their label and become mentally disordered.

## ■ Research

■ **Xia (2012)** reported that China has imprisoned political dissidents in psychiatric institutions and subjected them to forced treatments, such as electroconvulsive therapy (ECT), illustrating the use of diagnostic criteria to control dissidents.

■ **Curran & Parr (1957)** reported that only 9 out of 100 homosexual men treated with aversion therapy showed a later preference towards heterosexuality, illustrating the weak efficacy of the treatment and its unethical nature.

■ **Abelson & Langer (1974)** found that clinicians told that a young man in a video was a job applicant perceived him positively, but when told he was a mental patient, they perceived him negatively, demonstrating the stigmatizing effect of labelling.

## ■ Positive evaluation

■ In October 1973, the Australian and New Zealand College of Psychiatry Federal Council declared that homosexuality was not an illness, with homosexuality removed from DSM-II in December 1973.

## ■ Negative evaluation

■ The accusation remains that psychiatric drugs are used to control rather than treat people with abnormal conditions, with drug companies keen to promote their usage to boost profits. Sales of antipsychotic drugs topped £10 billion globally in 2008.

## ■ Practical application

■ Aversion therapy was a treatment used by psychiatrists to treat homosexuality. Electric shocks were given if patients became aroused by homosexual images. However, the treatment did not 'cure' homosexuals; instead patients often become stressed, depressed and suicidal.

## ■ Issues and debates

■ Cultural considerations in diagnosis are most important in multicultural societies, where several subcultures, each with their own perceptions of what constitutes normality, exist side by side.

---

**■ STRENGTHEN YOUR LEARNING**

1 Explain what is meant by cultural relativism.

2 Why are all definitions of abnormality culturally relative?

3 Outline ethical considerations in diagnosis.

4 Summarize what research evidence has suggested about cultural relativism and ethical considerations in diagnosis.

5 What other evaluative points, including practical applications and relevant issues and debates, can be made about cultural relativism and ethical considerations in diagnosis?

---

**Expert tip**

Be sure to read the wording of questions concerning ethical considerations in diagnosis carefully, as it is quite easy to construct an irrelevant answer. For instance, if a question asks about ethical implications, then an answer focusing solely on ethical issues/considerations would not really be creditworthy. Instead, you would need to talk about the consequences of ethical considerations, for individuals and society as a whole.

# Etiology of abnormal psychology

Revised ☐

## Description of OCD

Revised ☐

**Obsessive-compulsive disorder (OCD)** is an anxiety-related mental disorder characterized by fear reactions so high they become maladaptive. Two per cent of the population suffer from OCD.

**Obsessions** consist of inappropriate thoughts, beliefs and visual images – for example, contamination by germs – leading to feelings of extreme anxiety.

**Compulsions** consist of uncontrollable urges to repetitively perform behaviours, like constantly cleaning door handles, which decrease obsessional thoughts. These only reduce obsessional thoughts in the short term, with obsessional thoughts returning to trigger compulsive behaviours in a repeating cycle.

Most OCD sufferers realize their obsessions and compulsions are inappropriate but cannot consciously control them. OCD is perceived as a mental disorder when it negatively affects sufferers' ability to function effectively in everyday life.

> **Key terms**
>
> **Obsessive-compulsive disorder (OCD)** – an anxiety disorder characterized by persistent, recurring unpleasant thoughts and repetitive, ritualistic behaviours.
>
> **Obsessions** – forbidden or inappropriate ideas and visual images that lead to feelings of extreme anxiety.
>
> **Compulsions** – uncontrollable urges to repetitively perform specific tasks and behaviours.

### ■ Symptoms

#### ■ Obsessions

| Symptoms of obsessions | Description |
|---|---|
| Recurrent and persistent unwanted thoughts | Repeatedly experiencing inappropriate unwanted thoughts, beliefs and mental images that create anxiety. |
| Thoughts irrelevant to real life | Experiencing thoughts unconnected to real life. |
| Suppressed thoughts | Sufferer attempts to replace unwanted thoughts with more appropriate ones. |
| Thoughts recognized as self-generated | Realization that obsessional thoughts are self-invented. |

#### ■ Compulsions

| Symptoms of compulsions | Description |
|---|---|
| Repetitive actions | Desire to repeat behaviours and mental acts in response to obsessional thoughts. |
| Aimed at reducing distress | Repetitive behaviours and mental acts are oriented at reducing anxiety. |

#### ■ Other symptoms

| Symptoms of obsessions and disorders | Description |
|---|---|
| Recognized as excessive | Sufferers realize obsessions/compulsions are extreme. |
| Time-consuming | Obsessions/compulsions are so time-consuming that they interfere with the ability to effectively conduct everyday life. |

### ■ Gender variations in the prevalence of OCD

There are gender differences in types of OCD. Preoccupations with contamination and cleaning are more apparent in females, while male sufferers focus more on religious and sexual obsessions. OCD is more common among male children and males have an earlier, gradual onset with more severe symptoms, while females have a later, sudden onset with fewer severe symptoms.

### ■ Cultural variations in the prevalence of OCD

Sociocultural factors do not cause OCD, but they do increase chances of it developing and being maintained in vulnerable individuals, by raising anxiety levels, through influences like life crises and family tensions. Sociocultural influences help shape expression of the disorder; for instance, in religious environments obsessions often reflect the religious views of that cultural setting.

> **Key terms**
>
> **Gender variations in the prevalence of OCD** – differences between males and females in experiencing OCD.
>
> **Cultural variations in the prevalence of OCD** – the influence of sociocultural factors upon the experience of OCD.

KEY CONTEMPORARY STUDY

## 'THE INFLUENCE OF CULTURAL FACTORS ON OBSESSIVE-COMPULSIVE DISORDER: RELIGIOUS SYMPTOMS IN A RELIGIOUS SOCIETY'

**Greenberg & Witztum (1994)**

### Aim
- To assess rituals concerning cleanliness and exactness in presentations of OCD.

### Procedure
- Nineteen ultra-orthodox Jewish OCD outpatients and 15 non-ultra-orthodox Jewish outpatients attending a clinic in Jerusalem were assessed for symptoms of OCD.

### Results
- Religious symptoms pertaining to prayer, dietary practices, cleanliness and menstrual practices were found in 13 out of 19 ultra-orthodox participants and in none of the 15 non-ultra-orthodox participants.
- Repetitive performance of religious rituals by ultra-orthodox participants was perceived by their rabbis as abnormal rather than reflecting heightened spirituality.
- The presentation of religious obsessions resembled the presentation of OCD symptoms in non-religious patients.

### Conclusions
- Religious rituals do not cause OCD, but help shape its expression, supporting the idea that sociocultural factors help shape and maintain OCD symptoms, but do not cause the disorder.

### Evaluation
- The use of non-researchers, in the form of rabbis, to help interpret findings gives the study more validity, especially in terms of reducing investigator bias.
- Reliability of findings could be assessed by repeating the study with a different ultra-religious (non-Jewish) group of participants.

## ■ Research

- **Mathis et al. (2011)** found male OCD sufferers were more likely to have early onset OCD, social impairments and more sexual and religious symptoms, while females had later onset and more contamination and cleaning symptoms, illustrating gender differences in the onset and expression of OCD.

- **Lomax et al. (2009)** found that the brains of individuals with early onset OCD, who are generally male, showed a reduction in size of some brain areas, which is not apparent in those with later onset OCD, who tend to be female. This illustrates a gender difference in the expression of OCD and suggests that male OCD may be more biological in nature than female OCD.

- **Gothelf et al. (2004)** reported that anxiety-raising life crises preceded the onset of OCD, suggesting such events do not cause OCD but act as triggers in those predisposed to OCD, as not everyone subjected to such life crises develops the disorder.

- **Fontenelle et al. (2004)** found that, while symptoms of OCD can reflect sociocultural factors, there was no solid evidence that any particular sociocultural factor had a causal role, which implies that sociocultural factors shape the expression of OCD, but do not cause it.

## ■ Positive evaluation

- As OCD occurs in different cultures and has similar prevalence rates and a consistency in the forms that obsessions and compulsions take, OCD seems to be more biological than sociocultural in origin.

- Because research suggests that OCD is primarily biological in nature, but has sociocultural triggers that initiate its onset, it offers clinicians a chance to create individually targeted therapies to treat the disorder, by identifying the particular sociocultural triggers involved in each individual's case.

## ■ Negative evaluation

■ Not all patients with early onset OCD are male, nor are those with later onset OCD all female, weakening the argument that male OCD is more biological in nature.

■ Symptoms often overlap with those of other disorders, like Tourette's syndrome and autism, which suggests that OCD may not exist as a truly separate disorder.

## ■ Practical application

■ An understanding of the symptoms of OCD and variations in its prevalence among different subgroups has led to the development of increasingly effective treatments, like drugs and CBT.

## ■ Issues and debates

■ OCD is understood by reference to the cognitive approach, as sufferers endure persistent and intrusive thoughts occurring as obsessions or compulsions, or a combination of both.

---

### ■ STRENGTHEN YOUR LEARNING

1 What are:
  a obsessions,
  b compulsions?
2 When is OCD perceived as being a mental disorder?
3 Outline:
  a symptoms of obsessions,
  b symptoms of OCD,
  c other symptoms of OCD.
4 Outline gender and cultural variations in the prevalence of OCD.
5 For Greenberg & Witztum's (1994) twin study into the influence of cultural factors on OCD, in your own words, state the aims, procedure, results, conclusions and evaluative points.
6 Summarize what research evidence has suggested about OCD.
7 What other evaluative points, including practical applications and relevant issues and debates, can be made about OCD?

---

**Expert tip**

A common mistake is to write about sociocultural causes of OCD, but there is very little evidence of this. Instead, sociocultural factors seem to shape the expression of OCD (the differing forms it takes), with evidence suggesting the disorder is more biological in nature.

---

# The genetic explanation for OCD

Revised ☐

The **genetic explanation** sees individuals as having different genetic vulnerabilities to OCD, dependent upon the number of genes contributing to vulnerability that they inherit. Research originally centred on twin and adoption studies, to assess the concordance rate for OCD between individuals with varying degrees of genetic similarity, with more recent gene-profiling studies seeking to identify genes common to OCD sufferers. Research indicates some genetic similarity between OCD and Tourette's syndrome, but they are believed to be separate disorders. Research also suggests that childhood forms of OCD may have a greater genetic component than adult forms.

**Key term**

**Genetic explanation for OCD** – the idea that individuals have different vulnerabilities to developing OCD, dependent upon the number of genes contributing to vulnerability that they inherit.

## ■ Research

■ **Grootheest et al. (2005)** reviewed 28 twin studies of 10,034 twin pairs conducted between 1929 to the present day, to find a heritability component between 45 and 65 per cent in children and between 27 and 47 per cent in adults. This suggests a genetic component to OCD, especially in childhood forms.

- **Stewart *et al.* (2007)** found from gene-profiling studies that a variant of the OLIG-2 gene was common in OCD sufferers, indicating a genetic link to the disorder.

- **Samuels *et al.* (2007)** used gene mapping to compare OCD sufferers who exhibited compulsive hoarding behaviour with those who did not, to find a link to chromosome 14 marker D14S588, implying a genetic influence to compulsive hoarding behaviour, which suggests the existence of a separate OCD subtype.

- **Davis *et al.* (2013)** compared the genetic datasets of 1,500 OCD participants with those of 5,500 non-OCD sufferers, as well as 1,500 genetic datasets of 1,500 participants with Tourette's syndrome and 5,200 without Tourette's syndrome, to find OCD and Tourette's syndrome both had an inherited basis, with some genetic overlap, but that the two disorders had separate genetic architectures that indicated them to be separate disorders.

## Positive evaluation

- As genes seem to be especially at work in some forms of OCD, like obsessions focused on religion and contamination, and compulsions focused on ordering and washing, it may be that some types of OCD are more genetic than others.

- The advent of gene-profiling studies through the extraction and analysis of DNA has allowed psychologists to understand a lot more about the genetic basis to OCD and to assess whether there are varying heritability rates to different forms of the disorder, as well as being able to investigate whether OCD and Tourette's syndrome are separate disorders or not.

## Negative evaluation

- Although research indicates a genetic basis to OCD, little is known about actual genetic mechanisms underpinning the disorder.

- As family members with OCD often display different symptoms, e.g. an adult constantly washing and a child constantly arranging dolls, it weakens supports for the genetic viewpoint, otherwise behaviour would be similar.

## Practical application

- The identification of specific genes associated with OCD may lead to gene therapies for the disorder, where associated genes are removed or replaced with non-associated ones.

## Issues and debates

- As concordance rates between MZ twins are never 100 per cent, there must be environmental as well as genetic influences upon the onset of OCD, which suggests an interaction of nature and nurture.

---

**■ STRENGTHEN YOUR LEARNING**

1 Outline the genetic explanation for OCD.

2 Summarize what research evidence has suggested about the genetic explanation for OCD.

3 What other evaluative points, including practical applications and relevant issues and debates, can be made about the genetic explanation for OCD?

---

**Expert tip**

A common mistake is to see OCD as caused by a single gene, but instead evidence points more towards the existence of several genes, each of which contributes to an increased vulnerability to developing the disorder.

# The neural explanation for OCD

Some forms of OCD are linked to maladaptive immune system functioning, such as through contracting throat infections, Lyme's disease and influenza, indicating a biological explanation through damage to neural mechanisms. Such onset of OCD is seen more in children than adults.

PET scans show low levels of serotonin activity in the brains of OCD patients and as drugs increasing serotonin activity reduce the symptoms of OCD, it suggests the neurotransmitter is involved with the disorder. PET scans also show that OCD sufferers have high levels of activity in the orbital-frontal cortex, a brain area associated with higher level thought processes and the conversion of sensory information into thoughts. The brain area helps initiate activity upon receiving impulses to do so and then stops the activity when the impulse lessens. OCD sufferers have difficulty in switching off or ignoring impulses, such as to wash dirt from their hands, so that they turn into obsessions, resulting in compulsive behaviour.

> **Key term**
>
> **Neural explanation for OCD** – the perception of OCD as resulting from abnormally functioning brain mechanisms.

## ■ Research

- **Pichichero (2009)** reviewed case studies to find children with throat infections often displayed rapid onset of OCD symptoms shortly after becoming infected. Such children also often exhibited symptoms of Tourette's syndrome. This supports the idea that such infections may affect neural mechanisms underpinning OCD.

- **Fallon & Nields (1994)** reported that 40 per cent of people contracting Lyme's disease (a bacterial infection spread by ticks) incur neural damage resulting in psychiatric conditions, including OCD. This suggests that the **neural explanation** accounts for the onset of some cases of OCD.

- **Zohar et al. (1987)** found that that symptoms of OCD were enhanced in 12 OCD patients taking a drug that reduced serotonin levels, compared to 20 non-OCD patients who took the drug, which suggests that OCD is related to abnormal levels of serotonin.

- **Saxena & Rauch (2000)** reviewed studies of OCD using brain scans, to find an association between the orbital-frontal cortex brain area and OCD symptoms. This suggests that specific neural mechanisms are involved with the disorder.

## ■ Positive evaluation

- The neural and genetic explanations can be combined, as neural mechanisms, like levels of serotonin, may be regulated by genetic factors, with two mutations of the human serotonin transporter gene (hSERT), which lead to diminished levels of serotonin, associated with the disorder.

- Recent research into OCD, such as that identifying throat infections and influenza as triggers for the disorder, has advanced psychological understanding of the disorder, which may lead to more effective treatments.

## ■ Negative evaluation

- The extent to which abnormal levels of serotonin and activity within the orbital-frontal cortex are causes of OCD or effects of the disorder is not known.

- Not all OCD sufferers respond to serotonin-enhancing drugs, lessening support for the neurotransmitter being the cause of OCD.

## ■ Practical application

- Drug treatments that elevate serotonin levels to stimulate the orbital-frontal cortex to function more normally have proven a very effective treatment with OCD.

## ■ Issues and debates

■ The neural explanation for OCD sees the condition as a physiologically based disorder and as such is biologically determinist, acknowledging no role for environmental factors.

---

**■ STRENGTHEN YOUR LEARNING**

1 Outline the neural explanation for OCD.

2 Summarize what research evidence has suggested about the neural explanation for OCD.

3 What other evaluative points, including practical applications and relevant issues and debates, can be made about the neural explanation for OCD?

---

**Expert tip**

A common fault with answers that require description and evaluation is to overdo the amount of description produced – for example, description of the neural explanation for OCD – at the expense of evaluating the explanation. It is not necessary to describe everything you may know about the explanation in order to get all the marks available for description.

# The evolutionary explanation for OCD

Revised ▢

The **evolutionary explanation** sees OCD as having an adaptive survival value, as if it did not, natural selection would not have favoured it and it would have died out. Evolutionary theory, therefore, sees the disorder as fulfilling a useful purpose. For example, OCD involves repetitive behaviours, like constant washing and grooming, and these would have had an adaptive value in protecting against infection. Similar repetitive behaviours would have increased security through vigilance and alertness. So, behaviours like continually cleaning door handles may be exaggerations of prehistoric adaptations.

**Seligman (1971)** suggests the evolutionary idea of **biological preparedness**, where humans (and animals) have innate tendencies to more easily display anxieties that have an adaptive value linked to survival and reproduction abilities, like a fear of infection. This involves genetic and environmental components: a predisposition to learn a fear of infection being the inherited component, and a learning experience involving infection being the environmental component. It would be harder to develop anxieties about being shot, as such a risk did not exist in prehistoric times.

**Key term**

**Evolutionary explanation for OCD** – the perception of OCD as having being acted upon by natural selection through having an adaptive survival value.

**Biological preparedness** – the idea that people have innate tendencies to more easily display obsessions and compulsions that have an adaptive value linked to survival and reproduction abilities.

## ■ Research

■ **Chepko-Sade et al. (1989)** found that rhesus monkeys who performed the most grooming of others were retained within a group following group in-fighting, suggesting OCD tendencies have an adaptive value, as continued group membership is crucial to survival.

■ **Polimeni (2005)** reported that OCD tendencies like counting and checking possess the potential to benefit society, which suggests an ancient form of behavioural specialization with evolutionary origins.

■ **Garcia & Koelling (1966)** found that rats quickly learned not to drink a sweet-tasting liquid paired with an injection that made them sick, as this is a natural adaptive response, but they did not develop such a taste aversion when the sweet-tasting liquid was paired with an electric shock, as this would not be an adaptive response – electric shocks not being apparent in prehistoric times, thus supporting the evolutionary idea of biological preparedness.

## ■ Positive evaluation

■ The evolutionary explanation can be seen as an extension to the genetic explanation (and the neural explanation) rather than an opposing theory, as genes are the medium by which evolution occurs.

■ Gender differences in OCD behaviours reflect the evolutionary differences in male/female priorities, like mating and parenting.

## ■ Negative evaluation

■ It is difficult to see how OCD behaviours that prevent the ability to perform everyday activities could be seen as having an evolutionary survival value.

■ Much evidence supporting the evolutionary explanation comes from animal research, presenting problems of generalizing findings to humans, whose behaviour is affected more by cognitive processes.

## ■ Practical application

■ Evolutionary explanations help clinicians and patients gain a better understanding of causes and symptoms of OCD that could lead to more effective therapies.

## ■ Issues and debates

■ Although evolution, as a biological explanation, is generally viewed as supporting the nature side of the 'nature versus nurture' debate, the concept of biological preparedness actually takes an interactionist viewpoint, as it sees OCD developing through a combination of genetic (nature) and environmental (nurture) influences.

---

■ **STRENGTHEN YOUR LEARNING**

1 Outline the evolutionary explanation for OCD; make reference in your answer to Seligman's idea of biological preparedness.

2 Summarize what research evidence has suggested about the evolutionary explanation for OCD.

3 What other evaluative points, including practical applications and relevant issues and debates, can be made about the evolutionary explanation for OCD?

---

**Expert tip**

Do not just write a general description of evolutionary theory when outlining the evolutionary explanation for OCD (or a general evaluation of the theory), as this will not gain many marks. Your outline and evaluation must be specific to the evolutionary explanation of OCD to gain higher levels of credit.

---

# The behaviourist explanation for OCD

Revised ☐

The **behaviourist explanation** sees OCD as being a learned condition, through classical conditioning (CC), operant conditioning (OC) and social learning theory (SLT).

The **two-process model** uses CC and SLT to explain the onset of OCD, with OC explaining how OCD is maintained.

The onset of OCD is seen as occurring through CC, where a neutral stimulus becomes associated with threatening thoughts or experiences, leading to the development of anxiety. For example, the neutral stimulus of shaking hands becomes associated with thoughts of becoming contaminated with germs by doing so (or by actually being contaminated). This also occurs through SLT, where an individual experiences an anxiety response after witnessing someone else experience an anxiety-arousing event.

The maintenance of OCD is seen as occurring through OC, where an individual is reinforced for exhibiting a behaviour that reduces anxiety. For example, an individual washes their hands and this reduces the anxiety of being contaminated. This reinforces the behaviour as it increases the chances of it recurring, when anxiety returns. OCD becomes resistant to extinction because sufferers constantly make reinforcing avoidance responses.

## ■ Research

■ **Meyer & Cheeser (1970)** demonstrated how compulsions are learned responses, reducing the heightened anxiety levels brought on by obsessions, which supports a behaviourist explanation for this component of the disorder.

---

**Key terms**

**Behaviourist explanation for OCD** – the perception of OCD as being a condition learned from environmental experiences.

**The two-process model of OCD** – the perception of OCD as a condition learned through classical conditioning or social learning and maintained through operant conditioning.

- **Rachman & Hodgson (1980)** found that, when OCD patients were exposed to situations that triggered obsessional thoughts, they experienced high levels of anxiety, but when they then enacted their compulsive behaviours, levels of anxiety declined. This supports the two-process theory that CC explains the acquisition of OCD, while OC explains its maintenance.

- **De Rosnay *et al.* (2006)** found that previously non-anxious toddlers started to exhibit anxiety after observing their mothers' fearful reactions, illustrating how OCD can be acquired through social learning via observation and imitation of role models.

## Positive evaluation

- As behavioural therapies are effective in treating OCD, it suggests the behaviourist explanation upon which they are based is valid.

- The behaviourist explanation is good at explaining compulsions, but not obsessive thinking, which is better explained by the cognitive approach. Perhaps a better explanation, then, is one that combines the behaviourist and cognitive explanations.

## Negative evaluation

- Compulsive avoidance behaviours, performed to reduce anxiety, like persistent washing, actually create more anxiety. It is therefore difficult to view such behaviours as reinforced responses, weakening the behaviourist viewpoint.

- The explanation is oversimplified, as it only focuses on learning, thus ignoring other important aspects, such as cognitive and biological factors. For example, the evolutionary explanation explains why certain stimuli are easier to condition.

## Practical application

- The behavioural therapy of exposure and response prevention, where patients are exposed to things that stimulate their anxiety in gradual doses and taught how to tolerate it without using compulsive behaviours, has proved effective in treating OCD, especially with children.

## Issues and debates

- Although the behaviourist explanation comes from the sociocultural approach, as it focuses on social and environmental learning experiences, the SLT part of the explanation is also part of the cognitive approach, as it focuses on mental processes involved with OCD.

---

**■ STRENGTHEN YOUR LEARNING**

1 Outline the behaviourist explanation for OCD; make reference in your answer to the two-process model in order to explain:

   a the onset of OCD,

   b the maintenance of OCD.

2 Summarize what research evidence has suggested about the behaviourist explanation for OCD.

3 What other evaluative points, including practical applications and relevant issues and debates, can be made about the behaviourist explanation for OCD?

---

**Expert tip**

Although the two-process model generally refers to the acquisition of OCD as occurring through classical conditioning and its maintenance through operant conditioning, social learning theory can also be used to explain acquisition.

# The cognitive explanation for OCD

The **cognitive explanation** sees some people as vulnerable to OCD because of an attentional bias, where thought processes focus upon anxiety-generating stimuli in a maladaptive way, like assessing the risk of infection from shaking hands being much higher than in reality. Behaviours that reduce faulty obsessive thoughts then become compulsions because of their anxiety-reducing qualities.

The cognitive explanation also sees compulsive behaviours as due to **cognitive errors**, based on an elevated sense of personal responsibility, motivating sufferers to carry out compulsive behaviours to avoid negative outcomes. This has a behaviourist element, where compulsive behaviours are reinforcing by reducing anxiety. However, using compulsive behaviours means sufferers do not test out their faulty thinking to realize there are no negative consequences to not performing compulsive behaviours. Thus the behaviours continue, as even when sufferers feel less anxious as a result of compulsive behaviours, the cognitive doubts return.

> **Key terms**
>
> **Cognitive explanation for OCD** – the perception of OCD as resulting from maladaptive thought processes.
>
> **Cognitive errors** – thought processes that cause individuals to perceive reality wrongly.

## Research

- **Clark (1992)** found that intrusive thinking is more common in OCD sufferers than in non-sufferers, supporting the cognitive explanation that maladaptive thought patterns are responsible for the disorder.

- **Buttolph & Holland (1990)** found that 69 per cent of female OCD sufferers had an onset or worsening of symptoms during pregnancy, supporting the idea that sufferers have a heightened sense of personal responsibility, as the imminent birth of a child presents a big responsibility for the unborn child's welfare.

- **Barrett & Healey (2002)** found that children with OCD had higher levels of cognitive appraisals, like probability, and severity of events and the fusing of thoughts with actions than anxious and non-anxious children who did not have OCD. This suggests that the cognitive conceptualization of OCD occurs in childhood.

## Positive evaluation

- Because there are subtypes of OCD, each focusing upon different forms of anxiety arousal and faulty thought processes, this supports the idea of OCD being determined by cognitive rather than biological factors.

- Cognitive and biological theories can be combined to create a more incisive explanation of OCD. For instance, the fact that some individuals are more susceptible to obsessional thinking because of their increased vulnerability due to genetic factors links cognitive factors to the genetic explanation, while activity seen in the orbital-frontal cortex brain area of OCD sufferers that is not seen in non-sufferers also links the two models together.

## Negative evaluation

- Support for the cognitive explanation is lessened by the fact that it does not explain why OCD sufferers take personal responsibility for events with negative consequences but not those with positive consequences.

- If an inflated sense of personal responsibility was the prime factor in causing OCD, then many more people would have the disorder, again lessening support for the explanation.

## Practical application

- Cognitive behavioural therapy, which seeks to replace maladaptive obsessional thinking with rational thinking, is based upon the cognitive explanation and has proven effective in treating the disorder.

## ■ Issues and debates

■ The fact that maladaptive cognitive processes are similar in sufferers cross-culturally suggests a biological basis to the onset and maintenance of OCD, with cognitive features merely effects rather than causes of the disorder.

---

### ■ STRENGTHEN YOUR LEARNING

1 Outline the cognitive explanation for OCD.

2 Summarize what research evidence has suggested about the cognitive explanation for OCD.

3 What other evaluative points, including practical applications and relevant issues and debates, can be made about the cognitive explanation for OCD?

---

### Expert tip

An effective point to make about the cognitive explanation for OCD is that the high success rate of cognitive behavioural therapy in treating the disorder gives support to the cognitive explanation upon which the theory is based.

# The psychodynamic explanation for OCD

Revised ■

The **psychodynamic explanation** of OCD sees the ego as disturbed by obsessions and compulsions, leading to sufferers using ego defence mechanisms to reduce anxiety.

### Key term

**Psychodynamic explanation for OCD** – the perception of OCD as resulting from unresolved traumatic experiences occurring during childhood psychosexual stages of development.

| Ego defence mechanism | Description |
| --- | --- |
| Isolation | Ego of a sufferer separates itself from anxiety produced by unacceptable urges of the id, by perceiving such urges as not belonging to them, but urges intrude as obsessional thoughts. |
| Undoing | Anxiety resulting from undesirable urges is addressed by performing compulsive behaviours. |
| Reaction formation | Anxiety resulting from undesirable urges is dealt with by adopting behaviours that are the opposite of the undesirable urges. |

The explanation sees the anal stage of psychosexual development as linked to the onset of OCD. Individuals become anxious over conflicts about being controlled and clean and tidy (seen as arising during potty training). Conflict over sexual restriction also provides a similar route to developing OCD.

**Adler (1930)** argued for a different psychoanalytic explanation, where OCD develops from children being prevented, by over-strict parents, from developing a secure sense of competence, leading to an anally fixated personality. OCD therefore occurs through feelings of inferiority and a need for control, expressed through obsessive cleanliness and tidiness.

## ■ Research

■ **Leichsenring & Steinert (2016)** reviewed research to find that short-term psychodynamic therapy (STPT) is effective in treating OCD, which suggests that the psychodynamic explanation upon which the therapy is based is valid.

■ **Rachman & Hodgson (1980)** reported that a few people with OCD had anal personality traits, but many do not show these traits, and many who have them do not go on to develop OCD, weakening support for the explanation.

■ **Peterson et al. (1992)** found no evidence that people with obsessive personality types are more likely to develop OCD than those with non-obsessive personality types, lowering support for the explanation.

## ■ Positive evaluation

■ There is a common-sense element to the idea of childhood anxiety-forming experiences later manifesting themselves as OCD, giving the explanation face validity.

■ There is some evidence, like that from **Leichsenring & Steinert (2016)**, to suggest psychodynamic therapies are effective, giving the psychodynamic explanation upon which they are based some support.

## ■ Negative evaluation

■ The explanation only relates to certain obsessions and compulsions. It is difficult to see how checking and orderliness compulsions (such as compulsions to check that doors are locked or a need to be excessively tidy) could relate to potty training.

■ Psychodynamic concepts are difficult to objectively test in a scientifically credible way. For example, it would be difficult to measure the level of anxiety produced by conflicts over potty training.

## ■ Practical application

■ Psychodynamic therapies, like STPT, that give patients insight into the origins of their OCD have proven effective, although not as effective as other treatments, and there are some claims that such treatments actually make symptoms worse.

## ■ Issues and debates

■ Rather than viewing OCD as resulting from any single explanation, it is more sensible to explain it by reference to the diathesis-stress model, which combines biological and psychological factors. A genetic vulnerability for the disorder is inherited (diathesis), while psychological influences act as triggers (stress), such as personality factors determined in childhood, as explained by the psychodynamic explanation.

---

### ■ STRENGTHEN YOUR LEARNING

1 Outline the psychodynamic explanation for OCD; make reference in your answer to ego-defence mechanisms and Adler's explanation.

2 Summarize what research evidence has suggested about the psychodynamic explanation for OCD.

3 What other evaluative points, including practical applications and relevant issues and debates, can be made about the psychodynamic explanation for OCD?

---

### Expert tip

As with the evolutionary explanation, be careful not to just give a general outline and evaluation of psychodynamic theory. Only answers that are specifically centred on psychodynamic explanations of OCD will receive much in the way of credit.

---

# Description of anorexia nervosa

Revised ☐

**Anorexia nervosa (AN)** is a mental disorder characterized by self-starvation and motivation to lose weight through fear of being fat. Twenty per cent of sufferers recover after one episode, 60 per cent have periodic episodes, while 20 per cent are hospitalized for lengthy periods. About 15 per cent of sufferers die from starvation, suicide, electrolyte imbalances and organ failure. AN has the highest mortality rate of any mental disorder. Brain damage and infertility can also occur.

## ■ Symptoms

Symptoms and effects of AN include extreme thinness, elevated liver enzymes, irregular heart rate, low blood pressure, poor circulation, constipation, osteoporosis, dehydration, dizziness, cold sensations, fatigue, brittle nails, thin hair, absence of menstruation, lanugo, dry skin, blotches, bruising, bloated stomach, halitosis and aching joints.

### ■ Behaviour

Many sufferers have trouble sleeping, are self-obsessed, have little interest in sex and are facile liars. They often wear baggy clothing to hide their thinness, pretend to eat and vomit food that is eaten. They also use vast quantities of diuretics and

---

### Key terms

**Anorexia nervosa (AN)** – eating disorder characterized by an obsessional desire to lose weight by limiting food intake.

**Subtypes of AN** – the division of anorexia nervosa into related, but different types.

laxatives. Anorexics are very interested in food and enjoy cooking for others. Many will hoard food that they never eat. Vigorous exercise is often pursued, as is frequent self-weighing.

## ■ Subtypes of AN

Some clinicians divide anorexia into two **subtypes of AN**.

| Subtypes of anorexia nervosa | Description |
| --- | --- |
| *Restricting type* | Weight loss achieved through dieting, fasting and/or excessive exercise. No regular episodes of binging or purging. |
| *Binge-eating/purging type* | Regular episodes of binging and/or purging. Self-induced vomiting and use of laxatives, diuretics and enemas to elicit purging are evident. |

## ■ Gender variations in the prevalence of AN

One per cent of adolescent females, compared to 0.3 per cent of males, are hospitalized with AN. About 85 per cent of sufferers are female and 15 per cent male, though male prevalence is on the increase. A disproportionate number of male sufferers are homosexual. Male and female anorexia often has different environmental triggers, which can explain different prevalence rates, at different ages. There is a higher proportion of older females than older males who develop the disorder and most male sufferers develop the disorder in adolescence and early adulthood.

> **Key term**
>
> **Gender variations in the prevalence of AN** – differences between males and females in experiencing anorexia nervosa.

## ■ Cultural variations in the prevalence of AN

There are variations in prevalence rates in different cultures, which suggests that sociocultural factors are involved, like cultural perceptions of attractiveness and media pressure to conform to cultural body type stereotypes. Prevalence rates are higher in western cultures, which reflects their emphasis on slimness, especially for females, as being desirable. Media sources in western cultures promote examples of ultra-slim females as being something that females need to conform to in order to be attractive and have high self-esteem. Dieting is also heavily promoted in western cultures, as a route to attractiveness.

> **Key term**
>
> **Cultural variations in the prevalence of AN** – the effect of sociocultural factors upon the experience of anorexia nervosa.

## ■ Research

■ **Feldman (2007)** found that 15 per cent of American homosexual males had an eating disorder, compared to only 5 per cent of heterosexual males, supporting the idea that AN is more prevalent among homosexual males.

■ **Darcy & Lin (2012)** reported that assessment tests for AN are designed mainly for female use, which may therefore underestimate male sufferers, who are not seen as anorexic by such tests.

■ **Gunewardene et al. (2001)** reported that prevalence rates for AN in non-western cultures are increasing and this correlates with exposure to western cultural ideals of body image brought by globalization. This supports the idea that sociocultural factors are linked to the development of AN.

■ **Makino et al. (2004)** reviewed studies to find prevalence rates in western cultures of 2.6 per cent in Norway and 1.3 per cent in Italy, but lower in non-western cultures, at 0.05 per cent in Malaysia and 0.01 per cent in China. This supports the idea that prevalence rates are higher in western cultures where cultural ideals of slimness are held in higher regard.

## ■ Positive evaluation

■ Research has allowed psychologists to understand that AN is mainly environmentally determined, which has implications for which treatments may be more beneficial. As prevalence rates are dissimilar across cultures, it suggests the disorder is not biological in nature.

■ The idea that AN is influenced by sociocultural factors is supported by the fact that, when a culture becomes more westernized, or when people from non-western cultures move to western cultures and are exposed to western cultural ideals of body image, there are increases in levels of the disorder.

## ■ Negative evaluation

■ Research suggests that separate diagnostic assessment categories may need to be constructed for males and females (and possibly even for heterosexual and homosexual males) in order for more valid diagnoses of males to occur.

■ Many cross-cultural studies of AN only look at female prevalence rates in student populations. More representative samples are needed, especially ones including cross-cultural male prevalence rates, in order for more valid conclusions to be drawn.

■ Increasing numbers of females, but not males, are developing AN in middle age. This may be because divorce makes women feel pressurized to lose weight in order to be 'attractive' to potential new partners, or due to the stress of an aging body reducing female perceptions of 'attractiveness', the loneliness associated with children leaving home or the trauma of parents dying. It suggests that there are different triggers for AN between males and females, which diagnosis needs to consider.

## ■ Practical application

■ Research that highlights differences in prevalence rates across social groups and changes in prevalence rates has allowed resources and therapies to be targeted in more effective ways.

■ It is important that more research into AN in males is undertaken, as the mortality rate is much higher in males, usually due to suicide. Only through understanding the reasons for this will it be possible to devise effective treatment strategies.

## ■ Issues and debates

■ An issue with research into anorexia nervosa is that findings were originally generalized to whole populations. However, valid theories need to be able to explain differences in cross-cultural prevalence rates, as well as gender, age, social class and sexuality prevalence rates. More recent studies have been orientated at different populations, leading to an increased awareness of how anorexia affects different social groups.

---

### ■ STRENGTHEN YOUR LEARNING

1 Describe anorexia nervosa; include reference to symptoms and behaviour in your answer.

2 Outline subtypes of anorexia nervosa.

3 Outline gender and cultural differences in the prevalence of anorexia nervosa.

4 Summarize what research evidence has suggested about gender and cultural differences in the prevalence of anorexia nervosa.

5 What other evaluative points, including practical applications and relevant issues and debates, can be made about gender and cultural differences in the prevalence of anorexia nervosa?

---

### Expert tip

A common mistake is to describe AN in terms of symptoms, behaviours and facts about its frequency. However, if a question requires explanations for the disorder, none of this would really be relevant (unless shaped to be so). Always identify the 'command words' in a question (the words that tell you what kind of answer is required), before answering the question.

# The genetic explanation for AN

The **genetic explanation** sees AN as having an inherited component, with each individual's vulnerability to the disorder being determined by the number of genes they inherit that contribute to the development of the disorder. Whether AN actually develops depends on the presence or not of environmental triggers, like stress, family structure, etc.

Study methods involve examining the incidence of AN among individuals with different levels of genetic similarity, such as twin and adoption studies, as well as gene-profiling studies that search for common genes among sufferers.

> **Key term**
>
> **Genetic explanation for AN** – the idea that individuals have different vulnerabilities to developing anorexia nervosa, dependent upon the number of genes contributing to vulnerability that they inherit.

## ▨ Research

- **Kortegaard *et al.* (2001)** assessed 34,000 pairs of Danish twins, finding a concordance rate for MZ twins, who are 100 per cent genetically similar, of 0.18, compared to DZ twins, who are 50 per cent genetically similar, of 0.07. This supports the genetic explanation, while also indicating a role for environmental factors.

- **Hakonarson *et al.* (2010)** compared DNA material from 1,003 mainly female AN participants and 3,733 non-sufferers, finding variants of the OPRD1 gene and HTR1D gene were associated with the disorder, supporting the idea that genes contribute to vulnerability of developing AN.

- **Bulik *et al.* (2006)** used a sample of 31,406 Swedish twin pairs to find that the incidence of AN was 1.2 per cent for females and 0.29 per cent for males, with heritability of the disorder calculated as 56 per cent, suggesting a genetic influence in the development of the disorder, but with gender differences.

## ▨ Positive evaluation

- The fact that genes and environmental influences contribute to AN supports the diathesis-stress model, where genes (diathesis) set biological vulnerability and environmental factors (stress) determine if the disorder is triggered.

- Genes can be used to explain a non-direct influence upon the development of AN, where individuals with genetically determined perfectionist personality characteristics are more vulnerable to developing AN, through a desire to achieve a 'perfect' body image. This view was supported by **Bachner-Melman *et al.* (2007)**, finding three genes associated with AN that are also associated with having a perfectionist personality.

## ▨ Negative evaluation

- As multiple genes are involved in AN, it makes it difficult to quantify the role of individual genes, as each have different levels of influence and may exert different levels of influence in different individuals.

- The explanation cannot account for why incidence of AN is higher in females, nor why the disorder is on the increase when inheritance of genes has not greatly changed.

## ▨ Practical application

- As genes contribute to the development of AN, it may one day be possible to treat the disorder with gene therapies that add genes to a sufferer's cells to replace missing or malfunctioning genes in order to reduce vulnerability.

## ▨ Issues and debates

- The fact that both genes and environmental factors are involved in the onset of AN suggests that the disorder is not a result of nature or nurture, but an interaction of the two upon each other.

■ **STRENGTHEN YOUR LEARNING**

1 Outline the genetic explanation for AN.

2 What study methods are used to assess the genetic explanation; how do they operate?

3 Summarize what research evidence has suggested about the genetic explanation for AN.

4 What other evaluative points, including practical applications and relevant issues and debates, can be made about the genetic explanation for AN?

**Expert tip**

A common mistake is for students to write about an 'anorexic gene', when evidence suggests instead that there are multiple genes that contribute to an overall vulnerability to the disorder.

# The neural explanation for AN

Revised ☐

The **neural explanation** sees AN as linked to defective brain structures. Interest has focused on the lateral hypothalamus and the insula dysfunction hypothesis, which sees AN associated with the insula brain area.

Neural explanations also see faulty biochemistry involved in AN, with the neurotransmitter serotonin linked with the onset and maintenance of the disorder and noradrenaline linked to maintaining restriction of eating by influencing anxiety levels.

Leptin also attracts interest through its regulation of the neuroendocrine system during starvation.

**Key term**

**Neural explanation for AN** – the perception that anorexia nervosa results from defective brain structures and biochemistry.

## KEY CONTEMPORARY STUDY

### 'ANOREXIA LINKED TO DISTURBANCE IN BRAIN REGION'

**Oberndorfer *et al.* (2013)**

#### Aim
■ To investigate the degree to which brain structures play a role in the development of AN.

#### Procedure
■ Fourteen female recovered anorexics and 14 non-anorexic females fasted overnight and received a standardized breakfast of 604 calories, before having an fMRI scan to establish satiety fullness state.
■ fMRI scans then measured brain responses to calorific and non-calorific sweet tastes.

#### Results
■ Anorexics had reduced responses to sweet tastes, especially calorific ones, in the right anterior insula brain area.

#### Conclusions
■ There is a relationship between AN and neural processes in the insula brain region, which determines whether individuals feel hungry.
■ Anorexics have altered sensitivity in brain mechanisms signalling the calorific content of food.

#### Evaluation
■ It is not known whether faulty brain mechanisms cause anorexic behaviour or whether anorexic behaviour leads to changes in brain mechanisms.

## ■ Research

■ **Anand & Brobeck (1952)** found that lesions to the lateral hypothalamus led to weight loss, suggesting that damage to this brain area causes AN, a view supported by **Stellar (1954)**, finding that stimulating the lateral hypothalamus increased eating, but lesioning it decreased eating.

■ **Grinspoon *et al.* (1996)** found that leptin levels were lower in anorexics and that leptin levels correlated with body weight and percentage of body fat, supporting the idea of leptin being related to AN.

- **Bailer *et al.* (2005)** found heightened serotonin levels in the brains of anorexics, especially those with high anxiety, which suggests that prolonged disruption of serotonin produces heightened anxiety levels, which then triggers AN.

## Positive evaluation

- The neural theory can be combined with the genetic theory to provide a fuller biological explanation of AN, as the abnormal biochemistry seen in anorexics may be under genetic control.

- Research findings into leptin suggest a role for the hormone as a therapy to treat AN.

## Negative evaluation

- Abnormal levels of serotonin and leptin may not cause the onset of AN, but instead be an effect of the malnutrition associated with the disorder.

- Much research into AN is performed on females, presenting generalization problems to males, who have different distributions and amounts of body fat, so the relationship between male anorexics and neurotransmitter levels may be different to that of female sufferers.

## Practical application

- Research findings concerning the insula brain area suggest treatments for AN through enhancing insula activity through biofeedback or by mindfulness training to adjust the brain's response to food stimuli.

## Issues and debates

- Neural and biochemical explanations see AN as biologically determined, with little if any role for free will in the onset and maintenance of the disorder.

---

### ■ STRENGTHEN YOUR LEARNING

1  Outline the neural explanation for AN; include reference in your answer to brain structures and biochemistry.

2  For Oberndorfer *et al.*'s (2013) twin study into AN, in your own words, state the aims, procedure, results, conclusions and evaluative points.

3  Summarize what research evidence has suggested about the neural explanation for AN.

4  What other evaluative points, including practical applications and relevant issues and debates, can be made about the neural explanation for AN?

---

**Expert tip**

Less creditworthy answers on the neural explanation tend to only focus on the lateral hypothalamus and the insula dysfunction hypothesis. More creditworthy answers tend to also focus on faulty biochemistry, such as the influence of serotonin, noradrenaline and leptin.

# The evolutionary explanation for AN

Revised ▢

The **evolutionary explanation** sees AN as having an adaptive survival value acted upon by natural selection, which explains why AN continues to be apparent in the population.

## ■ The reproduction suppression hypothesis: Surbey (1987)

The **reproduction suppression hypothesis** (RSH) sees AN as an evolutionary adaptation of females suspending sexual maturity so that they do not get pregnant in times when food supplies are too scarce to feed infants. When young females are stressed, it makes them react in a genetically pre-programmed way, as if food supplies were low, by dieting, in order to suppress getting pregnant until environmental conditions improve, allowing them to successfully raise children.

**Key terms**

**Evolutionary explanation for AN** – the perception that anorexia nervosa has been acted upon by natural selection through having an adaptive survival value.

**Reproduction suppression hypothesis** – the perception that anorexia nervosa incurs an adaptive survival value by females suspending sexual maturity in order not to get pregnant in times when food supplies are too scarce to feed infants.

## Adaptive response to famine: Guisinger (2003)

The **adaptive response to famine** (ARF) explanation sees AN as an adaptive response to times of food scarcity, where populations migrate to find food, with the hyperactivity found in anorexics forming a 'migratory restlessness': a motivation to move to a more food-rich environment through loss of weight.

## Research

- **Frisch & Barbieri (2002)** reported that most women need 17–22 per cent of their body weight to be fat in order to be able to menstruate and ovulate, supporting the RSH that AN is related to a suppression of reproductive ability.

- **Rakison (2002)** used an eating attitudes and attitudes to sex and marriage questionnaire with anorexics and non-anorexics, to find a negative correlation between high levels of disordered eating and low levels of attraction to sexual attention, supporting the evolutionary idea that AN is linked to a suppression of reproductive behaviour.

- **Arcelus et al. (2011)** reviewed 36 studies to find AN, at 4 per cent, has the highest death rate of any mental disorder, especially from suicide, weakening support for evolutionary explanations, as these findings suggest anorexia does not have an adaptive survival value.

## Positive evaluation

- The RSH gains support from the fact that AN does restrict physical signs of puberty – for example, the stopping of periods – which means that sufferers cannot get pregnant, in line with the theory.

- Evolutionary explanations gain support from the fact that, if AN was maladaptive, natural selection would have acted to remove the condition from the gene pool.

## Negative evaluation

- The fact that many anorexics are male, and indeed homosexual, goes against the RSH, which sees AN as an evolutionary adaptive response of females suppressing their chances of getting pregnant during times of food scarcity.

- There is little support for the ARF explanation. Guisinger herself provided no research evidence. Other explanations have more research support, which suggests the explanation has less validity.

## Practical application

- Getting sufferers to understand the biological evolutionary origins of their condition can help in formulating individual treatment plans to address the negative symptoms of the disorder.

## Issues and debates

- Evolutionary explanations are simplistic in neglecting other factors involved in AN, like media influences. It is better to include evolutionary explanations as part of a diathesis-stress explanation, where some individuals, through evolution, have a greater genetic vulnerability to developing AN, with environmental factors determining whether the condition is triggered.

---

**Key term**

**Adaptive response to famine** – the perception that anorexia nervosa is an adaptive response to food scarcity, through an energized motivation to migrate to more food-rich environments

■ **STRENGTHEN YOUR LEARNING**

1 What is the main principle underpinning evolutionary explanations for AN?

2 Outline the following evolutionary explanations for AN:

   a the reproduction suppression hypothesis,

   b adaptive response to famine.

3 Summarize what research evidence has suggested about evolutionary explanations for AN.

4 What other evaluative points, including practical applications and relevant issues and debates, can be made about evolutionary explanations for AN?

**Expert tip**

A valid theory should be able to explain all instances of a phenomenon. The fact that both the RSH and the ARF theories cannot really explain why males develop AN makes both theories somewhat invalid.

# Family systems theory: Minuchin (1979)

Revised ☐

**Family systems theory** (FST) sees the behaviour of family members as affecting the functioning of other members and that AN develops within one family member as a means of reducing tensions within the whole family – for example, by drawing attention to an anorexic individual and away from arguing parents.

## ■ Enmeshment

**Enmeshment** involves dysfunctional family interactions inhibiting each family member's sense of individuality. This tends to occur in families where children are not allowed to develop individuality, with restriction of eating a protest against this.

## ■ Autonomy and control

Autonomy concerns choice and freedom in relation to oneself and others, and involves the development of control, identity, competence and effectiveness. The major aspect of achieving **autonomy and control** is to develop a sense of self. The FST sees disturbances in the development of autonomy as a central feature of AN, which manifests as distortions of body image, misperceptions of internal states and a paralysing sense of ineffectiveness.

The FST lists five qualities of dysfunctional families that hinder the development of autonomy:

1 enmeshment,

2 over-protectiveness,

3 rigidity of style,

4 conflict avoidance,

5 involvement of the anorexic in parental conflict.

## ■ Research

■ **Minuchin *et al.* (1978)** found that families of anorexics had higher levels of enmeshment, over-protectiveness, conflict avoidance and rigidity of style, supporting the idea of enmeshment and lack of autonomy being features of AN, in line with the FST.

■ **Strauss & Ryan (1987)** found that anorexics had less sense of autonomy, poorer self-concept and more disturbed family interactions than non-anorexics, supporting the FST, especially the idea of autonomy disturbance.

■ **Karwautz *et al.* (2003)** compared anorexic and non-anorexic sisters, finding that anorexic sisters had lower levels of autonomy, related mainly to their relationships with their mothers (and to a lesser extent their fathers), supporting the idea of autonomy being a central feature of AN.

**Key terms**

**Family systems theory of AN** – the perception that anorexia nervosa results from dysfunctional patterns of family interaction.

**Enmeshment** – the idea that anorexia nervosa results from a family interactive style that inhibits each family member's sense of individuality.

**Autonomy and control** – the perception of anorexia nervosa as resulting from a struggle for self-management identity and effectiveness.

## ■ Positive evaluation

■ There is a wealth of research evidence for the FST, which lends the explanation considerable support.

■ The success of family-based therapy in treating AN, where family dynamics are worked upon in order to restore an anorexic's development towards autonomy, gives support for the FST upon which the treatment is based.

## ■ Negative evaluation

■ Heightened tensions within families of anorexics, rather than being a trigger for the development of AN, could be the result of having an anorexic in the family.

■ Deficiencies in autonomy are central to many abnormal conditions and therefore it is not known how such deficiencies relate specifically to AN.

## ■ Practical application

■ Family-based therapies have proven effective when they are tailor-made to fit individual circumstances, as uniform features of dysfunctional anorexic families do not really exist, and when they treat the family, not as the cause of AN but as a resource to help a sufferer recover from their disorder.

## ■ Issues and debates

■ The FST relates to the sociocultural approach, as it focuses on social and environmental learning experiences, and the cognitive approach, as it focuses on the idea of identity and self, which involves mental processes, like self-perception.

---

**■ STRENGTHEN YOUR LEARNING**

1 Outline the family systems theory explanation for AN; include reference in your answer to enmeshment and autonomy and control.

2 Summarize what research evidence has suggested about the family system theory explanation for AN.

3 What other evaluative points, including practical applications and relevant issues and debates, can be made about the family systems explanation for AN?

---

**Expert tip**

A sophisticated evaluative point to make about the FST is that it includes elements of both the sociocultural and the cognitive approaches. Theories that include elements of more than one approach tend to be regarded as having greater validity.

---

# The social learning theory explanation for AN

Revised ☐

The **social learning theory explanation for AN** is based around the idea that individuals observe and imitate popular people's thinness in order to be popular themselves. Young people are especially vulnerable, as they are searching for an identity and heightened self-esteem.

SLT explains why AN occurs more in cultures where attractiveness is associated with thinness and why it is more of a female disorder, as low body weight is associated with attractiveness in females. Similarly, it explains the high incidence of AN in homosexual men, as gay men value thinness more than heterosexual men.

## ■ Reinforcement

Observed behaviours are imitated if others vicariously reinforce behaviour by responding favourably, increasing the chances of the behaviour occurring again. **Reinforcement** can be external, like gaining approval from others for losing weight, or internal, like feeling better about oneself. Reinforcements can be positive, like receiving compliments for being skinny, or negative, such as not being mocked for being chubby.

---

**Key terms**

**Social learning theory explanation for AN** – the perception of anorexia nervosa as being learned through observation and imitation.

**Reinforcement** – the consequence of a behaviour, which strengthens the chances of the behaviour occurring again.

## Media

In western cultures, the **media** portray thinness as desirable. These images are observed and imitated to the point where AN develops. This explains why women are more likely to be anorexic, as women are bombarded by more 'desirable' media images of thinness than men.

## Research

- **Bemis (1978)** found, from reviewing 20 years of *Playboy* centrefolds, that the weight of models progressively decreased, while **Garner & Garfinkel (1980)** found that Miss America beauty queen winners have become slimmer over time, illustrating how media sources present female thinness as attractive.

- **Herzog *et al.* (1991)** found that homosexual men had role models who were much lighter in weight than heterosexual role models, supporting the idea that heightened levels of AN among gay men can be explained by reference to SLT.

- **Lai (2000)** found that AN increased among Chinese people in Hong Kong as the region became more westernized, which suggests that SLT affects cultural influences upon AN, in this case by western media images promoting female thinness as desirable.

## Positive evaluation

- SLT is better able than biological explanations or the FST to explain why the prevalence of AN has increased and why it occurs more in females and certain cultures (due to the increased promotion of female thinness in western cultures).

- SLT has a wealth of research support, which supports it as a valid explanation for AN.

## Negative evaluation

- SLT cannot explain why dieting continues after compliments for losing weight stop, or indeed when negative comments commence.

- SLT does not explain why only some women develop AN, when all women are subjected to the same media images of thinness being attractive.

## Practical application

- Presenting positive images of media role models, such as females with fuller-sized figures as models, should encourage females to develop such a figure themselves due to the vicarious reinforcement received by such models.

## Issues and debates

- Although the SLT explanation of AN is environmentally determinist, as it sees the condition as caused by learning experiences outside of an individual's control, there is a cognitive element too, as there is focus upon memory and attention, when observing and imitating anorexic behaviour.

---

**Key term**

**Media** – public forms of communication that promote observation and imitation of thinness.

---

### ■ STRENGTHEN YOUR LEARNING

1 Outline the social learning theory explanation for AN; include reference in your answer to reinforcement and media.

2 Summarize what research evidence has suggested about the social learning theory explanation for AN.

3 What other evaluative points, including practical applications and relevant issues and debates, can be made about the social learning theory explanation for AN?

---

**Expert tip**

An effective way of evaluating the SLT explanation of AN is to compare it against other explanations to draw out strengths and weaknesses. For instance, SLT is better able than the biological theory to explain the increased incidence of AN and why it occurs more in females and in certain cultures.

# The cognitive explanation for AN

The **cognitive explanation** sees AN as caused by maladaptive thought processes, like wishing to attain unreal levels of perfection by developing a thin body type, in order to be acceptable.

## ■ Distortions

Distorted thought processes involve errors in thinking that negatively affect perceptions of body image. These **distortions** lead to individuals adopting strict rules about eating, with any breaking of rules creating a sense of guilt that lowers self-esteem and creates self-disgust. This results in increased anorexic behaviour.

## ■ Irrational beliefs

**Irrational beliefs** are maladaptive ideas leading to the development and maintenance of AN, with such irrational beliefs resulting in anorexics misperceiving body image and seeing themselves as fatter than they are. Anorexics also possess flawed reasoning behind their eating habits.

Anorexics demonstrate both distortions and errors in thinking.

| Distortions in thinking |
| --- |
| Misperceiving one's body as overweight when it is underweight. |
| Basing self-worth on physical appearance. |
| Having flawed beliefs about eating and dieting. |

| Errors in thinking |
| --- |
| All or nothing thinking, e.g. 'I ate a chip, now I'm fat'. |
| Overgeneralizing, e.g. 'If I cannot restrict my eating, I am a failure'. |
| Magnification/minimization, e.g. 'Gaining any weight is not acceptable/My weight loss is not harmful'. |
| Magical thinking, e.g. 'If I weighed below five stone, I would be happy'. |

## ■ Research

- **Bemis-Vitouesk & Orimoto (1993)** found that anorexics have a distorted body image and feel they must continually lose weight to be in control of their bodies, illustrating the key role that distortions play in the maintenance of AN.

- **Konstantakopoulos et al. (2012)** found that 28.8 per cent of anorexics had delusional body image beliefs associated with restricted eating and body dissatisfaction, linking irrational thinking to the onset and maintenance of AN.

- **Halmi et al. (2000)** tested anorexics to find that the higher the need for perfection, the more severe symptoms were, which supports the cognitive theory that anorexics wish to attain an unreal level of perfectionism to be acceptable.

## ■ Positive evaluation

- Cognitive behavioural therapies are effective in treating AN, lending support to the cognitive theory upon which they are based.

- The multiple factors of AN converge into two key elements: low self-esteem and a high need for perfectionism, both explicable by reference to the cognitive theory.

## ■ Negative evaluation

- Cognitive theory has not established if maladaptive thought processes are a cause of AN or a result of being anorexic.

- Many people express dissatisfaction with their bodies and have been on diets, but only a few develop AN, which cognitive theory cannot explain.

**Key terms**

**Cognitive explanation for AN** – the perception of anorexia nervosa as resulting from maladaptive thought processes.

**Distortions** – faulty thought processes that negatively affect perceptions of body image.

**Irrational beliefs** – maladaptive ideas that lead to the development and maintenance of anorexia nervosa.

## ■ Practical application

■ Cognitive behavioural therapy, which identifies and replaces maladaptive with rational ways of thinking about food and eating, has proven to be an effective therapy for AN, especially in addressing the mental processes that underpin the condition.

## ■ Issues and debates

■ The cognitive theory does not consider other explanations, many of which have research support. A better way, therefore, of understanding AN is to combine explanations into one interconnected theory. For example, the high drive for perfectionism exhibited by many anorexics and which is a key part of the cognitive theory may be genetically transmitted.

---

■ **STRENGTHEN YOUR LEARNING**

1 Outline the cognitive explanation for AN; include reference in your answer to distortions and irrational beliefs.

2 Explain the types of errors and distortions in thinking that anorexics make.

3 Summarize what research evidence has suggested about the cognitive explanation for AN.

4 What other evaluative points, including practical applications and relevant issues and debates, can be made about the cognitive explanation for AN?

---

**Expert tip**

When outlining the cognitive explanation for AN, detail can be achieved by reference to the various distortions and errors in thinking. This then provides opportunities to evaluate through a wide range of research studies that specifically focus on such errors and distortions.

# Treatment of mental disorders and their effectiveness

Revised ☐

## Biological treatments of OCD

Revised ☐

### ■ Drug therapy

Antidepressant SSRIs elevate levels of serotonin, causing the orbital-frontal cortex to function more normally. Anxiolytics drugs are used due to their anxiety-lowering properties, while antipsychotic drugs with a dopamine-lowering effect are used when treatment with SSRIs is not effective. Beta-blockers reduce physical symptoms of OCD by lowering adrenaline and noradrenaline production that elevates blood pressure and heart rate to cause anxiety.

### ■ Psychosurgery and deep-brain stimulation

**Psychosurgery** destroys brain tissue to disrupt the cortico-striatal circuit by the use of radio frequency waves to reduce symptoms. **Deep-brain stimulation** focuses magnetic pulses on the supplementary motor area of the brain, associated with blocking out irrelevant thoughts and obsessions.

### ■ Research

■ **Mallett et al. (2008)** found symptom reduction with deep-brain stimulation, which was replicated by **Greenberg et al. (2008)**, finding symptom reduction and functional improvement in 18 out of 26 OCD patients, suggesting the treatment is effective.

■ **Julien et al. (2007)** found that with SSRIs, although symptoms do not fully disappear, 50 to 80 per cent of OCD patients improve, allowing them a fairly normal lifestyle, which would not be possible without the treatment.

■ **Liu et al. (2008)** found, from 35 OCD patients non-responsive to other treatments, that psychosurgery allowed 57 per cent to become symptom-free, 29 per cent to have symptom reduction, with 14 per cent showing no improvements, suggesting the treatment to be safe and effective.

**Key terms**

**Biological treatments for OCD** – therapies based upon the medical model, which perceive cures as emanating from addressing the physical causes of the disorder.

**Drug therapy** – treatment of OCD by chemical means.

**Psychosurgery** – treatment of OCD by irreversible destruction of brain tissue.

**Deep-brain stimulation** – treatment of OCD by application of magnetic pulses to specific brain areas.

## KEY CONTEMPORARY STUDY

### 'OLANZAPINE AUGMENTATION FOR TREATMENT-RESISTANT OBSESSIVE-COMPULSIVE DISORDER'

**Ringold *et al.* (2000)**

### Aims

■ To assess the ability of olanzapine in treating resistant forms of OCD.

### Procedure

■ Ten adults with non-treatment-responsive OCD continued with SSRI fluoxetine treatment, but with the addition of the antipsychotic drug olanzapine.

### Results

■ Of the nine participants who completed the trial, there was a 16 per cent reduction in symptoms.

■ Only one patient was 'much improved' and maintained the improvement over six months.

■ Six patients suffered weight increase.

### Conclusions

■ Adding olanzapine to SSRI treatment has positive effects in treatment of resistant forms of OCD.

■ Simultaneous drug therapies are more effective than single drug treatments.

### Evaluation

■ A cost–benefit analysis needs to assess whether the improvement in symptoms justified the weight increase seen in 60 per cent of patients.

■ The response of the patients supports the idea of a biological cause to OCD.

## ■ Positive evaluation

■ Antidepressant medication is more suitable for adults, as they are more able to tolerate and understand side effects.

■ Drug treatments are effective as they are relatively cheap, do not require a therapist to administer them and are user-friendly, with people used to taking pills.

## ■ Negative evaluation

■ Psychosurgery is not a cure for OCD. Patients will continue to need psychiatric support following the procedure.

■ Some argue that drug treatments should not be used due to the risk of side effects, the tendency of antidepressants to produce suicidal thinking and the effectiveness of psychological treatments.

## ■ Practical application

■ Cannabidol, an ingredient in marijuana, is as effective as antipsychotics in treating OCD, but with fewer side effects. However, it is cheap and does not generate big profits for drug companies.

## ■ Issues and debates

■ Drug therapies, psychosurgery and deep-brain stimulation all relate to the biological approach, as they exert a physiological effect to reduce OCD symptoms.

■ **STRENGTHEN YOUR LEARNING**

1 Outline the following biological treatments for OCD:

  a drug therapy,

  b psychosurgery,

  c deep-brain stimulation.

2 For Ringold *et al.*'s (2000) twin study into olanzapine treatment for OCD, in your own words, state the aims, procedure, results, conclusions and evaluative points.

3 Summarize what research evidence has suggested about biological treatments for OCD.

4 What other evaluative points, including practical applications and relevant issues and debates, can be made about biological treatments for OCD?

### Expert tip

An effective way to draw conclusions from research studies, such as **Ringold *et al.*'s (2000)** study into olanzapine augmentation, is to assess how much the aims of the study have been realized. As the ability of olanzapine in treating resistant forms of OCD was seen to be high, the treatment can be concluded to be effective.

# Psychological treatments of OCD

Revised ☐

## ■ Cognitive behavioural therapy

With **cognitive behavioural therapy** (CBT), sufferers learn to realistically assess the likelihood of obsessional ideas occurring and practise new adaptive beliefs, while disregarding their former maladaptive ones. All types of maladaptive thoughts can be addressed with CBT; intrusive thoughts are shown to be normal and patients learn that thinking about a behaviour is not the same as doing it. CBT occurs as an individual treatment, or as a group therapy, where interaction with fellow sufferers provides additional support and encouragement, decreasing the feelings of isolation that can aggravate symptoms.

## ■ Psychodynamic therapies

**Psychodynamic therapies** (PDTs) are used with patients who have been non-responsive to other treatments, who have comorbid conditions and suffer from borderline personality disorder and whose OCD developed in adulthood due to stressors based upon interpersonal relationships, as well as patients whose OCD originates from unresolved childhood crises.

Dynamic deconstructive psychotherapy gets patients to identify emotions experienced in relation to their condition and encourages them to explore other ways of interpreting their interactions with people. This deconstructs how individuals regard themselves and builds more positive attributions.

## ■ Research

■ **Cordioli (2008)** reviewed clinical trials and meta-analyses of CBT, finding it effective in reducing OCD symptoms in 70 per cent of patients who complied with treatment, suggesting that the therapy has useful therapeutic value, though the reasons why many sufferers are non-responsive were not identifiable.

■ **Chlebowski & Gregory (2009)** reviewed five cases studies of individuals suffering from OCD, to find psychotherapy useful for patients with comorbid OCD and bipolar disorder and for patients whose OCD started in adulthood due to interpersonal stressors and whose symptoms have symbolic significance. This suggests PDTs are effective in specific instances.

■ **Leichsenring & Steinert (2016)** reviewed research to find that short-term psychodynamic therapy is effective in treating OCD, which suggests that the treatment is beneficial.

■ **Jónsson & Hougaard (2009)** found that group CBT was better than drug treatments in reducing OCD symptoms, which suggests it is a plausible therapeutic procedure.

### Key terms

**Cognitive behavioural therapy** – treatment of OCD through modification of thought processes in order to alter behavioural and emotional states.

**Psychodynamic therapies** – treatment of OCD through identifying and resolving related childhood traumatic experiences.

## Positive evaluation

- The feelings of isolation that OCD incur can be addressed by the social support that group therapies provide and the realization that others have similar problems.

- Old forms of psychotherapy often worsened rather than improved symptoms, but more modern types targeted at improving interpersonal relationships in specific patients are effective, elevating their regard among clinicians.

## Negative evaluation

- CBT and psychotherapy are not suitable for OCD patients who have difficulties talking about inner feelings, or who do not possess the verbal skills to do so.

- There is an ethical issue of harm with PDTs, as such treatments can involve revisiting traumatic emotional experiences seen to relate to the condition. This could worsen rather than improve symptoms.

## Practical application

- Drug treatment followed by CBT produces more symptom reduction than drugs or CBT alone, which suggests that, while CBT is effective, it is most effective when used as a combined treatment.

## Issues and debates

- An issue with CBT and psychodynamic treatments for OCD is that, while proven to be effective, both are costly, requiring trained clinicians to deliver them. Therefore, drugs are arguably more cost-effective.

> **Expert tip**
>
> A good way of evaluating CBT and psychodynamic therapies for OCD (or any other treatments for that matter) is to compare their effectiveness against each other. It should be noted though that some treatments are more effective against particular types of OCD, such as psychodynamic therapies being effective against OCD cases that originated in adulthood due to interpersonal stressors.

---

### ■ STRENGTHEN YOUR LEARNING

1 Outline the following psychological treatments for OCD:
   a cognitive behavioural therapy,
   b psychodynamic therapies.
2 Summarize what research evidence has suggested about psychological treatments for OCD.
3 What other evaluative points, including practical applications and relevant issues and debates, can be made about psychological treatments for OCD?

---

# Biological treatments of AN

`Revised` ☐

## Drug therapy

Drugs are not effective on their own (though they reduce excessive focus on food and dieting), but they contribute to effectiveness when combined with other treatments. Antidepressant SSRIs are useful in treating anorexics with comorbid anxiety disorders and/or depression, with the antipsychotic olanzapine also used to reduce anxiety related to weight and dieting in patients non-responsive to other treatments. SSRIs are prescribed to patients who have increased in weight, as the risk of side effects is heightened in underweight patients, who may experience loss of appetite and further weight loss.

As well as reducing low mood in anorexics by elevating serotonin levels, SSRIs help patients maintain weight once control over weight and eating is established.

## Other biological therapies

1 **Mandometer** – a device giving patients feedback on their eating rate, which is used to accelerate rate of eating in anorexics.

2 **Repetitive transcranial magnetic stimulation** (rTMS) – a form of brain stimulation involving targeted magnetic pulses, which induces an electrical current in specific nerve cells to positively affect mood. Used on anorexics with high levels of anxiety.

> **Key terms**
>
> **Biological therapies for anorexia nervosa** – treatment of anorexia nervosa based on the medical model, which perceives cures as resulting from addressing the physical causes of the disorder.
>
> **Drug therapy** – treatment of anorexia nervosa by chemical means.
>
> **Mandometer** – treatment of anorexia nervosa by use of a device that provides feedback on an individual's feeding rate.
>
> **Repetitive transcranial magnetic stimulation** – treatment of anorexia nervosa through application of targeted magnetic pulses to positively affect mood.

## ■ Research

- **Biederman *et al*. (1985)** reported that treating AN using only antidepressants produced little weight gain, and often incurred side effects, causing patients to stop taking them. This was supported by **Holtkamp *et al*. (2005)**, who found treatment with SSRIs alone had no beneficial effects. This suggests drug therapies alone are not effective in treating AN.

- **Boachie *et al*. (2003)** found that the treatment of anorexics aged 10–12 years with the antipsychotic drug olanzapine lessened anxiety and increased weight gain, suggesting the treatment was useful for young patients.

- **Van Elburg *et al*. (2012)** found that 63 per cent of mandometer patients reached normal weight compared to 85 per cent with other treatments. Also, after two years, more mandometer patients than patients with other treatments were still in treatment and more had relapsed, which suggests MT is not an effective long-term treatment.

- **Van den Eynde *et al*. (2011)** found that rTMS treatment reduced anorexics' urges to restrict eating and reduced their feelings of fullness, which restricted eating. This suggests the treatment is effective in treating AN.

## ■ Positive evaluation

- Drugs are effective in keeping anxiety levels low in recovering patients. Elevated anxiety levels could cause fear of eating/weight increase to return, leading to spiralling back into AN.

- rTMS offers a non-invasive, biological way of treating AN without the side effects associated with drug therapies and could act as a replacement for drugs in combined treatments.

## ■ Negative evaluation

- Clinicians are reluctant to prescribe SSRIs due to their side effects, especially causing low appetite and weight loss, which could worsen symptoms.

- Drug companies, keen to boost profits, have promoted research into drug therapies, but with little indication of their effectiveness.

## ■ Practical application

- Drug treatments are useful for treating AN when combined with other psychological treatments. Drugs reduce symptoms of AN, like anxiety, allowing psychological treatments more chance of success.

## ■ Issues and debates

- Drug therapies, the mandometer and repetitive transcranial magnetic stimulation all relate to the biological approach, as they see AN as physiologically determined. However, as none of these treatments is effective by itself, this suggests AN is not biologically determined.

---

**■ STRENGTHEN YOUR LEARNING**

1 Outline the following biological treatments for AN:
   a drug therapy,
   b mandometer,
   c repetitive transcranial magnetic stimulation.
2 Summarize what research evidence has suggested about biological treatments for OCD.
3 What other evaluative points, including practical applications and relevant issues and debates, can be made about biological treatments for OCD?

---

**Expert tip**

Better responses to exam questions about biological therapies for AN will include reference to treatments other than just drug therapies – for example, the mandometer and repetitive transcranial magnetic stimulation. This will then give an opportunity to use a wider range of research studies in any evaluation of biological therapies.

# Psychological treatments of AN

## ■ Cognitive behavioural therapy

**Cognitive behavioural therapy** (CBT) sees individuals with negative, distorted perceptions of themselves developing feelings of shame and disgust that trigger weight control behaviours and a repeating cycle of negative self-evaluation. CBT gives sufferers insight into the factors that maintain their anorexic behaviour and teaches skills to develop more adaptive ways of thinking and behaving in order to maintain a healthy weight.

CBT for AN has three phases:

| Phases | Description |
| --- | --- |
| *Behavioural phase* | Therapist and patient create a plan for stabilizing eating behaviour and reducing anorexic symptoms. Coping strategies are taught and practised to help deal with negative emotions. |
| *Cognitive phase* | Cognitive restructuring skills to alter negative thinking patterns are taught. Relationship, body image and self-worth problems are addressed, as well as methods of controlling one's emotions. |
| *Maintenance and relapse prevention phase* | Focus on reducing factors that trigger anorexic thoughts and behaviour and developing strategies to prevent relapsing back into AN. |

> **Key terms**
>
> **Cognitive behavioural therapy** – treatment of anorexia nervosa through modification of thought processes associated with the disorder in order to positively affect behaviour and mood.
>
> **Psychodynamic therapies** – treatment of anorexia nervosa through identifying and resolving childhood traumatic experiences associated with the disorder.

## ■ Psychodynamic therapies

**Psychodynamic therapies** (PDTs), such as focal psychodynamic therapy (FPT), see AN as linked to unresolved conflicts occurring in childhood. Psychotherapists help patients understand their unconscious thoughts, feelings and behaviour, with such insight helping them to repair relationships with themselves and others.

Interpersonal therapy (IT) sees AN as related to perceptions of low self-worth and high anxiety, caused by problems with interpersonal relationships. Therapist helps patients assess negative factors associated with interpersonal relationships and form and practise strategies to resolve them.

## ■ Research

- **Pike (2003)** found that after one year, 22 per cent of patients receiving CBT had either dropped out of treatment or relapsed, compared to 77 per cent of patients receiving nutritional advice, which suggests CBT is effective.

- **Carter et al. (2009)** found that after one year, 35 per cent of CBT patients who had regained a healthy weight had relapsed, compared to 66 per cent of group therapy patients, which suggests CBT is an effective long-term maintenance treatment for recovering anorexics.

- **Egger et al. (2016)** found that FPT had lower average costs than CBT, which suggests that FPT is a cost-effective treatment.

- **McIntosh et al. (2005)** found that, compared to CBT or outpatient support, IT was ineffective in reducing symptoms by the end of treatment, but at a 6.7-year follow-up had a similar recovery rate to the other treatments, suggesting IT has some long-term effectiveness.

## ■ Positive evaluation

- A positive aspect of psychodynamic therapies is that they do not incur any side effects, unlike drug therapies.

- Both PDTs and CBT are supported by research evidence, which suggests they have effectiveness as treatments for AN.

## ■ Negative evaluation

- Both psychotherapies and CBT need trained therapists to administer treatment, increasing the cost of treatment.

- A problem with assessing the effectiveness of CBT is the high drop-out rate. This reduces sample sizes, making generalization of findings less valid, obscuring whether treatments are effective or not.

## ■ Practical application

- PDTs are becoming more acceptable with clinicians, which is beneficial, as AN is difficult to treat, so new methods of treatment would be most welcome.

## ■ Issues and debates

- A methodological issue in assessing treatments of AN is that patients have different severities of AN, which makes it difficult to assess how effective treatments are.

---

### ■ STRENGTHEN YOUR LEARNING

1 Outline cognitive behavioural therapy for treatment of AN; make reference in your answer to the behavioural, cognitive and maintenance and relapse prevention phases.

2 Outline psychodynamic therapies for the treatment of AN; include reference in your answer to focal psychodynamic therapy and interpersonal therapy.

3 Summarize what research evidence has suggested about psychological treatments for AN.

4 What other evaluative points, including practical applications and relevant issues and debates, can be made about psychological treatments for AN?

---

### Expert tip

In answers outlining CBT for AN, detail can be achieved by description of the three specific phases of the treatment: the behavioural, cognitive and maintenance and relapse prevention phases. This will also demonstrate a greater understanding of the treatment and thus attract a higher level of credit.

---

# The role of culture in treatment

Revised ☐

Mental health care reflects culture. For example, western cultures stress the medical model, hence the emphasis on biological treatments.

How different cultures perceive mental disorders affects whether individuals seek treatment. In cultures with a stigma of shame about mental disorders, there is less likelihood of seeking treatment. The way patients present symptoms, and thus the diagnosis and treatment given, differ cross-culturally.

In some cultures, individuals with mental disorders are more likely to seek help from religious figures or traditional healers, negatively affecting recovery prospects.

For people from ethnic minorities, it is often not possible to have a therapist of the same ethnicity, and this affects the chances of committing to a treatment, or even seeking treatment.

Cost of treatment affects type of therapies received. People in many cultures cannot afford specialist treatments and so only receive low-cost treatments, unless in countries like Great Britain, where mental health care is free.

### Key term

**The role of culture in treatment** – the influence of a group's shared beliefs, norms and values upon the perception, application and effectiveness of therapies for mental disorders.

## ■ Research

- **Lin & Cheung (1999)** found that Asian patients report physical symptoms more than emotional ones, but when questioned further admit to having emotional symptoms. This suggests that people of different cultures express (or not) symptoms in a culturally acceptable way, affecting the treatment prescribed.

- **Peifer et al. (2000)** reported that many cultural groups turn to informal sources of care, like clergy, traditional healers and family and friends, instead of health professionals, when encountering mental health problems. This suggests that such cultural groups have lower chances of recovery.

■ **Vega et al. (1998)** reported that ethnic minorities in the USA are less likely than white people to seek mental health treatment, due to negative perceptions of being mentally disordered, illustrating cultural differences in perceptions about mental health treatments.

■ **Sussman et al. (1987)** found that nearly 50 per cent of black Americans suffering from depression feared hospitalization and mental health treatments, compared to 20 per cent of white Americans, and these fears led to them often not seeking treatment. This suggests that black Americans are more likely to have lower prospects of recovery from mental disorders.

## ■ Positive evaluation

■ Revisions of classification systems of mental health and its treatment have increasingly taken into account cultural factors, improving the effectiveness of treatments.

■ Increasingly, clinicians are being taught how cultural factors affect the treatment of mental disorders and incorporate such training into their mental health care provision to improve patients' chances of recovery.

## ■ Negative evaluation

■ The consequences of individuals not seeking treatment due to culturally determined negative perceptions of mental disorders are serious. Patients' conditions can worsen and the risk of suicide grows.

■ Gaining valid data about mental health care in different cultures is problematic, as health care systems vary greatly cross-culturally, making comparisons difficult.

## ■ Practical application

■ Having clinicians from many cultures helps in the delivery of mental health care, as people can have a clinician of their own cultural background who better understands their needs and perceptions.

## ■ Issues and debates

■ There is a danger, with the delivery of mental health care to people of different cultures, of an imposed etic, where clinicians apply their own cultural viewpoints concerning mental health treatment inappropriately to people of other cultures.

---

■ **STRENGTHEN YOUR LEARNING**

1  In bullet-point form, outline the various ways in which culture can affect the treatment of mental disorders.
2  Summarize what research evidence has suggested about the ways in which culture can affect the treatment of mental disorders.
3  What other evaluative points, including practical applications and relevant issues and debates, can be made about the ways in which culture can affect the treatment of mental disorders?

---

**Expert tip**

Be careful with answers on this topic area to not just describe the role of culture in treatment (unless a question only calls for a descriptive answer). Evaluation, in the form of research evidence, effectiveness of treatments, etc. will generally be equally important.

## EXAM-TYPE QUESTIONS

| | |
|---|---|
| 1 Discuss classification systems used in the diagnosis of abnormality. | (22 marks) |
| 2 Discuss the role of clinical biases in diagnosis of abnormality. | (22 marks) |
| 3 Discuss psychologists' attempts to define abnormality. | (22 marks) |
| 4 Evaluate the reliability and validity of diagnosis in abnormality. | (22 marks) |
| 5 Discuss one or more studies relating to the reliability and validity of diagnosis in abnormality. | (22 marks) |
| 6 Discuss ethical considerations in the diagnosis of abnormality. | (22 marks) |
| 7 Discuss one or more biological explanations for one abnormal disorder. | (22 marks) |
| 8 Evaluate one sociocultural explanation of one abnormal disorder. | (22 marks) |
| 9 Discuss cognitive explanations of one or more abnormal disorders. | (22 marks) |
| 10 With the use of suitable examples, discuss the prevalence rates for one abnormal disorder. | (22 marks) |
| 11 Discuss one or more research studies of the explanation of one abnormal disorder. | (22 marks) |
| 12 Evaluate one or more etiologies of one abnormal disorder. | (22 marks) |
| 13 Contrast one biological and one cognitive explanation of one or more abnormal disorders. | (22 marks) |
| 14 Discuss one or more biological treatments for one abnormal disorder. | (22 marks) |
| 15 Evaluate cognitive treatment of one or more abnormal disorders. | (22 marks) |
| 16 Discuss the sociocultural approach to the treatment of one or more abnormal disorders. | (22 marks) |
| 17 Discuss one or more research studies of the treatment of one abnormal disorder. | (22 marks) |
| 18 Discuss ethical considerations in the treatment of one or more abnormal disorders. | (22 marks) |
| 19 Evaluate the role of culture in diagnosis. | (22 marks) |
| 20 Discuss research studies of the role of culture in diagnosis. | (22 marks) |

# Influences on cognitive and social development

## Influences of peers

### ■ Influences of peers on cognitive development

Piaget and Vygotsky both acknowledged the importance of **peers** in stimulating **cognitive development**, especially Vygotsky, who saw children with superior cognitive skills as tutoring those with inferior ones.

Social learning theory is applicable to the influence of peers, where children imitate observed peer behaviour if it has rewarding consequences, especially if a child identifies with a model, like being of the same gender.

### ■ Influences of peers on social development

Initially, parents exert the greatest influence on children's **social development**, but peers become increasingly more influential and, by adolescence, they are the biggest socialization influence.

Interactions with peers influence the development of **theory of mind** (ToM), the ability to empathize and adopt someone else's perspective. This is apparent from three years of age, with the ability to see someone else's viewpoint stimulated by interactions with peers.

### ■ Research

- **Senghas & Coppola (2011)** reported that when a group of deaf Nicaraguan children, with no language, were put together as a group, they developed their own sign language, which they taught to newcomers to the group, illustrating the powerful influence of peers upon cognitive development.

- **Azmitia & Hesser (1993)** found that younger children observed and followed guidance from older siblings more than they did with older peers, and that older siblings helped younger children more than older peers did, without prompting to do so. This suggests that older siblings are more influential upon cognitive development than older peers. The research also highlights the importance of identification within social learning. The young children observed their siblings, who were role models that they identify with. The effect was not so strong with peers who they identify with less.

### ■ Positive evaluation

- Peer influence upon both social and cognitive development is especially beneficial for children disadvantaged through their home life or intellectually, as it compensates for such disadvantages.

- The benefits of peer influence to a learner are well documented, but it is a two-way effect, as the peer exerting the influence also benefits socially, through learning to help others, and cognitively, by learning to adapt language to explain a skill to someone less able.

### ■ Negative evaluation

- It is difficult to see if peers exert a social or cognitive influence due to the amount of interaction between the two, as in the development of language. It is more sensible to see them acting in unison.

---

**Key terms**

**Peers** – individuals of equal status.

**Cognitive development** – process by which the ability to think and perceive matures in an individual.

**Social development** – process by which interaction with and understanding of others mature in an individual.

**Theory of mind** – the ability to attribute mental states to oneself and others.

■ Research into the influence of peers on social and cognitive development often neglects the contribution of biological maturation, as biological maturation tends to run parallel to peer influence.

## Practical application

■ Vygotsky's technique of collaborative learning, where children of similar levels of ability work collectively, promotes the use of language to bring about cognitive development, with knowledge socially constructed by working together on common tasks.

## Issues and debates

■ The contribution of the social environment to cognitive development is debatable. Vygotsky sees social environment as exerting an important influence through culture and language, while Piaget emphasizes biological factors more.

---

### ■ STRENGTHEN YOUR LEARNING

1 What are peers?

2 Outline the influence of peers on:

  a cognitive development,

  b social development.

3 Summarize what research evidence has suggested about the influence of peers on cognitive and social development.

4 What other evaluative points, including practical applications and relevant issues and debates, can be made about the influence of peers on cognitive and social development?

---

**Expert tip**

Always identify the 'command words' in a question (the words that inform what kind of answer is required) before beginning an answer. For instance, if a question asks specifically about the influence of peers on cognitive development, then material on the influence of peers on social development would not be relevant.

# Influences of play

Revised ▢

## ■ Influences of play on cognitive development

Piaget believed that children develop cognitively through interaction with the environment, with **play** being important, as it allows children to construct and test ideas of how the world works (their schemas). Their understanding of the world changes as their interactions, such as through play, allow them to discover new truths about the world around them. Play also stimulates creative skills, especially those promoting new and advanced ways of thinking. Social play may also stimulate the development of ToM through role playing, which allows children to see the world from someone else's perspective.

## ■ Influence of play on social development

The social form of play, where children interact with others, is a powerful vehicle for teaching social skills, such as turn taking and working cooperatively. Pretend play, like playing with dolls, enhances emotional security, as it allows children to work through anxiety-creating situations.

## ■ Research

■ **Howard-Jones et al. (2010)** found that children were more creative in building a collage if they had been allowed previously to free play with modelling dough, as opposed to doing a structured activity of copying text. This illustrates the value of free play in stimulating creative ways of thinking.

■ **Lillard (1993)** found that pretend play allowed children to view the world from someone else's viewpoint by acting out their role, which suggests pretend play is an important factor in developing ToM in children.

■ **Pellis et al. (2010)** found a relationship between the amount of time rats played when young and how socially competent they were as adults. This seemed to have an effect on actual brain structures, which suggests that play aids social development from a biological perspective.

---

**Key term**

**Play** – the participation in activities for pleasure and recreation.

■ **Lillard et al. (2013)** found a relationship between the amount of time spent in parallel play (where children copy each other's activities) and language, intelligence and creativity development, suggesting it is a useful stimulus for development.

## Positive evaluation

■ Structured play, where a child's environment is enhanced with appropriate toys that help stimulation of cognitive and social skills, is especially beneficial to development. Free play is then beneficial, as it allows children to practise and enhance their newly learned skills.

■ Different types of play stimulate development in different areas. For instance, social play stimulates cognitive development in terms of language development and understanding others. Other forms of play are more appropriate in other developmental areas.

## Negative evaluation

■ The argument that social play facilitates development of ToM is not supported by research. ToM develops without social play, so play is not an important influence.

■ Not all play influences development positively. War play encourages aggressiveness and can have negative social effects on difficult-to-manage children, making their social skills even more problematic.

## Practical application

■ Getting children to pretend play being a role model, like Batman, while learning a new skill helps them to concentrate and work for longer on that skill.

## Issues and debates

■ The extent to which play is an influence upon child development has consequences for educational systems. If play is a major influence, it should be incorporated into school timetables and activities more than it often is.

> ### ■ STRENGTHEN YOUR LEARNING
>
> 1 Outline the influence of play on:
>    a cognitive development,
>    b social development.
> 2 Summarize what research evidence has suggested about the influence of play on cognitive and social development.
> 3 What other evaluative points, including practical applications and relevant issues and debates, can be made about the influence of play on cognitive and social development?

> **Expert tip**
>
> A common mistake students make is to create too much descriptive content when answering questions on the influence of play on development. You would not have to write everything you know about the topic to secure all the marks available for description. Remember to leave sufficient time to provide an evaluation too (as long as the question requires evaluation).

# The effects of childhood trauma

Revised ☐

The effects of childhood **trauma** include increased anxiety, **substance abuse**, sleep disorders and **somatic (body) problems**.

## Increased anxiety

Post-traumatic stress disorder (PTSD) can occur in cases of trauma. Sufferers experience flashbacks, nightmares and repeatedly relive the trauma. A constant state of tension makes relaxation difficult, with additional physical effects, like aching muscles. Flashbacks can be triggered by sounds, smells and other sensory input.

## Substance abuse

One possible effect of PTSD is heavy drinking and drug use, often painkillers due to the physical pain associated with the condition.

> **Key terms**
>
> **Trauma** – the psychological and/ or physical effects of experiencing distressing events.
>
> **Substance abuse** – the harmful use of psychoactive substances, including alcohol and drugs.
>
> **Somatic problems** – negative bodily effects associated with the experience of childhood trauma.

## KEY CLASSIC STUDY

### 'RELATIONSHIP OF CHILDHOOD ABUSE AND HOUSEHOLD DYSFUNCTION TO MANY OF THE LEADING CAUSES OF DEATH IN ADULTS'

Felitti *et al.* (1998)

#### Aim

■ To assess the relationship between childhood trauma and long-term effects.

#### Procedure

■ A total of 13,494 adults self-reported on childhood adverse experiences, such as sexual abuse.

■ Participants were assessed for health risk factors and current health state.

#### Results

■ More than 50 per cent experienced one adverse childhood experience, with 25 per cent experiencing two or more experiences.

■ The numbers of adverse experiences correlated with level of risky behaviour.

■ Those with four or more adverse experiences were sexually promiscuous, less likely to exercise and had increased health risks, like drug abuse and suicide risks.

#### Conclusions

■ Childhood trauma has serious long-term negative effects on health.

#### Evaluation

■ The study prompted much follow-up research, which validated the findings.

## ■ Somatic problems

Childhood trauma is associated with adult obesity, connected to emotional eating as a desire to arrest sexual attention. Sleep disorders are also common, lasting into adulthood, possibly due to staying alert to avoid abuse or because of the high anxiety incurred.

## ■ Research

■ The National Child Traumatic Stress Network found that individuals experiencing abuse were three times more likely to incur substance abuse than those not experiencing trauma, illustrating a link between trauma and later behavioural problems (**Dierkhising *et al.* 2013**).

■ **Powers *et al.* (2016)** found an association between amount of childhood trauma participants and PTSD symptoms and psychotic episodes, illustrating how childhood trauma can lead to mental health problems in adulthood.

■ **Danese & Tan (2014)** found that suffering trauma as a child was a risk factor for obesity, while **Greenfield *et al.* (2011)** found childhood abuse related to disturbances of sleep into adulthood, suggesting a relationship between childhood abuse and negative somatic effects.

## ■ Positive evaluation

■ Most evidence linking trauma to adverse effects is only correlational. However, evidence of the trauma causing the adverse effects comes from studies showing the brains of trauma victims have incurred developmental changes that may incur adverse effects.

## ■ Negative evaluation

■ Trauma can incur an adverse effect on memory, making studying trauma difficult, as memories of traumatic events may be incomplete or even missing.

## ■ Practical application

■ Rhythmic eye-movement therapy involves moving your eyes side to side while reliving a traumatic event to desensitize the memory and then replacing negative thoughts with positive ones.

## ■ Issues and debates

■ There is an ethical consideration of harm when researching into people who have experienced trauma. Such research should only be undertaken by those qualified to do so and for the purpose of gaining insight towards formulating effective therapies.

---

**■ STRENGTHEN YOUR LEARNING**

1 What is meant by trauma?

2 Explain how the following can occur as a result of trauma:

  a  anxiety,

  b  substance abuse,

  c  somatic problems.

3 For Felitti's (1998) study into the long-term effects of trauma, in your own words, state the aims, procedure, results, conclusions and evaluative points.

4 Summarize what research evidence has suggested about the effects of childhood trauma.

5 What other evaluative points, including practical applications and relevant issues and debates, can be made about the effects of childhood trauma?

---

**Expert tip**

As trauma is a sensitive topic, it would be relevant to comment on the ethical considerations of conducting research in this area. For instance, the risk of further harming participants who have suffered trauma.

---

# Childhood resilience

Revised ☐

**Resilience** concerns the capability to recover from adversity and is usually assessed through self-report measures.

## ■ Strengthening resilience

**Educational interventions** for resilience aim to make individuals persevere more when facing challenges, such as fostering a growth mindset, where individuals feel more competent, believe they learn from failure and can meet challenges. Other educational interventions include developing student–teacher relationships, a caring environment, cooperation and peer tutoring, as well as student abilities, such as life skills, extracurricular activities and literacy. The basic idea is to 'inoculate' children against later difficulties.

---

**Key terms**

**Resilience** – characteristics that permit individuals to resist and recover quickly from difficulties experienced.

**Educational interventions** – a programme of steps designed to foster and build resilience.

---

## ■ Research

■ **Hines (2015)** performed a meta-analysis of 17 studies to find that resilience was key to coping with adverse home environments, such as homes with frequent incidents of violence. Prime resilience factors were found to be cultivation of support and the belief in hope for the future. This illustrates the importance of resilience in very different threatening conditions for children and how it can help them cope with being in such an environment.

■ **Lin et al. (2014)** found from research into those suffering childhood trauma that low resilience was linked to vulnerability to suicide, though other factors, such as level of available social support, were important too. The relationship was apparent into mid-life (ages 48 to 52 years), which illustrates the long-term nature of the relationship between resilience and coping with the effects of childhood trauma.

■ **Allen et al. (2016)** found that childhood trauma sufferers who took part in intervention programmes felt more confident about dealing with their problems and had lower numbers of emotional and behavioural problems than those not participating in such programmes, which suggests such intervention programmes are effective.

## Positive evaluation

■ Research into resilience has led to the development of many effective resilience development programmes, such as those promoting a growth mindset.

■ The establishment of resilience has proven to be a most effective means of alleviating negative physical and psychological problems in individuals who have suffered childhood abuse.

## Negative evaluation

■ Assessment of resilience is usually through self-reports, which have the problem of being context-based. So if tested at a time of crisis, reported resilience may be artificially low, providing invalid results.

■ Resilience is made up of several components, which work in unison with each other, such as levels of hope, perseverance and optimism. As these are difficult to test in isolation, it is not possible to know which components exert the greatest influence.

## Practical application

■ Osiris is a six-day growth mindset development programme for schools, delivered by trained instructors, which aims to embed a sustainable culture of success into students through resilience.

## Issues and debates

■ Resilience seems to be a cross-cultural construct recognized as a means of well-being and dealing with trauma. For example, there is the Finnish concept of 'Sisu', which is a type of inner grit, bravery and hardiness, and the Welsh concept of 'Hwyl', an inner strength in the face of adversity. As resilience is cross-cultural, it suggests a biological origin.

> **Expert tip**
>
> As the topic of resilience is mainly researched through self-reports, it would be acceptable to comment on the limitations of this method, such as the risk of idealized and socially sensitive answers, as well as findings being context-based. However, such comments should be focused on the reduction of the validity of findings in order to be creditworthy.

> ■ **STRENGTHEN YOUR LEARNING**
>
> 1 What is resilience and how is it measured?
> 2 Explain how resilience can be strengthened.
> 3 Summarize what research evidence has suggested about childhood resilience.
> 4 What other evaluative points, including practical applications and relevant issues and debates, can be made about childhood resilience?

# The influence of poverty/socio-economic status on development

Revised ☐

Development is influenced by **poverty** in three ways: education, health and environment.

> **Key term**
>
> **Poverty** – a lack of resources and means to be able to meet personal needs.

## Education

Children of poverty lag behind those from affluent families, attaining lower educational levels. One factor is poorer attendance levels, which affects children's ability to learn, causing them to fall behind. Quality of home life is often not conducive to learning, with few books available and little parental stimulation, nor is there any reinforcement of the value of education. Parents are often low achievers and so not good educational role models. Poverty is also associated with low-quality food, stress and risk factors, all of which inhibit educational progress.

## Health

Poverty negatively affects health, which adversely affects development. Poor health is linked to low school attendance, due to frequent illness, slower brain growth, due to poor diet, and cognitive and social impairments, due to impoverished learning and social environments. Children of poverty especially struggle to process information and regulate their emotions.

## ▨ Environment

Development is affected by children of poverty facing more environmental risks, like violence and abuse. Environmental risk leads to children feeling unsafe, which affects self-esteem and health, which in turn impinges on development. Children of poverty also have poorer quality play, as play facilities may be missing or unsafe and this negatively affects development by reducing opportunities for cognitive and social stimulation.

## ▨ Research

- **Bradley & Corwyn (2002)** found that children of poverty in high-stress environments display higher levels of disruptive behaviour and are less able to experience a positive school life due to the inability to develop healthy academic and social skills. This illustrates how poverty can negatively affect education.

- **Gunnar *et al.* (2009)** found that children growing up in a stressful environment were less likely to be able to regulate their emotions due to atypical brain development, illustrating how negative environmental factors associated with poverty can have biological consequences that affect development.

- **Emery & Laumann-Billings (1998)** found high levels of stress in communities dominated by low-income households, which produced negativity and low mood in parents, resulting in them not parenting their children effectively. There were also higher levels of disruption, separation and violence within the households, illustrating a relationship between environment and negative outcomes in children.

## ▨ Positive evaluation

- The fact that poverty is linked to negative outcomes in development gives an opportunity for vulnerable children to be identified and targeted with specific interventions to alleviate such effects.

## ▨ Negative evaluation

- Poverty clearly inhibits development, but there are so many other factors affecting children's development that the actual contribution of poverty to negative outcomes is difficult to assess.

## ▨ Practical application

- Interventionist programmes, like 'Headstart' in the USA, provide pre-school children of poverty with better diet and educational stimulation in the home and advise parents on how best to raise children. IQ levels were elevated, though often declined when intervention ceased.

## ▨ Issues and debates

- The fact that poverty retards brain growth, which then impinges on children's development, indicates a biological origin to the negative effects of poverty, though environment evidently plays a part too, which suggests effects result from an interaction of nature and nurture.

---

**▨ STRENGTHEN YOUR LEARNING**

1  Explain the effects poverty can have on:
   a  education,
   b  health,
   c  environment.
2  Summarize what research evidence has suggested about the effects of poverty on development.
3  What other evaluative points, including practical applications and relevant issues and debates, can be made about the effects of poverty on development?

---

**Expert tip**

When answering questions on the influence of poverty/socio-economic status on development, detail can be built into answers by focusing on the different ways in which development is affected, such as by education, health and environment. Access would then be created to a wide range of research studies to act as evaluation in your answer.

# Developing an identity

Revised ☐

## Attachments

Revised ☐

An **attachment** is a two-way, emotional tie to a specific other person and their emergence in early life is pivotal to identity development.

Attachments form in set phases and are stimulated by interactions and bodily contact. A first attachment occurs around 7–8 months of age, with most children then forming multiple attachments to different people for different purposes.

### Bowlby's theory of monotropy

Bowlby saw infants as having an innate tendency to form a bond with one prime attachment figure who responds sensitively to their needs. Infants have **innate social releasers**, like crying, smiling and vocalizations, which stimulate adult caregiving. Bowlby believed in a **critical period**, a set time in which attachments must form, otherwise they never would, and that attachments formed an **internal working model**, a blueprint for future relationships.

### Bowlby's maternal deprivation hypothesis

Bowlby believed that if attachments are broken, even temporarily, negative, irreversible damage occurs to children's emotional, social and cognitive development. Separation concerns short-term bond disruption, like day care, while deprivation concerns long-term disruption, like divorce, and privation concerns never having formed an attachment.

### Research

- **Lorenz (1935)** reported that goslings imprinted upon the first moving thing they encountered within a critical period, prompting Bowlby to argue that attachment is a human form of imprinting.

- **Schaffer & Emerson (1964)** found that multiple attachments are the norm and that 39 per cent of children had a prime attachment to someone other than their main carer, which suggests it is the formation of attachments that is important to the formation of identity, not the primary attachment.

- **Hazan & Shaver (1987)** found a continuity between early attachment style and later adult relationship types, supporting the internal working model.

### Positive evaluation

- Bowlby's idea of attachment has an evolutionary survival value, as keeping close proximity to an attachment figure would keep an infant from danger.

### Negative evaluation

- Bowlby's theory has an over-reliance on animal studies. Animals that imprint are precocial, born at an advanced stage, while humans are altricial, born at an immature state of development, making generalization difficult.

### Practical application

- Research shows that maternal deprivation effects are avoidable if opportunities for alternative attachments to form are given, leading to nurses' work practices changing so that children in hospital could form attachments to them.

### Issues and debates

- Bowlby showed how the process of science works, by amending his idea of the critical period to that of a sensitive period, when **Sluckin et al. (1966)** demonstrated that imprinting was possible beyond a set time period.

---

#### Key terms

**Attachments** – enduring two-way emotional ties to specific individuals.

**Bowlby's theory of monotropy** – an evolutionary explanation of attachment that perceives infants as having an innate tendency to form an emotional bond with one primary caregiver who responds appropriately and sensitively to their needs.

**Innate social releasers** – inherited infant behaviours that stimulate adult interaction and caregiving.

**Critical period** – a set amount of time in which an attachment is able to be formed.

**Internal working model** – a cognitive framework used to make sense of others, self and the world around us, formed from attachment experiences, which acts as a template for future relationships.

**Bowlby's maternal deprivation hypothesis** – an explanation of the effects of disruption of the attachment bond leading to permanent, negative outcomes.

## KEY CLASSIC STUDY

### '44 THIEVES STUDY OF MATERNAL DEPRIVATION'

**Bowlby (1944)**

### Aim

- To assess whether juvenile delinquents had experienced maternal deprivation.

### Procedure

- Interviews were carried out with 44 juvenile thieves and 44 juvenile non-thieves (and their mothers) to ascertain their personalities and whether they had experienced maternal separation.

### Results

- Thirty-two per cent of thieves exhibited affectionless psychopathy (lacking a social conscience) compared to 0 per cent of the non-thieves.
- Eighty-six per cent of affectionless psychopaths had experienced maternal separation compared to 17 per cent of thieves not classed as affectionless psychopaths.

### Conclusions

- Maternal deprivation can have serious, negative consequences.

### Evaluation

- The results may have been due to privation, rather than maternal deprivation.

---

### ■ STRENGTHEN YOUR LEARNING

1 Define attachment.
2 Explain the process by which attachments are formed.
3 Outline:
   a Bowlby's theory of monotropy,
   b Bowlby's maternal deprivation hypothesis.
4 For Bowlby's (1944) study into maternal deprivation, in your own words, state the aims, procedure, results, conclusions and evaluative points.
5 Summarize what research evidence has suggested about attachments.
6 What other evaluative points, including practical applications and relevant issues and debates, can be made about attachments?

### Expert tip

Bowlby's two theories are very different in origin and should be written about as such. His maternal deprivation hypothesis is a psychodynamic theory, based on Freudian ideas, while his later theory of monotropy is more of an evolutionary theory based on the survival value that forming an attachment brings.

## Types of attachment

Revised ☐

From interviews and observations of mother–child relationships in Uganda and the USA, Ainsworth identified three **types of attachments**. Ainsworth then designed **the 'Strange Situation'**, a naturalistic observation technique to assess her findings, which confirmed them to be valid.

### Key terms

**Types of attachment** – the various forms of attachment that develop with different patterns of mother–infant interactions.

**The Strange Situation** – an observational testing method for the measurement of types of attachment.

| Type of attachment | Description |
| --- | --- |
| Type A: Insecure–avoidant | Infants are willing to explore, have low stranger anxiety, are unconcerned by separation and avoid contact at the return of their caregiver. Caregivers are indifferent to infants' needs. |
| Type B: Securely attached | Infants are keen to explore, have high stranger anxiety, are easy to calm and are enthusiastic at the return of their carer. Caregivers are sensitive to infants' needs. |
| Type C: Insecure–resistant | Infants are unwilling to explore, have high stranger anxiety, are upset by separation and seek and reject contact at the return of their caregiver. Caregivers are ambivalent to infants' needs, demonstrating simultaneous opposite feelings and behaviours. |

## KEY CLASSIC STUDY

## 'THE STRANGE SITUATION'

### Ainsworth *et al.* (1978)

### Aim

- To assess individual differences in the quality of mother–infant pairs' attachments.

### Procedure

- Eight episodes of interactions in an unfamiliar environment, between 106 mothers, strangers and infants, were observed through a one-way window.

- Stranger anxiety, separation anxiety, reunion behaviours and exploration behaviour (as a measurement of attachment security) were recorded.

### Results

- Type A = 15 per cent, Type B = 70 per cent, Type C = 15 per cent.

### Conclusions

- Sensitive responsiveness is the major factor determining the quality of attachments, with sensitive mothers correctly interpreting infants' needs and responding appropriately. Sensitive mothers have securely attached babies.

- Individual differences in attachment underpin identity formation.

### Evaluation

- Ainsworth's findings are reliable, as they were confirmed by other studies, but are invalid as attachment type changes with different caregivers and contexts.

- The Strange Situation focuses too much on children's behaviour and not enough on mothers' behaviour.

- The method is ethical; it produces harmful stress, but no greater than everyday life, like being left with an unfamiliar babysitter.

## Research

- **McMahon (2001)** found no existence of Type A in the Dogon people of Mali due to their natural childrearing practices, which were not studied by Ainsworth, which suggests the Strange Situation is not suitable for all cultures.

- **Main & Solomon (1986)** found a fourth attachment type, insecure–disorganized (Type D), a rare, confusing mix of approach and avoidance behaviours.

## Positive evaluation

- The Strange Situation became a paradigm study, the accepted method of assessing attachment behaviours that underpin the development of identity.

## Negative evaluation

- The Strange Situation methodology, being laboratory-based and unfamiliar, lacks ecological validity. **Brofenbrenner (1979)** found attachment behaviour is stronger in the laboratory than at home.

## Practical application

- The Strange Situation is used to assess whether children are being inappropriately parented and should be placed in care. This can be controversial when done in cultural groupings with different childrearing practices, like the Aborigines of Australia.

## Issues and debates

- Attachment types appear generally to be cross-cultural. **Van IJzendoorn & Kroonenberg (1988)** found similar results across cultures, with some variations due to childrearing practices and within cultures due to socio-economic differences.

■ **STRENGTHEN YOUR LEARNING**

1   What was Ainsworth's 'Strange Situation'?

2   Outline Ainsworth's types of attachment.

3   For Ainsworth *et al.*'s (1978) 'Strange Situation' study, in your own words, state the aims, procedure, results, conclusions and evaluative points.

4   Summarize what research evidence has suggested about types of attachment.

5   What other evaluative points, including practical applications and relevant issues and debates, can be made about types of attachment?

**Expert tip**

Types of attachment should not be described just in terms of infant characteristics, but also in terms of the caregiver's characteristics. For example, children with the secure–avoidant attachment type have caregivers who are indifferent to infants' needs.

# Gender identity and social roles

Revised ☐

## Biological explanation of the development of gender identity

Revised ☐

Biological sex is determined by **sex chromosomes**, XX for females and XY for males. The XY chromosome triggers gonads in males to become testes, which produce high levels of testosterone to develop a foetus as male. A surge in male hormones in male babies occurs again after birth and in puberty. The biological explanation sees physical differences between the sexes as underpinning gender behavioural differences. Girls with **congenital adrenal hyperplasia** (CAH) have an enlarged adrenal gland, which triggers high levels of testosterone that cause male physical features and male-type behaviours, including choosing males as playmates. These differences persist despite CAH individuals being raised as girls, suggesting **gender identity** is biologically determined. Additionally, a girl's testosterone levels in adolescence dictate how stereotypically feminine behaviour is, again indicating a biological basis to gender identity.

### ■ Research

- **Hines et al. (2002)** found that women with higher testosterone levels during pregnancy had daughters who displayed male-typical preferences in play choice and toy preference, supporting the idea of a biological basis to gender identity.

- **Hines & Kaufmann (1994)** found that girls with CAH chose more male playmates than non-CAH girls, suggesting a biological reason for such gender preferences.

### ■ Positive evaluation

- There is a degree of evidence to support biological factors, like sex hormones, exerting an influence on the development of gender identity.

- Research into atypical sex conditions has led to effective hormonal treatments to alleviate behavioural and physical problems encountered.

### ■ Negative evaluation

- Teasing apart the influences of biology from the cognitive and sociocultural influences is difficult. It seems likely that a combination of factors explain development of gender identity.

- Evidence indicating a relationship between male hormonal levels and gender identity is often correlational, presenting problems in establishing causality.

### ■ Practical application

- Research into Turner's syndrome, a biologically determined typical female sex condition, where sufferers are normally infertile, has led to a treatment involving pre-pubescent egg extraction, so that they can later achieve pregnancy.

**Key terms**

**Sex chromosomes** – structures of nucleic acids containing genetic material that determines an individual's sex.

**Congenital adrenal hyperplasia** – an inherited condition caused by genetic mutations, which leads to excess amounts of male sex hormones being produced by the adrenal glands.

**Gender identity** – an understanding and recognition of an individual's gender that is formed from experience.

**Bem Sex Role Inventory** – a self-report measure of masculinity–femininity and gender role.

## KEY CONTEMPORARY STUDY

### 'SEX ROLE IDENTITY RELATED TO THE RATIO OF SECOND TO FOURTH DIGIT LENGTH IN WOMEN'

Csathó *et al.* (2003)

#### Aim

- To assess the extent to which male hormones influence sex role identity in women.

#### Procedure

- The ratio between the second and fourth fingers was examined in female adults to assess degree of exposure to testosterone in the womb. A low ratio (ring finger longer than the index finger) indicates high prenatal testosterone levels.
- Participants completed the **Bem Sex Role Inventory** to assess masculinity/femininity.

#### Results

- The researchers found that both men and women with low ratios on the right hand were more likely to be masculine on the Sex Role Inventory. The effect was not significant on the left hand.

#### Conclusions

- Gender identity appears to have a biological origin.

#### Evaluation

- The Bem Sex Role Inventory is criticized for being a measure of personality more than one of sex role identity.
- It is not explained why the effects should be more predominate on the right than left hand.

## ■ Issues and debates

- Much research into the biological explanation is conducted on individuals with atypical sex conditions, which raises generalization issues to individuals without such conditions, upon whom biological differences may exert different influences.

---

### ■ STRENGTHEN YOUR LEARNING

1 Outline the biological explanation for the development of gender identity; include reference in your answer to chromosomes and congenital adrenal hyperplasia.

2 For Csathó *et al.*'s (2003) sex role identity study, in your own words, state the aims, procedure, results, conclusions and evaluative points.

3 Summarize what research evidence has suggested about the biological explanation for the development of gender identity.

4 What other evaluative points, including practical applications and relevant issues and debates, can be made about the biological explanation for the development of gender identity?

---

### Expert tip

A common mistake when dealing with the biological explanation of gender identity is to include explanations based on other explanations. This would not be creditworthy, unless used as a comparison to highlight relative strengths and weaknesses of the biological explanation.

## Kohlberg's (1966) cognitive explanation of the development of gender identity

Revised ▢

**Kohlberg's cognitive theory of gender development** focuses on how children's thinking about gender changes and sees children developing an understanding of gender in three stages, with gender role behaviour apparent only after an understanding emerges that gender is fixed and constant.

Once gender constancy is reached, children value the behaviours and attitudes associated with their gender and identify with and imitate adult role models possessing these qualities in a process known as self-socialization.

### Key term

**Kohlberg's cognitive theory of gender development** – an explanation of gender development that perceives children as building an understanding of gender in stages, with gender-role behaviour apparent only after a comprehension emerges that gender is fixed and constant.

| Stage of gender development | Description |
| --- | --- |
| *Gender labelling* | 18 months–3 years. Children's understanding of gender is merely labels of 'male' and 'female'. |
| *Gender stability* | 3–5 years. Recognition that gender is for life, but relies on physical signs to determine gender, e.g. a woman with short hair changes to a man. |
| *Gender constancy* | By about 6–7 years, children realize gender is permanent and that individuals retain their gender. |

## Research

- **Slaby & Frey (1975)** found that children with high levels of gender constancy focused more on same-sex models than children with low levels. This supports the idea that children in the gender constancy stage observe people of the same gender to gain a full understanding of their gender.

- **Rabban (1950)** found children at age three could name their gender, but could not say why they were that gender or whether they would retain that gender. Their understanding, however, developed with age, supporting Kohlberg's idea that gender development occurs in stages.

- **Thompson (1975)** found that, at two years of age, children given pictures of boys and girls could successfully select same-sex ones, which showed they could identify genders in themselves and others. Older children illustrated that a greater understanding of gender identity developed over time. This suggests that understanding of gender develops over time, in a set order of stages, as explained by Kohlberg.

## Positive evaluation

- The concepts of gender identity, stability and constancy occur in that order in all cultures at similar ages, regardless of upbringing, giving the theory validity and suggesting a biological mechanism.

- Although not without criticism, Kohlberg's theory is supported by a wealth of evidence that suggests gender understanding does indeed develop in set stages.

- **Gender schema theory** shares a similar cognitive view of gender understanding, though perceives children as having schemas for gender at an earlier stage than Kohlberg.

## Negative evaluation

- Although cognitive and biological factors are included, the theory neglects important cultural and social factors, like the influence of family and friends.

- Kohlberg's theory is mainly descriptive, but it does not explain how the developments occur and so lacks depth as an explanation.

- Kohlberg predicts that gender-specific behaviours will only occur once children reach gender constancy, but it occurs earlier than this, calling the ages and stages of his theory into question.

## Practical application

- As gender understanding develops in set stages at set ages, it has allowed educationalists to produce materials relating to gender that match a child's understanding of their age.

> **Key term**
>
> **Gender schema theory** – an explanation of gender development that sees gender identity alone as providing children with motivation to assume sex-typed behaviour patterns.

## ■ Issues and debates

■ Kohlberg's theory is more holistic than reductionist, as it combines social learning and biological developmental factors.

> **Expert tip**
>
> A sophisticated point to make about Kohlberg's theory, which shows high-level comprehension, is to comment on its similarity to gender schema theory in having a cognitive basis to gender understanding, but also that the two theories differ in that gender schema theory perceives children as developing schemas for gender at an earlier stage than Kohlberg's theory.

> **■ STRENGTHEN YOUR LEARNING**
>
> 1 Outline Kohlberg's theory of cognitive development; include reference in your answer to his stages of development.
> 2 Summarize what research evidence has suggested about Kohlberg's theory.
> 3 What other evaluative points, including practical applications and relevant issues and debates, can be made about Kohlberg's theory?

# The sociocultural explanation of the development of gender identity

Revised ☐

Social learning theory (SLT) sees gender development occurring through the observation of influential models, like parents and peers. Behaviour reinforced for being gender appropriate is copied and thus gender roles are acquired. SLT explains boys and girls learning different gender roles as parents only reinforce gender-appropriate behaviour and children select same-sex models to observe and imitate. Children then show preference for same-sex groups and police each other's gender behaviour, with gender-inappropriate behaviour being ridiculed.

The media acts as a powerful socializing agent, with TV, magazines, etc. portraying both sexes in **gender stereotypical** ways to be observed and imitated.

## ■ Research

■ **Block (1983)** found that boys are reinforced more for imitating behaviours reflecting masculinity, while girls are reinforced for those reflecting femininity. This illustrates how SLT can explain why males and females acquire different gender roles, as the reinforced roles fit the gender roles prevalent in society.

■ **Renold (2001)** found that schoolgirls who sought academic success were bullied and ostracized by both boys and girls and had problems establishing feminine roles that did not revolve around boys and presenting their body in certain ways. This illustrates how peers play a strong role in policing stereotypical gender roles, supporting SLT.

> **Key terms**
>
> **The sociocultural explanation of the development of gender identity** – an explanation that sees gender development as explicable by reference to social learning theory, where a child observes and imitates role models of the same gender.
>
> **Gender identity** – a person's perception of having a particular gender, which may or may not correspond with their birth sex.
>
> **Gender stereotypes** – pre-set expectations of what behaviours, values, beliefs, etc. are appropriate for males and females.

## ■ Positive evaluation

■ As gender stereotypes and roles are fairly consistent across cultures, it suggests that gender is more biological in origin, although, as there is some cross-cultural variation, environment plays a role too.

■ Research shows that, although parents exert the stronger social learning influence for young children, peers become increasingly influential, illustrating the changing nature of social learning influences.

## ■ Negative evaluation

■ SLT cannot explain gender changes with age; indeed SLT assumes no developmental stages, while evidence suggests there are.

■ It is simplistic to see children as passive recipients of media. Children select characters to watch, suggesting more of a cognitive input than a purely social learning effect.

## ■ Practical application

■ SLT allows for the creation of positive gender stereotyping through observation and imitation of media role models, such as by portraying female sports stars in TV programmes.

## 'GENDER STEREOTYPES OF SCIENTIST CHARACTERS IN TV PROGRAMMES'

**Steinke (2008)**

### Aim

- To examine gender stereotyping in TV portrayals of scientist characters.

### Procedure

- One hundred and twelve episodes of 14 TV programmes popular with children aged 12–17 were analysed for details of scientist characters.

### Results

- Of 196 scientist characters, 113 were male and 83 female.
- Male scientists were portrayed of higher status than female ones and with qualities of independence and dominance.

### Conclusions

- Male scientist characters are more common than female ones on TV and are more likely to be portrayed with masculine qualities.

### Evaluation

- Female scientific status has improved; an earlier study found females more likely to be portrayed as assistants.
- Most programmes with female scientist characters were funded by educational groups, implying mainstream media is more culpable for gender stereotyping.

## ■ Issues and debates

- Studies of SLT tend not to be gender-biased, as they consider the different aspects of peers, parents and the media upon gender development in both boys and girls.

### ■ STRENGTHEN YOUR LEARNING

1 Outline the sociocultural explanation for the development of gender identity.
2 For Steinke's (2008) study of gender stereotypes, in your own words, state the aims, procedure, results, conclusions and evaluative points.
3 Summarize what research evidence has suggested about the development of gender identity.
4 What other evaluative points, including practical applications and relevant issues and debates, can be made about the development of gender identity?

**Expert tip**

SLT forms the basis of the sociocultural explanation of the development of gender identity, but care should be taken not to outline and evaluate SLT in general terms, as this would not accumulate much credit. Instead, the SLT should be presented and evaluated in a way that is specifically focused as an explanation of the development of gender identity.

# Social roles

Revised ☐

**Social roles** are behaviours expected of someone in a particular context, which therefore vary across situations, cultures, ages and genders. At a cognitive level, social roles are a type of internal script, which allows individuals to understand how people should behave in a certain context. Gender behaviour involves social roles where there is an expectation of how males and females are expected to act in different contexts. Such gender social roles are socialized on to males and females from an early age and are reinforced when utilized in expected ways.

The Bem Sex Role Inventory (BSRI) measures whether an individual's personality fits gender roles, by measuring levels of masculinity (e.g. independent, competitive, ambitious), femininity (e.g. yielding, sensitive, nurturing) and androgyny (elements of both masculinity and femininity). Anyone displaying elements of low masculinity and femininity is classed as differentiated. Androgyny is perceived to be a desirable, healthy state of gender personality.

**Key term**

**Social roles** – patterns of behaviour, beliefs and norms that an individual adopts when given a role in society.

---

KEY CLASSIC STUDY

## 'PSYCHOLOGICAL ANDROGYNY AND PERSONALITY ADJUSTMENT IN NORMAL AND CLINICAL POPULATIONS'

Burchardt & Serbin (1982)

### Aim

- To assess whether androgyny is associated with positive mental health.

### Procedure

- Male and female undergraduates and psychiatric patients completed personality tests, including the BSRI.

### Results

- Androgynous females scored lower for depression and social introversion than feminine females; undergraduate females also scored lower on schizophrenia and mania scales.
- In male psychiatric patients androgynous and masculine males scored lower for deviance than feminine males and lower on depression, while undergraduate males scored lower on social introversion than feminine males.

### Conclusions

- Androgyny and masculinity are associated with positive mental health, especially with respect to depression.

### Evaluation

- Sex-role conformity may relate differently to personality development and psychological functioning for males and females.

## Research

- **Haney et al. (1973)** found that participants quickly conformed to playing assigned roles of prisoners and guards in a simulated prison environment, even though behavioural consequences were generally negative, illustrating the power that social roles play upon determining behaviour.
- **Urberg (1982)** read children aged 3–7 years stories stressing sex-role stereotypical characteristics, but without stating the gender of characters, to find bravery was attributed to male characters and caring to female ones. This suggests that sex-role stereotypes are learned from an early age.

## Positive evaluation

- The socialization of gender roles for different contexts allows individuals to know what behaviour is expected of them and others in specific situations, which allows interactions to occur in more effective and predictable ways.

## Negative evaluation

- Research into gender identity and social roles tends to use imagined scenarios and thus may lack ecological validity by not reflecting real-life occurrences.

## Practical application

- Getting children to role play social roles reflecting gender identities is an effective manner of teaching children which roles are desirable and positive and which are undesirable and negative.

## Issues and debates

- Globalization, which has led to the breaking down of cultural beliefs and practices, may be prompting a movement towards more uniform gender identities and social roles across cultures.

■ **STRENGTHEN YOUR LEARNING**

1 Explain what is meant by gender identity and social roles.

2 Outline the Bem Sex Role Inventory.

3 For Burchardt & Serbin's (1982) study of psychological androgyny, in your own words, state the aims, procedure, results, conclusions and evaluative points.

4 Summarize what research evidence has suggested about gender identity and social roles.

5 What other evaluative points, including practical applications and relevant issues and debates, can be made about gender identity and social roles?

**Expert tip**

Description of the rationale (how it works) behind Bem's Sex Role Inventory, such as a score of high femininity and high masculinity indicating androgyny, will gain marks for description in questions about gender identity and social roles. Do take care though to 'shape' your answer to fit the needs of the question.

# Development of empathy and theory of mind

Revised ☐

## Development of empathy

Revised ☐

**Empathy** is the ability to understand and share others' feelings. The biological underpinning of empathy is believed to be mirror neurons, specific nerve cells activated in the brain when observing others that mimic those of the people being observed. Understanding thinking and emotion in others may occur by observing someone's **non-verbal communication** (NVC), which activates mirror neurons so that the observer empathizes with their thoughts and feelings. As emotion is expressed in NVC, regardless of language, empathy can occur cross-culturally.

**Key terms**

**Empathy** – the ability to understand and experience or share the feelings of others.

**Non-verbal communication** – the process of conveying meaning without the use of words, by the use of such things as pitch, speed, tone and volume of voice, gestures and facial expressions, body posture, stance and proximity to the listener, eye movements and contact, as well as dress and appearance.

## Development of theory of mind

Revised ☐

**Theory of mind** (ToM) involves understanding that others have different feelings and experiences from oneself, with ToM a key aspect in the development of empathy. From birth, children exhibit egocentric thinking, that their experience is the world and their experience is the same as everyone else's. From four years old, ToM is apparent, with children realizing that others have a mind that is different to theirs. With the development of ToM comes the ability to manipulate and deceive others by hiding one's true emotions and intentions. An earlier version of ToM, shared attention mechanism (SAM), develops from 9–18 months of age, allowing two people to realize that they are witnessing the same thing.

**Key term**

**Theory of mind** – an ability to attribute mental states to oneself and others.

ToM is investigated by presenting children with false belief tasks involving witnessing a scenario and interpreting it from the viewpoint of a character in the scenario. If they can interpret the situation from another's viewpoint, they have a ToM, but if they interpret the scene from their own egocentric viewpoint, they do not.

### ■ Research

■ **Schulte-Rüther et al. (2007)** found using fMRI scans that mirror neurons were implicated in both motor and interpersonal cognition when observing others' NVC, which supports the idea that face-to-face interpersonal interactions are mimicked by the mirror neuron system and so are important for experiencing empathy.

■ **Wicker (2003)** found smelling a horrible aroma activated the same brain areas as observing someone else's expression of disgust, indicating mirror neuron activity in the experience of empathy.

■ **Wimmer & Perner (1983)** found that most 6–8-year-olds could give an answer in a false belief task that reflected someone else's belief, about where chocolate was hidden, rather than their own, suggesting they had ToM. As most four-year-olds could not, it suggests they had not developed ToM.

## ■ Positive evaluation

■ A lack of ToM gives a plausible explanation for **autism**. For example, not understanding others' thoughts may explain the difficulties autistic people have in empathizing.

## ■ Negative evaluation

■ There may be more to ToM than passing false belief tasks. Children below the age of two years, who fail false belief tasks, can initiate pretend play and understand the pretending of others, suggesting an ability to empathize with others.

## ■ Practical application

■ As research indicates autistic people have poor empathy skills due to a lack of ToM, therapies have centred on developing strategies to develop empathy in sufferers by encouraging them to experience the feelings and intentions of others.

## ■ Issues and debates

■ There are parallels in the movement from egocentric thinking to development of ToM and Piaget's cognitive development theory, which sees similar movement from egocentrism to decentring by experiencing others' thoughts and feelings.

> **Key term**
>
> **Autism** – a developmental disability characterized by problems in communicating and building relationships with others and in using language and abstract concepts.

---

**■ STRENGTHEN YOUR LEARNING**

1 Explain what is meant by empathy.
2 Outline the development of empathy.
3 Explain what is meant by ToM.
4 Outline the development of ToM.
5 How is ToM investigated?
6 Summarize what research evidence has suggested about the development of empathy and ToM.
7 What other evaluative points, including practical applications and relevant issues and debates, can be made about the development of empathy and ToM?

---

> **Expert tip**
>
> The theory of mind can generally be used in two ways: first, as an explanation for the development of empathy (from about four years) and second, as an explanation for autism. Although there are overlaps, these should be treated as two separate explanations.

# Developing as a learner

Revised ☐

## Piaget's theory of cognitive development

Revised ☐

Piaget saw knowledge as discovered using:

1 **Functional invariants** – structures remaining the same throughout development. There are two of these:
   a the process of *adaption* – involving **assimilation** (fitting new environmental experiences into existing schemas) and **accommodation** (altering existing schemas to fit in new experiences)
   b the process of **equilibration** – involving swinging between **equilibrium**, a pleasant state of balance, and **disequilibrium**, an unpleasant state of imbalance motivating a return to equilibrium.

> **Key terms**
>
> **Piaget's theory of cognitive development** – an explanation that sees thought processes undergoing qualitative changes as children age, with biological processes directing these changes.
>
> **Functional invariants** – structures that remain the same during development.
>
> **Assimilation** – fitting new environmental experiences into existing schemas.
>
> **Accommodation** – altering existing schemas to fit in new experiences.

2  **Variant structures** – structures that develop as knowledge is discovered. There are two of these:
   a  **schemas** – ways of understanding the world
   b  **operations** – logical strings of schemas.

Thus, cognitive development involves constantly swinging between equilibrium and disequilibrium, through a continuous series of assimilation and accommodation.

There are four stages of cognitive development:

- *sensorimotor stage* (0–2 years), where **object permanence** develops, an understanding that objects that are not being perceived or acted upon still exist

- *pre-operational stage* (2–7 years), where children are **egocentric** (cannot see a situation from another's point of view)

- *concrete operational* (7–11 years), where **conservation** develops, an understanding that changing the appearance of something does not affect its mass, number or volume, as well as **class inclusion**, an understanding that some sets of objects or subsets can be sets of other larger classes of objects

- *formal operational stage* (11+ years), where abstract reasoning develops.

## Research

- **Bower & Wishart (1972)** found that one-month-old babies show surprise when toys disappear, suggesting that Piaget witnessed immature motor skills, not a lack of object permanence.

- **Piaget & Cook (1952)** got seven-year-old children to agree that two identically shaped beakers, A and B, contained equal amounts of liquid. Having witnessed beaker A being poured into beaker C, a taller, thinner beaker that contained the same amount, the children stated that C contained more, which suggests they cannot conserve.

- **Inhelder & Piaget (1958)** got participants to consider which of three factors was the most important in assessing the speed of swing of a pendulum. The solution was to vary one variable at a time and children in the formal operational stage were able to do this, but younger children could not, as they tried several variables at once. This suggests that children in the formal operational stage can think logically in an abstract manner in order to see the relationships between things.

## Positive evaluation

- Piaget's theory became the starting point for many later theories and research. **Schaffer (2004)** argues it is the most comprehensive account of how children come to understand the world.

- Piaget was not rigid in his beliefs. His theory was constantly adapted in response to criticism. In later life, he referred to his stages of development as 'spirals of development' to reflect evidence that there were transitional periods in which children's thinking was a combination of the stage they were leaving and the stage they were progressing on to.

- Piaget's work fundamentally changed the way in which children's thinking and how they learn was understood and led to huge changes in schooling, through the creation of child-centred educational environments centred on children discovering knowledge themselves through interaction with their environment.

---

### Key terms

**Equilibration** – the process of swinging between equilibrium and disequilibrium.

**Equilibrium** – a pleasant state of balance.

**Disequilibrium** – an unpleasant state of imbalance that motivates a return to equilibrium.

**Variant structures** – structures that develop as knowledge is discovered.

**Schemas** – ways of understanding the world that change with experience.

**Operations** – strings of schemas assembled in logical order.

**Object permanence** – an understanding that objects that are not being perceived or acted upon still exist.

**Egocentrism** – an inability to see a situation from another's viewpoint.

**Conservation** – an understanding that changing the appearance of something does not affect its mass, number or volume.

**Class inclusion** – an understanding that some sets of objects or subsets can be sets of other larger classes of objects.

KEY CLASSIC STUDY

## 'THE SWISS MOUNTAIN SCENE STUDY'
**Piaget & Inhelder (1956)**

### Aim
- To assess at what age children are egocentric and cannot see the model of a mountain scene from someone else's viewpoint.

### Procedure
- Children aged 4–8 years were shown a model of three different Swiss mountains, each with something different on the top: a red cross, snow or a chalet.
- Children explored the model, then sat on one side while a doll was placed on the other side.
- Children were shown ten pictures of different views of the model, including the doll's and their own. They were asked to select the picture representing the doll's view.

### Results
- Four-year-olds chose the picture matching their own view.
- Six-year olds sometimes chose the picture representing the doll's view.
- Seven- and eight-year-olds chose the picture representing the doll's view.

### Conclusions
- Four-year-olds are egotistic, as they are unaware that there are viewpoints other than their own.
- Children of seven or older can decentre and understand others' viewpoints.

### Evaluation
- Swiss mountains are unfamiliar to children; therefore, what Piaget witnessed, due to his poor methodology, was not egocentrism but a lack of understanding. Other studies found that, when a familiar scenario was used, children of three and a half could decentre, so Piaget may have underestimated the age at which children stop being egocentric.
- The study is not an experiment, as it has no independent variable, but is a 'controlled observation'.

## Negative evaluation

- Piaget used his own children as participants in many of his studies, which has led to accusations of researcher bias. Risk of demand characteristics is also increased when people familiar to a researcher are used as participants.

- Piaget neglected the important role of emotional and social factors in intellectual development and in doing so overemphasized cognitive aspects of development.

- Piaget saw language ability as reflecting an individual's level of cognitive development, while theorists like Bruner argued it was the other way round, with language development preceding cognitive development.

- Piaget believed the rate at which a child's cognitive development occurred could not be accelerated, as it was under biological control. However, **Meadows (1995)** found that direct tuition could speed up development, which suggests that environmental influences do exert an influence upon learning.

## Practical application

- Piaget's theory has wide applications in primary education, especially *discovery learning*, where children learn through independent exploration, and the idea of *curriculum*, where certain skills are taught at certain ages to reflect a child's level of cognitive development.

## Issues and debates

- Cross-cultural evidence implies that the stages of development (except formal operations) occur as a universal, invariant sequence, suggesting cognitive development is a biological process and therefore more of a product of nature than nurture.

■ **STRENGTHEN YOUR LEARNING**

1   Outline Piaget's theory of cognitive development in terms of the process of adaption and the process of equilibration.

2   Outline Piaget's stages of cognitive development, including the ages at which the stages occur.

3   For Piaget & Inhelder's (1956) Swiss mountain study, in your own words, state the aims, procedure, results, conclusions and evaluative points.

4   Summarize what research evidence has suggested about Piaget's theory of cognitive development.

5   What other evaluative points, including practical applications and relevant issues and debates, can be made about Piaget's theory of cognitive development?

**Expert tip**

There is a lot of terminology associated with Piaget's theory, such as 'egocentrism', 'assimilation', etc. When using such terms, to show your understanding, ensure that you explain what they mean – you can refer to the key terms included above to achieve this.

# Vygotsky's theory of cognitive development

Revised ☐

Vygotsky saw cognitive development as affected by the learning of norms and attitudes of the culture a child is raised in. At the *cultural level*, children benefit from the knowledge of previous generations, gained through interactions with caregivers, while at the *interpersonal level* cognitive development occurs first on a social level, through interaction between people (*interpsychological*), and second on an individual level within a child (*intrapsychological*).

A key part of Vygotsky's theory is the **zone of proximal development** (ZPD): the distance between current and potential ability. Cultural influences and knowledgeable others acting as mentors push children through the ZPD and on to tasks beyond their current ability. Another key concept is **scaffolding**, where cognitive development is assisted by sensitive guidance, with children given clues as to how to solve a problem, rather than being given the actual solution. Vygotsky saw **semiotics** as assisting cognitive development through the use of language and other cultural symbols, acting as a medium for knowledge to be transmitted, which turn elementary mental functions into higher ones. Such development occurs in several phases:

- *social speech* (birth to 3 years) – involving pre-intellectual language

- *egocentric speech* (3–7 years) – involving self-talk/thinking aloud

- *inner speech* (7+ years) – where self-talk becomes silent and internal and language is used for social communications.

Vygotsky also proposed four stages of concept formation:

**Key terms**

**Vygotsky's theory of cognitive development** – an explanation that sees thought processes as affected by the learning of norms and values of whichever culture a child is raised in.

**Zone of proximal development** – the distance between current and potential intellectual ability.

**Scaffolding** – tuition given by more knowledgeable others.

**Semiotics** – the use of signs and symbols to convey meaning.

| | |
|---|---|
| **Vague syncretic** | ● Trial-and-error formation of concepts without comprehension of them. |
| | ● Similar to Piaget's pre-operational stage. |
| **Complex** | ● Use of some strategies to comprehend concepts, but not very systematic. |
| **Potential concept** | ● More systematic use of strategies, with one attribute being focused on at a time – for example, weight. |
| **Mature concept** | ● Several attributes can be dealt with systematically – for example, weight and colour. |
| | ● Similar to Piaget's formal operations stage. |

## KEY CLASSIC STUDY

# 'A STUDY OF ASSISTED PROBLEM-SOLVING'
## Wood & Middleton (1975)

### Aim
- To assess the role of the ZPD in children's problem-solving abilities.

### Procedure
- Twelve mothers were observed using various strategies to support their four-year-old children in building a model of blocks and pegs that resembled one in a picture and that was too difficult for the children to achieve by themselves.
- Supporting strategies used were: general encouragement, e.g. 'now you have a go', specific instructions, e.g. 'get four big blocks', and direct demonstration, e.g. showing a child how to put blocks together.

### Results
- No single strategy was best for helping children. Most effective assistance came from mothers who varied their strategy according to how their child was doing. When doing well, mothers became less specific with their help. When struggling, mothers gave increasingly specific instructions until their child started to make progress.

### Conclusions
- The study illustrates the use of the ZPD in action, thus verifying its existence.
- Scaffolding is most effective when matched to the needs of a learner, so that they are assisted to achieve success in a task that previously they could not have completed alone.

### Evaluation
- There is a possibility of observational bias where researchers unconsciously interpret behaviour to support the concept of a ZPD.

## Research

- **Wertsch *et al*. (1980)** found that the amount of time children under five years of age spent looking at their mothers when assembling jigsaws decreased with age, illustrating the progression through scaffolding to self-regulation.

- **McNaughton & Leyland (1990)** observed mothers giving increasingly explicit help to children assembling progressively harder jigsaws, which illustrates how scaffolding and sensitivity to a child's ZPD aids learning.

- **Freund (1990)** got three- and five-year-old children to help a puppet decide what furniture should be put in different rooms of a doll's house. Half the children worked alone, while half worked with their mothers providing guidance. The results showed that children given guidance performed best, which suggests that Vygotsky's idea of scaffolding, where children work with guidance, is superior to Piaget's idea of discovery learning, where children learn through independent exploration.

- **Berk (1994)** found that children talked to themselves more when doing difficult tasks, supporting the idea of egocentric speech. This decreased with age, in line with Vygotsky's idea of progression to inner speech.

- **Gredler & Gilbert (1992)** reported that in New Guinea the symbolic use of fingers and arms when counting among natives limited learning, supporting the idea of cultural influence on cognitive development, in line with Vygotsky's theory.

## Positive evaluation

- Different cultures emphasize different skills and learning goals and yet Vygotsky's concepts of sensitive guidance, scaffolding and ZPD are applicable in all cultures, suggesting his concepts to be 'culture-fair'.

- Unlike Piaget's theory, Vygotsky's theory can explain the influence of the social environment, through culture and language, upon cognitive development.

- There are strong central similarities between Piaget's and Vygotsky's theories, and it has been suggested that combining the two may be desirable and feasible to gain a fuller understanding of children's cognitive development.

- Like Piaget's theory, Vygotsky's theory has stimulated research into cognitive development that has greatly increased our knowledge of this area.

## Negative evaluation

- Although there is relatively less research evidence to support Vygotsky's theory, the fact that it focuses more upon the processes involved in, rather than the outcomes of, cognitive development makes it harder to test.

- **Schaffer (2004)** criticizes Vygotsky's theory for failing to recognize the influence of emotional factors, such as the frustrations of failure and the joys of success, as well as failing to identify the motivational factors children use to achieve particular goals.

## Practical application

- Like Piaget's theory, Vygotsky's theory has applications in education, especially his concepts of scaffolding and peer-tutoring, where a child is perceived as an apprentice learner who is assisted in their learning, rather than directly taught.

## Issues and debates

- Vygotsky's theory was developed within a collectivist culture and is more suited to such cultures, with their stronger element of social learning than individualistic western cultures. The theory can also be accused of overemphasizing the role of social factors at the expense of biological and individual ones. Learning would be faster if development depended only on social factors.

---

### ■ STRENGTHEN YOUR LEARNING

1  Outline Vygotsky's theory of cognitive development, including reference in your answer to the cultural level, the interpersonal level, the zone of proximal development, scaffolding and semiotics (including social speech, egocentric speech and inner speech).

2  Outline Vygotsky's four stages of concept formation.

3  For Wood & Middleton's (1975) study of assisted problem-solving, in your own words, state the aims, procedure, results, conclusions and evaluative points.

4  Summarize what research evidence has suggested about Vygotsky's theory of cognitive development.

5  What other evaluative points, including practical applications and relevant issues and debates, can be made about Vygotsky's theory of cognitive development?

---

**Expert tip**

A key difference between Vygotsky and Piaget's theories, which is worth stressing in any evaluative comparison, is that Vygotsky sees cognitive development coming after and being dependent upon language development, while for Piaget language development comes after and is dependent upon cognitive development.

---

# Brain development

Revised ▢

The brain, a bodily organ associated with many mental faculties, develops over the course of an individual's life due to biological and environmental influences.

## ■ The physical developmental trajectory of the brain

Brain growth follows a typical developmental trajectory. Brain size increases as a child grows in size, but halts at around 11 years old for girls and 15 years old for boys. The **grey matter** volume, which is the brain tissue containing synapses, increases and then decreases in size a few years earlier than total

---

**Key terms**

**Brain development** – the physical maturation of the brain, which occurs in a common pathway of growth.

**Grey matter** – the darker tissue of the brain and spinal cord, consisting mainly of nerve cell bodies and branching dendrites.

brain size. The **white matter**, which is brain tissue containing the connections between grey matter, continues to increase in size throughout childhood and adolescence.

**Key term**
**White matter** – the paler tissue of the brain and spinal cord, consisting mainly of nerve fibres and their myelin sheaths.

The grey matter varies in terms of maturation, with different areas of brain function. The motor and sensory areas develop first, with the prefrontal cortex, which enables higher order thinking, such as judgement, decision-making and impulse control, being the last area to develop. This helps to moderate emotional decision-making and occurs during adolescence.

The increase in white matter throughout childhood and adolescence increases connectivity to accommodate increased learning. The more a connection is used, the thicker the size of that connection. In adolescence, pruning occurs, where some connections are discarded and important connections made stronger, as the brain refines its activity in response to learning.

# Influences on the developmental trajectory of the brain

## Genes and environment

Genes determine the changes in grey and white matter, but are influenced by age, with genetic influence increasing with age for white matter development, but lessening for grey matter.

## Gender differences

There are gender differences in the vulnerability to developing neuropsychiatric disorders and the development of such disorders. Also, the average male brain has greater size in terms of grey and white matter and the cortical structure of the brain is different between genders. This impacts on the capacity for learning different skills – for example, males have a greater ability for some spatial skills and females for verbal skills.

## Toxins

Pollutants in the environment can affect brain development – for example, heavy metals like lead, and organophosphates found in insecticides, as well as alcohol and some drugs. Such pollutants can permeate the womb and affect the brain development of unborn children, affecting learning potential – for example, foetal alcohol syndrome.

# Research

- **Esquivel-Alvarez & Shahdiani (2015)** found that brain development of participants with Autistic Spectrum Disorder (ASD) differed in terms of grey and white matter growth, cortical thickness and myelination (the production of myelin sheaths, which helps in conducting messages along the axon of the neuron). This suggests that ASD could be a manifestation of abnormal brain development.

- **Albert *et al.* (2013)** reviewed studies to find that brain development in adolescence affects decision-making and risk-taking behaviour through maturation of the frontal lobe and that, as other areas of the brain mature that facilitate self-regulation, it permits individuals to increasingly be able to resist peer influence in motivating risk-taking behaviour. This suggests that brain development has a social as well as biological influence.

- **Lopez-Larson *et al.* (2011)** found significant gender differences in male and female brain development from the age of 11 to 35 years. The key difference was a greater amount of neuronal connections in the amygdala, associated with emotion, and the hippocampus, associated with memory. This suggests that gender differences have a biological basis.

## KEY CONTEMPORARY STUDY

### 'A WINDOW OF OPPORTUNITY FOR COGNITIVE TRAINING IN ADOLESCENCE'
Knoll *et al.* (2016)

#### Aim
- To assess the extent to which brain development facilitates learning beyond childhood.

#### Procedure
- There were 633 11- to 33-year-olds, divided into four age groups, and assigned to one of three training groups focused on different cognitive skills.
- All groups completed 20 days of training on either perception of quantity, reasoning or facial recognition.

#### Results
- Training worked in different ways for each cognitive skill: for perception of quantity, training improved only the abilities of late adolescents and adults; training for reasoning was successful across all ages; while training did not improve for facial recognition abilities at any age.

#### Conclusions
- For some cognitive skills, learning is superior in late adolescence and adulthood.
- The early adolescent brain is not as receptive to development.

#### Evaluation
- Educationalists should take into account when designing school courses that learning will occur at different speeds at different ages for different cognitive abilities.
- The research has not taken into account possible gender differences in how brain development affects age-related changes in learning.

## Positive evaluation

- Research has tended to find general developmental trends in human brains of all cultures. This has allowed the establishment of age 'norms' for brain development that individuals can be compared with to ascertain progress and to identify those with possible developmental problems.

- A range of effective practical applications have emerged from research into brain development. For example, production of water pipes made from lead ceased after research into the effects of toxins showed the metal to have a negative effect on brain development.

## Negative evaluation

- The influence of the environment on the developing brain is widely acknowledged. However, the degree to which innate biological factors and environmental factors affect brain development is difficult to ascertain. Indeed, developmental influence may result from an interaction of biological and environmental factors rather than as separate influences.

- Brain imaging research traditionally uses small samples, owing to participant availability, cost and equipment availability. This means that generalizing findings to the whole population is difficult.

- The study of brain development has focused mainly on childhood. However, the idea that this should be the main focus is questionable following findings that the brain learns effectively and develops further across the whole lifespan.

## Practical application

- Research into how toxins can affect brain development in the womb has led to advice for pregnant woman, such as not drinking alcohol in pregnancy, which has positively affected brain development in children.

## ■ Issues and debates

■ The understanding of brain development is not gender-biased, as differences in brain structure development and their effects on learning have generally been taken into account and documented.

### ■ STRENGTHEN YOUR LEARNING

1 Outline the physical developmental trajectory of the brain.

2 Outline the following influences upon the physical developmental trajectory of the brain:

  a genes and environment,

  b gender differences,

  c toxins.

3 For Knoll *et al.*'s (2016) study of cognitive training, in your own words, state the aims, procedure, results, conclusions and evaluative points.

4 Summarize what research evidence has suggested about the physical developmental trajectory of the brain.

5 What other evaluative points, including practical applications and relevant issues and debates, can be made about the physical developmental trajectory of the brain?

### Expert tip

When outlining the developmental trajectory of the brain, organize your answer by reference to the various different influences upon this process, such as genes and environment, gender differences and toxins. Each of these can then be evaluated by reference to specific research studies, as well as more general evaluative comments.

## EXAM-TYPE QUESTIONS

1 Discuss the role of peers or play as influences on cognitive and social development. (22 marks)

2 Evaluate the role of play on social development. (22 marks)

3 Evaluate childhood trauma and resilience as influences on social development. (22 marks)

4 Discuss the influence of poverty/socio-economic status on social development. (22 marks)

5 Discuss how children develop an identity. (22 marks)

6 Evaluate one or more explanations of gender identity. (22 marks)

7 Discuss research studies of attachment. (22 marks)

8 Discuss the development of empathy and theory of mind. (22 marks)

9 Contrast theories of cognitive development. (22 marks)

10 Discuss brain development. (22 marks)

# Determinants of health

Revised ☐

## Biopsychosocial model of health and well-being – Engel (1978)

Revised ☐

The model acknowledges the influence of biology, psychology and environmental factors in health and illness. Three key elements are stressed:

1 *The biological element* – focuses on physiological influences upon health, including viruses, bacteria and physiological damage, like brain lesions caused by a stroke.

2 *The psychological element* – focuses on behavioural lifestyle, like level of alcohol consumption, and thought processes in terms of beliefs, as well as resilience in terms of coping strategies and perceived levels of stress and pain.

3 *The social element* – focuses on social influences, like class and ethnicity. Social influences can create differences in how different individuals experience vulnerability to the same illness.

The model also acknowledges the influence of **behavioural norms**, such as what are considered healthy levels of alcohol consumption, as well as **cultural norms**, as different cultures view health practices and the treatment of illnesses differently.

> **Key terms**
>
> **Biopsychosocial model of health and well-being** – an explanation of health that stresses biomedical elements, based on biology and medicine, as well as psychosomatic elements, based on mental factors.
>
> **Behavioural norms** – expected modes of conduct.
>
> **Cultural norms** – the shared and accepted beliefs, values and behaviours found within a cultural group.

### ■ Research

- **Miró et al. (2009)** asked 182 participants with muscular dystrophy to complete questionnaires, finding that biological, psychological and social elements all played roles in determining individual pain experience, which supports the biopsychosocial model and allowed identification of key factors in pain management for sufferers of the condition.

- **Habtewold et al. (2016)** applied the biopsychosocial model to patients affected physically by diabetes and psychologically with depression and found that social factors of marital status, negative life events and poor social support played key roles in the level of depression experienced. This illustrates the importance of social factors and that all three elements of the model need to be considered when determining treatment for patients.

- **McNamara & McCabe (2012)** found that Australian athletes diagnosed as 'exercise dependent' had differences at the biological level, in terms of higher body mass, at the psychological level, in terms of cognitive beliefs relating to exercise, and at the social level, in terms of lower amounts of social support and higher levels of pressure from coaches, giving support to the idea of understanding illness by reference to the three elements of the biopsychosocial model.

### ■ Positive evaluation

- The model is widely accepted by clinicians, who perceive it is a valid explanation from their everyday experiences with patients.

- The model focuses on a wide range of health influences, not just biological ones, giving greater insight into individual experiences of illness.

### ■ Negative evaluation

- Due to limited time and resources, clinicians often cannot find out about all elements of patients and their illnesses and focus on biological elements as they are easier and cheaper to treat.

■ The emphasis on non-biological elements is perceived by some as shifting the blame for illness on to patients through focusing on elements within their control.

## ■ Practical application

■ The biopsychosocial model led to greater use of eclectic methods of treatment, rather than single treatments. For example, with schizophrenia, antipsychotic drugs are often applied first to reduce physiological symptoms, with psychological therapies then given, like cognitive behavioural therapy, to modify maladaptive thought processes.

## ■ Issues and debates

■ The biopsychosocial model takes a holistic viewpoint of health and well-being, as it sees the health of individuals as being due to a complex system of interacting influences.

---

### ■ STRENGTHEN YOUR LEARNING

1  Outline the biopsychosocial model of health and well-being; make reference in your answer to the biological element, the psychological element, the social element, behavioural norms and cultural norms.

2  Summarize what research evidence has suggested about the biopsychosocial model of health and well-being.

3  What other evaluative points, including practical applications and relevant issues and debates, can be made about the biopsychosocial model of health and well-being?

---

**Expert tip**

It is quite important, in order to show your understanding, when explaining the biopsychosocial model of health and well-being, to outline the model in terms of its key elements: the biological, psychological and social elements, as well as behavioural norms. Doing this will give you access to a higher level of marks.

---

# Genetic vulnerability

Revised ☐

Genetics are an internal health factor and thus outside of an individual's control. Addiction is an area of health where individuals have different levels of genetic vulnerability. There is no single 'addiction' gene that determines whether or not individuals will be addicts; instead, there are a number of genes that each exert small influences on addictive tendencies. The more of these genes an individual has, the more vulnerable they will be to becoming an addict. However, the presence of such genes by themselves will not cause addiction, as environmental triggers – for example, peer pressure – will additionally be needed to activate addictive behaviour. Genetic vulnerability is therefore determined by an interaction of biology and environment.

Genes can affect whether addictive substances are positively or negatively experienced, thus affecting the chances of becoming addicted. For instance, in many Asian people, genes exert an influence over the way alcohol is metabolized in the body so that they feel nauseous when drinking it, decreasing vulnerability to alcohol addiction.

Genetic vulnerability is measured through **twin** and **adoption studies** that examine concordance rates between individuals of varying levels of genetic relatedness, and **gene-profiling studies** that identify common genes in sufferers of different conditions

## ■ Research

■ **Tsuang *et al.* (1996)** found a much higher concordance rate for drug usage between Vietnamese MZ twins (who are 100 per cent genetically similar) and DZ twins (50 per cent genetically similar), suggesting a genetic component to addiction.

■ **Greengard (2004)** found that addiction to cocaine, opiates and amphetamines was associated with abnormal functioning of the genetically controlled brain protein DARPP-32, which supports the idea of a genetic component to addiction.

---

**Key terms**

**Twin studies** – the examination of concordance rates between identical MZ twins (who have 100 per cent genetic similarity) and non-identical DZ twins (who have 50 per cent genetic similarity), upon a particular quality, to assess whether such a quality is more genetic or environmental in nature.

**Adoption studies** – the examination of concordance rates between adopted children and their biological and adoptive parents, upon a particular quality, to assess whether such a quality is more genetic or environmental in nature.

**Gene-profiling studies** – the examination of DNA samples to identify common genes in particular groups of people.

- **Nielsen *et al*. (2009)** found similarities in DNA between former heroin addicts that were not present in non-addicts, again suggesting genes are involved in addiction.
- **Kendler & Prescott (1998)** found a concordance rate for cannabis dependence of 35 per cent for MZ twins compared to 0 per cent for DZ twins, indicating a genetic basis to cannabis addiction.

## Positive evaluation

- Research into genetic vulnerability has highlighted the importance of environmental triggers in initiating addictive behaviour, rather than just seeing such behaviour as genetically determined.
- There is a wealth of research evidence indicating that addictive behaviours have a strong genetic component.

## Negative evaluation

- MZ twins tend to get treated more similarly than DZ twins, so it could be their shared environmental influences rather than their biological ones that create higher concordance rates for addiction than for DZ twins.
- The genetic link to addiction varies with different forms of addiction, which means that genetic vulnerability is not general, as often believed, but varies with different behaviours, substances, etc.

## Practical application

- DNA profiling can be used to indicate individuals with high genetic vulnerability to addiction so that interventions can be more specifically targeted at them.

## Issues and debates

- Genetic influences on health suggest a biological origin, but as genetic vulnerability requires environmental triggers to produce addictive behaviour, such behaviour results from an interaction of nature and nurture and not just nature alone.

> **Expert tip**
>
> When explaining genetic vulnerability, in terms of the number of genes associated with a behaviour (such as addiction) that an individual possesses, it would be creditworthy to describe the rationale (how they work) behind related research methods, such as twin, adoption and gene-profiling studies. The conclusions drawn from such studies could then help form an evaluative appraisal of genetic vulnerability.

> ■ **STRENGTHEN YOUR LEARNING**
>
> 1  Explain genetic vulnerability to addiction.
> 2  Explain how genetic vulnerability is studied.
> 3  Summarize what research evidence has suggested about genetic vulnerability to addiction.
> 4  What other evaluative points, including practical applications and relevant issues and debates, can be made about genetic vulnerability to addiction?

# Personality factors

Revised ☐

Individuals with pathological personalities are easily stressed and have a negative outlook on life and so are more likely to develop dependencies.

## Addictive personality

**Eysenck (1997)** argued that individuals displaying **neuroticism** (high levels of anxiety and irritability) and those displaying **psychoticism** (high levels of aggression and emotional detachment) are more vulnerable to dependencies, as addictive substances and behaviours bring temporary relief. As Eysenck saw personality as innate, dependency behaviours were therefore an inherited tendency.

**Cloninger's (1987) tri-dimensional theory** of addictive behaviour states that there are three key traits to vulnerability to dependency:

■ *novelty seeking* – individuals with a low boredom threshold and a need for excitement

■ *harm avoidance* – individuals who do not perceive the negative elements of a situation

■ *reward dependence* – individuals who experience rewarding effects more easily.

## ■ Research

■ **Howard *et al.* (1997)** reviewed studies to find that novelty seeking does predict alcohol abuse in teenagers and young adults and anti-social behaviour in such alcoholics, but harm avoidance and reward dependence were not clearly linked to addictive behaviours. This suggests that the three dimensions of Cloninger's theory do not contribute equally to addictive behaviour.

■ **Zuckerman (1983)** studied addictive behaviour and reported a link between the need for novelty and dependencies. As sensation seeking is closely related to novelty seeking, the findings give support to that element of Cloninger's theory.

## ■ Positive evaluation

■ Research evidence indicates high levels of neuroticism and psychoticism, as well as novelty seeking, are involved in dependency behaviours, as predicted.

## ■ Negative evaluation

■ The possession of certain traits does not automatically mean that addiction will occur; it is merely a predisposition, other factors play a part too.

### Key terms

**Personality factors** – internal elements that affect health and are characteristics of a person.

**Addictive personality** – a personality type characterized by high levels of neuroticism and psychoticism.

**Neuroticism** – a personality characteristic typified by high levels of anxiety and depressed mood.

**Psychoticism** – a personality characteristic typified by high levels of aggressiveness and hostility to others.

**Tri-dimensional theory** – an explanation that sees vulnerability to addictive behaviour as dependent upon characteristics of novelty seeking, harm avoidance and reward dependence.

---

## KEY CONTEMPORARY STUDY

### 'THE RELATIONSHIP BETWEEN STRESS, PERSONALITY, FAMILY FUNCTIONING AND INTERNET ADDICTION IN COLLEGE STUDENTS'

Yan *et al.* (2014)

### Aim

■ To assess the relationship between stress, personality and family relations in regard to internet addiction.

### Procedure

■ The sample consisted of 892 Chinese participants, who completed questionnaires measuring personal data, family functioning, internet addiction level, personality and stress levels.

### Results

■ Ten per cent of participants had severe internet addiction and 11 per cent mild internet addiction.

■ Severe addicts had poor family relationships, high neuroticism and psychoticism and low extroversion levels, as well as high stress levels over the last year.

■ Mild addicts scored similarly to non-addicts on all measures.

### Conclusion

■ Personality, stress and family functioning are influential in dependency behaviour.

■ Eysenck's predictions of addiction being linked to high levels of neuroticism and psychoticism were supported.

### Evaluation

■ Poor family relations could be an effect of, rather than a cause of, addiction.

■ Many participants were not included as they did not complete questionnaires, which could bias results, as they may have been individuals wishing not to disclose addictive tendencies.

## ■ Practical application

■ Personality tests can indicate which individuals may be more vulnerable to dependency behaviours so that preventative interventions could be more targeted at them, though there is a danger of creating a self-fulfilling prophecy by doing so.

## ■ Issues and debates

■ As Eysenck saw personality factors as innate, it suggests that addictive personalities result from biological determinism, with addicts having no free will over their dependencies.

---

### ■ STRENGTHEN YOUR LEARNING

1 Outline Eysenck's theory of addictive personality.

2 Outline Cloninger's tri-dimensional theory of addictive behaviour, including reference to novelty seeking, harm avoidance and reward dependence.

3 For Yan *et al.*'s (2014) study into internet addiction, in your own words, state the aims, procedure, results, conclusions and evaluative points.

4 Summarize what research evidence has suggested about personality factors and addiction.

5 What other evaluative points, including practical applications and relevant issues and debates, can be made about personality factors and addiction?

**Expert tip**

Eysenck's theory was a general theory of personality that was adapted as an explanation of addiction. However, Cloninger's theory is probably a more relevant theory, as it was especially designed to explain addictive behaviour.

# Health belief model

Revised ☐

The model was generated through attempts to understand why individuals did not use preventative behaviours to protect their health, such as attending health check-ups. The model aims to assess the likelihood of someone using facilities and services available to them and to gain insight into people's health behaviours. Likelihood of engagement is established by looking at how at risk individuals feel they are and how much they perceive services and facilities positively.

Key elements of the model centre on:

■ *individual perceptions* – the perceived susceptibility to the consequences of not acting and the perceived severity of not acting

■ *modifying factors* – the benefits of acting, demographic variables like age, the threat level to health and cues to action, like death of a loved one

■ *likelihood of action* – the costs, barriers and benefits of acting.

**Key term**

**Health belief model** – an explanation of the reasons why individuals do not always use preventative behaviours to protect their health, which focuses on the degree of personal risk individuals perceive to their health and whether they evaluate available facilities and services positively or negatively.

## ■ Research

■ **De Wit & Stroebe (2004)** reviewed the model to find that questionnaires designed for the model measure individual components but do not test the model in its entirety, which means the model's predictive validity (how good it is at predicting health behaviours) cannot be assessed.

■ **Gorin & Heck (2005)** found that the model predicted the uptake for a cervical cancer screening programme accurately, with demographic variables, like age and marital status, playing a large role in uptake, thus supporting the model.

■ **Wringe *et al.* (2009)** found that the biggest determinant for uptake on to a HIV programme in rural Tasmania was its accessibility, which was a big limiting factor. This illustrates how influential factors in the model vary across countries.

## ■ Positive evaluation

■ A positive feature of the model is how it sees a variety of key elements as involved in health-related decision-making. This reflects most people's experience of such decision-making in real-life situations, which suggests the model has face validity.

■ The model is good at explaining individual behaviours, such as attending a screening test or being inoculated against diseases.

## ■ Negative evaluation

■ A limitation of the model is its failure to fully recognize the role of emotions in making decisions about health-related behaviour, as emotional states can act as a mediating factor in making such decisions.

■ The health belief model is not really able to explain general attitudes to health, as it concentrates mainly on the likelihood of uptake of individual behaviours, such as the possibility that someone will attend a health check-up.

## ■ Practical application

■ The model can identify reasons specific to an individual as to why they may not participate in a particular health-related preventative behaviour, which gives clinicians an understanding of how to go about promoting that behaviour in a way that will be seen more positively, thus increasing the chances of that individual subsequently participating in the behaviour.

## ■ Issues and debates

■ The model has cross-cultural validity, as it recognizes that the most influential factors of the model vary across different cultures.

> **Expert tip**
>
> Rather than just using research evidence to assess the validity of the health belief model, a higher level form of evaluation (as with any theory/model/explanation) is to also incorporate other forms of evaluation, such as strengths and weaknesses, practical applications, as well as relevant issues and debates, and build these together into an effective commentary.

> **■ STRENGTHEN YOUR LEARNING**
>
> 1 Outline the health belief model, including reference to individual perceptions, modifying factors and likelihood of action.
> 2 Summarize what research evidence has suggested about the health belief model.
> 3 What other evaluative points, including practical applications and relevant issues and debates, can be made about the health belief model?

# Theory of planned behaviour – Ajzen (1991)

Revised

The **theory of planned behaviour** (TPB) sees attempts to abstain from dependency behaviours as due to factors supporting decision-making, rather than predisposing factors, with an added component where addicts need confidence in their abilities and available resources to quit. The model explains how beliefs affect behaviour change and is applicable to many health behaviours, including addiction. In terms of addiction, the model explains why someone might be successful in quitting addiction and why someone else might not. The core idea is that, in order to predict the outcome of a treatment programme, the beliefs, influences and motivation of an addict to the proposed change need to be considered. There are four parts to the model:

1 *Behavioural beliefs*, involving the subjective probability that behaviour will produce abstention.

> **Key term**
>
> **Theory of planned behaviour** – an explanation of the likelihood of success of health treatment programmes that focuses on the beliefs, influences and motivation of an individual to the proposed change in health behaviour.

2 *Normative beliefs*, involving the degree of perceived social pressure to quit.

3 *Control beliefs*, involving individual beliefs about the ability to abstain.

4 *Behavioural intentions*, involving a combination of the other three factors to create level of motivation to quit.

The TPB assesses an individual's motives for continuing dependency and their resolve to abstain. The higher their level of perceived behavioural control, the more likely they are to quit.

## Research

- **Webb & Sheeran (2006),** from a meta-analysis of 47 studies of the model, found that a high level of intention to quit resulted in a small behavioural change, suggesting the model has validity, but to a lesser extent than expected.

- **Godin & Kok (1996)** found the model predicted the relationship between levels of behaviour and intention and that the level of perceived behavioural control made a significant contribution towards predicting behaviour in some cases, giving some support to the model.

- **Oh & Hsu (2001),** from questionnaires, found a positive correlation between attitudes and behavioural intentions and actual behaviour, supporting the model.

- **Walker *et al.* (2006)** found that behavioural beliefs and normative beliefs were important in explaining gambling behaviour, but that control beliefs were not. Intention was, however, a good predictor of behavioural change. This gives support to some elements of the model.

## Positive evaluation

- Practitioners in health psychology and health economics perceive the TPB as valid and value its predictive power as an effective tool in treating addiction.

- A strength of the model is its acknowledgement of the role of peers in influencing behaviour and thus in predicting outcomes of behaviour change programmes.

## Negative evaluation

- There is no consideration of emotion within the TPB, which can affect likelihood of behavioural change, especially so with addiction, a vulnerable condition affected by mood.

- The model relies on self-report measures, which is a potential problem as addicts can be irrational and liable to downplay the level of their dependency, making such measures unreliable.

## Practical application

- The TPB is used to decide whether an intervention may be effective, saving money, time and effort if it finds interventions not to be suitable.

## Issues and debates

- The theory can be considered to be holistic, as it includes a range of influences upon behaviour, including social and environmental ones, rather than just focusing on one area of influence.

---

**■ STRENGTHEN YOUR LEARNING**

1 Outline the TPB, including reference to behavioural beliefs, normative beliefs, control beliefs and behavioural intentions.

2 Summarize what research evidence has suggested about the TPB.

3 What other evaluative points, including practical applications and relevant issues and debates, can be made about the TPB?

---

**Expert tip**

There is quite a lot of theoretical terminology associated with the TPB, such as behavioural beliefs, normative beliefs, etc. When using such terminology, to show your understanding, be sure to explain what these terms mean.

# Prochaska's (1977) six-stage model of behaviour change

Prochaska's model details the process of changing from unhealthy to healthy behaviours in a series of six stages of alteration in thinking and behaviour. The model acknowledges the importance of people's confidence in their ability to change, their level of social support and rewards for change being greater than those from continuing unhealthy behaviours, as well as acknowledging that relapse can occur at any stage.

> **Key term**
>
> **Prochaska's six-stage model of behaviour change** – an explanation of the process of changing from unhealthy to healthy behaviours, which perceives such change as a series of stages in thinking and action.

| Stage of behaviour change | Description |
|---|---|
| Pre-contemplation | Recognition of unhealthy behaviour, but with no compulsion to address it. |
| Contemplation | An admission that action is needed. |
| Preparation | Planning for how such action will occur. |
| Action | Putting the plan into action – usually involves cutting down or withdrawing from the dependency behaviour. |
| Maintenance | Use of strategies to prevent relapse, such as focusing on the benefits of withdrawal. |
| Termination | Reaching a state where temptation is no longer experienced. |

## KEY CONTEMPORARY STUDY

### 'DEMOGRAPHIC VARIABLES, SMOKING VARIABLES AND OUTCOME ACROSS FIVE STUDIES'

**Velicer *et al.* (2007)**

### Aim

- To assess the effectiveness of Prochaska's model in predicting behaviour change.

### Procedure

- A meta-analysis of five studies totalling 58,454 participants was conducted that investigated the success levels of smoking cessation programmes based upon Prochaska's model.

### Results

- A 22 to 26 per cent success rate in maintaining cessation of smoking six months after first stopping was found.

- There were no demographic differences in success rates, like gender or age-related factors.

- Success was generally dependent on how frequent smoking behaviour had originally been.

### Conclusions

- The model is applicable to all types of people.

- As the success levels compare favourably with other types of intervention in addressing nicotine addiction, it suggests Prochaska's model is effective.

### Evaluation

- The strength of cigarettes smoked was not assessed, which may have affected whether people were able to quit or not.

- Self-report methods were used, so participants may have given idealized answers about the success of their quitting smoking, rather than truthful answers.

## ■ Research

■ **Parker & Parikh (2001)** found the model performed well and helped facilitate the organizing and planning of successful programmes, which suggests it has effective real-world applications.

■ **Aveyard et al. (2009)** contradicted Velicer's study, by finding no increase in effectiveness if an intervention was tailored to the stages of change of the individual trying to stop smoking. This suggests further research is required.

## ■ Positive evaluation

■ The model has led to questionnaires being developed that allow classification on which stage individuals are currently in, such as the URICA (University of Rhode Island Change Assessment scale).

## ■ Negative evaluation

■ Rather than being in distinct changes of behavioural change, individuals may be influenced to different degrees by several stages at once.

## ■ Practical application

■ Prochaska's model permits interventions to be tailored to which stage of change an individual is in, increasing chances of success of behavioural change.

## ■ Issues and debates

■ Variations in research support for the model may be due to the model not acknowledging individual differences, which means the model suits some individuals more than others.

---

■ **STRENGTHEN YOUR LEARNING**

1 Outline Prochaska's six-stage model of behavioural change, including reference to the individual stages of the model.
2 For Velicer et al.'s (2007) meta-analysis of Prochaska's model, in your own words, state the aims, procedure, results, conclusions and evaluative points.
3 Summarize what research evidence has suggested about Prochaska's model.
4 What other evaluative points, including practical applications and relevant issues and debates, can be made about Prochaska's model?

---

**Expert tip**

A common mistake is to refer to Prochaska's model as a form of therapy. It isn't. Although generally applied to addiction, it is an explanation of behaviour change and should be referred to as such.

# Stress

Revised ☐

**Stress**, especially chronic, long-term stress, increases **vulnerability to addiction**, as dependency behaviours often act as coping mechanisms to give temporary relief from stressors. Urban environments tend to have more stressors, such as poverty, poor housing and social tensions, and so are associated with higher vulnerability to dependency behaviours, especially as drugs may be more readily available in such environments. There are mediating factors, though, that affect vulnerability to stress, such as degree and types of social support and individual differences in how people respond to stress, with some reacting more negatively and so being more at risk of developing dependencies. Having an addiction can in itself be stressful – for example, causing strained relationships and financial difficulties in maintaining dependency behaviours.

**Key terms**

**Stress** – a lack of balance between the perceived demands of a situation and an individual's perceived ability to cope with such demands.

**Vulnerability to addiction** – an individual's level of susceptibility to indulging in dependency behaviours.

## ■ Research

■ **Tavolacci et al. (2013)** found that students who were highly stressed had greater levels of smoking, alcohol abuse and internet addiction than students with low stress levels, which suggests stress and vulnerability to addiction are positively correlated.

- **Sinha (2001)** reviewed research to find that stress played a role in maintaining drug abuse and relapse. However, the mechanism by which this occurred was not identified in the research, which suggests that there is a link between stress and addiction, but further investigation is required.
- **Piazza *et al.* (1989)** found that rats, stressed by pinching their tails, became more likely to seek out and ingest amphetamines the more stressed they became. This indicates a relationship between degree of stress experienced and level of dependency behaviour exhibited.
- **Kosten (2000)** found that neonate rats, subjected to isolation stress for one hour a day between their second and ninth day of life, had a greater tendency for cocaine usage when adult, compared to rats who were not subjected to such stress. This suggests early childhood stress can impact on later vulnerability to addiction.

## Positive evaluation

- The identification of which stressors, and at what levels, are linked to dependency behaviours has led to the establishment of stress measures for addiction that can be applied to vulnerable individuals to assess their level of risk.

## Negative evaluation

- Much research evidence linking stress and addiction is correlational, making causality difficult to establish. High stress levels may be linked to the likelihood of becoming addicted, but they could equally be a by-product of being addicted in the first place.
- There is a need for research into possible gender differences and vulnerability to addiction. Stressors may have different effects on males and females in terms of how they affect dependency behaviours.

## Practical application

- Residents of nursing homes are screened for risk of addiction through vulnerability to stressors at key times, such as death of a loved one or being prescribed painkillers following surgery. If vulnerability is high, appropriate preventative measures are put in place.

## Issues and debates

- Much research linking stress to addiction is performed upon animals, such as rats. However, this presents an issue of representativeness, as findings may not be generalizable to humans, whose experience of stress is affected by cognitive processes that would not occur in such animals.

---

**■ STRENGTHEN YOUR LEARNING**

1   Explain the relationship between stress and vulnerability to addiction.
2   Summarize what research evidence has suggested about the relationship between stress and vulnerability to addiction.
3   What other evaluative points, including practical applications and relevant issues and debates, can be made about the relationship between stress and vulnerability to addiction?

---

**Expert tip**

It is important to remember that stress does not affect individuals in a uniform way. Vulnerability to stress has wide-ranging individual differences and this should be stressed in exam answers.

# Family and peer influences

Revised ☐

## Family influences

Families influence addictive behaviour through **social learning** and creation of **expectancies** about dependency behaviours, which either put individuals at risk of dependency or protect them from developing dependencies.

Social learning involves observation and imitation of individuals modelling addictive behaviour (or modelling non-addictive behaviour). If **vicarious reinforcement** occurs, the addictive behaviour (or non-addictive behaviour) is likely to be imitated. Expectancies involve what individuals believe will be the consequences of participating in dependency behaviours. If expectancies are positive, it increases chances of participation in the behaviour.

## Peers

As with families, peers influence addictive behaviour through social learning and creation of expectancies, especially during adolescence. However, choosing a peer group that indulges in dependency behaviours may be influenced by a desire to participate in such behaviour in the first place, and the fact that such peers will not be judgemental. Peers can promote opportunities for relapse too when attempting to quit dependency behaviours.

## Research

- **Akers & Lee (1996)** assessed smoking behaviour in 454 young adults aged 12–17, to find that social learning processes were involved in initiation, maintenance and cessation of smoking, with family influences especially influential. This illustrates the important role of families in dependency behaviours.

- **Bullers et al. (2001)** performed a longitudinal study to find that selection of a peer group often came after someone became an addict and that social influence from peer groups had a lesser effect. This suggests that peer influence may not be that strong.

- **Kobus (2003)** reviewed studies to find that, although peers influenced both encouragement and determent of smoking, the media, family and neighbourhood were also influential, which suggests that the psychological processes behind smoking behaviour may involve a combination of interacting factors.

- **Bauman & Ennett (1996)** reviewed studies to find that, although peer influence was stated as a reason underpinning substance abuse, such statements were not accompanied by research evidence, which suggests peer influence may have been overstated as an influence upon dependency behaviours.

## Positive evaluation

- Peer influence is seen to increase over time, especially as individuals enter adolescence, with risk of addiction greatly influenced by peers from that point onwards.

- SLT can explain individual differences in the extent to which dependency behaviours modelled by peers and family are imitated, by recourse to the mediating cognitive processes of attention, retention, reproduction and motivation.

## Negative evaluation

- It is difficult to assess the specific influence of peers and family upon addiction as they vary over time and occur in conjunction with other risk factors, such as biological and personality considerations.

- Research into family and peer influences tends to be non-experimental and therefore does not establish cause-and-effect relationships about their influences.

## Practical application

- Treatment strategies include social context elements, as well as biological and behavioural ones, due to the threat of relapse when released from hospitalization from family and peer influences. Recovering addicts are encouraged to stay away from such influences.

---

**Key terms**

**Family influences** – the ways in which family members affect health-related behaviours.

**Social learning** – acquiring behaviours through observation and imitation of role models.

**Expectancies** – the associations that are learned from observations of environmental experiences.

**Vicarious reinforcement** – observation of another person being rewarded for their behaviour, which increases the chances of that behaviour being imitated.

## Issues and debates

- Seeing addiction as resulting from family and peer influences takes a reductionist viewpoint, as it fails to consider, as a more holistic approach would, other types of influences, like biological factors.

> ### STRENGTHEN YOUR LEARNING
>
> 1 Explain how family influences can affect vulnerability to addiction.
> 2 Explain how peers can affect vulnerability to addiction.
> 3 Summarize what research evidence has suggested about how family influences and peers can affect vulnerability to addiction.
> 4 What other evaluative points, including practical applications and relevant issues and debates, can be made about how family influences and peers can affect vulnerability to addiction?

> **Expert tip**
>
> 'Family influences' is a fairly general term, so better answers will focus on the specific ways in which families influence addictive behaviour, such as through social learning and creation of expectancies. Peer influence should be explained as a separate form of influence that becomes more influential in adolescence.

# Health problems

Revised ☐

## The dopamine explanation of addiction

Revised ☐

The neurotransmitter **dopamine** is associated with dependency, as addictive substances and behaviours create a high by elevating activity in the **brain's reward system**, found in the centre of the brain and consisting of a complex circuit of neurons that produces a sensation of euphoria. Production of this sensation increases the chances of the behaviour continuing into dependency.

This is known as 'the common reward pathway', with activation occurring specifically in the ventral tegmental brain area (VTA), containing many dopamine neurons, which triggers activation in the nucleus accumbens (located in the limbic system), which then heightens activity in the prefrontal cortex.

Over time, due to changes in the neural structure in the pathway, increased levels of dependency substances/behaviours are required to elicit the reaction, heightening tolerance levels and cravings, resulting in addiction.

### Research

- **Dani & Biasi (2001)** performed research on rats to find that nicotine acts upon dopaminergic systems in the brain to reinforce further nicotine consumption. This illustrates the relationship between neural mechanisms in the brain and the rewarding effects of smoking that lead to addiction.

- **Watkins *et al.* (2000)** reviewed research into the neurobiology of nicotine addiction to find that dopamine release was reduced following long-term exposure to nicotine, which suggests that heightened tolerance of nicotine occurs (and thus a desire for greater consumption) due to the level of perceived reward decreasing.

- **Calvert *et al.* (2010)** found that smokers, when shown a cigarette packet, experienced activation in the ventral tegmental and nucleus accumbens brain areas, suggesting a biological reason for cravings.

### Positive evaluation

- The role of dopamine within the common reward pathway offers a plausible explanation of why certain substances, like drugs, and behaviours, like gambling, create feelings of euphoria so elevated as to exert a powerful addictive influence.

- The role of dopamine could be associated with a genetic link to addiction, with the dopaminergic mechanism in individuals with certain genes causing them to feel the rewarding aspects of drugs to a greater level and thus be more vulnerable to addiction.

> **Key terms**
>
> **Dopamine explanation of addiction** – a biological explanation of addiction centred upon the elevation of dopamine levels, through participation in dependency behaviours, in the brain's reward system.
>
> **Dopamine** – a neurotransmitter associated with feelings of joy.
>
> **The brain's reward system (common reward pathway)** – an area in the centre of the brain consisting of a complex circuit of neurons that creates feelings of euphoria.

## ■ Negative evaluation

■ The role of dopamine is only part of the neural action concerning dependency behaviours and so should not be seen as the only factor in the biochemical influence upon addiction.

■ Research into the effect of dopamine on addiction often uses animals and so findings may not generalize to humans, as the higher level of cognitive functioning in humans means that we experience the effects of drugs differently.

## ■ Practical application

■ Methadone is a medication used to treat addiction to opiate drugs, like heroin. It works by changing the way the common reward pathway operates, blocking out the euphoric highs of opiate drugs, while working on the nervous system to reduce withdrawal effects.

## ■ Issues and debates

■ The dopamine theory is a reductionist, rather than holistic, explanation, as it focuses on the single biological factor of biochemistry at the expense of other contributing factors, such as psychological influences.

---

**■ STRENGTHEN YOUR LEARNING**

1  Outline the dopamine explanation of addiction.

2  Summarize what research evidence has suggested about the dopamine explanation of addiction.

3  What other evaluative points, including practical applications and relevant issues and debates, can be made about the dopamine explanation of addiction?

---

**Expert tip**

The dopamine explanation of addiction can be used to explain not just how addictions are formed, but also how they are maintained, the formation of higher tolerance levels and relapse from quitting due to cravings.

# The cognitive theory of addiction

Revised

The **cognitive theory** sees dependency behaviours as arising from and being maintained by **cognitive distortions** and maladaptive thought processes. Such thought processes negatively affect mood to the point where it is believed that only by participation in a dependency behaviour will emotions be elevated.

Expectancies about dependency behaviours arise from learning experiences to become a type of schema about such behaviours. Therefore, if positive expectancies are formed, it increases the chances of addictions forming through continual participation in such behaviours.

Addicts also tend to have a cognitive bias where they focus on positive aspects of dependency behaviours and ignore the negative sides. Several such cognitive distortions have been identified, such as those below associated with gambling addiction.

| Cognitive distortion | Description |
|---|---|
| *Availability* | Positive experiences of gambling recalled more easily than negative ones. |
| *Confirmation bias* | Focus on information consistent with irrational beliefs about gambling, like being 'lucky'. |
| *Hindsight bias* | Belief that wins/losses were expected. |
| *Flexible attribution* | Belief that wins are due to skill and losses are due to bad luck. |
| *Illusion of control* | Belief that personal control can be exerted over outcomes. |
| *Concrete information bias* | Over-focus on wins and downplay of losses. |

**Key terms**

**Cognitive theory of addiction** – an explanation that sees dependency behaviours as arising from and being maintained by cognitive distortions and maladaptive thought processes.

**Cognitive distortions** – forms of cognitive bias where addicts focus on positive aspects of dependency behaviours and ignore the negative sides.

**Cognitive behavioural therapy** – a treatment for addiction that seeks to identify irrational thinking patterns and change them to rational ones in order to modify behaviour.

# ■ Research

■ **Dunn & Goldman (1998)** found that the expectancies of 7–18-year-olds matched those of adults, which suggests a child's learning environment helps form schemas of dependency behaviours that influence whether they later participate in such behaviours.

■ **Griffiths (1994)** found that gambling addicts perceived themselves as more skilful than they actually were and had irrational beliefs about losses, like seeing them as 'near wins', illustrating the association of cognitive distortions with dependency behaviours.

■ **Toneatto (1999)** reviewed studies to find that cognitive biases were prominent in the thinking of gamblers, especially exaggerating their own skill, downplaying others' skill and irrational beliefs about predicting outcomes. This suggests gambling addiction is driven by distorted beliefs.

# ■ Positive evaluation

■ The success of **cognitive behavioural therapy** (CBT) in treating addiction suggests that addiction does have a cognitive component to it.

■ The cognitive explanation explains how dependencies may form through expectancies, but also how they are maintained and why addicts relapse through cognitive distortions.

# ■ Negative evaluation

■ Schemas are known to be powerful influences on behaviour; however, the extent to which they are influential in addictive behaviour is difficult to assess precisely.

■ Much research into cognitive biases and addiction uses self-reports, bringing problems of validity with regards to the extent that participants are aware of their own level of cognitive processing regarding dependency behaviours.

# ■ Practical application

■ CBT is used to restructure the thought processes of addicts and to equip them with the cognitive skills to resist temptations to indulge in dependency behaviours.

# ■ Issues and debates

■ An issue with the cognitive theory of gambling addiction is that it cannot explain the physiological withdrawal symptoms experienced when addicts try to quit. This indicates the same brain mechanisms are involved as with substance dependencies, suggesting a biological explanation.

---

**■ STRENGTHEN YOUR LEARNING**

1 Outline the cognitive explanation of addiction; include reference to cognitive distortions.

2 Summarize what research evidence has suggested about the cognitive explanation of addiction.

3 What other evaluative points, including practical applications and relevant issues and debates, can be made about the cognitive explanation of addiction?

---

**Expert tip**

In explanations of the cognitive theory, detail can be achieved by reference to specific cognitive distortions, such as availability, hindsight bias, etc. Answers that are structured and organized like this will gain access to a higher level of marks.

# The sociocultural theory of addiction

Revised ☐

Sociocultural explanations focus on how **classical conditioning, operant conditioning** and **social learning theory** can be used to explain addiction.

## ■ Social learning theory

Social learning theory (SLT) sees dependency as learned from observation and imitation of individuals modelling dependency behaviours who are **vicariously reinforced** for their behaviour. For example, someone taking drugs is praised for being 'cool' for doing so and is imitated to gain the same response from others.

## ■ Operant conditioning

Participation in dependency behaviours is reinforcing (rewarding), increasing the chances of the behaviour recurring to gain further reinforcement. This occurs through positive reinforcement, like gaining a 'high' from taking drugs, and negative reinforcement, like smoking cigarettes to lower stress levels. Operant conditioning thus explains how dependency behaviours are maintained.

## ■ Classical conditioning (cue reactivity)

Classical conditioning involves learning to associate an originally neutral stimulus with a particular response – for example, learning through repetition of the experience to associate smoking with having finished eating food. Once the association has been made, cravings can occur, such as finishing eating and craving a cigarette.

## ■ Research

■ **Brynner (1969)** found that media images portraying smoking as attractive and making smokers look tough increased the motivation for wanting to smoke and that role models of smoking in the media provided opportunities for social learning. This supports SLT being implicated in initiating dependency behaviours.

■ **Goldberg et al. (1981)** found that monkeys would press a lever to receive nicotine at a rate similar to one they had learned previously to receive cocaine. This suggests that addictions can be explained by reference to the reinforcing effects of operant conditioning.

■ **Calvert et al. (2010)** reported that showing smokers a cigarette packet created cravings for smoking, which suggests that the originally neutral stimulus of the cigarette packet had become associated with the pleasure of smoking, in line with the cue reactivity explanation of classical conditioning.

## ■ Positive evaluation

■ A combination of SLT, which explains how dependency behaviours can be initiated, and classical and operant conditioning, which explain how they are maintained, offers a plausible explanation for addiction.

■ The success of behaviourist therapies in getting addicts to quit, such as the use of positive reinforcements, suggests that there is a learning element to addiction.

## ■ Negative evaluation

■ Learning theory cannot explain why, when different individuals participate in dependency behaviours, only some go on to become addicted. Other vulnerability factors must be exerting an influence.

■ Learning explanations especially neglect the role of biology in addiction. Research has shown several brain areas are activated in response to dependency behaviours that explain the pleasurable effects of such behaviours and the physiological cravings that result from trying to quit, which learning theory by itself cannot explain.

---

**Key terms**

**The sociocultural theory of addiction** – an explanation of addiction that sees dependency behaviours being learned from environmental experiences.

**Classical conditioning** – where addictions are learned through an association being formed between a previously neutral stimulus and a positive emotional response.

**Operant conditioning** – where addictions are learned due to the positive or negative consequences of participating in dependency behaviours.

**Social learning theory** – where addictions are learned through observation and imitation of individuals modelling dependency behaviours who are seen to be vicariously reinforced for their behaviour.

**Vicarious reinforcement** – observation of another person being rewarded for their behaviour, which increases the chances of that behaviour being imitated.

## ■ Practical application

■ Media images of role models who do not display positive attitudes to dependency behaviours can help to prevent individuals from being initiated into such behaviours.

## ■ Issues and debates

■ The notion that addictions can be explained via reference to SLT and classical and operant conditioning concerns the idea of environmental determinism, where behaviour is created by external influences that individuals have no free will to control.

> **Expert tip**
>
> As the sociocultural theory mainly involves the behavioural approach, comparisons can be made with other approaches to highlight strengths and weaknesses of the approach. For example, how the behavioural approach neglects the role of biology in addiction, thus favouring the biological approach more.

> ■ **STRENGTHEN YOUR LEARNING**
>
> 1  Outline the sociocultural explanation of addiction; include reference to social learning theory, operant conditioning and classical conditioning.
> 2  Summarize what research evidence has suggested about the sociocultural explanation of addiction.
> 3  What other evaluative points, including practical applications and relevant issues and debates, can be made about the sociocultural explanation of addiction?

# Prevalence rates of health problems

Revised ☐

Prevalence concerns the rate of occurrence of health problems. Knowledge of how common problems are raises public awareness and helps to target resources. DSM-V described alcohol addiction in the USA as common in 2013 (12.4 per cent in men and 4.9 per cent in women), with the highest rates among young adults and 40 per cent of Native Americans reported to have 'alcohol use disorder'. Gambling addiction was a lesser issue, at 0.3 per cent of the general population, while 0.6 per cent of the population had a drug dependency and 17 per cent were habitual smokers.

> **Key term**
>
> **Prevalence rates of health problems** – the level of occurrence of health-related issues.

## KEY CONTEMPORARY STUDY

### 'A CASE STUDY OF MENTAL HEALTH PREVALENCE STATISTICS'

**McManus et al. (2016)**

#### Aim
■ To assess the prevalence rates of mental health problems.
■ To gather data on services providing mental health treatments.

#### Procedure
■ The Adult Psychiatric Morbidity Survey was used to gather data on treated and untreated psychiatric disorders.
■ Findings were compared to those of the two previous surveys.

#### Results
■ Seventeen per cent of people experienced a common mental disorder, like depression, in the previous week.
■ Common mental disorders, like depression, are more common among women, especially those aged 16–24.
■ People reporting a common mental disorder rose from 15.5 per cent in 1993 to 18.9 per cent by 2014.
■ Unemployed people are most likely to report common mental disorders.

#### Conclusions
■ Mental health issues are rising in the general population with specific groups especially experiencing problems.

#### Evaluation
■ The sample benefited from being from the general population and not just patients, and included demographic details, enabling a fuller picture of the prevalence of mental health problems to be established.
■ There are generalization problems, as certain groups were excluded, like the homeless, who are known to have high levels of mental health issues, and only 57 per cent of people contacted responded, which may have biased results, as non-respondents may have higher levels of mental health issues.

## ■ Research

■ **Keyes *et al.* (2010)** found that the perceived level of stigma associated with being treated for alcoholism affected the willingness of alcoholics to receive treatment or admit to addiction problems. This suggests that reported prevalence rates are lower than the actual rates.

■ **Hoffman & Kopak (2015)** found the criteria listed in the DSM and ICD classification systems differ for mild and moderate alcohol misuse, affecting the validity of reported prevalence rates.

## ■ Positive evaluation

■ Regular collecting of prevalence rates allows comparisons to identify long-term trends in health problems.

## ■ Negative evaluation

■ Addicts may be reluctant to acknowledge dependency, as this means facing withdrawal, something they may not be prepared to do. This negatively impacts on the validity of reported prevalence rates.

## ■ Practical application

■ Prevalence rates are used to focus resources on health issues of most need in the most affected demographic groups.

## ■ Issues and debates

■ An issue with prevalence rates is definition of health issues – for example, the differences between casual use of addictive substances and actual dependency. Recommendations of limits for safe usage differ between cultures, again making valid data hard to amass.

---

### ■ STRENGTHEN YOUR LEARNING

1 Outline prevalence rates of health problems.

2 For McManus *et al.*'s (2016) case study of mental health prevalence, in your own words, state the aims, procedure, results, conclusions and evaluative points.

3 Summarize what research evidence has suggested about prevalence rates of health problems.

4 What other evaluative points, including practical applications and relevant issues and debates, can be made about prevalence rates of health problems?

---

**Expert tip**

The topic of prevalence rates of health problems, unlike many other topics, does not involve explanations. Therefore, description in answers can instead be formed from details of research studies that illustrate prevalence rates, with evaluation formed around methodological and other problems in collecting valid data.

# Promoting health

Revised ☐

## Health promotion

Revised ☐

**Health promotion** divides into three categories: **self-empowerment**, **community development** and **behaviour change**.

## ■ Self-empowerment

This approach focuses on the control of the individual over their body and environment. The more control they feel they have, the more likely they are to take action about their health. Encouragements are made to get people to take positive lifestyle choices and to believe that by taking personal control improvements will occur. For example, the 'This Girl Can' campaign directly confronted women's concerns about their appearance as a reason for not participating in exercise, with slogans such as 'I'm sweating like a pig' and 'I jiggle therefore I am'.

**Key terms**

**Health promotion** – communication with targeted groups that aims to encourage positive health behaviours.

**Self-empowerment** – the development of control by an individual over their body and environment.

## Community development

Community development involves promoting health among local groups, especially through social support of each other and shared activities. For example, in China, large groups of people gather in the morning in local environments to perform group activities, like tai chi and choral singing. This fosters a sense of well-being and companionship that contributes to heightened self-esteem and positive health.

## Behaviour change

Behaviour change concerns a cognitive approach to health promotion, as faulty thinking is seen as contributing to negative health – for instance, that smoking is not a health risk to an individual as they do some exercise, which counteracts the bad effects. Public health campaigns are used to address this misperception by presenting facts and highlighting those at risk. This is seen to be most effective if all sides of an issue are presented, so that an individual feels they retain an element of control over personal health decisions, as this will make necessary changes seem more attractive.

The general idea is that presenting facts in an honest fashion will alter people's misperceptions that specific health issues do not apply to them or affect them in a lesser way. This will increase the chances of an individual making necessary lifestyle changes to counteract unhealthy behaviours. For example, the British Heart Foundation challenged the idea that heart disease was a male-only problem by putting up cardboard gravestones in five British cities with 'Mum', 'Grandma', etc. written on them and inscriptions that related their deaths to heart disease.

> **Key terms**
>
> **Community development** – the promotion of health among locally based groups.
>
> **Behaviour change** – a cognitive approach to health promotion, which argues that presenting health-related information honestly reduces individuals' beliefs that specific health issues do not concern them or affect them in a lesser way, which increases the chances of individuals making lifestyle changes to reduce unhealthy behaviours.

---

### KEY CONTEMPORARY STUDY

### 'WHEN SCARY MESSAGES BACKFIRE: INFLUENCE OF DISPOSITIONAL COGNITIVE AVOIDANCE ON THE EFFECTIVENESS OF THREAT COMMUNICATIONS'

**Nestler & Egloff (2010)**

#### Aim

- To assess why health promotions do not always work in the intended manner.

#### Procedure

- Two hypothetical health messages were given to participants that talked about the risk of caffeine consumption leading to a fictional condition called xyelinenteritis. In the high-threat condition, participants were told that caffeine could cause 'xyelinenteritis', which would lead to stomach cancer. In the low-threat condition, the link to cancer was not mentioned. Both groups were told that they should reduce caffeine consumption.

- Reactions of participants to the two health messages were examined, with an expectation that the 'high-threat' message would prompt healthier choices due to the consequences of maintaining unhealthy choices.

- Thinking styles were examined, especially the level of cognitive avoidance (the amount of disregarding of threatening and unpleasant information).

#### Results

- Cognitive avoidance levels affected participants' reactions and the level of threat they perceived, with high-cognitive avoiders underplaying the threat level in the high-threat condition to below that of the low-threat message and being less likely to reduce caffeine intake.

#### Conclusions

- There are individual differences in reactions to health promotion campaigns because of differing cognitive styles.

#### Evaluation

- The use of deceit in terms of creating a fictional disease with serious health consequences is unethical, especially as it may have caused psychological distress.

- The findings have implications for how health promotion campaigns should be targeted in order to maximize their effectiveness, especially in altering the thought processes involved in health-related behaviours.

## Research

- **Wallerstein (1992)** reviewed research to find that a lack of control is a risk factor for disease, illustrating how self-empowerment is an important factor in health promotion.

- **Armstrong (2000)** found that garden programmes in New York State, designed to facilitate better health, were four times more likely to help the communities they served, in terms of social support and health benefits, when located in low-income areas. This illustrates that community health and well-being can be enhanced by a better social and physical environment.

## Positive evaluation

- Self-empowerment health promotion campaigns not only help to initiate healthy behaviour, but they also increase the likelihood of the behaviour continuing.

- Health promotion campaigns tend to assume that their 'message' will be perceived and acted upon in a positively predictable way. However, as research like that by **Nestler & Egloff (2010)** shows, there are no guarantees that the target population will react how they 'should'. This means that campaigns are very difficult to design and execute effectively.

## Negative evaluation

- Self-empowerment strategies to improve health can be seen as placing the blame of poor health on to the individual. This is especially true for those whose personality characteristics make them perceive health outcomes as beyond their control.

- Measuring self-empowerment is difficult to do in a valid and reliable way, so the exact effect is difficult to ascertain.

## Practical application

- Addressing cognitive avoidance is crucial to changing health behaviour. A successful British health promotion campaign challenged the idea that AIDS only affected homosexual men. By addressing the misperception, it got heterosexuals to change their thinking (and behaviour) regarding risks of contracting AIDS through unprotected sex.

## Issues and debates

- There can be cultural bias with health promotion, as different cultures place varying emphasis on the duty of the state to influence health, with collectivist cultures seeing it as more of a social duty to promote general well-being.

---

**■ STRENGTHEN YOUR LEARNING**

1 Outline health promotion in terms of:
   a self-empowerment,
   b community development,
   c behaviour change.
2 For Nestler & Egloff's (2010) study of dispositional cognitive avoidance, in your own words, state the aims, procedure, results, conclusions and evaluative points.
3 Summarize what research evidence has suggested about health promotion.
4 What other evaluative points, including practical applications and relevant issues and debates, can be made about health promotion?

**Expert tip**

Rather than writing generally about health promotion, better answers will be structured and organized around categories of health promotion, such as self-empowerment, community development and behaviour change. Evaluation can then be focused on specific research studies for each of these areas.

# Tools for promoting health

## ■ The mass media

The **mass media** consists of modes of public communication, like TV, radio, printed and digital media. It is a key tool for health promotion, due to its ability to reach large audiences quickly. Health promotions directed through mass media are targeted at specific audiences and convey simple, clear messages that are easy to remember.

## ■ Legislation

**Legislation** is used to promote health behaviours by restricting the availability of potentially unhealthy products, like alcohol and cigarettes – for example, by putting age restrictions on their sale. More indirect methods of restriction include increasing prices by raising taxation on unhealthy goods or by legislating to ban adverts that make unhealthy products seem glamorous.

## ■ Source characteristics

The choice of person giving a message in a health promotion affects the likelihood of it being effective, thus celebrities who target audiences admire, identify with and respect are often used, as are people known for their honesty, as this increases the chances of the message being believed. Sports stars are often used for health promotions, due to their connection with health and fitness. Different types of celebrities will be used when promotions are targeted at specific audiences – for example, female celebrities for campaigns aimed specifically at females.

## ■ Research

- **Sharf (1997)** found that online discussion forums for breast cancer awareness helped create awareness and self-empowerment in women and social support for each other, highlighting the role that social media can play in promoting positive health behaviours.

- **Meyers et al. (2009)** reported a 17 per cent decrease in hospital admissions for heart attacks following a smoking ban in public places in the USA, which illustrates the effectiveness of direct use of legislation in promoting health-related behaviours.

- **Chapman & Leask (2001)** reported that using famous cricketer and smoker Shane Warne to promote giving up smoking did not succeed, as it became known that Warne received a large payment for the promotion and did not give up smoking himself. This illustrates how using celebrities and role models can be counterproductive.

## ■ Positive evaluation

- The growth of social media since the introduction of the internet has proven invaluable as a means of conveying health promotions to large numbers of people in a quick fashion.

- The success of legislation in promoting health, such as the ban on smoking in public places, has led to increased legislative action, such as taxation on unhealthy foods.

## ■ Negative evaluation

- A problem with mass media is false information that can lead to false beliefs about health-related behaviour. For example, untrue social media suggestions that vaccination can cause autism led to higher levels of illnesses like measles, due to children not being vaccinated.

---

**Key terms**

**Tools for promoting health** – the means by which health-related behaviours are encouraged.

**The mass media** – the promotion of health via public forms of communication.

**Legislation** – the promotion of healthy behaviours and restriction of unhealthy behaviours through the creation of laws.

**Source characteristics** – the use of specific individuals, such as celebrities, to promote health.

## ■ Practical application

■ Research, such as that by **Chapman & Leask (2001)**, has illustrated that, when using celebrities for health promotions, the message must be honestly conveyed and celebrities not motivated to take part by large personal gain.

## ■ Issues and debates

■ The effectiveness of media in promoting health is not universal across cultures due to the differing levels of state control and censorship over forms of media.

---

■ **STRENGTHEN YOUR LEARNING**

1   Explain the following as tools of health promotion:
    a   mass media,
    b   legislation,
    c   source characteristics.
2   Summarize what research evidence has suggested about tools of health promotion.
3   What other evaluative points, including practical applications and relevant issues and debates, can be made about tools of health promotion?

---

**Expert tip**

When writing about tools for promoting health, organize and structure your answer around different types of tools, such as legislation, the mass media and source characteristics. Evaluation can then be centred on research studies that deal specifically with each of these tools.

---

# Effectiveness of health promotion programmes

Revised ☐

Health promotion programmes are assessed for their cost-effectiveness and the extent to which they meet their aims by changing health behaviour positively.

A baseline measurement is needed, so that 'before' and 'after' measures can be compared to assess effectiveness, with measurements taken from target populations. For instance, if a promotion is aimed at changing health behaviours in 16–24-year-old females, then that gender and age group form the target population to be assessed.

Key term

**Effectiveness of health promotion programmes** – the degree to which health promotions are successful in meeting their aims.

## ■ Research

■ **Van Hasselt et al. (2015)** reviewed health promotion effectiveness evaluation in severe mental illness, to find there were key areas that were not being assessed, such as level of restlessness, an important characteristic in many mental patients. There were also inappropriate measures, such as self-reports of behaviour, notoriously invalid for mental health patients. This suggests that evaluation of health promotion programmes may often be suspect.

## ■ Positive evaluation

■ The use of baseline measurements permits an objective assessment of whether health promotions have been effective.

## ■ Negative evaluation

■ Assessing whether changes in behaviour as a result of promotions are significant can be difficult to achieve. Changing the behaviour of relatively small amounts of people can be considered a success when other methods have failed to work.

## ■ Practical application

■ **Pommier et al. (2010)** reviewed evaluations of health promotion in schools to produce a research protocol based on good practice. Key aspects were ensuring that both qualitative and quantitative methods were used and ensuring that designs were realistic so that promotions would be completed properly and with good levels of uptake.

KEY CONTEMPORARY STUDY

### 'HOW EFFECTIVE AND COST-EFFECTIVE WAS THE NATIONAL MASS MEDIA SMOKING CESSATION CAMPAIGN *STOPTOBER*?'

Brown *et al.* (2014)

### Aim

■ To assess the effectiveness of the Stoptober smoking cessation campaign.

### Procedure

■ 31,366 smokers were asked about attempts to quit smoking before the Stoptober campaign in October 2012. Details were also taken of their age, gender, social grade and degree of smoking behaviour.

■ The number of attempts to stop during the campaign was recorded and compared with the average number during the preceding months, including peak times for quitting, such as New Year.

### Results

■ Quit attempts were higher in October 2012 than previously.

■ During Stoptober, attempts to stop increased by 4.15 per cent compared to previous Octobers.

■ The effect was seen uniformly across all demographic groups.

■ Cost-effectiveness of the promotion was greatest for people aged 35–44 years and least cost-effective for those under 35 years.

■ The number of participants who gave up smoking as a result of the campaign was 8,817.

### Evaluation

■ A cause-and-effect relationship between the campaign and quitting cannot be made, as there may have been other uncontrolled factors that affected its effectiveness.

■ Although cessation rates were impressive, the number of people who attempted to quit due to the promotion was relatively small when compared to the total number of British smokers.

## ■ Issues and debates

■ Researcher bias is an issue when assessing the effectiveness of health promotions, as the desire to show positive effects can unconsciously affect accuracy and honesty, lowering the reliability of evaluations.

---

### ■ STRENGTHEN YOUR LEARNING

1 How is the effectiveness of health promotion campaigns evaluated?

2 For Brown *et al.*'s (2014) study of the effectiveness of 'Stoptober', in your own words, state the aims, procedure, results, conclusions and evaluative points.

3 Summarize what research evidence has suggested about the effectiveness of health promotion campaigns.

4 What other evaluative points, including practical applications and relevant issues and debates, can be made about the effectiveness of health promotion campaigns?

### Expert tip

Descriptive content for answers on the effectiveness of health promotion programmes will generally come from outlining research studies that assess such programmes, with evaluation formed around the conclusions of such studies, as well as methodological considerations, practical applications and relevant issues and debates.

## EXAM-TYPE QUESTIONS

1 Evaluate the biopsychosocial model of health and well-being. (22 marks)
2 Discuss research studies related to the biopsychosocial model of health. (22 marks)
3 Discuss the influence of dispositional factors on health-related behaviour. (22 marks)
4 Evaluate health beliefs as determinants of health. (22 marks)
5 Discuss one or more research studies of determinants of health. (22 marks)
6 Discuss risk and protective factors as determinants of health. (22 marks)
7 Contrast explanations of health problems. (22 marks)
8 Discuss research studies related to one or more explanations of health problems. (22 marks)
9 Discuss one explanation of health problems. (22 marks)
10 Discuss prevalence rates of health problems. (22 marks)
11 Evaluate research studies related to prevalence rates of health problems. (22 marks)
12 With the use of suitable examples, discuss ethical considerations of research into health problems. (22 marks)
13 Discuss the ethical considerations of research into health promotion. (22 marks)
14 Discuss health promotion. (22 marks)
15 Discuss one or more studies related to the effectiveness of health promotion programmes. (22 marks)
16 Evaluate the effectiveness of health promotion programmes. (22 marks)
17 Discuss the effectiveness of two health promotion programmes. (22 marks)

# Formation of personal relationships

## Evolutionary theory of reproductive strategies

The evolutionary explanation sees males and females as under different selective pressures. Different male and female reproductive strategies evolved due to males producing lots of sperm, but not being sure of paternity, and females possessing limited eggs, but being assured of maternity. Natural selection primed males to have sex with as many females as possible, while priming females to choose genetically strong, resource-rich males, in order to produce healthy offspring with enhanced chances of developing to sexual maturity.

### ■ Male and female reproductive strategies

| Male strategies | Description | Female strategies | Description |
|---|---|---|---|
| *Courtship* | Gives opportunities to display genetic fitness, e.g. health, body symmetry, and resource richness, e.g. giving presents and kindness (indicates willingness to share resources). | *Courtship* | Gives opportunities to assess males on genetic fitness and resource richness, and makes males invest time and resources, lowering their chances of deserting after successful matings. |
| *Size* | Emphasize strength and muscularity compared to other males. | *Handicap hypothesis* | Favour males who demonstrate genetic strength despite handicaps, e.g. being able to tolerate high levels of alcohol. |
| *Sperm competition* | Males with larger testicles, bigger ejaculations and fast-swimming sperm have more reproductive success. | *Reducing attractiveness of other females* | Decrease mating opportunities of rival females by emphasizing their unattractiveness and unfaithfulness. |
| *Mate guarding* | Females are prevented from having mating opportunities with other males to lower chances of **cuckoldry** and spending resources raising another male's genes. | *Sexy sons hypothesis* | Favour males with signs of genetic fitness, e.g. body symmetry, as offspring will have same features. |
| *Sneak copulation* | Mate with other females other than one's partner to increase reproductive chances. | *Display fertility and health* | Advertise signs of health, e.g. shiny hair, and fertility, e.g. youthfulness, body symmetry, big breasts, large hip–waist ratio. |

### ■ Research

- **Buss (1989)** found using participants from 37 cultures that males prefer young, physically attractive females, while females prefer resource-rich, ambitious, industrious males, which suggests that gender differences in attractiveness are biological in nature.

- **Cartwright (2000)** found that women with symmetrical breasts were more fertile than more asymmetrically breasted women, supporting the idea that body symmetry indicates reproductive fitness. Additionally **Penton-Voak et al. (2001)** found females prefer males with greater facial symmetry, an indication of developmental stability that would be passed on to their sons, supporting the sexy sons hypothesis.

> **Key terms**
>
> **Evolutionary theory of reproductive strategies** – an explanation of heterosexual relationships that sees males and females as subjected to different selective pressures, which prompts them to use different mating strategies to maximize reproductive success.
>
> **Cuckoldry** – where a female becomes pregnant by a non-partner male.

## 'SEX DIFFERENCES IN JEALOUSY: THE RECALL OF CUES TO SEXUAL AND EMOTIONAL INFIDELITY IN PERSONALLY MORE AND LESS THREATENING CONTEXT CONDITIONS'

### Schutzwohl & Koch (2004)

### Aim
- To assess gender differences in sexual and emotional **jealousy**.

### Procedure
- Two hundred male and female German students decided whether their partner forming a sexual and emotional relationship with someone else would cause them more sexual or emotional jealousy. Choices and time taken to make a decision were recorded.

### Results
- Emotional jealousy was greater for males and females, but more males (37 per cent) were primarily sexually jealous than females (20 per cent).
- Women who selected emotional **infidelity** reached their decision faster than women selecting sexual infidelity.
- Men who selected sexual infidelity reached their decision faster than men selecting emotional infidelity.

### Conclusions
- Males who are more jealous of sexual infidelity use simpler decision-making strategies than males who are more jealous of emotional infidelity, while females who are more jealous of emotional infidelity use simpler decision-making strategies than females who are more jealous of sexual infidelity.
- Males and females who choose their adaptive primary infidelity type – sexual for men, emotional for women – rely on their immediate response tendency suggested by their respective jealousy mechanisms, while males and females selecting their adaptive secondary infidelity type engage in additional thinking that leads them to override their initial response tendency.

### Evaluation
- Previous results suggesting that women who select the emotional infidelity option use more complex decision-making than women selecting sexual infidelity are contradicted by this study.
- The exact nature of the decision-making processes used, especially by men, when selecting their adaptive secondary infidelity type is not identified.

---

- **Singh (1993)** used data from 50 years of beauty contest winners and *Playboy* centrefolds to find that a small waist set against full hips was a consistent feature of female attractiveness, supporting the idea of waist-to-hip ratio advertising reproductive ability.

## ▮ Positive evaluation

- **Diamond (1992)** argues that young males indulge in risky behaviours, like drugs and bungee jumping, to advertise their reproductive fitness in the face of adversity, supporting the handicap hypothesis.

- Checking partners' mobile phone records, email accounts, etc. is a modern form of mate guarding, where checks are made on partners to see if they have been sexually/emotionally unfaithful, in line with evolutionary theory.

- Females often use make-up and cosmetic surgery and lie about their age in order to appear younger and more fertile, while males exaggerate their resource richness and pretend to be in love to get females to mate with them. This supports the idea of males and females using different strategies to maximize reproductive potential.

## ▮ Negative evaluation

- The evolutionary explanation is oversimplified as it presumes heterosexuality and that all heterosexual relationships are sexual. It also cannot explain couples choosing not to have children, as it assumes a desire to reproduce.

> **Key terms**
>
> **Jealousy** – an emotional state characterized by suspicion of infidelity.
>
> **Infidelity** – sexual and/or emotional unfaithfulness towards a romantic partner.

- Evolutionary theory explains female choosiness and male competitiveness in terms of maximizing reproductive potential. However, this can also be explained socioculturally by gender role socialization.

- **Simmons et al. (2003)** found 28 per cent of Australian males admitted to cheating on partners, but 22 per cent of females did too, which refutes the idea of sneak copulation being a male reproductive strategy, especially as, if such females are caught being unfaithful, they risk abandonment and having to raise children without male resources.

## Practical application

- Relationship counselling advises jealous individuals that sexual and emotional jealousy are natural, evolutionary responses, which can help those who feel threatened by such intense feelings to come to terms with them and develop trust within their relationships.

## Issues and debates

- 'Pick-up' coaches in the USA teach men how to trick women into having casual sex using evolutionary theory. Such practices are ethically questionable, as they involve deceit and manipulation.

---

### ■ STRENGTHEN YOUR LEARNING

1. Explain, from an evolutionary viewpoint, why males and females have different reproductive strategies to maximize reproductive success.

2. Outline male and female reproductive strategies.

3. For Schutzwohl & Koch's (2004) study of sex differences in jealousy, in your own words, state the aims, procedure, results, conclusions and evaluative points.

4. Summarize what research evidence has suggested about evolutionary explanations of reproductive strategies.

5. What other evaluative points, including practical applications and relevant issues and debates, can be made about evolutionary explanations of reproductive strategies?

---

### Expert tip

When writing about the evolutionary theory of reproductive strategies, take care not just to present a general outline and evaluation of evolutionary theory, as this will not attract much credit. You should be writing about how the theory specifically relates to relationships, such as differences between male and female strategies.

# The matching hypothesis

Revised ▢

The **matching hypothesis** (Walster *et al.*, 1966) sees individuals as forming an impression of their own level of attractiveness and then seeking others with similar levels of attraction.

Securing a partner of similar attractiveness reduces the chances of rejection (for someone more attractive) and thus increases feelings of relationship security.

### Key term

**Matching hypothesis** – the idea that individuals are attracted to people of similar perceived attractiveness.

## Research

- **Walster & Walster (1969)** found participants randomly paired with dance partners of similar attractiveness liked their partner more than those randomly paired with dance partners of greater or lesser attractiveness, supporting the matching hypothesis.

- **Taylor et al. (2011)** used profiles and photographs from an online dating site to find that initial attraction was based on physical attractiveness, which did not support the matching hypothesis. However, replies were more likely to be sent to individuals who were perceived as of similar levels of physical attractiveness and agreements to 'communicate' were also more likely to occur among couples of similar physical attractiveness, which suggests the matching hypothesis applies more to later stages of the dating process rather than to initial attraction.

## Positive evaluation

- The matching hypothesis is supported by research evidence, for both heterosexual and homosexual relationships, and is applicable for relationships ranging from dating couples to long-term marriages.

KEY CLASSIC STUDY

## 'THE MATCHING HYPOTHESIS OF INTERPERSONAL ATTRACTION'

Murstein (1972)

### Aim
- To assess similarity of physical attractiveness in heterosexual couples.

### Procedure
- Eight judges rated the attractiveness levels from photographs of 99 real couples who were dating or engaged. Each individual was rated separately, with judges not knowing who their partner was. Judges also rated attractiveness levels from photographs of 98 couples formed by random pairings. Individuals additionally rated their own and their partner's levels of attractiveness.

### Results
- Real couples had more similar levels of attractiveness than randomly paired couples.
- Individuals from real couples rated their own and their partner's levels of attractiveness as more similar than individuals in randomly paired couples.

### Conclusions
- Individuals form relationships with partners of similar levels of attractiveness more than with individuals of dissimilar levels of attractiveness.

### Evaluation
- Participants were generally young and not in long-term relationships, creating generalization problems. However, **Price & Vandenberg (1979)** found similar results using married couples aged 28–60, suggesting the results are reliable.
- Participants were generally those of a western cultural background, forming voluntary relationships, which suggests results are not representative of couples from non-western cultural backgrounds forming arranged marriages.

- Although physical beauty is important in attractiveness, those without it can compensate through complex matching, by pairing up with more physically attractive partners by being attractive in other ways, like being rich or domestically skilled.

## ■ Negative evaluation
- According to evolutionary theory, females should be more physically attractive than males, as males value attractiveness more in females than females do in males, which refutes the matching hypothesis.

## ■ Practical application
- Dating agencies match individuals with similar levels of attractiveness as a proven way of pairing individuals into lasting relationships.

## ■ Issues and debates
- Being attracted to people with similar attractiveness may be genetically coded and part of our unconscious biological nature, or it may be learned through socialization processes as a result of nurture.

■ STRENGTHEN YOUR LEARNING

1 Explain the matching hypothesis as an explanation of relationship formation.
2 For Murstein's (1972) study of the matching hypothesis, in your own words, state the aims, procedure, results, conclusions and evaluative points.
3 Summarize what research evidence has suggested about the matching hypothesis.
4 What other evaluative points, including practical applications and relevant issues and debates, can be made about the matching hypothesis?

Expert tip

A useful point to make about the matching hypothesis is that it is more of an explanation of initial attraction than long-term relationship maintenance. The stability of relationships over time is based on a lot more factors than just levels of attractiveness.

# Social exchange theory

Revised

**Social exchange theory** (SET) focuses on the economics of maximizing profits and minimizing costs in maintaining relationships. There is an exchange of rewards like affection and positive experiences, and costs, like freedoms given up and negative experiences. The greater the rewards and the lower the costs, the bigger the profit and therefore the more the desire to maintain the relationship. The greater the level of affection, the more highly rewards are perceived and the lesser costs are regarded.

> **Key term**
>
> **Social exchange theory** – an economic explanation of relationship maintenance based on maximizing profits and minimizing costs.

Rewards are assessed by making two comparisons:

1 The *comparison level* (CL) – rewards are compared against costs to judge profits.

2 The *comparison level for alternative relationships* (CLalt) – rewards and costs are compared against perceived rewards and costs for possible alternative relationships.

Relationships are maintained if rewards exceed costs and profit level is not exceeded by possible alternative relationships.

**Thibaut & Kelley's (1959)** four-stage model of SET sees people developing mutually beneficial patterns of exchanges that assist relationship maintenance.

## Thibaut & Kelley's four-stage model

| Stage | Description |
|---|---|
| *Sampling* | Rewards and costs are assessed in a number of relationships. |
| *Bargaining* | A relationship is 'costed out' and sources of profit and loss are identified. |
| *Commitment* | A relationship is established and maintained by a predictable exchange of rewards. |
| *Institutionalization* | Interactions are established and the couple 'settles down'. |

## Research

■ **Mills & Clark (1980)** found communal couples give rewards out of concern for each other without expecting anything in return, while exchange couples keep mental records of who is 'ahead' and 'behind'. This suggests that SET applies only to some types of relationship.

■ **Rusbult (1983)** found that costs and rewards of relationships were compared against costs and rewards of potential alternative relationships to assess whether relationships should be continued, which implies, in support of SET, that individuals do evaluate relationships by making comparisons.

## Positive evaluation

■ SET applies to 'scorekeepers', who **Murstein *et al.* (1977)** identified, through the exchange orientation tool, as suspicious and insecure individuals, illustrating the validity of the theory for relationships lacking in confidence and trust.

■ SET provided the basis and inspiration for equity theory, which concerns balance and stability in relationships, and is a logical progression from SET.

## Negative evaluation

■ **Sedikides (2005)** argues against SET, as the idea that humans only seek profit is simplistic and inaccurate. Many people are unselfish by doing things for others without expecting anything in return, especially in emotionally close relationships, where they willingly help partners when they are faced with difficulty and stress.

- Research into SET has focused mainly on the initial formation stages of relationships, rather than the more important, long-term maintenance of relationships.

## Practical application

- Relationship counsellors use the idea of profit to help maintain relationships by focusing on rewards rather than costs, especially less noticeable rewards, like emotional security.

## Issues and debates

- SET is *nomothetic* in seeing people as assessing maintenance of relationships by considering rewards and costs. However, **Mills & Clark (1980)** found this is not generalizable to everyone and so is more *idiographic* where individuals' relationships are unique and not representative of others.

> **■ STRENGTHEN YOUR LEARNING**
>
> 1  Outline SET, including reference to comparison levels and Thibaut & Kelley's four-stage model of SET.
>
> 2  Summarize what research evidence has suggested about SET.
>
> 3  What other evaluative points, including practical applications and relevant issues and debates, can be made about SET?

**Expert tip**

SET, equity theory and Rusbult's investment theory are all explanations of relationship maintenance and so can be compared against each other to highlight relative strengths and weaknesses, as a form of evaluation.

# Equity theory

Revised ☐

**Equity theory** (ET) sees dissatisfaction occurring with relationship *inequity* (unfairness), which motivates attempts to attain *equity* (fairness), with maintenance of relationships occurring through achieving balance and stability within relationships.

Definitions of equity differ between relationships, with inequitable relationships occurring where individuals put in more than they receive, or receive more than they put in.

When inequity is not resolved, **dissolution** occurs. However, recognizing inequity gives opportunities for relationships to be saved by making adjustments to return to equity.

Relationships swing between periods of equity and inequity, but if individuals remain motivated to achieving equity, relationships will be maintained. The greater the inequity, the greater the efforts to return to equity, so long as it is perceived as achievable.

**Key terms**

**Equity theory** – an explanation of relationship maintenance based upon a motivation to achieve fairness and balance.

**Dissolution** – the process by which romantic relationships break down.

## ■ Walster *et al.*'s (1978) four principles of equity

| Principle | Description |
|---|---|
| *Profit* | Rewards are maximized and costs minimized. |
| *Distribution* | Trade-offs and compensations are negotiated to achieve fairness in a relationship. |
| *Dissatisfaction* | The greater the degree of perceived unfairness, the greater the sense of dissatisfaction. |
| *Realignment* | If restoring equity is possible, maintenance will continue, with attempts made to realign equity. |

## KEY CONTEMPORARY STUDY

### 'CULTURAL DIFFERENCES IN EQUITY THEORY'

Yum *et al.* (2009)

#### Aim

■ To assess whether equity theory predicts maintenance in relationships in different cultures.

#### Procedure

■ Participants from the USA, Spain, Japan, South Korea, the Czech Republic and China reported levels of equity and maintenance strategies.

#### Results

■ As predicted by ET, maintenance strategies differed. Individuals in equitable relationships engaged in most maintenance strategies, followed by those in over-benefited and under-benefited relationships.

■ Most participants who were equitably treated reported greater use of maintenance strategies than those who reported not being equitably treated.

#### Conclusions

■ As cultural factors had little effect, equity theory explains the maintenance of relationships across cultures.

#### Evaluation

■ There were some variations cross-culturally in the use of maintenance strategies, illustrating that cultural factors do have a little influence.

■ Not all cultures were assessed, limiting the generalizability of the findings.

## Research

■ **Canary & Stafford (1992)** found a correlation between amount of perceived equity and the frequency of maintenance strategies, giving support to ET.

■ **Dainton (2003)** found that individuals in relationships of perceived inequity had low relationship satisfaction, but were motivated to return to equity, implying that equity is important in relationship satisfaction and maintenance.

## Positive evaluation

■ Equity is especially applicable to females, as the main motivation for and efforts towards achieving equity are female-generated.

■ Research supports the central idea of perceived inequity, be it from under-benefiting or over-benefiting, motivating maintenance strategies that seek a return to equity.

## Negative evaluation

■ **Sprecher (1986)** believes close relationships are too complex to permit calculation of rewards and costs involved in establishing and maintaining equity.

■ **Moghaddam *et al.* (1993)** found that US students prefer equity, but European students prefer equality in relationships, suggesting that ET is not culturally universal.

## Practical application

■ Relationship counsellors emphasize that a lack of equity does not mean relationships are doomed, but that adjustments need to be made for equity to be re-established.

## Issues and debates

■ If ET is cross-cultural, it suggests the principles of relationship maintenance are genetically coded from evolution, as maintaining relationships to successfully raise children has a survival value. This suggests equity results from nature rather than nurture.

---

■ **STRENGTHEN YOUR LEARNING**

1   Outline equity theory, including reference to Walster *et al.*'s four principles of equity.

2   For Yum *et al.*'s (2009) study of cultural differences in equity, in your own words, state the aims, procedure, results, conclusions and evaluative points.

3   Summarize what research evidence has suggested about equity theory.

4   What other evaluative points, including practical applications and relevant issues and debates, can be made about equity theory?

**Expert tip**

A common mistake is to see equity theory as concerning equality between partners in a relationship. It doesn't; it concerns balance, fairness and stability between romantic partners.

# Rusbult's investment model of commitment

Revised ☐

**Rusbult's investment model of commitment** (RIMOC) sees relationship satisfaction as dependent upon perceived benefits, costs and the quality of possible alternative relationships, with three important factors: *satisfaction level*, *comparison with alternatives* and *size of investment*.

**Key term**

**Rusbult's investment model of commitment** – an explanation that sees relationship satisfaction as dependent upon a consideration of perceived benefits, costs and the quality of possible alternative relationships.

| Factors | Description |
|---|---|
| *Satisfaction level* | ● Consideration of positive and negative effects of being in a relationship.<br>● Satisfaction determined by how much a partner meets requirements. |
| *Comparison with alternatives* | ● Contrast current relationship with how needs could be met within an alternative relationship.<br>● If needs are met best in current relationship, commitment to that relationship is strong. |
| *Investment size* | ● Level and importance of resources associated with a relationship, both *direct* and *indirect* and how much they would decline if relationship ended.<br>● Investments heighten relationship commitment, as dissolution becomes more costly. |

RIMOC sees two variables associated with commitment:

| Variable | Description |
|---|---|
| *Equity* | ● The degree of balance within a relationship.<br>● Inequity creates lack of relationship satisfaction and less commitment. |
| *Social support* | ● Level of support available from others.<br>● Relationship approval from others increases relationship commitment. |

## ▦ Research

■ **Rusbult *et al.* (1998)** found all three factors of the model in homosexual relationships, suggesting the model has validity in explaining maintenance over a variety of relationships.

■ **Van Lange *et al.* (1997)** found evidence for all three factors of RIMOC in Taiwanese participants and, with **Lin & Rusbult (1995)** obtaining similar results with Dutch participants, it implies the model has cross-cultural validity.

## ▦ Positive evaluation

■ RIMOC appears a better explanation than ET, as its focus on commitment and investments better predicts long-term maintenance.

■ RIMOC explains why individuals stay in abusive relationships, because they have a large investment and commitment to a relationship, with no potential better alternative relationships on offer.

## 'THE INVESTMENT MODEL SCALE: MEASURING COMMITMENT LEVEL, SATISFACTION LEVEL, QUALITY OF ALTERNATIVES AND INVESTMENT SIZE'

### Rusbult, Martz & Agnew (1998)

### Aim

- To assess reliability and validity of the investment model scale (IMS) questionnaire in assessing relationship maintenance.

### Procedure

- The IMS questionnaire was completed by 914 participants in relationships ranging from casual dating to marriage. The questionnaire measured commitment level, satisfaction level, quality of alternatives and investment size. Follow-up interviews were carried out with 136 participants.

### Results

- The higher the relationship satisfaction, the higher the commitment to relationship maintenance.

- The higher the quality of potential alternative relationships, the lower the commitment to relationship maintenance.

- The higher the relationship satisfaction, the higher the level of investment in relationships.

### Conclusions

- All three factors of RIMOC are supported, suggesting the IMS questionnaire is reliable and valid.

### Evaluation

- Gender differences occur, as females report greater relationship satisfaction, lower quality of potential alternative relationships, greater investment and higher commitment than males.

## Negative evaluation

- RIMOC is culture-biased, as its main factors ignore some characteristics of more collectivist cultures, like a high level of involvement with one's extended family.

- There are issues with measuring Rusbult's three factors – for example, how low would commitment to a relationship need to be before dissolution and not maintenance occurred?

## Practical application

- Relationship counsellors ask partners to focus on meeting each other's needs and on the direct and indirect investments they have made in order to increase commitment.

## Issues and debates

- Levels of commitment and investment are higher in females and only factors relevant to western cultures are considered by RIMOC, suggesting it is gender and culture-biased.

### ■ STRENGTHEN YOUR LEARNING

1. Outline Rusbult's investment model of commitment, including reference to satisfaction level, comparison with alternatives, size of investment, equity and social support.

2. For Rusbult, Martz & Agnew's (1998) study of the investment model, in your own words, state the aims, procedure, results, conclusions and evaluative points.

3. Summarize what research evidence has suggested about Rusbult's model.

4. What other evaluative points, including practical applications and relevant issues and debates, can be made about Rusbult's model?

### Expert tip

When writing about Rusbult's model, organize your answer around the different factors and variables associated with relationship satisfaction and commitment. This will demonstrate a high level of understanding and give your answer an effective structure.

# Role of communication in personal relationships

Revised ☐

## Attribution theory

Revised ☐

Humans analyse behaviour to attribute (explain) reasons for it. There are two basic attributions:

1 *Internal attribution* – behaviour occurs because of something personal, like attitude or character.

2 *External attribution* – behaviour occurs due to elements of the situation one is in.

Others' behaviour is analysed by reference to whether they normally act this way and whether there is an intention to the behaviour that reflects that person's personality (internal attribution), or whether an identifiable event motivated the behaviour (external attribution). Attributions are affected by emotional and motivational states, with individuals using attributions to portray themselves positively and others negatively. Intentional behaviour is seen as more informative than unthinking behaviour.

Attribution serves as a type of persuasion and communication, which influences relationship development and maintenance. With negative outcomes, individuals use **egocentric bias** by perceiving their own behaviour as due to external attributions (factors in the external environment), while perceiving their partner's behaviour as due to internal attributions (elements of their personality). This protects self-esteem and controls/punishes the partner.

**Minding the close relationship theory** sees partners in healthy relationships making accurate, positive attributions about each other, with communication acting as a mutual, constant process of seeking and giving self-disclosure. Flexibility in response to new information is important, as is sometimes making negative attributions to stimulate discussion and overcome relationship problems.

Gender differences exist, with women analysing reasons for issues and events more than males, who only indulge in extensive attribution when they perceive relationship problems.

### ■ Research

- **Orvis *et al.* (1976)** researched examples of behaviour for which partners had different explanations, finding for negative outcomes that participants saw themselves as blameless and their partners guilty, with this more so in problematic relationships, though not in tranquil relationships, where negative outcomes were attributed more to the situation than to their partner's personality. This highlights the role of egocentric bias in attribution and how motivational factors are involved in making attributions in relationships.

- **Holtzworth-Monroe (1988)** found that women in violent relationships blamed external factors, with their husbands also giving external attributions for their violence, which suggests that attribution theory can explain the quality of interpersonal relationships.

### ■ Positive evaluation

- As there are gender differences in how and when males and females use attribution processes, it supports the idea that there are also gender differences in how males and females experience relationship breakdown.

### ■ Negative evaluation

- Although egocentric bias may negatively affect relationships by itself, through the assigning of attributions, it could, however, just be highlighting that the relationship already has problems.

---

**Key terms**

**Attribution theory** – an explanation that sees communication within relationships as dependent upon a process by which individuals explain the causes of behaviour and events.

**Egocentric bias** – where individuals perceive their own behaviour as due to external attributions (factors in the external environment), while perceiving their partner's behaviour, as due to elements of their personality.

**Minding the close relationship theory** – the idea that, in healthy relationships, individuals mutually take care to make positive but accurate attributions about their partners.

## ■ Practical application

■ Relationship counsellors teach couples how inappropriate attributions can create and maintain problems in relationships and how creating positive attributions about partners can build trust and admiration for each other.

## ■ Issues and debates

■ Attribution theory is not gender-biased, as it acknowledges differences in how attributions are made between males and females for behaviour within relationships. Individual differences are acknowledged too, as attributions are not seen as being made in an identical fashion by everyone.

---

**■ STRENGTHEN YOUR LEARNING**

1 Outline attribution theory as an explanation for communication within relationships. Make reference in your answer to internal attributions, external attributions, egocentric bias and minding the close relationship theory.

2 Summarize what research evidence has suggested about attribution theory.

3 What other evaluative points, including practical applications and relevant issues and debates, can be made about attribution theory?

---

**Expert tip**

Attribution theory has quite a lot of terminology associated with it, so take care when using these terms to fully explain their meaning in order to demonstrate your understanding of the theory. This will help give you access to a higher level of marks.

# Self-disclosure

Revised ☐

**Self-disclosure** (SD) involves communicating personal information about oneself, which helps build intimacy to develop and maintain relationships. SD is important in **virtual relationships** (VRs), where interpersonal relationships form through social media. SD occurs easily in VRs due to less fear of social embarrassment and, as VRs allow continual interaction, intimate relationships build more quickly than with **face-to-face (FTF) relationships**. SD in VRs is based on meaningful factors, like shared interests, rather than the superficial factors of FTF relationships, like physical attractiveness. Due to the anonymity of VRs, SD concerns the 'true' self rather than a publicly presented 'false' self, with such real intimacies constructing a stronger relationship.

High levels of affection created in VRs through SD are maintained if people physically meet, as false impressions created by physical levels of attractiveness (as in FTF relationships) do not occur. VRs permit more intimate communication due to the lack of *gating*, the limiting factors that influence the formation and maintenance of FTF relationships, like shyness.

VRs can be harmful due to their anonymous nature, with people misrepresenting themselves.

**Key terms**

**Self-disclosure** – the revealing of personal information about oneself to another.

**Virtual relationships** – non-physical interactions between people communicating via social media.

**Face-to-face relationships** – physical interactions between individuals.

## ■ Research

■ **McKenna et al. (2002)** got participants to interact with a partner via an internet chat room or FTF and found paired participants liked each other more meeting via the internet rather than FTF, as communications were more intimate. This suggests that, in FTF interactions, superficial gating features, like level of physical attractiveness, overwhelm other factors that lead to more intimate disclosure and greater attraction.

■ **Peter et al. (2005)** found shy people were attracted to VRs as communicating online compensated for lack of FTF social skills, allowing intimate relationships to develop through SD. As extroverts also self-disclose more in VR, leading them to develop intimate VRs, it highlights how personality is important in shaping the formation of VRs.

## ■ Positive evaluation

■ As gating features are absent from VRs, it creates a bigger group of people to form relationships with than FTF relationships, as VRs form from communications based on common interests rather than being limited by superficial gating features, like level of physical attractiveness.

■ VRs are attractive to people who live remotely, like in rural locations, who may experience difficulties physically meeting individuals with shared interests. Without VRs, they might never find a suitable partner.

## ■ Negative evaluation

■ A negative of SD in VRs is the presentation of an ideal self to a virtual partner, which the person cannot live up to in reality.

■ Social media can create social pressure for individuals to conform to high levels of intimate disclosures they are uncomfortable with. For example, being pressured to send sexts (sexually explicit images of oneself).

## ■ Practical application

■ Encouraging socially inept people to form VRs based on ever-increasing levels of SD has proven an effective means of such people learning communication skills and attaining levels of confidence necessary to form meaningful FTF relationships.

## ■ Issues and debates

■ Research conducted into SD in VRs can be accused of culture bias, as findings tend to be from participants in western cultures, which are then generalized universally.

---

**■ STRENGTHEN YOUR LEARNING**

1 Outline self-disclosure as a factor affecting communication within relationships, including reference to virtual relationships, face-to-face relationships and gating.

2 Summarize what research evidence has suggested about self-disclosure as a factor affecting communication within relationships.

3 What other evaluative points, including practical applications and relevant issues and debates, can be made about self-disclosure as a factor affecting communication within relationships?

---

**Expert tip**

An effective evaluative point to make about virtual relationships is their practical applications, such as helping people who lack social skills or who live in remote areas to form relationships.

---

# Explanations for why relationships change or end

Revised ☐

## Duck's phase model of dissolution

Revised ☐

**Duck (2001)** gave three reasons for **dissolution**, with several other factors contributing to dissolution:

| Reasons for dissolution | Description |
|---|---|
| *Pre-existing doom* | Incompatibility exists from beginning of relationship. |
| *Mechanical failure* | Partners 'grow apart' from each other. |
| *Sudden death* | Traumatic incident, e.g. infidelity leads to instant ending of relationship. |

| Factors contributing to dissolution | Description |
|---|---|
| *Predisposing personal factors* | Personal characteristics that harm a relationship, e.g. emotional instability. |
| *Precipitating factors* | Influences that trigger relationship crises, e.g. mismatched working hours. |
| *Lack of skills* | Deficiency of necessary abilities, e.g. sexual inexperience. |
| *Lack of motivation* | Absence of enthusiasm for contributing to a relationship. |
| *Lack of maintenance* | Failure to sustain relationship, e.g. being absent for long periods. |

Duck sees dissolution as a 'managed process', as partners consider how dissolution will seem to others, in order to present themselves favourably towards possible new relationships. Duck saw this as occurring in four sequential phases:

| Phases of dissolution | Description of phases |
|---|---|
| Intrapsychic | • One partner is privately dissatisfied with the relationship.<br>• Costs of withdrawal are considered. |
| Dyadic | • Dissatisfaction is revealed and discussed.<br>• If dissatisfaction is not resolved, there is a move to the next phase. |
| Social | • Break up is made public.<br>• Negotiation about finances, children, etc. occurs, with family and friends becoming involved. |
| Grave dressing | • Post-relationship view of the break up is created in order to protect self-esteem and move positively towards potential new relationships. |

**Key terms**

**Duck's phase model of dissolution** – an explanation that sees relationship breakdown as occurring through a series of four sequential stages.

**Dissolution** – the process by which relationships break down.

In the *grave-dressing phase*, partners attempt to portray themselves as blameless, and esteem-building activities begin.

**Rollie & Duck (2006)** added *resurrection*: a period of reinvention and preparation for new relationships. They also added the factor of *communication* into the phases, which gave an opportunity to return to more positive times rather than inevitable progression on to the next phase of dissolution.

## Research

- **Hatfield *et al*. (1984)** reported that discontentment makes individuals feel 'under-benefited', which makes them consider their position, supporting the idea of the intrapsychic phase.

- **Tashiro & Frazier (2003)** found dissolution prompted personal growth factors, like feeling wiser and emotionally strong, which aided future relationships and strengthened friendships, supporting the idea of grave dressing, where individuals gradually progress after dissolution.

## Positive evaluation

- Duck's theory has face validity as people recognize the phases of dissolution from their own experiences.

- Perceiving dissolution as a process, rather than an event, is seen as true and applicable to ending friendships, as well as romantic relationships from dating to marriage.

## Negative evaluation

- Duck's theory starts when dissatisfaction has already occurred, so does not fully explain dissolution, as to why dissatisfaction originally occurred.

- The phases are not universal. They do not apply in every relationship breakdown, nor do they always occur in a set order.

## Practical application

- The addition of the resurrection phase allows relationship counsellors to save troubled relationships by identifying which phase partners are in and then providing opportunities for communication, to facilitate a return to more favourable times.

## ■ Issues and debates

■ Duck's model is gender-biased, as it does not acknowledge gender differences in dissolution. For example, women often initiate dissolution due to incompatibility and unhappiness, while men do so due to lack of sex.

---

### ■ STRENGTHEN YOUR LEARNING

1 Outline Duck's
   a three reasons for relationship breakdown,
   b factors that contribute to dissolution.
2 Outline Duck's theory of dissolution, making reference to his four stages of relationship dissolution and resurrection.
3 Summarize what research evidence has suggested about Duck's theory of dissolution.
4 What other evaluative points, including practical applications and relevant issues and debates, can be made about Duck's theory of resolution?

---

**Expert tip**

A common mistake with Duck's theory is for students to confuse factors that contribute to relationship breakdown with his phases of dissolution. Factors concern things that influence breakdown, while phases refer to the stages of dissolution individuals go through.

# Lee's stage theory of relationship breakdown

Revised ☐

Lee analysed data from relationship breakdowns to produce an explanation similar to Duck's, in perceiving dissolution as developing in stages and in being a process that unfolds gradually, rather than being an event happening at a given time.

Lee's theory has five sequential stages:

| Stages of dissolution | Description |
| --- | --- |
| Dissatisfaction | One partner perceives dissatisfaction with the relationship. |
| Exposure | The dissatisfaction is communicated to the other partner. |
| Negotiation | Discussion occurs about the nature of the dissatisfaction. |
| Resolution | Attempts are made to overcome the dissatisfaction. |
| Termination | If the dissatisfaction is not overcome, the relationship ends. |

**Key term**

**Lee's stage theory of relationship breakdown** – an explanation that sees dissolution as occurring through a series of five sequential stages.

## ■ Research

■ **Argyle & Henderson (1984)** found that 'rule violations', like jealousy and publicly criticizing partners, were often responsible for dissolution. As these factors are not included in Lee's theory, it suggests it is incomplete.

■ *Research studies focused on Duck's model that deal similarly with stages of dissolution can also be used to assess the validity of Lee's theory.*

## ■ Positive evaluation

■ Lee's explanation of dissolution is more optimistic than Duck's, as it perceives greater opportunities for dissatisfaction in troubled relationships to be resolved.

■ Lee's theory is supported by his major research study that was targeted specifically at assessing the validity of his theory.

## ■ Negative evaluation

■ Lee's theory is oversimplified, as it cannot account for all types of relationships and the many reasons for dissolution.

## KEY CLASSIC STUDY

### 'INVESTIGATING THE ENDINGS OF RELATIONSHIPS'

#### Lee (1984)

#### Aim

■ To identify the stages of relationship dissolution.

#### Procedure

■ Participants from 112 non-marital, heterosexual romantic relationships completed a survey investigating reasons for the breakdown of their relationships.

#### Findings

■ Five sequential stages were identified: dissatisfaction, exposure, negotiation, resolution and termination.

■ The most distressing and emotionally fatiguing stages were exposure and negotiation.

■ Not all couples experienced all five stages.

■ Participants who went straight from dissatisfaction to termination (i.e. just abandoned the relationship) reported less intimacy with their partner, even when the relationship was satisfactory.

■ Participants who spent longest progressing from dissatisfaction to termination reported more attraction for partners and more loneliness after dissolution.

#### Conclusions

■ Dissolution is a process occurring over time rather than being an event occurring at a specific time.

#### Evaluation

■ Individual differences exist in how people progress through the stages and in which stages they experience.

■ As only student dissolutions were studied, generalizing to long-term relationships, like those involving children and shared resources, is difficult.

■ Lee's theory especially cannot explain why individuals, like those in relationships where they are being abused, do not express dissatisfaction, but just terminate the relationship without warning.

### ■ Practical application

■ Within the exposure, negotiation and resolution stages of dissolution, relationship counsellors try and re-establish affection, trust and equity, in order to restore harmony between individuals.

### ■ Issues and debates

■ Lee's theory is culturally biased, as it is based on western cultural ideals, where relationships are generally voluntary and between two individuals, with cultural acceptance of dissolution. It does not apply to collectivist cultures that favour arranged marriages where whole families are involved and where dissolution is often not an option.

---

#### ■ STRENGTHEN YOUR LEARNING

1 Outline Lee's theory of relationship breakdown, including reference to his five sequential stages.

2 For Lee's (1984) study of relationship dissolution, in your own words, state the aims, procedure, results, conclusions and evaluative points.

3 Summarize what research evidence has suggested about Lee's theory of relationship breakdown.

4 What other evaluative points, including practical applications and relevant issues and debates, can be made about Lee's theory of relationship breakdown?

---

#### Expert tip

When outlining Lee's theory, refer closely to his 1984 study, as it was the basis from which the explanation was formed.

# Social responsibility

Revised ☐

## Bystanderism

Revised ☐

**Bystanders** are people who witness events without intervening or offering assistance.

### ■ Reasons for bystanderism

#### ■ Number of witnesses

The more witnesses, the less likely others will intervene. Three reasons are given for this:

1 *Diffusion of responsibility* – the belief that the more witnesses there are, the more likely someone else will help. Each bystander, therefore, does not feel pressure to intervene.

2 *Pluralistic ignorance* – the belief that, if others are not helping, the situation cannot be an emergency and so help is not needed.

3 *Evaluation apprehension* – the belief that, if an individual intervenes, their actions will be rated by others, creating a reluctance to help.

#### ■ Type of emergency

If a situation is perceived as an emergency, even at a risk to personal safety, bystanders feel obliged to help.

#### ■ Emotional arousal

The **arousal: cost–reward model** sees bystanders feeling obliged to intervene as dependent on whether intervening is seen as lowering the emotional arousal caused by an event. To assess this, a cost–reward analysis is undertaken, where the costs of helping, like risk of harm etc., are compared with the costs of not helping, like criticism from others etc.

#### ■ Cognitive appraisals

**Darley & Latane's (1970) five-stage model of bystander behaviour** believes individuals make several rapid appraisals in deciding whether to help. At each stage, a positive appraisal moves an individual on to the next stage. If all appraisals are positive, help is given, but if any appraisal is negative, no help is given. The model sees individuals making logical decisions about situations, and not just acting from instinct or emotion:

| Stage | Description |
|---|---|
| *Stage one* | Attention is directed to the situation. |
| *Stage two* | Assess whether the situation is an emergency. |
| *Stage three* | Personal responsibility is assumed for dealing with the situation. |
| *Stage four* | Assess whether the individual has the necessary skills to help, e.g. medical skills. |
| *Stage five* | Action to help is given. |

#### ■ Social identity

An individual's *social identity* (the perception of which groups they belong to) affects chances of bystander intervention. If someone in need is perceived as a member of an in-group (belongs to an individual's social group), help is more likely to be given than if they are seen as a member of an out-group (they do not belong to an individual's social group).

**Key terms**

**Bystanderism** – the effects of bystanders upon the likelihood of an individual intervening in a situation.

**Bystanders** – people who witness events without intervening or offering assistance.

**Arousal: cost–reward model** – an explanation of bystanderism that sees the chances of intervention as being dependent upon whether such intervention would reduce the emotional arousal caused by the situation.

**Cognitive appraisals** – an individual's interpretations of an emotional situation in terms of how it will affect them.

**Darley & Latane's five-stage model of bystander behaviour** – an explanation of bystanderism that sees individuals as making a series of cognitive appraisals as whether or not to intervene in a situation.

## KEY CLASSIC STUDY

## 'BYSTANDER INTERVENTION IN EMERGENCIES: DIFFUSION OF RESPONSIBILITY'

### Darley & Latane (1968)

### Aim

- To assess the effect of the number of witnesses to an event on whether individuals would intervene.

### Procedure

- Participants believed they were taking part in an intercom discussion with either one other, two other or five other individuals.
- An emergency is created by a pseudo-participant asking for assistance over the intercom, by claiming they are having an epileptic fit.
- Measurements were taken of a) the percentage of participants in each condition who intervened within four minutes, and b) how long it took participants to intervene.

### Results

- *One-to-one intercom discussion*: 100 per cent of participants intervened, with an average time for intervention of 52 seconds.
- *One-to-two intercom discussion*: 85 per cent of participants intervened, with an average time for intervention of two minutes.
- *One-to-five intercom discussion*: 62 per cent of participants intervened, with an average time for intervention of nearly three minutes.

### Conclusions

- As the number of people in a group increases, the chances of an individual intervening in an emergency decreases, due to *diffusion of responsibility*, where individuals feel less personal responsibility for taking action.

### Evaluation

- Evaluation apprehension could explain why intervention does not occur, as an individual fears being rated by others if they do. The bigger the group, the greater the evaluation apprehension, so the less chance of intervention.
- The use of pseudo-participants, deceit (claiming to have an epileptic fit) and creating distress are unethical.
- The findings lack ecological validity. In real-life situations, attention might be distracted elsewhere, causing the situation to not be seen as an emergency, lowering the chances of intervention.

## Research

- **Piliavin *et al*. (1969)** found that if a confederate, pretending to be partially sighted, collapsed on a train, nearly everyone gave help rapidly, while if he pretended to be drunk and collapsed, only 50 per cent helped and less rapidly. As the numbers of passengers had no effect on helping behaviour, the findings do not support *diffusion of responsibility*, but instead the *cost–reward model*, because the cost of helping someone partially sighted is low (little chance of them being violent) and the cost of not helping would be high (negative opinions of others), while the cost of helping a drunk is high (high chance of them being violent) and the cost of not helping is low (little chance of negative opinions from others).

- **Darley & Latane (1969)** found 75 per cent of participants alone in a room filling with smoke reported the incident, but only 10 per cent did so when two pseudo-participants were present who ignored the smoke. This supports *pluralistic ignorance*, where if others do not react to an incident it is not seen as an emergency and so bystander intervention does not occur.

## Positive evaluation

- Research has identified the role that specific factors play in determining the extent of helping behaviour, like pluralistic ignorance, social identity and cost–reward assessments, leading to a greater understanding of the phenomenon.

- Research into bystander intervention has led to effective practical applications that promote helping behaviours, such as by getting people to take personal responsibility for the welfare of others in possible distress.

## ◼ Negative evaluation

- Research tries to find single reasons for bystander behaviour, when in real life, several factors may determine the level of helping behaviour.

- Darley and Latane's five-stage model is unrealistic, as people do not systematically work through a series of appraisals, but instead act unthinkingly and immediately.

## ◼ Practical application

- In Germany, it is illegal to not intervene when a person needs medical assistance, with several successful prosecutions. It is hoped to create a 'social norm' of helping behaviour that people will automatically conform to.

## ◼ Issues and debates

- Much bystander research would not occur now due to ethical considerations. The presence of confederates means that deceit was used, which means informed consent could not be gained. High levels of distress were also common.

> ◼ **STRENGTHEN YOUR LEARNING**
>
> 1 What are bystanders?
> 2 Outline reasons for bystanderism in terms of:
>    a number of witnesses,
>    b type of emergency,
>    c emotional arousal,
>    d cognitive appraisals (including reference to Darley & Latane's five-stage model of bystander behaviour),
>    e social identity.
> 3 For Darley & Latane's (1968) study of bystander intervention, in your own words, state the aims, procedure, results, conclusions and evaluative points.
> 4 Summarize what research evidence has suggested about bystanderism.
> 5 What other evaluative points, including practical applications and relevant issues and debates, can be made about bystanderism?

> **Expert tip**
>
> When revising the reasons for bystanderism, make sure you have a research study that illustrates each reason. For example, **Darley & Latane's (1968)** study highlights diffusion of responsibility, while **Darley & Latane's (1969)** study highlights pluralistic ignorance.

# Prosocial behaviour

Revised ☐

**Prosocial behaviour** concerns voluntary behaviour intended to help others, motivated by concern for the welfare of others, due to feelings of empathy (sharing feelings).

Altruism concerns unselfish prosocial behaviour, where behaviour is performed at a cost to oneself in order to benefit another.

## ◼ Hamilton's kin selection theory (1964)

Kin selection is an evolutionary explanation that considers the effect of behaviour on an individual's survival chances (*direct fitness*) and those of relatives (*indirect fitness*), as individuals share genetic material with relatives. Performing actions at a cost to oneself, but that benefit one's relatives, increases the possibility of their survival and reproduction chances and thus the chances of one's genes, which are shared with that individual's relatives, being passed on and becoming more widespread in a population.

The closer the genetic relationship between an individual and others, and the more that relatives will benefit from an individual's altruistic behaviour, the greater the risks an individual will make to benefit those others, as the reward in terms of shared genes will be greater.

> **Key terms**
>
> **Prosocial behaviour** – actions that are intended to benefit others.
>
> **Hamilton's kin selection theory** – an explanation that sees helping behaviour as directed at increasing the reproductive chances of genetically related individuals.

## Research

- **Smith (2007)** found that, when sea rocket plants had to share a pot, genetically unrelated plants competed for soil nutrients by sprouting aggressive root growth, but this did not happen between genetically related plants. This suggests that, as kin selection occurs in varied life forms, it is evolutionary.

- **Madsen *et al.* (2007)** found, using British and Zulu participants, that the greater the level of genetic relatedness between two individuals, then the greater length of time one individual would hold a painful body position in order for the other individual to receive food or money, thus supporting kin selection theory that prosocial behaviour is based upon genetic relatedness.

- **Whiting & Whiting (1975)** found differences in levels of helping behaviour between children of six different cultures, from 100 per cent in Kenyan children down to 8 per cent in American children, which suggests prosocial behaviour is learned, not innate, refuting kin selection theory.

## Positive evaluation

- The fact that examples of kin selection are found among animal and plant species supports the validity of the theory as having an evolutionary basis.

- The theory has face validity from observing everyday behaviour – for example, individuals leave sums of money to relatives in their will that reflect how closely related they are.

## Negative evaluation

- Calculations would be involved to decide which related individuals to sacrifice oneself for; for instance, for three children (as they collectively contain 150 per cent of one's genes) but not one child and two cousins (as they only collectively contain 75 per cent of an individual's genes). In dangerous situations, sacrificial reactions would be instantaneous and could not involve such calculations.

- Many human relationships do not involve genetic relatedness, like that between adoptive parents and adopted children, so kin selection cannot explain acts of sacrifice between such persons.

## Practical application

- Related individuals could be put into the same army units, as they would be more inclined to sacrificial behaviour for each other than non-related individuals, giving such armies an advantage. This policy was adopted by the USA in the Second World War.

## Issues and debates

- Kin selection theory is deterministic, as it sees helping behaviour as an unconscious, innate response programmed genetically into individuals through evolution, with no role for free will.

---

### ■ STRENGTHEN YOUR LEARNING

1 What is prosocial behaviour?
2 Outline Hamilton's kin selection theory, including reference to direct fitness and indirect fitness.
3 Summarize what research evidence has suggested about kin selection theory.
4 What other evaluative points, including practical applications and relevant issues and debates, can be made about kin selection theory?

---

**Expert tip**

Hamilton's kin selection theory is an evolutionary explanation of prosocial behaviour, so in order to highlight this, explain what the adaptive survival value of prosocial behaviour is in terms of direct and indirect fitness.

## ■ Batson's empathy–altruism theory (1987)

Individuals help others, despite personal cost, if *empathy* occurs through *perspective taking*. If empathy is not felt, helping only occurs if benefits of behaviour outweigh costs.

When people need help, two types of emotional reaction occur:

1 *Personal distress* – feelings of concern for others motivate *egoistic* helping to reduce one's own feelings of discomfort.

2 *Empathetic concern* – feelings of sympathy motivate altruistic helping to reduce others' discomfort.

> **Key term**
>
> **Batson's empathy–altruism theory** – an explanation that sees helping behaviour as motivated by unselfish concern for the needs of others.

---

### KEY CLASSIC STUDY

### 'IS EMPATHIC EMOTION A SOURCE OF ALTRUISTIC MOTIVATION?'

**Batson *et al.* (1981)**

#### Aim

■ To assess whether empathy would lead to altruistic, rather than egoistic, motivation to help someone in distress.

#### Procedure

■ Forty-four female participants filled in a questionnaire measuring attitudes etc. and witness Elaine, a fellow student, receive electric shocks (and believe it was only by random choice that they were not receiving the shocks). Elaine explains that she fears electric shocks, having received them before.

■ Participants can receive the remaining shocks, rather than Elaine. If they do not, they have to watch her get shocked (*difficult escape condition*) or they can leave and not see her get shocked (*easy escape condition*).

■ Participants see Elaine's questionnaire responses, which are similar to theirs (*similar victim condition*) or dissimilar (*dissimilar victim condition*).

■ Whether participants would swap was recorded, as well as the number of shocks they would take.

#### Results

■ When Elaine has similar attitudes etc., 91 per cent in the easy escape condition would swap with her and 82 per cent in the difficult escape condition.

■ When Elaine has dissimilar attitudes etc., 18 per cent in the easy escape condition would swap with her and 64 per cent in the difficult escape condition.

#### Conclusions

■ Empathy leads to altruistic, not egoistic helping, as people with high empathy help just as much when escape is easy as they do when it is difficult, but people with low empathy help more when escape is difficult than they do when it is easy.

#### Evaluation

■ The findings lack ecological validity, as the situation was not true to life.

■ The study was unethical as deceit and harmful distress occurred.

---

## ■ Research

■ **Batson *et al.* (1981),** in a second study, found when empathy was high, people help regardless of it being difficult to escape, while when empathy was low, people only help when it is difficult to escape without helping.

■ **Singer *et al.* (2013)** found the right supramarginal brain area was involved in experiencing empathy, suggesting empathy has a biological component. Only those with naturally high empathy were capable of unselfish altruistic behaviour.

## ■ Positive evaluation

■ Empathy–altruism has research support, allowing predictions to be made about circumstances necessary for empathy–altruism to occur.

## ▨ Negative evaluation

- It is not known whether altruistic behaviour is motivated by empathy for others or by the desire to escape from one's own negative emotions.

- Although there is research support for empathy–altruism, Batson himself admits such behaviour is rare.

## ▨ Practical application

- Prosocial behaviour is promoted by providing opportunities to develop empathy, especially in instances of others being in distress.

## ▨ Issues and debates

- Empathy results from an interaction of nature and nurture rather than being determined solely by one of them.

---

**▨ STRENGTHEN YOUR LEARNING**

1 Outline Batson's empathy–altruism theory, including reference to personal distress and empathetic concern.

2 For Batson *et al.*'s (1981) study of empathy–altruism, in your own words, state the aims, procedure, results, conclusions and evaluative points.

3 Summarize what research evidence has suggested about empathy–altruism theory.

4 What other evaluative points, including practical applications and relevant issues and debates, can be made about empathy–altruism theory?

---

## ▨ Promoting prosocial behaviour

Being prosocial is associated with high levels of social competence, doing well academically and reducing anti-social behaviour. Several factors help develop prosocial behaviour:

1 **Perspective taking** – empathetic individuals develop more prosocial behaviours, through concern for others.

2 **Prosocial moral reasoning** – individuals basing behaviour on belief systems centred on the welfare of others more easily develop prosocial behaviours from concern for others.

3 **High self-esteem** – competent individuals with high self-worth interact effectively with others and so develop prosocial behaviour.

4 **Emotional well-being** – individuals with good mental health function effectively and so develop prosocial behaviours.

5 **Attributional style** – responsible individuals believe they influence events through personal efforts (internal attribution) and perceive events more positively than people who believe they cannot influence events (external attribution), and so develop more prosocial behaviours.

### ▨ Schools

Schools develop prosocial behaviour directly through educational programmes and indirectly through peer interactions that develop necessary social and cognitive skills. Prosocial behaviour is promoted through lessons providing cooperative learning activities that develop perspective taking, empathy and prosocial moral reasoning.

### ▨ Parenting styles

'Positive' parenting styles help develop prosocial behaviours in young children, but even more so in adolescents. Important factors are developing secure attachment patterns with parents in early childhood and using balanced positive discipline to develop a conscience focused on compassion for others.

---

**Expert tip**

A common mistake when detailing Batson's empathy–altruism theory is to over-describe **Batson et al.'s (1981)** 'Elaine' study. Only details that illustrate the explanation and the level to which the theory is supported should be referred to. It will, therefore, not be necessary to outline all of the procedure of the study.

---

**Key terms**

**Perspective taking** – individuals who can perceive the viewpoints of others are seen as more able to develop prosocial behaviours.

**Prosocial moral behaviour** – individuals whose actions are based on belief systems centred on the welfare of others are seen as more able to develop prosocial behaviours.

**High self-esteem** – those with elevated levels of self-worth are seen as more able to develop prosocial behaviours.

**Emotional well-being** – individuals with positive mental health are seen as more able to develop prosocial behaviours.

**Attributional style** – individuals who believe they influence events through personal effort are seen as more able to develop prosocial behaviours.

'Authoritarian' parenting incurs negative outcomes, through instilling fear and shame in children, associated with increased anti-social behaviour. Authoritarian parenting also weakens trust between parents and children, harming the attachment bond.

## Research

- **Spivak & Dulak (2015)** found schools that used cooperative learning, provided opportunities for prosocial learning and role models, demonstrated prosocial behaviours and emphasized caring relationships with teachers and peers developed higher levels of prosocial behaviour. This suggest prosocial behaviour is nurtured through education.

- **Knafo-Noam et al. (2015)** found high levels of prosocial behaviour among adolescents whose parents demonstrated prosocial behaviour and gave their children opportunities to develop prosocial behaviour. Positive parenting styles and balanced positive discipline were also important, supporting the importance of parenting upon prosocial behaviour.

## Positive evaluation

- Promoting prosocial behaviour within schools reduces the time and cost of dealing with maladaptive behaviours, as such behaviours are much reduced.

- Giving students even short programmes of lessons to increase mindfulness (empathy) and prosocial behaviour is effective, although more long-term benefits are gained when such lessons are a regular part of students' timetables.

## Negative evaluation

- Prosocial programmes are rare, as they are costly and difficult to place within crowded timetables. More traditional subjects, like mathematics, often receive more resources.

- Twin studies indicate that prosocial behaviour has a genetic component, which suggests there is a limit to the effect that parenting and schooling can have on its development.

## Practical application

- The effectiveness of teaching programmes and parenting styles for promoting prosocial behaviour has led to their wider acceptance and usage.

## Issues and debates

- Research into prosocial behaviour programmes has not assessed whether gender and cultural differences exist in their effectiveness.

---

**■ STRENGTHEN YOUR LEARNING**

1 Explain why prosocial behaviour is advantageous.
2 Outline factors that help develop prosocial behaviour.
3 Explain how prosocial behaviour can be promoted by:
   a   schools,
   b   parenting styles.
4 Summarize what research evidence has suggested about promoting prosocial behaviour.
5 What other evaluative points, including practical applications and relevant issues and debates, can be made about promoting prosocial behaviour?

---

**Expert tip**

The topic of promoting prosocial behaviour contains quite a lot of psychological terminology, such as prosocial moral reasoning etc. Be sure when using these terms to fully explain them in order to demonstrate your understanding of them. This will help give you access to a higher level of marks.

# Group dynamics

## Cooperation and competition

**Cooperation** and **competition** are separate and opposite factors, performing contributory influences on each other in producing behaviour. For example, team members cooperate to win games, but compete against each other to be the best player. Cooperation would not be a powerful force without the pressure of competition that motivates individuals to cooperate.

### ■ The theory of cooperation and competition: Deutsch (1949)

Deutsch proposed that the degree to which group members see goals as shared affects how goals are pursued and their chances of success. Cooperation leads to group processes that produce better outcomes than if individuals individually compete against each other, with cooperation producing positive effects like effective communication, helpfulness, coordination of effort, respect, agreement and empathy. Competition produces negative effects like poor communication, obstructiveness, disagreement and conflict. Thus cooperation is superior in producing better outcomes and a more caring society.

Deutsch saw cooperative and competitive goals as interdependent and actions taken towards goals as either *effective* (ones that increase the chances of individuals achieving goals) or *bungling* (ones that decrease individuals' chances of achieving goals), with these actions affected by:

- *substitutability* – how much a person's actions meet the intentions of another

- *cathexis* – how effectively an individual can evaluate themselves and their environment

- *inducibility* – how ready an individual is to accept the influence of another.

Deutsch's **Crude Law of Social Relations** states that being cooperative leads to individuals cooperating again in the future, while being competitive leads to more competition. So the effects of cooperation, like creating more helpfulness and trust, and the effects of competition, like poorer communication and increased suspicion of others, are factors that lead to people originally being cooperative and competitive. This is a *self-reinforcing feedback loop*, where the effects of something heighten the chances of it recurring repetitively.

### ■ Research

- **Johnson & Johnson (1989)** found that cooperation produced greater group productivity, more favourable interpersonal relations, better psychological health and higher self-esteem than competition. Cooperation also created more constructive resolution of conflicts, demonstrating the superiority of cooperation over competition in producing a better functioning society.

- **Aronson *et al.* (1978)** found students using cooperative techniques had increased self-esteem, motivation, interpersonal attraction and empathy, and improved academic performance, especially among ethnic minority students, compared to those using competitive techniques, which supports Deutsch's theory that cooperation produces better outcomes than competition.

### ■ Positive evaluation

- Deutsch's theory led to research into cooperation and competition and an understanding of how they interact. Subsequent theories, like game theory, originate from Deutsch's theory.

- As Deutsch's theory led to applications in a wide range of real-life settings, it can be considered valid.

> **Key terms**
>
> **Cooperation** – when two or more people work together towards the same end.
>
> **Competition** – when two or more individuals struggle against each other for a goal that cannot be shared.
>
> **Theory of cooperation and competition** – an explanation that sees the degree to which group members perceive their goals as being shared as affecting the manner in which those goals are pursued and their chances of success.
>
> **Crude Law of Social Relations** – the idea that cooperation leads individuals to being cooperative again in the future, while being competitive leads to more competitive behaviour in the future.

### Negative evaluation

- Deutsch's theory lacks ecological validity, as much research was laboratory-based and not applicable to real-world situations.

### Practical application

- Deutsch's theory produced strategies that successfully resolved conflicts through the use of cooperative rather than competitive techniques in schools, industry, business and in military and sporting settings.

### Issues and debates

- The theory is nomothetic in seeing cooperative and competitive techniques as affecting people similarly, but there are important individual differences in how cooperation affects people, so it is more idiographic.

---

**■ STRENGTHEN YOUR LEARNING**

1 Explain the relationship of cooperation and competition to each other.
2 Outline Deutsch's theory of cooperation and competition, including substitutability, cathexis, inducibility, Crude Law of Social Relations and self-reinforcing feedback loop.
3 Summarize what research evidence has suggested about cooperation and competition.
4 What other evaluative points, including practical applications and relevant issues and debates, can be made about cooperation and competition?

---

**Expert tip**

Rather than seeing cooperation and competition as separate concepts, they should be viewed as opposite ends of a continuum. This is backed up by the fact that they often have a contributory effect upon each other in producing behaviour.

---

# Evolution and cooperation

*Revised* ☐

Cooperation can be seen as evolutionary through **kin selection**, as cooperatively working with genetically related others boosts the survival and reproduction chances of our own genes, which we share with them.

Cooperation is also evolutionary as group members work better together in competing against other groups for limited resources, like in warfare, where a cooperative body of warriors competes against another cooperative body of warriors to gain territory, resources, etc. The resources cannot be won by one individual, so working together and sharing resources won is the best method of securing some resources. Group members are often related, which again has an evolutionary survival value, in line with kin selection theory.

Humans have also evolved ways of detecting shirkers and cheaters, group members who do not contribute fully, or try to gain resources at the expense of other group members. This led to social punishments to deter such behaviour, like members being excluded from the benefits of group membership.

### Research

- **Boyd & Richerson (2009)** reported that cultural differences between groups led to competition and to natural selection favouring behaviours that increase competitive ability. Within cultural groups, natural selection favoured genes that increased cooperative behaviours, as such behaviour increased reproductive success. This suggests that competitive and cooperative behaviour co-evolved, with both having a complementary influence upon each other.

- **Binmore (2007)** highlighted a problem with cooperative behaviour, known as *by-product benefit*, where 'free-riders' (those who do not contribute to cooperative behaviour, but share in the rewards) take advantage of the fact that cooperation, like when hunting, produces greater rewards than just competitively hunting on your own. **Gardner et al. (2009)** showed how this problem is dealt with by *enforcement*, where free-riders are punished for not being cooperative, by not having resources shared with them or being excluded from the group, and through *reciprocal cooperation*, where individuals cooperate only with those who have previously cooperated fully.

---

**Key terms**

**Evolution and cooperation** – the explanation of cooperation by reference to its adaptive survival value.

**Kin selection** – working cooperatively with genetically related others.

## Positive evaluation

■ Evolution explains how cooperation and competition interact to heighten reproductive success and how such behaviours arose in the first place.

■ Evolutionary theory is supported by the fact that a wide range of cooperative and competitive behaviours in animals and humans are seen in a wide range of situations.

## Negative evaluation

■ As cooperative and competitive skills can be taught, it suggests that they are not as biologically determined as evolutionary theory suggests.

■ Much research into evolutionary explanations of cooperation and competition are animal-based, presenting problems of generalization of findings to humans. Human cooperative and competitive behaviour often involves higher-order cognitive processing, which animal behaviour does not.

## Practical application

■ Getting individuals who are socially punished for non-cooperative behaviour within a group to understand that their behaviour may have a biological origin can help them to then over ride such temptations to not contribute to group activities.

## Issues and debates

■ Evolutionary theory suggests that cooperative and competitive behaviour is biologically determined. However, humans can also use their higher-level cognitive processing to exert free will over their actions.

---

■ **STRENGTHEN YOUR LEARNING**

1 Explain the different ways in which cooperation can be seen as evolutionary.

2 Summarize what research evidence has suggested about the evolutionary nature of cooperation and competition.

3 What other evaluative points, including practical applications and relevant issues and debates, can be made about the evolutionary nature of cooperation and competition?

---

### Expert tip

When writing about evolution and cooperation through kin selection, reference can be made to Hamilton's kin selection theory of prosocial behaviour (see page 194), as there are relevant overlaps.

# Game theory

Revised ☐

**Game theory** explains how people interact cooperatively and competitively to achieve goals. Game theory has two aspects:

■ *cooperative game theory* – how individuals cooperate in groups in competition against other groups to achieve goals

■ *non-cooperative game theory* – how individuals interact to achieve personal goals.

The **prisoner's dilemma** assesses the influence of cooperation and competition upon behaviour. Each player is accused of a crime and, if neither confesses, each gets a one-year sentence, while if both confess, each gets a 40-year sentence. If one confesses, that player gets a three-month sentence, while the other gets a 20-year sentence. From this and similar games, it was found that competition is favoured in some situations and cooperation in others, with important factors being the level of communication between individuals, size of groups and the level of reciprocal behaviour.

Personality is also important, with some people always competing, some always cooperating and some being conformist by mirroring others' behaviour, like cooperating initially, but then competing if others do.

### Key terms

**Game theory** – an explanation of social behaviour that focuses on how individuals interact cooperatively and competitively in the pursuit of goals.

**Prisoner's dilemma** – a game played between individuals that is designed to identify the important factors in determining whether behaviour is cooperative or competitive.

Game theory highlights that individuals do not always maximize gaining rewards, indicating human social behaviour is not always logical.

## Research

- **Davis (1997)** found with the prisoner's dilemma that, although there is a good payoff if players cooperate and do not confess (only getting one year each), players generally compete by confessing and hoping the other one does not, in the expectation of only getting three months. This demonstrates that people compete in some situations where cooperating would be more profitable.

- **Wichman (1970)** found that, if players in the prisoner's dilemma cannot communicate with each other, 40 per cent of responses were cooperative, increasing to 70 per cent when they could communicate, illustrating the role communication plays in cooperative and competitive behaviour.

- **Deutsch & Krauss (1960)** got two participants to play a game delivering goods quickly either along a longer route or a shorter one-lane route, with players having to cooperate to use the shorter route by taking turns, or compete by shutting a gate to stop the other player using that route. Although being cooperative is most profitable, players generally compete and shut the gate, demonstrating how sometimes, even when it is inferior, people compete rather than cooperate.

## Positive evaluation

- Games like the prisoner's dilemma have provided a paradigm method (an accepted means of studying a phenomenon) that has proven valuable in understanding the relationship between cooperation and competition.

- Game theory research suggests cultural factors play a role in determining if behaviour is cooperative or competitive. **Werner (1979)** found that Americans generally learn during childhood to be competitive.

## Negative evaluation

- Game theory research lacks ecological validity through playing artificial games that do not reflect real-life situations.

- Game theory is simplistic in not considering that behaving cooperatively or competitively depends on a complex interaction of external and internal factors.

## Practical application

- Games like the prisoner's dilemma tutor individuals how to behave cooperatively and competitively in order to attain goals.

## Issues and debates

- As research into game theory shows cultural differences exist in how much people behave cooperatively and competitively, it suggests such behaviour results from nurture not nature.

---

**■ STRENGTHEN YOUR LEARNING**

1  Outline game theory; include reference to cooperative game theory, non-cooperative game theory and the prisoner's dilemma.

2  Summarize what research evidence has suggested about game theory.

3  What other evaluative points, including practical applications and relevant issues and debates, can be made about game theory?

---

**Expert tip**

Explaining the rationale behind the prisoner's dilemma and other similar games (how they assess the influence of cooperation and competition upon behaviour) would be a legitimate means of gaining marks for description in questions about game theory.

# Cohesion

Effective groups have **cohesion** (work together well), with cohesion affecting leadership, inter-group relationships and role definition.

Group cohesion can affect or cause cooperation between group members, and works in two ways:

- the total sum of forces binding a group together
- resistance by the group to disruptive forces.

Cohesion does not guarantee cooperative group success. Often effective group performance creates greater cohesion.

There is a difference between:

- *task cohesion* – how well cooperative groups work as units to achieve goals
- *social cohesion* – how well group members like each other and identify with the group.

Successful performance relies more on task cohesion, with the relation between cohesion and performance dependent on the type of group structure involved. Group structure can be:

- *co-active* – members perform identical tasks at different times and do not require others to be successful for them to be successful, e.g. batting at cricket
- *interactive* – members perform different tasks simultaneously in situations requiring high collective work effort, e.g. hockey.

Interactive groups are more successful with high cohesion, with high cohesion more important than individuals' skill levels.

Co-active groups can be successful with low social cohesion, as rivalries and competitive behaviour between members are motivational, inspiring individuals to better performances.

The more group members are dependent on each other and the more group performance depends on cooperative action, the greater the role for cohesion.

Cohesion can negatively affect performance, as in small groups high cohesion prevents individuals expressing individuality. High group cohesion also leads to individuals performing to similar standards, minimizing healthy competition within a group.

Overall, cohesive cooperative groups are successful, as they possess strong group identity and stay together longer, allowing development of skills and strategies and resistance to adversity. Therefore, establishing and maintaining cohesion is desirable.

> **Key term**
>
> **Cohesion** – the degree of unity between members of a social group.

## ▓ Research

- **Mullen & Copper (1994)** found the relationship between cohesion and performance was due to task commitment rather than interpersonal attraction or group pride, suggesting task (not social) cohesion is crucial for performance.
- **Rovio *et al.* (2009)** found that high cohesion in ice hockey teams led to impaired performances, due to pressures for individuals to perform similarly and conform to group norms, illustrating how high cohesion can negatively affect performance.

## ▓ Positive evaluation

- Much group cohesion research occurs in real-life situations, like studies performed on competitive sports teams, so findings have high ecological validity.

## ■ Negative evaluation

■ Cohesion is difficult to assess, as situations differ in terms of levels of team cohesion. Additionally, cohesiveness is unstable, and adjustments are needed to address changes in cohesion, like through alterations in group members, group goals, etc.

## ■ Practical application

■ Cohesion is measured through sociograms: diagrams showing interpersonal relationships between group members. These highlight less-preferred group members and cliques, providing opportunities for harmful cliques to be broken up and 'outsiders' to be included more effectively into a group.

## ■ Issues and debates

■ Cohesion research may be gender-biased, as few studies have assessed whether cohesion affects males and females differently. Females have a higher need to agree and cooperate, suggesting such differences may exist.

---

### ■ STRENGTHEN YOUR LEARNING

1 What is meant by cohesion?

2 Explain the two ways in which group cohesion can affect or cause cooperation between group members.

3 Explain how group structure can be:

 a co-active,

 b interactive.

4 Outline the effects of cohesion on performance.

5 Explain the difference between task and social cohesion.

6 Summarize what research evidence has suggested about the relationship between cohesion and performance.

7 What other evaluative points, including practical applications and relevant issues and debates, can be made about cohesion and performance?

---

**Expert tip**

When writing about cohesion, care should be taken to separate social cohesion from task cohesion, as they exert very different effects on behaviour, with task cohesion generally linked more to successful group performance.

---

# Social loafing

Revised ☐

The greater the size of a group, the less effort that is put in by individual members. For instance, if one person pulls on a rope, they put in 100 per cent effort, but if two people pull they put in 93 per cent average individual effort, while eight people put in just 49 per cent individual effort.

**Social loafing** involves cohesion via **diffusion of responsibility**, where decreased effort occurs due to the lack of identifiability of individual efforts. This can be overcome by setting group members identifiable individual roles, monitoring individual performances and giving individual feedback to reinforce good practice. If individual members are more identifiable, a group situation provides a social incentive, through group cohesion, to perform better. Creating individual roles also helps prevent group cohesion lowering performance due to a loss of individuality within the group and the loss of healthy competition between group members.

**Key terms**

**Social loafing** – the phenomenon of people exerting less individual effort in a group than when on their own.

**Diffusion of responsibility** – a phenomenon whereby individuals are less likely to take responsibility for a situation when others are present.

## ■ Research

■ **Ingram et al. (1974)** asked blindfolded participants to pull on a rope in the belief that other people were also pulling. As the perceived size of the group increased, individual effort decreased, in line with **Ringelman's (1913)** idea of social loafing.

■ **Gross (1982)** found that sports players who received feedback about individual performances performed better than those who did not, demonstrating how the negative effects of social loafing can be reduced in cooperative groups.

## Positive evaluation

■ The phenomenon of social loafing is supported by the analysis of results from sporting competitions. For example, Olympic coxed fours rowing teams are only 13 per cent faster than coxed pairs and coxed eights are only 23 per cent faster than coxed pairs.

## Negative evaluation

■ Other factors contribute to social loafing, as well as cohesion, like loss of control, distraction of the group, etc. Therefore, the effect is not just due to a lack of cohesion.

## Practical application

■ Sports coaches, business managers, etc. address social loafing by giving individual members set roles and emphasize the importance of each person's contribution to overall group success.

## Issues and debates

■ Seeing lack of cohesion as solely due to social loafing is somewhat reductionist, as it does not consider other factors that also contribute to lowered cohesion.

---

### ■ STRENGTHEN YOUR LEARNING

1 What is meant by social loafing?

2 Explain the effect of social loafing on performance; include reference to diffusion of responsibility.

3 Summarize what research evidence has suggested about the effect of social loafing on performance.

4 What other evaluative points, including practical applications and relevant issues and debates, can be made about the effect of social loafing on performance?

---

### Expert tip

Do not be confused by the fact that some books refer to social loafing as the 'Ringelman effect' – they both essentially explain that the greater the size of a group, the less effort that is put in by individual members.

# Prejudice and explanations for prejudice

Revised ☐

**Prejudice** involves attitudes towards things and people not based on fact. Attitudes have three components: *cognitive* (beliefs about an attitude object, whether false or true), *affective* (emotions concerned with an attitude object) and *behavioural* (actions towards an attitude object). For example:

■ *Cognitive*: 'All blondes are stupid.'

■ *Affective*: 'Blondes really frustrate me.'

■ *Behavioural*: 'I own a company, but I wouldn't employ any blondes.'

Prejudices are generally negative due to the discrimination created towards the people that prejudiced attitudes are held about – for example, racial discrimination, where people from ethnic minorities are distrusted and abused. Psychologists study prejudice in order to develop effective strategies to reduce its negative effects upon society.

### Key terms

**Prejudice** – an unfair or unreasonable idea or feeling that is not based on fact.

**Authoritarian personality** – an explanation that sees prejudice as arising in individuals with a set pattern of personality characteristics.

## ■ The authoritarian personality: Fromm (1941)

The **authoritarian personality** (AP) sees prejudiced people as being highly conformist and obedient, with such individuals trusting authority figures and fearing and discriminating against minorities. **Adorno et al. (1950)** saw such people as having insecurities, formed in childhood through strict, authoritarian parenting. He created the F-scale questionnaire to measure an individual's degree of authoritarian personality.

**Jost et al. (2003)** see the authoritarian personality as a more cognitive construction, motivated by thought processes that reflect a desire to reduce the fear that other social groups will introduce harmful social change.

## ■ Research

- **Adorno** *et al.* **(1950)** found that high scorers on the F-scale had more prejudiced beliefs about people from minority social groups. This supports the idea that prejudice can arise from having an authoritarian personality.

- **Akrami (2005)** found that Finnish students' levels of different forms of prejudice, including homophobia, sexism and prejudice against disabled people, were highly correlated with each other, which supports AP in that prejudice is formed from personality characteristics disposing individuals to be hostile to minority groups.

- **Harding** *et al.* **(1969)** reviewed studies to find that individuals prejudiced towards Jews were also prejudiced towards black people and ethnic minorities, supporting the idea that those with an AP are generally disposed to prejudice against minority groups.

## ■ Positive evaluation

- A later form of AP measurement, the Right-Wing Authoritarian Scale, is superior to the F-scale, as it has an equal number of pro-and anti- statements, making it less prone to demand characteristics.

- There is a wide range of research support for the general idea that personality characteristics are related to some forms of prejudice.

## ■ Negative evaluation

- The AP explains prejudice towards minority social groups, but has difficulty in explaining other forms of prejudice, such as ageism and sexism.

- Although the F-scale has some research support, authoritarian individuals do not always score highly on the characteristics that the theory would predict.

## ■ Practical application

- As an authoritarian personality appears to form in childhood, it suggests that parenting styles that favour strict, authoritarian forms of parenting should be discouraged in favour of more liberal, child-centred ones in order to produce less prejudicial individuals.

## ■ Issues and debates

- If an authoritarian personality does indeed form in childhood as a result of strict parenting, it suggests that it is a result of nurture rather than nature.

---

**■ STRENGTHEN YOUR LEARNING**

1 Explain how prejudice is an attitude comprised of three components.
2 Why are prejudices generally negative?
3 Explain Fromm's theory of the authoritarian personality.
4 Explain how Jost *et al.* (2003) saw the authoritarian personality as more of a cognitive construction.
5 Summarize what research evidence has suggested about the authoritarian personality.
6 What other evaluative points, including practical applications and relevant issues and debates, can be made about the authoritarian personality?

---

**Expert tip**

The 'authoritarian personality' can be used to explain conformity and obedience, as well as prejudice, so take care when using it to answer a question on explanations for prejudice, to shape it to specifically explain prejudice.

## ■ Stereotyping

**Stereotyping** is a cognitive bias where certain types of individuals are grouped together on the incorrect basis that they possess similar qualities – for example, that all blondes are stupid. This involves cognitively classifying groups on their similarities and differences from other groups.

Stereotyping has an evolutionary survival value in simplifying the world, making it easier to deal with people. However, such mental 'short cuts' of out-groups can be negative, leading to fear and discrimination against out-group members.

Conversely, stereotypes of in-group members are positive, leading to preferential discriminatory behaviour towards group members. How stereotypes develop is explicable through social identity theory, as part of the social categorization, social identification and social comparison process.

Prejudiced attitudes and discrimination towards minorities, like homosexuals, is often based on incorrect stereotyped beliefs generalized to members of a minority group. Stereotypical behaviour, like blondes behaving stupidly, is portrayed as 'typical blonde behaviour', while non-stereotypical behaviour, like blondes behaving intelligently, is ignored. Thus stereotyping maintains prejudiced views against out-group members and the discrimination resulting from such views.

## Social identity theory: Tajfel & Turner (1979)

**Social identity theory** (SIT) sees self-esteem as central to individual identity and that, in order to feel good about ourselves, we need to feel good about the social groups we identify with. The theory has three components:

1 *Social categorization* – a person perceives themselves as having similar characteristics to members of a social group.

2 *Social identification* – a person classifies themselves as a member of that in-group by adopting the group's norms.

3 *Social comparison* – a person compares themselves, as a member of their in-group, as superior to out-group members, leading to prejudiced and discriminatory treatment of out-groups.

SIT includes the out-group homogeneity effect, where members of out-groups are seen as not only different from in-group members, but as more similar to each other than in-group members.

## Research

- **Crandall & Stangor (2005)** found that when participants were told in-group members held a belief, they were more likely to report the belief themselves than those not told this. This supports SIT, where individuals adhere to in-group norms.

- **Jones et al. (1981)** found that participants rated members of other out-group dining clubs as more similar to each other than their own in-group dining club. This illustrates SIT's out-group homogeneity effect also demonstrates a stereotyping effect, where people are grouped together by similarities, whether they are true or not.

- **Nelson et al. (1990)** found, even when told pictures of men and women had been matched for height and offering cash for making accurate judgements, male images were perceived as taller than female ones, suggesting individuals cannot free themselves of gender stereotypes, illustrating the strength of stereotyping in maintaining prejudice.

## Positive evaluation

- SIT explains why prejudice occurs even when an out-group poses no threat to an in-group, owing to a need to discriminate against others to boost self-esteem.

- Stereotyping has an evolutionary survival value, as simplifying people into 'types' makes it easier to make decisions on how to deal with them based on their potential harmful or beneficial qualities.

## Negative evaluation

- Although stereotypes automatically trigger how we treat people, personality also plays a part, as 'low-stereotype' people block out such stereotypes, while 'high-stereotype' people do not. This relates to Adorno's concept of the authoritarian personality.

**Key terms**

**Stereotyping** – a type of cognitive bias that concerns grouping types of individuals together on the incorrect basis that they all possess the same quality.

**Social identity theory** – an explanation for prejudice that argues that individuals discriminate positively towards in-group members and negatively to out-group members.

## KEY CLASSIC STUDY

### 'EXPERIMENTS IN INTERGROUP DISCRIMINATION: THE MINIMAL GROUP PARADIGM'

Tajfel (1970)

### Aim

- To see whether prejudice arises between people with no previous prejudice towards each other, by placing them into different groups.

### Procedure

- Sixty-four English schoolboys aged 14–15 years were put into groups on the basis of tasks of limited interest. Two experiments were then conducted.

- *Experiment one* – boys had to say how many dots were on a screen. They were told they were being put into groups of either 'over-estimators' or 'under-estimators' (all groupings were done randomly). Participants then gave small rewards of money to a pair of boys who were either in-group or out-group members, using a book of matrices. Each matrix had a pair of numbers that converted into money (1 point = 1 pence).

- *Experiment two* – boys were put into two groups on the basis of preferences for paintings (all groupings were done randomly). Participants choose from matrices of pairs of numbers, but this time participants had three choices:

  a   *maximum joint profit* – giving the largest amount to members of both groups

  b   *maximum in-group profit* – giving the largest amount to an in-group member, regardless of the amount to an out-group member

  c   *maximum difference* – giving the largest possible difference in amounts between an in-group and an out-group member.

### Results

- *Experiment one* – amounts allocated were similar if pairs consisted of two in-group or two out-group members, but when allocating money to an in-group and an out-group member, most boys gave more to an in-group member.

- *Experiment two* – amounts allocated were similar if pairs consisted of two in-group or two out-group members, but when allocating money to an in-group and an out-group member, the maximum difference was chosen, even if it meant giving the in-group member less money than choosing the 'maximum in-group profit' option.

### Conclusions

- Prejudice can be created by getting individuals to identify with an in-group and see others as out-group members.

- Discrimination against out-group members is more important than rewarding in-group members.

### Evaluation

- The studies lack ecological validity as the tasks were not everyday life ones. In real-life situations, where consequences are greater, stronger prejudice and discrimination might be expected.

- Demand characteristics could occur through the matrices being seen as a game to 'win', and it was this expectation that shaped behaviour.

---

- Research into stereotyping and SIT is often laboratory-based and so lacks ecological validity, with results not generalizable to real-life situations.

## Practical application

- Emphasizing positive, non-stereotypical behaviours of prejudiced group members can help break down discrimination towards such groups.

## Issues and debates

- The evolutionary aspects of stereotyping and SIT suggest a biological origin to prejudice, explicable through biological determinism. However, as prejudice can be consciously reduced, there also seems to be a role for free will.

■ **STRENGTHEN YOUR LEARNING**

1   What is a stereotype?

2   Explain the relationship between stereotyping and prejudice.

3   Outline social identity theory, including reference to social categorization, social identification and social comparison.

4   For Tajfel's (1970) study of intergroup discrimination, in your own words, state the aims, procedure, results, conclusions and evaluative points.

5   Summarize what research evidence has suggested about stereotyping and social identity theory.

6   What other evaluative points, including practical applications and relevant issues and debates, can be made about stereotyping and social identity theory?

**Expert tip**

When using **Tajfel's (1970)** study to discuss social identity theory, take care, if a question requires you to focus on explanations of prejudice, not to over-describe the study in terms of its procedure. Instead, use the findings of the study to assess the validity of the theory in explaining prejudice.

## ▨ Conformity

**Conformity** involves adhering to the norms of in-groups and not those of out-groups. Therefore, individuals adopt, in line with SIT, prejudiced, stereotypical beliefs about out-group members and conform to discriminating against such people. This concerns **normative social influence** and involves **compliance**, where individuals, publicly but not privately, adopt the norms of a social group in order to be accepted. **Identification**, a stronger form of conformity, involving both public and private agreement with a group, occurs where membership of an in-group has desirable outcomes, as in the social identification component of SIT. The strongest form of conformity is **internalization**, where individuals adopt the belief system of in-groups (including their beliefs about and behaviours towards members of out-groups), even when individuals are not with other in-group members. Individuals with low self-esteem have a greater need for social acceptance into in-groups and so conform more to social norms of prejudice to out-groups.

## ▨ Research

■ **Crandall & Stangor (2005)** found that when participants were told that in-group members held a belief, they were more likely to hold this belief than those not told this, supporting the idea that, in line with SIT, people conform to in-group norms.

■ **Minard (1952)** found 80 per cent of white miners were friendly to black miners below ground, where there was a social norm of co-worker friendliness, but only 20 per cent were above ground, where the social norm was one of racial prejudice. This supports the idea of prejudice due to conformity, where people adopt the norms of a given situation to fit in.

■ **Pettigrew (1959)** found highly conformist white South African students were more prejudiced against black people than those less conformist. This suggests that highly conformist people have more need for social approval and show more prejudice to achieve it. This adds a personality dimension to the conformist explanation of prejudice.

## ▨ Positive evaluation

■ SIT explains that prejudice can occur to out-groups, even when they pose no threat, due to needing to discriminate against others to boost self-esteem.

■ Compliance, identification and internalization differ in terms of degree of private acceptance and how much they affect belief systems, which explains the different degrees of prejudice towards out-group members.

## ▨ Negative evaluation

■ Some individuals have more need for self-esteem and social acceptance and so more easily conform to prejudiced views, with authoritarian personality theory better explaining such people's discriminatory beliefs. **Devine (1989)** reinforces this by arguing that individuals with a 'low-stereotype' personality can block out prejudiced stereotypes, while 'high-stereotype' individuals cannot.

**Key terms**

**Conformity** – yielding to group pressure (majority influence).

**Normative social influence** – a motivational force to be liked and accepted by a group.

**Compliance** – publicly but not privately going along with majority influence to gain approval.

**Identification** – public and private acceptance of majority influence in order to gain group acceptance.

**Internalization** – public and private acceptance of majority influence through adoption of a group's belief system.

- Although conformity offers a plausible explanation for prejudice, social norms change over time, which therefore does not explain why such prejudiced views are maintained.

## Practical application

- As people discriminate against others by conforming to in-group prejudice against them, it offers a way of reducing such prejudice by creating and emphasizing positive social norms of behaviour towards out-group members.

## Issues and debates

- As conformity to in-group prejudices seemingly has an evolutionary origin, it suggests such behaviour results from biological determinism and is not a product of free will, although, if true, this offers little scope for reducing such behaviour.

---

**■ STRENGTHEN YOUR LEARNING**

1  Outline how conformity can be used to explain prejudice; make reference to SIT, in-groups and out-groups, normative social influence and types of conformity.

2  Summarize what research evidence has suggested about conformity, as an explanation for prejudice.

3  What other evaluative points, including practical applications and relevant issues and debates, can be made about conformity, as an explanation for prejudice?

---

## Realistic conflict theory

**Realistic conflict theory (RCT)** explains how inter-group rivalry over conflicting goals and competition for valuable resources leads to prejudice. Inter-group conflicts occur over competition for goals and resources, leading to discriminatory behaviour, with prejudice level determined by the degree of importance placed upon achieving goals and securing resources, and the degree of inter-group conflicts to secure such goals and resources.

## Research

- The **Michigan National Election Studies (1972)** found that white people generally opposed racial integration in schools, as they did not want black children getting access to the better educational resources they possessed. This supports RCT that prejudice arises between groups competing for the same limited resources.

## Positive evaluation

- RCT explains why competition for resources in communities comprising different social groups can incur harmful, discriminatory consequences.

- RCT explains real-life prejudice and hostility that occurs over valuable resources, like that between Ukraine and Russia over who controls Europe's gas pipelines.

## Negative evaluation

- RCT cannot explain how prejudice arises between groups of unequal status, where groups of lower status either accept being dominated or reject it by responding with resistance, like by the Catholic minority in Protestant-dominated Northern Ireland.

## Practical application

- **Sherif *et al.*'s (1961)** study illustrates that discrimination can be broken down by getting opposing groups to indulge in mutually rewarding, cooperative tasks.

---

**Expert tip**

Conformity is a topic in itself, so take care, when using conformity as an explanation for prejudice, to shape your answer specifically to prejudice. A general description of conformity would not earn many marks.

---

Key terms

**Realistic conflict theory** – an explanation that sees prejudice arising through competition between in- and out-group members.

**In-groups** – social groups an individual identifies with.

**Out-groups** – social groups an individual does not identify with.

## KEY CLASSIC STUDY

### 'INTER-GROUP CONFLICT AND COOPERATION: THE ROBBERS CAVE EXPERIMENT'

Sherif *et al.* (1961)

### Aim

- To find out whether inter-group conflict could be created through competition and group frustration.

### Procedure

- Two groups of 12 boys were given cooperative tasks to perform.
- The groups engaged in competitive activities, with a trophy, knives and medals for the winning group. Results were fixed so that one group won.
- Situations were introduced where both groups had to interact and cooperate, like eating together and repairing the broken water supply.

### Results

- Two separate groups, the 'Eagles' and 'Rattlers', formed, each with a leader, group hierarchy and social norms.
- Inter-group tensions formed, with a fight occurring and the losing group stealing the winner's medals and knives. **In-group** members were positively stereotyped and **out-group** members negatively stereotyped by both groups.
- Interaction had little effect, but gradually, cooperation reduced hostility – 65 per cent of friendship choices now came from out-group members and out-group stereotypes became more positive.

### Conclusions

- Out-group prejudice can occur through competition for resources.
- Contact with an out-group is insufficient by itself for prejudice to be reduced.
- Prejudice can be reduced and positive relationships established between previously hostile groups by working towards goals that require cooperative action.

### Evaluation

- Manipulation within the study, like encouraging cooperation, may have created demand characteristics where the boys formed impressions of how they should act.
- The study was unethical; deceit occurred, with the boys not knowing they were in a study, so there was no informed consent, nor was there a right to withdraw. Harm occurred too, due to the creation of hostility and prejudice. No debriefing was given either.

## ■ Issues and debates

- RCT is gender-biased, as it has not explored whether there are differences in the explanation's application to males and females, with little research in this area.

---

### ■ STRENGTHEN YOUR LEARNING

1 Outline realistic conflict theory, as an explanation for prejudice; include reference to inter-group conflicts in your answer.
2 For Sherif *et al.*'s (1961) Robbers Cave study, in your own words, state the aims, procedure, results, conclusions and evaluative points.
3 Summarize what research evidence has suggested about realistic conflict theory, as an explanation for prejudice.
4 What other evaluative points, including practical applications and relevant issues and debates, can be made about realistic conflict theory, as an explanation for prejudice?

### Expert tip

It would be a good idea to include **Sherif *et al.*'s (1961)** 'Robbers Cave' study when using realistic conflict theory as an explanation of prejudice, as the study was crucial to the construction and initial assessment of the theory.

# Origins of conflict and conflict resolution

Conflicts are disputes arising from human interactions. Conflicts are cognitive, as they arise from a perception of incompatibility between groups and are resolved by removing that perception and replacing it with one of compatibility.

Conflicts are characterized by 1) the presence of two or more separate parties, 2) a scarce or valuable resource, 3) mutually opposed goals and 4) the possibility of behaviour designed to injure others. Conflicts occur between individuals (inter-personal), social groups (inter-group) and nations (international).

Conflicts arise over *issues of interest*, where conflicting groups agree on goals, but disagree on how to achieve them, and over *issues of value*, where conflict arises over fundamental, *zero sum conflicts*, where one group wins all of a resource – these are the hardest to resolve.

Conflicts managed in a *structured environment*, where behaviour occurs through agreed norms, are carried out in a cooperative manner that seeks to find shared goals. Conflicts occurring in an *unstructured environment* of no shared goals concern zero sum conflicts and are conducted in a hostile, competitive manner that can lead to violence.

Three types of behaviour arise from conflicts:

| Type of behaviour arising from conflict | Description |
|---|---|
| *Persuasion* | Use of reason, references to shared values and norms of fairness. Verbal discussions occur. Low cost to all parties. |
| *Coercion* | Reference to unacceptable costs and/or threats of violence. Verbal and physical behaviour occur. High cost to all parties. |
| *Reward* | Promises of benefits to other groups. Use of verbal and physical behaviour. Some costs incurred in paying out rewards. |

Conflicts are resolved by replacing disagreement and incompatibility between groups with cooperation and interdependent goals.

## Explanations of conflict origin

### ■ Social identity theory

**Social identity theory** (SIT) sees prejudice as explaining the origins of conflict, where conflict against out-groups arises from individuals identifying themselves as members of in-groups. If the status of an in-group is low or gaining access to valuable resources difficult, conflict between groups arises.

### ■ Realistic conflict theory

**Realistic conflict theory** (RCT) sees conflict arising from social groups competing for resources that only one group can win, with out-group members negatively stereotyped and treated with hostility. Conflict is reduced by forming shared, interdependent goals, as cooperatively working towards goals reduces negative stereotypes and hostility.

### ■ Research

- **Tajfel (1970)** (see page 208) suggests that perceiving in-group members as superior to out-group members leads to conflict, supporting SIT.

> **Key term**
>
> **Origins of conflict and conflict resolution** – the bases from which disputes arise and are settled.

> **Key terms**
>
> **Social identity theory** – an explanation that sees conflict arising through hostility against out-group members where the status of an in-group is low or access to desired resources difficult.
>
> **Realistic conflict theory** – an explanation that sees conflicts arising from groups competing for resources that only one group can win, with out-group members being negatively stereotyped, and being reduced by opposing groups forming shared, interdependent goals.

■ **Sherif *et al.* (1961)** (see page 211) suggests conflict arises from hostile groups competing for resources, with conflict resolved through cooperatively working towards shared goals, which supports RCT.

## Positive evaluation

■ Research has identified the key factors involved in the origins of conflicts, permitting effective means of resolution to be constructed.

## Negative evaluation

■ Research into conflict origins tends to be laboratory-based and so lacking in ecological validity, making generalizations to real-life situations difficult.

## Practical application

■ The three-step collaborative conflict resolution and interactive conflict resolution methods are effective means of dealing with conflict (see page 214).

## Issues and debates

■ Methods of conflict resolution lack culture bias, as differences in cultural backgrounds and perceptions are taken into account in order to amicably settle disputes between dissimilar groups.

---

### ■ STRENGTHEN YOUR LEARNING

1 What are conflicts?
2 Name and describe the four conditions that characterize conflicts.
3 Explain the two ways in which conflicts can arise.
4 How does the environment in which they occur affect conflicts?
5 Outline, in your own words, the three basic types of behaviour that arise from conflicts.
6 Explain how the following theories explain the origins of conflict:
    a social identity theory,
    b realistic conflict theory.
7 Summarize what research evidence has suggested about social identity theory and realistic conflict theory, as explanations for the origins of conflict and conflict resolution.
8 What other evaluative points, including practical applications and relevant issues and debates, can be made about origins of conflict and conflict resolution?

---

**Expert tip**

Take care to shape social identity theory and realistic conflict theory specifically to explain the origins of conflict and conflict resolution in questions on this topic, as more general descriptions of the theories would not attract high-level credit.

---

# Methods of conflict resolution

`Revised`

## ■ Deutsch (1949)

Deutsch sees cooperation as leading to conflict resolution. Constructive resolution is more likely when goals are reframed into shared ones, with the conflict then becoming a joint problem. This occurs with cooperative norms, like honesty and respect for others, based on shared values of equality and non-violence, which creates common ground between opposed groups.

Conflict management requires skills to create and maintain effective working relationships between groups, skills to sustain cooperative behaviours throughout a conflict and skills for group problem-solving and decision-making.

These skills can be learned and must be expressed within an environment supportive of all groups, if cooperative attitudes and behaviours are to be maintained.

## ■ Three-step collaborative conflict resolution

■ **Step 1:** *Recognition of a conflict* – each group outlines what the problem is and what they want. Other groups listen respectfully and attempt to empathize.

- **Step 2:** *Exploration of underlying concerns* – each group outlines fears, desires and factors of importance. Other parties listen, with an attitude of finding resolution factors agreeable to all. Conflicts are explored in depth rather than seeking a quick fix.

- **Step 3:** *Creation of mutually agreeable solution* – an agreed plan of action that meets all parties' concerns is negotiated. This may require modification to suggestions outlined in Step 1.

## Interactive conflict resolution: Kelman (2008)

In **interactive conflict resolution** (ICR), trained conflict managers are used to resolve complex and lengthy disputes.

1 In workshops, groups are separately taught cooperative means of interaction and how to resist negative forms of interaction.

2 In workshops, using agreed norms of behaviour, reasons for conflicts are explored, especially ones concerning needs for recognition, security and justice.

3 Solutions are sought that meet all parties' needs, by taking part in joint problem-solving. Agreements are reached between the parties themselves.

## Research

- **Fisher (1997)** found that ICR workshops improved attitudes in conflict disputes and improved complexity of thinking about conflicts and possible ways of resolving them, which suggests that ICR is a valid means of resolving conflicts.

- **Deutsch (1973)** found that, while competition was associated with negativity and highlighting differences between groups, which did not lead to conflict resolution, cooperation was associated with positivity and de-emphasizing differences, which did lead to successful conflict resolution, supporting the Crude Law of Social Relations that cooperation is the best way to solve disputes.

## Positive evaluation

- Research suggests conflict management can effectively resolve disputes between opposing groups.

- Psychological methods of conflict resolution generally create long-term rather than short-term solutions, adding to their effectiveness.

## Negative evaluation

- Conflict resolution is only appropriate in certain situations and is of little value when disputing groups have different beliefs and little common ground.

- It may not be possible to develop a general model of conflict resolution applicable across different types and levels of conflict.

## Practical application

- Effective methods of resolution have improved relationships between groups and ended harmful conflicts in a harmonious manner.

## Issues and debates

- There are cultural differences in how conflicts are perceived. People from individualistic cultures are more confrontational in conflicts than people from collectivist cultures, who are more cooperative.

---

**Key terms**

**Methods of conflict resolution** – the means by which disputes are settled.

**Three-step collaborative conflict resolution** – an explanation that sees dispute settlements as occurring in set stages in order to find mutually acceptable resolutions.

**Interactive conflict resolution** – a method of dispute settlement that uses trained conflict managers to settle complex and lengthy disputes.

■ STRENGTHEN YOUR LEARNING

1 Outline:
   a Deutsch's theory of conflict resolution,
   b three-step collaborative conflict resolution,
   c interactive conflict resolution.
2 Summarize what research evidence has suggested about methods of conflict resolution.
3 What other evaluative points, including practical applications and relevant issues and debates, can be made about methods of conflict resolution?

### Expert tip

A common mistake when constructing answers on methods of conflict resolution is to spend too much time describing methods. Remember to leave sufficient time to assess the methods too (if a question requires evaluative content), in terms of research support, strengths and weaknesses, practical applications, as well as issues and debates.

## EXAM-TYPE QUESTIONS

1 Discuss two explanations for the formation of personal relationships. (22 marks)
2 Evaluate one explanation for the formation of personal relationships. (22 marks)
3 Discuss the role of communication in personal relationships. (22 marks)
4 Discuss what research studies have suggested about the role of communication in personal relationships. (22 marks)
5 Outline and evaluate two explanations for why relationships change or end. (22 marks)
6 Discuss what research studies have suggested about explanations for why relationships change or end. (22 marks)
7 Discuss one or more explanations of bystanderism. (22 marks)
8 Outline and evaluate research studies of bystanderism. (22 marks)
9 Discuss research studies of bystanderism. (22 marks)
10 Evaluate theories of prosocial behaviour. (22 marks)
11 Outline and evaluate one biological and one non-biological theory of prosocial behaviour. (22 marks)
12 Discuss what research studies have suggested about promoting prosocial behaviour. (22 marks)
13 Evaluate methods of promoting prosocial behaviour. (22 marks)
14 Discuss cooperation and competition in human relationships. (22 marks)
15 Discuss what research studies have suggested about cooperation and competition in human relationships. (22 marks)
16 Evaluate explanations for prejudice and discrimination. (22 marks)
17 Outline and evaluate research studies of prejudice and discrimination. (22 marks)
18 Discuss origins of conflict and conflict resolution. (22 marks)
19 Outline and evaluate methods of conflict resolution. (22 marks)
20 Discuss what research studies have suggested about the origins of conflict and conflict resolution. (22 marks)

## Research methods

### The experimental method

With the **experimental method**, researchers manipulate an **independent variable** (IV) between experimental conditions to see its effect on a **dependent variable** (DV), always a measurement of some kind. Controls prevent **extraneous variables** (variables other than the IV that could affect the value of the DV) from becoming **confounding variables** that 'confuse' the results. *Standardization* involves each participant performing an experiment under controlled (the same) conditions to reduce the chances of confounding variables. *Replication* (repeating the experiment in exactly the same way) to check the results is thus possible. *Causality* (a cause-and-effect relationship) is thus established. For instance, caffeine consumption (IV) could be manipulated to assess the effect on reaction times (DV), with all other variables, like amount of sleep, food consumed, etc. kept constant between participants.

#### ■ Operationalization of variables

**Operationalization** concerns objectively defining variables in an easily understandable manner, so that an IV can be manipulated (altered between testing conditions) and its effect on a DV measured. For example, if researching the effect of sleep on concentration, the IV could be operationalized as the amount of sleep the previous night and the DV the score on a test of concentration. Without accurate operationalization, results may be unreliable and invalid; therefore, it is crucial to operationalize IVs and DVs accurately, but this can be difficult. For example, how can 'anger' be accurately operationalized?

#### ■ Demand characteristics

Research involves social interactions between investigators and participants, which can influence and bias findings so that they are not valid. One such research effect is **demand characteristics**, where participants form impressions of the research purpose and unknowingly alter behaviour accordingly. Demand characteristics affect research findings in several ways: 1) where participants guess the purpose of research and try to please researchers by giving them their expected results, 2) where participants guess the purpose of research and try to sabotage it by giving non-expected results, 3) where participants, out of nervousness or fear of evaluation, act unnaturally and 4) where participants respond to a *social desirability bias* and give answers/exhibit behaviour that show them in a socially acceptable manner.

Demand characteristics are reduced by the *single-blind procedure*, where participants are not aware of which testing condition they are in. For example, in a drug trial, participants would not know if they had swallowed a real pill or a placebo.

#### ■ Investigator effects

**Investigator effects** concern the ways in which researchers can unconsciously influence research. These can occur in several ways: 1) *major physical characteristics*, like the age and gender of researchers, 2) *minor physical characteristics*, like their accent and tone of voice, and 3) *unconscious bias* in the interpretation of data.

The *double-blind technique* reduces investigator effects by neither participants nor researchers knowing which conditions participants are in.

---

#### Key terms

**Experimental method** – a research method using random allocation of participants and the manipulation of variables to determine cause and effect.

**Independent variable** – the factor manipulated by researchers in an investigation.

**Dependent variable** – the factor measured by researchers in an investigation.

**Extraneous variables** – factors other than the independent variable that might affect the dependent variable.

**Confounding variables** – uncontrolled extraneous variables that affect the dependent variable and make findings invalid.

**Operationalization of variables** – the process of defining variables into measureable factors.

**Demand characteristics** – a research effect where participants form impressions of the research purpose and unconsciously alter their behaviour accordingly.

**Investigator effects** – a research effect where features of a researcher influence participants' behaviour.

■ **STRENGTHEN YOUR LEARNING**

1 Using an example of your own, outline the experimental method; make reference in your answer to independent and dependent variables, extraneous and confounding variables, standardization, replication and causality.

2 Explain what is meant by operationalization of variables.

3 Explain:

   a what demand characteristics are,

   b the ways in which demand characteristics can affect research findings,

   c how demand characteristics can be reduced.

4 Explain:

   a what investigator effects are,

   b the ways in which investigator effects influence research,

   c how investigator effects can be reduced.

> **Expert tip**
>
> A common mistake is to perceive extraneous and confounding variables as separate things. However, they are related, as extraneous variables are variables that could confound results if they are not controlled, while confounding variables are extraneous variables that were not controlled and did therefore confound results.

# Types of experiments

Revised ☐

## ■ Laboratory

**Laboratory experiments** are performed in a controlled environment, permitting variables other than the IV to be kept the same for all participants, who are randomly allocated to testing groups. The variable being tested (the IV) is manipulated by the researcher and tested in isolation.

## ■ Field

**Field experiments** are performed in the 'real world' rather than a laboratory, with the IV manipulated by researchers and other variables controlled. Participants are unaware of being tested and are not randomly allocated to the conditions.

## ■ Natural

**Natural experiments** occur where the IV varies naturally, with the researcher recording the effect on the DV. Participants are not randomly allocated to the conditions.

## ■ Quasi

**Quasi-experiments** occur where the IV occurs naturally, like whether participants are male or female. Participants therefore are not randomly allocated to the conditions. This method is often used when it is unethical to manipulate an IV.

## ■ Strengths of experiments

- With extraneous variables being controlled, causality can be established, i.e. that changes in the value of the DV are due to manipulation of the IV. This is especially so with laboratory experiments where control is highest (though with other types of experiment it is more difficult to control extraneous variables, so causality is harder to establish).

- Other researchers can replicate the study exactly to check results, again more so with laboratory experiments, where control is highest.

- Field experiments have high **ecological validity** and no risk of demand characteristics, as they are conducted in real-life settings with participants unaware of being tested, and so findings are generalizable to target populations.

## ■ Weaknesses of experiments

- The artificial nature of experiments (except for field experiments) makes the results lack ecological validity and they are unrepresentative to other settings.

- High degrees of control are artificial, which also makes results unrepresentative and difficult to generalize to real-life settings.

> **Key terms**
>
> **Laboratory experiment** – an experiment that is conducted in a controlled environment, with participants randomly allocated to the testing conditions, allowing the establishment of causality.
>
> **Field experiment** – an experiment conducted in a naturalistic environment where the researchers manipulate the independent variable.
>
> **Natural experiment** – an experiment where the independent variable varies naturally.
>
> **Quasi-experiment** – an experiment where the independent variable occurs naturally without manipulation from the researchers.
>
> **Ecological validity** – the degree to which findings from a study can be generalized to other settings.

■ Demand characteristics may occur (except in field experiments), where participants are aware of being tested and so may attempt to guess the purpose of the study and respond accordingly.

## ■ Pilot studies

**Pilot studies** are small-scale 'practice' investigations allowing procedural improvements and removal of methodological errors. Participants can point out flaws, like the presence of demand characteristics. Pilot studies show what kinds of results are expected and if there is any possibility of significant results. Pilot studies permit the quality of research to be improved and help avoid unnecessary time and effort being wasted – for example, by performing lengthy studies only to find that, due to unexpected errors and problems, the results are invalid and the study will have to be altered and repeated.

**Key term**

**Pilot studies** – small-scale practice investigations.

---

**■ STRENGTHEN YOUR LEARNING**

1 Outline the following types of experiment:
  a  laboratory,
  b  field,
  c  natural,
  d  quasi.
2 Explain the strengths and weaknesses of experiments.
3 Explain:
  a  what pilot studies are,
  b  the reasons for conducting pilot studies.

---

**Expert tip**

Some psychologists do not regard natural and quasi-experiments as actually being experiments, as random allocation of participants to testing conditions does not occur and the researchers do not manipulate the IV.

# Observations

Revised ☐

**Naturalistic observations** involve measuring naturally occurring behaviour in real-world situations, like **Festinger's (1957)** study where he infiltrated a cult that was predicting the end of the world, to observe their behaviour. **Controlled observations** are conducted under controlled laboratory conditions, like **Ainsworth *et al.*'s (1978)** 'Strange Situation' study where infants' behaviour was observed in various scenarios (see page 137). **Participant observations** involve researchers being actively involved in the behaviour being assessed, such as in Zimbardo's prison simulation study (**Haney *et al.*, 1973**, see page 143), where Zimbardo was the 'superintendent' of a prison containing students assigned roles of guards and prisoners. **Non-participant observations** involve researchers not being actively involved in the behaviour being assessed, such as **Ainsworth *et al.* (1978)**. **Overt observations** involve the participants knowing they are being observed, as with **Haney *et al.* (1973)**, while **covert observations** do not, such as **Festinger (1957)**.

## ■ Strengths

■ Observations have high **external validity**, as they involve natural behaviour in a real-life setting and so can be generalized to other settings.

■ As participants are usually unaware of being observed there are few demand characteristics.

■ When manipulation of variables would be impractical or unethical (as when studying football hooliganism), an observational study may be more suitable.

## ■ Weaknesses

■ It can be difficult to remain unobserved and make accurate, full observations.

■ As observations are not conducted under controlled conditions, they are difficult to replicate to check the reliability and validity of findings and cannot show causality.

**Key terms**

**Naturalistic observations** – surveillance and recording of naturally occurring events.

**Controlled observations** – surveillance of events under controlled conditions.

**Participant observations** – observations conducted with the observers being involved in the event under surveillance.

**Non-participant observations** – observations conducted with the observers not being involved in the event under surveillance.

**Overt observations** – observations that are conducted without participants being aware they are under surveillance.

**Covert observations** – observations that are conducted with participants being aware they are under surveillance.

**External validity** – the extent to which findings of a study can be generalized to other settings, other people and over time.

- Observer bias may occur where observers 'see' what they want or expect to see, though this can be reduced by establishing **inter-observer reliability**.

- If participants are unaware of being observed, issues of informed consent and invasion of privacy can occur, while if they are aware, then demand characteristics can occur.

## Observational design

There are several ways to gather data from observations, including visual and audio recordings, and 'on-the-spot' notetaking using rating scales and coding categories. Observational studies work best when time is taken to create effective **behavioural categories**.

### Behavioural categories

Observers need to agree upon a grid or coding sheet that truly represents the behaviour being observed. For instance, if observers wish to observe the effect of age and gender on the speed of driving, they might wish to create behavioural categories like *distracted, talking, using mobile phone* and *concentrating* (see table below) and then code individual drivers' behaviour using agreed scales. Coding can involve numbers, like the apparent age of the driver, or letters to denote characteristics such as gender, e.g. 'M' for male, as well as observed behaviours, like using 'T' for a driver that was talking. Observed behaviours can also be rated on structured scales, like from 1 to 5 to indicate the degree of safe driving.

**Key terms**

**Inter-observer reliability** – where observers consistently and independently code behaviour in the same way

**Behavioural categories** – the division of target behaviours into subsets through the use of coding systems.

| Driver | Sex (M/F) | Age (estimate) | Number of passengers | Observed behaviour | Type of car | Speed (estimate in km per hour) | Safe driving rating 1 = very unsafe 5 = very safe |
|---|---|---|---|---|---|---|---|
| A | M | 55 | 0 | M-P | Ford | 40 | 2 |
| B | F | 21 | 2 | T | VW | 30 | 5 |
| C | F | 39 | 3 | D | BMW | 50 | 3 |
| D etc. | M | 70 | 0 | C | Jensen | 60 | 5 |

**Observed behaviour code:**
**D** = Distracted, **M-P** = Using mobile phone, **T** = Talking, **C** = Concentrating

### Sampling procedures

It is often difficult to observe all behaviour, especially continuous behaviour (non-stop). Placing behaviour into categories helps, but there are also different types of **sampling procedure** (methods of recording data) that can be used, which involve selecting some of the behaviour to observe and record, with the aim being to select representative behaviour. One sampling procedure is *event sampling*, where the number of times a behaviour occurs in a target individual (or individuals) is recorded. Another sampling procedure is *time sampling*, where behaviour is recorded at a set interval – for instance, what behaviour is seen every 30 seconds.

**Key term**

**Sampling procedures** – the different methods of recording observational data.

### Inter-observer reliability

Inter-observer reliability occurs when independent observers code behaviour in the same way. This lessens the chance of observer bias, where an observer sees what they want/expects to see. To establish inter-observer reliability, clearly described behavioural categories need to be created that do not overlap with each other. Video-taping observed behaviour means inter-observer reliability can be checked at a later date.

■ **STRENGTHEN YOUR LEARNING**

1 What are:
   a naturalistic observations,
   b controlled observations?
2 Explain the difference between:
   a participant and non-participant observations,
   b overt and covert observations.
3 Explain the strengths and weaknesses of observational studies.
4 What methods are used to collect data from observational studies?
5 Explain:
   a what is meant by behavioural categories,
   b how (using an example of your own) behavioural categories can be created.
6 Explain what is meant by sampling procedures; include reference in your answer to event sampling and time sampling.
7 Explain:
   a what is meant by inter-observer reliability,
   b what is meant by observer bias,
   c how inter-observer reliability can be established.

**Expert tip**

A common mistake is for students to believe all observations occur naturalistically (in real-life environments), but actually some famous observations, like Ainsworth's 'Strange Situation' and Milgram's original obedience study, occur under controlled laboratory conditions.

# Questionnaires

Revised ☐

**Questionnaires** are a **self-report** method where participants answer written questions involving opinions, attitudes, beliefs and behaviour, e.g. **Adorno et al.'s (1950)** F-scale questionnaire (see page 205). **Closed questions** involve limited responses set by researchers, with 'yes/no' tick boxes or a range of fixed responses. Answers are easy to quantify, but answers are restricted. **Open questions** allow participants to express feelings, opinions, etc. in their own words and thus give greater depth and freedom of expression, but are less easy to quantify.

## ■ Strengths

- Large samples are generated by mailing questionnaires, which also means researchers do not have to be present when they are completed.

- As questionnaires are standardized (use the same questions for everyone), they can be replicated to check results.

- Questionnaires obtain lots of data in a relatively quick time.

- There is a lack of investigator effects if questionnaires are completed without researchers present.

## ■ Weaknesses

- There is a possibility of **idealized** and **socially desirable answers**, with participants answering how they think they should, rather than honestly.

- Questionnaires, especially those with closed questions, are not suitable for sensitive issues requiring careful and detailed understanding.

- Only certain 'types' of people may complete questionnaires, making findings unrepresentative.

## ■ Questionnaire construction

Questionnaires can have a low response rate, so are constructed to maximize the chances of completion:

- *Aims* – having a precise aim not only allows participants to understand the purpose of the questionnaire, but also helps in constructing questions that fit the aim.

**Key terms**

**Questionnaires** – self-report method where participants record their own responses to a pre-set list of questions.

**Self-reports** – research method where participants give information about themselves without researcher interference.

**Closed questions** – where fixed questions are asked that involve yes/no answers, thus producing quantitative data.

**Open questions** – questions are asked that allow participants to answer in their own words, thus producing qualitative data.

**Idealized answers** – where participants give responses that relate to how they would like to behave rather than how they actually behave.

**Socially desirable answers** – where participants give responses that society would expect of them.

- *Length* – having unnecessary questions and over-long questions increases the chances that participants will not give the questions full consideration, or will not even complete the questionnaire.

- *Previous questionnaires* – questionnaires that have proved successful in gaining high return rates and generating useful answers should be used as a basis for the construction of a new questionnaire.

- *Question formation* – to generate meaningful answers and to increase completion rates, questions should be concise, unambiguous and easy to understand. It is also best if questions stick to single points to avoid becoming over-complex and confusing.

- *Pilot study* – a questionnaire should be tested out on a small group of individuals who provide detailed and honest feedback on all aspects of the questionnaire's design. This means corrections/adjustments can be made before the questionnaire is used on the actual sample of participants.

- *Measurement scales* – questionnaires often use measurement scales involving a series of statements, with participants choosing a score that reflects the statement they opt for. However, if participants do not fully understand a question, they will tend to choose the middle score, which can give a false impression of their actual attitude to that question. Therefore, when constructing such questions, it is important that the question and the statements to choose from are easy to understand.

**Rate your level of agreement with the following statement: 'Vigorous regular exercise is good for your health.'**

| 1 | 2 | 3 | 4 | 5 |
|---|---|---|---|---|
| Strongly agree | Agree | Undecided | Disagree | Strongly disagree |

Effective questionnaires use closed questions, with a limited range of responses that generate **quantitative data**, and open questions, where participants answer in their own words, generating **qualitative data**.

**Key terms**

**Quantitative data** – numerical data.

**Qualitative data** – non-numerical data.

---

> ### ■ STRENGTHEN YOUR LEARNING
>
> 1. What are questionnaires? Include reference in your answer to open questions and closed questions.
> 2. Explain the strengths and weaknesses of questionnaires; ensure your answers are fully justified.
> 3. Explain questionnaire construction in terms of aims, length, previous questionnaires, question formation, pilot studies and measurement scales.
> 4. Explain why effective questionnaires use both open and closed questions.

**Expert tip**

A common mistake is for students to perceive idealized answers, socially desirable answers and demand characteristics as different things. But actually, idealized and socially desirable answers are a type of demand characteristic, where participants respond in a way they believe a researcher wishes them to, or in a way that is expected of them.

## Interviews

Revised ▢

**Interviews** are a form of self-report (like questionnaires), but that involve asking participants face-to-face questions, such as with **Bowlby's (1944)** study of maternal deprivation in juvenile thieves (see page 136). There are four main types of interview:

1. **Structured interviews** involve asking identical, simple, quantitative questions to all participants, to which the interviewer writes the answers down. Little training is needed as such interviews are easy to conduct.

**Key terms**

**Interviews** – self-report method where participants answer questions in face-to-face situations.

**Structured interviews** – identical closed questions are asked to all participants, thus producing quantitative data.

2 **Unstructured interviews** involve an informal discussion on set topics, producing mainly qualitative data. Unstructured interviews require training and skill to conduct effectively.

3 **Semi-structured interviews** involve a mixture of structured and unstructured questions and thus produce quantitative and qualitative data. With both unstructured and semi-structured interviews, follow-up questions can be asked to further explore interesting answers.

4 **Focus group interviews** are done with specific groups of people about a particular issue, with participants interacting with each other when producing answers.

## Strengths

- Both quantitative and qualitative data is produced, which produces a greater variety and depth of findings.

- Complex and sensitive issues can be effectively dealt with by putting participants at ease and thus able to talk freely. This is especially so with unstructured interviews.

- Due to the face-to-face nature of the method, any questions that are not understood can be explained clearly so that relevant answers are gained.

- As structured interviews are standardized (all participants are asked the same questions), they can be replicated to check the validity of findings.

- Focus group interviews process several people at once on a particular topic, which produces a lot of data relatively quickly.

## Weaknesses

- Interviewers can bias responses through their appearance, age, gender, etc.

- Interviews can produce demand characteristics, where participants give answers they think are required.

- Some participants may not have the verbal skills to fully express themselves.

- A lot of skill is required to be a good interviewer, especially with unstructured interviewers, and such skilled people are not easy to find.

- With focus group interviews, there is less control than with one-to-one interviews, so time can be spent on irrelevant discussion.

- There is an ethical issue of participants revealing more than they wish on sensitive topics.

## Design of interviews

The effectiveness of interviews is dependent on the appropriateness of the interviewer and the choice of such is affected by several factors:

- *Gender and age* – can specially affect answers on questions of a sensitive sexual nature.

- *Ethnicity* – fuller, more honest answers are gained with interviewers of the same ethnic background as the interviewee.

- *Personal characteristics* – appearance, accent, amount of formality, etc. of an interviewer can all affect the answers gained. Effective interviewers adapt their style to suit different interviewees.

Interviews can be followed by a more targeted survey, which ask questions focused on areas of interest identified from an interview and that are framed in a manner as to produce quantitative data.

---

**Key terms**

**Unstructured interviews** – involve an informal discussion on a particular topic, with the possibility of follow-up questions to explore interesting responses, thus generally producing qualitative data.

**Semi-structured interviews** – involve a mixture of structured and unstructured techniques, thus producing quantitative and qualitative data.

**Focus group interviews** – involve asking questions to a particular group of people on a particular issue, with group members able to interact when giving answers.

■ **STRENGTHEN YOUR LEARNING**

1 What are interviews?

2 Outline the following types of interviews:

   a structured,

   b unstructured,

   c semi-structured,

   d focus group interviews.

3 Explain strengths and weaknesses of interviews; ensure your answers are fully justified.

4 Outline how the following factors determine the effectiveness of interviews through the appropriateness of choice of interviewer:

   a gender and age,

   b ethnicity,

   c personal characteristics.

5 How can areas of interest that arise from an interview be investigated in a way that produces quantitative data?

**Expert tip**

Structured interviews can be considered as similar to a questionnaire, as both techniques involve participants answering identical, simple, quantitative questions.

# Correlational analysis

Revised ▢

**Correlational analysis** involves assessing the degree of relationship between two or more **co-variables** – for example, **Murstein's (1972)** correlational study of the matching hypothesis (see page 180) where similarity between male and female couples' ratings of attractiveness was assessed. A **positive correlation** occurs when one co-variable increases as another co-variable increases – for example, sales of umbrellas increase as the number of days it rains increases. A **negative correlation** occurs when one co-variable decreases while another increases – for example, sales of bikinis decrease as the number of days it rains increases. Zero correlations occur when there is no association between co-variables. A **correlation co-efficient** is a numerical value expressing the degree to which co-variables are related. Measurements range between +1.0, a perfect positive correlation, and –1.0, a perfect negative correlation.

## ▨ Strengths

■ Correlations do not require manipulation of variables and so are used when experiments would be unethical.

■ Once correlations are established, predictions can be made, like how many umbrellas will be sold on rainy days.

■ Quantification of relationships is possible, which permits statistical analysis to see if relationships are significant (beyond the boundaries of chance).

## ▨ Weaknesses

■ Correlations are not conducted under controlled conditions and therefore do not show causality.

■ Correlations that at first inspection seem low can actually be statistically significant if the number of scores used is sufficiently high enough, while correlations that seem initially high may be statistically not significant if the number of scores is low.

■ Extraneous variables may influence co-variables and thus skew results, leading to incorrect conclusions regarding relationships.

■ Correlations can only measure linear relationships, not curvilinear ones – for example, a relationship where aggression increases as temperature increases, but then declines after a certain temperature is reached.

**Key terms**

**Correlational analysis** – a research method that measures the strength and direction of relationships between co-variables.

**Co-variables** – the factors being measured in a correlational analysis.

**Positive correlation** – as the value of one co-variable increases, the value of the other co-variable also increases (or both co-variables decrease).

**Negative correlation** – as the value of one co-variable increases, the value of the other co-variable decreases.

**Correlation co-efficient** – the numerical degree to which co-variables are related.

# Case studies

Revised

**Case studies** involve detailed, in-depth investigation of one person or a small group, usually involving biographical details, behaviour and experiences of interest, with qualitative data about feelings, experiences, etc. generally recorded, though quantitative data can be generated too. For example, **Koluchova's (1972)** study of twins suffering privation, which studied their experiences and assessed their progress to recovery. Case studies are often **longitudinal** (conducted over long periods to show changes over time).

> **Key terms**
>
> **Case studies** – a research method that involves the in-depth study of an individual, or small group of individuals, that is unique in some way.
>
> **Longitudinal studies** – studies conducted over a long period of time at regular intervals to show trends (changes over time).

## ■ Strengths

- Case studies allow 'difficult' areas to be investigated where other methods would be unethical, such as sexual abuse.

- Case studies allow research of unique behaviours that would not be possible by other means.

- Data relates specifically to one person, not an average produced from many people.

- As case studies are about real people and experiences, they have a level of 'truth' about them that relates to a real person and is not an 'average' gained from many people.

- Case studies can be useful for theory contradiction, where the findings of just one case study can disprove a theory.

## ■ Weaknesses

- Findings only relate to one person and cannot be generalized to others.

- Case studies are usually reliant on full and accurate memories, which can often be selective and affected by researcher bias.

- Researcher bias can occur where researchers interpret findings in a subjective way that matches their expectations or desires.

---

**■ STRENGTHEN YOUR LEARNING**

1. Explain what is meant by correlational analysis; include reference in your answer to positive, negative and zero correlations and correlation co-efficients.
2. Explain strengths and weaknesses of correlational analysis.
3. Explain the case study research method; include reference in your answer to why case studies are often longitudinal.
4. Explain strengths and weaknesses of case studies.

---

> **Expert tip**
>
> Correlational studies and experiments can be linked together, as correlational studies are often used to identify areas worthy of further study conducted under experimental controlled conditions.

# Scientific processes

Revised

## Aims and hypotheses

Revised

### ■ Aims

**Aims** are research objectives, exact statements of why studies are conducted – for instance, to investigate whether differing amounts of sleep affect concentration levels. Aims should incorporate what is being studied and what studies are trying to achieve. The hypotheses of a study generally incorporate the aims of a study. At the end of a study, conclusions will be drawn that assess whether aims have been met.

> **Key term**
>
> **Aims** – precise statements of why a study is being conducted.

## ■ Hypotheses

**Hypotheses** are more objectively precise than aims and are testable predictions of what is expected to happen. There are two types of hypotheses:

1 The **experimental hypothesis**, which predicts that differences in the DV will be outside the boundaries of chance (known as **significant differences**), as a result of manipulation of the IV. The term 'experimental hypothesis' is used with experiments; other research methods refer to 'alternative hypotheses'. For example, 'participants receiving eight hours' sleep last night will perform significantly better on a test of concentration than those receiving four hours' sleep last night'.

2 The **null hypothesis**, which predicts that the IV will not affect the DV and that any differences found will not be outside the boundaries of chance, i.e. will not be significantly different. For example, 'participants receiving eight hours sleep' last night will not perform significantly better on a test of concentration than those receiving four hours' sleep last night. Any differences found will be due to chance factors.'

One of these two hypotheses will be supported by the findings and accepted, while the other will be rejected.

There are two types of experimental/alternative hypotheses:

1 **Directional (one-tailed) hypothesis**, which predicts the direction that the results will lie in. For instance, 'participants running 400 metres on an athletics track while being watched by an audience of their peers will run significantly quicker times than those running without an audience'.

2 **Non-directional (two-tailed) hypothesis**, which predicts a difference in the results, but not the direction the results will lie in. For instance, 'there will be a significant difference in times achieved between participants running 400 metres on an athletics track while being watched by an audience of their peers and those running without an audience'. Directional hypotheses are used when previous research gives an indication of which way findings will lay.

Correlational studies use **correlational hypotheses** that predict (or not) a relationship between co-variables. As with experimental hypotheses, these can be one- or two-tailed. For example, 'as the amount of hours a child spends in day care increases, the amount of aggressive responses displayed will significantly increase' (one-tailed), and 'there will be a significant relationship between the amount of hours a child spends in day care and the amount of aggressive responses displayed' (two-tailed). A correlational null hypothesis would predict no significant relationship between co-variables. For example, 'there will be no significant relationship between the amount of hours a child spends in day care and the amount of aggressive responses displayed'.

> **Key terms**
>
> **Hypotheses** – testable research predictions.
>
> **Experimental hypothesis** – a hypothesis that predicts difference in the dependent variable will be beyond the boundaries of chance.
>
> **Significant difference** – a difference in values of a dependent variable that are beyond chance factors.
>
> **Null hypothesis** – a hypothesis that predicts differences in the dependent variable will not be beyond the boundaries of chance.
>
> **Directional (one-tailed) hypothesis** – a hypothesis that predicts not only a significant difference, but also the direction of the difference.
>
> **Non-directional (two-tailed) hypothesis** – a hypothesis that predicts a significant difference, but not the direction of the difference.
>
> **Correlational hypotheses** – hypotheses that predict relationships (or not) between co-variables.

---

### ■ STRENGTHEN YOUR LEARNING

1 Explain:
   a what a research aim is,
   b the purpose of having a research aim.

2 Explain what hypotheses are; include reference in your answer to experimental and null hypotheses, significant difference, directional (one-tailed) and non-directional (two-tailed) hypotheses and correlational hypotheses.

> **Expert tip**
>
> Students often do not realize that, like experiments, correlational studies have hypotheses too. Hypotheses in experiments predict differences between variables, while in correlational studies hypotheses predict relationships between co-variables.

## Sampling techniques

Revised ▢

A population consists of all the people within a certain grouping. A sample is a part of that population with the selection of that sample aiming to be as unbiased and thus as representative as possible, i.e. the sample should possess the same characteristics as the population from which it is drawn. Several **sampling** techniques exist, all of which have strengths and weaknesses.

> **Key term**
>
> **Sampling** – the selecting of participants to represent a wider population.

# Random sampling

**Random sampling** occurs where all members of a target population have an equal chance of being selected and are chosen without bias. Computer-generated random number lists can be used or the 'names out of a hat' method (all the names of a population are placed in a container and the required number of names drawn out).

## Strengths

- Selection is unbiased, which increases the chances of a **representative sample** being selected.

- As the sample is selected without bias, it should be fairly representative and therefore the results should be fairly generalizable to the target population.

## Weaknesses

- Sometimes random sampling is impractical, e.g. not all members of a population are available for selection or wish to be considered for selection. As these probably would consist of certain types of people (e.g. ill people and shy people), this would make the sample not representative of a population and thus the findings would be unrepresentative and lack generalizability.

- Unbiased selection does not guarantee that a representative sample will be created. Samples can still be unrepresentative, e.g. all females may be selected or people of one particular age group.

> **Key terms**
>
> **Random sampling** – where each member of a population has an equal chance of being selected.
>
> **Representative sample** – a sample that possesses the same characteristics as the population from which it is drawn.

# Opportunity sampling

**Opportunity sampling** involves using whoever is willing and available to take part – for example, those present in town during day time. **Sears (1986)** found 75 per cent of research conducted in universities (where most research occurs) uses undergraduates as participants, as it is convenient to do so.

## Strengths

- Such samples are relatively easy to obtain as they use those willing and available.

- It is the only sampling type available with natural experiments, where researchers have no control over who they can study.

## Weaknesses

- It is often unrepresentative as certain 'types' of participant may be excluded, e.g. a sample gathered in town during the day might not include students, people at work, etc.

- As participants can decline to take part, it can turn into self-selected sampling rather than opportunity sampling.

> **Key term**
>
> **Opportunity sampling** – selection of participants who are available.

# Self-selected sampling

**Self-selected sampling** (also known as **volunteer sampling**) involves using people who 'volunteer' themselves for selection. This usually involves potential participants responding to advertisements or posters, i.e. they select themselves.

## Strengths

- As self-selection sampling is self-generating, it involves minimal effort on the part of researchers (other than placing an advertisement, or producing and putting up a poster) to obtain participants.

- As volunteers are generally keen to please, there is less chance of the 'screw you' phenomenon (where participants attempt to deliberately sabotage the study).

> **Key term**
>
> **Self-selected (volunteer) sampling** – where participants volunteer themselves to participate in a study.

■ **Weaknesses**

■ As volunteers tend to wish to be helpful, there is an increased risk of demand characteristics, where volunteers give answers/behave in a way they think the researchers wish them to.

■ Volunteers tend to be certain 'types' of people, e.g. those interested in the focus of the study. This can make a sample unrepresentative and the findings lack generalizability to a target population.

## ■ Purposive sampling

**Purposive sampling** (selected sampling) involves selecting participants that have qualities specifically relevant to a research study. There are several subtypes:

| Subtype of purposive sampling | Description |
|---|---|
| *Maximum variation type* | As many different types of people as possible in a population are included to get a wide range of views/behaviour. |
| *Homogenous type* | People of a certain 'type' are selected, so as to get a representative view of that 'type'. |
| *Typical case sampling* | Selecting the most 'average' people from a population to get a 'typical' opinion/behaviour. |
| *Extreme case sampling* | Selecting non-typical people of a population to obtain the full range of opinions/behaviour. |
| *Critical case sampling* | Selecting one 'typical' person to study, so as to get a representative view. |
| *Total population sampling* | Selecting everyone in a population who has one or more shared characteristics, so as to get summaries of opinions/behaviour. |
| *Expert sampling* | Selecting members of a population with a certain type of skill/characteristic, so as to become better informed about a specific area of study. |

> **Key term**
> **Purposive sampling** – selection of participants that possess qualities relevant to a study.

■ **Strengths**

■ The method is focused, allowing selection of participants for a particular research purpose, with different types of purposive sampling possible for different research purposes.

■ Purposive sampling is relatively quick, as it does not waste time on selecting and testing participants whose data will not be of use.

■ **Weaknesses**

■ As selection is not unbiased, findings are unrepresentative and cannot be generalized to target populations.

■ Some forms of purposive sampling, such as critical case sampling, generate very small samples, which can make them unrepresentative and difficult to generalize from.

## ■ Snowball sampling

**Snowball sampling** is when initial participants (selected by other means) generate additional participants themselves, e.g. friends and acquaintances. Like a snowball rolling down a hill, it gets bigger and bigger with time.

> **Key term**
> **Snowball sampling** – where initial participants, selected by other methods, generate additional participants themselves.

### ■ Strengths

■ The method can locate examples of participants 'hidden' to researchers that they would never have located on their own, making the findings more representative.

■ Aside from the selection of the initial participants, the sample is self-generating, making it relatively easy to assemble.

### ■ Weaknesses

■ As selection is generally biased in participants selecting whoever they wish to include (and thus excluding those that do not wish to include), findings are unrepresentative and non-generalizable.

■ The participants initially selected may go on to only select people like themselves, thus 'anchoring' the sample to one particular type of person, making the findings unrepresentative and non-generalizable.

---

**■ STRENGTHEN YOUR LEARNING**

1 What is:
   a a population,
   b a sample?
2 What is a random sample? How can a random sample be created?
3 Explain strengths and weaknesses of random samples.
4 What is an opportunity sample?
5 Explain strengths and weaknesses of opportunity samples.
6 What is a self-selected (volunteer) sample? How can a self-selected sample be created?
7 Explain strengths and weaknesses of self-selected samples.
8 What are purposive samples? Include reference in your answer to the various types of purposive sampling.
9 Explain strengths and weaknesses of purposive samples.
10 What is snowball sampling?
11 Explain strengths and weaknesses of snowballing sampling.

---

**Expert tip**

A common mistake with random sampling is for students to describe how to obtain a random sample when a question actually asks for an explanation of what a random sample is (or vice versa). Always identify the 'command words' in a question (the words that specify what kind of answer is required) before composing your answer.

---

# Experimental design

Revised ☐

Experimental conditions have different forms of the IV, with the *control condition* acting as a comparison against the *experimental condition*. There are three types of experimental design, each with strengths and weaknesses.

## ■ Repeated measures design

In a **repeated measures design (RMD)**, the same participants perform in all conditions of an experiment; therefore, participants are tested against themselves under different forms of the IV. This is regarded as the most preferred design, as the lack of **participant variables** (see 'Strengths' below) is seen as generating the most valid results, unless it is impractical to use this design, such as when testing males and females, as their gender would form the different versions of the IV, and when **counterbalancing** (see 'Weaknesses' below) would be impossible.

### ■ Strengths

■ As each participant performs in all conditions, they are compared against themselves, so there are no participant variables (individual differences between participants) and differences in findings are due to manipulations of the IV.

---

**Key terms**

**Repeated measures design** – experimental design where each participant performs all conditions of an experiment.

**Participant variables** – individual differences between participants that may act as extraneous variables to invalidate findings.

**Counterbalancing** – a technique to address order effects, whereby half of participants perform one condition first and half of participants perform the other condition first.

- Each participant produces two pieces of data (or even more if there are multiple conditions of the IV), which is twice as much as an independent groups design.

### Weaknesses

- **Order effects** occur, where the order in which participants perform conditions affects findings, e.g. performing worse in the second condition due to fatigue or performing better due to a learning effect. Order effects are counterbalanced, where half the participants do one condition first and half the other condition first.

- Demand characteristics are more likely, as by participating in all conditions it is more likely participants will form an impression of the aims of the study and act as they believe the researcher wishes them to.

## Matched participants design

The **matched participants design (MPD)** is a special kind of RMD with participants pre-tested and matched on important variables for the study and then placed into similar pairs. One of each pair is randomly allocated into the experimental condition and one into the control condition. Identical twins are often used as they form perfect matched pairs, sharing identical genetic characteristics.

### Strengths

- As different participants perform different conditions, there are no order effects.

- Demand characteristics are reduced, as participants only perform one condition each.

### Weaknesses

- As participants only perform one condition, more participants are required to produce the same amount of data as a RMD.

- There is a risk of participant variables, as findings may be due to participants' individual differences, rather than manipulations of the IV.

## Independent groups design

In an **independent groups design (IGD)**, different participants perform in each experimental condition (i.e. each participant does only one condition), making them independent of each other, with participants randomly allocated to different conditions. Therefore, different participants are being tested against each other.

### Strengths

- As different participants do all conditions, there are no order effects.

- As different participants perform different conditions, there is less chance of demand characteristics.

### Weaknesses

- As each participant only performs in one condition, twice as many participants are required than with a RMD.

- There is a risk of participant variables, as findings may be due to participants' individual differences rather than manipulations of the IV.

> **Key terms**
>
> **Order effects** – where, in a repeated measures design, the order in which participants perform the experimental conditions may act as an extraneous variable to invalidate findings.
>
> **Matched participants design** – experimental design where participants are placed in similar pairs, with one of each pair performing one condition.

> **Key term**
>
> **Independent groups design** – experimental design in which each participant performs one condition of an experiment.

■ **STRENGTHEN YOUR LEARNING**

1 Explain the purpose of having experimental and control conditions in an experiment.

2 Outline the following types of experimental design:
   a independent groups design,
   b repeated measures design,
   c matched participants design.

3 Explain strengths and weaknesses of the following types of experimental design:
   a independent groups design,
   b repeated measures design,
   c matched participants design.

**Expert tip**

A way to simplify learning the strengths and weaknesses of the independent groups design and the repeated measures design is to remember that the strengths of an independent groups design are the weaknesses of a repeated measures design, while the weaknesses of an independent groups design are the strengths of a repeated measures design.

# Ethical issues

Revised

To protect the dignity and safety of participants, as well as the integrity of psychology, research should be conducted in an ethical manner. Full details of research should be submitted to the appropriate ethical committee for approval before commencing. The British Psychological Society publishes a code of ethics that researchers should follow:

**Key term**

**Ethical issues** – the moralistic rules governing the conduct of researchers in investigations.

1 *Informed consent* – participants should be fully informed of the objectives and details of research to make a considered decision about whether to participate. Parental consent needs to be obtained for under 16s. Informed consent cannot be gained from those under the influence of alcohol or drugs or mentally unfit to do so.

2 *Deception* – misleading of participants and withholding information should be avoided, especially if debriefing after a study has finished would leave participants distressed.

3 *Protection of participants* – participants should not be put at risk of harm and should leave a study in the same state they entered it.

4 *Right to withdraw* – participants should be aware that they can leave at any time, including withdrawing their data in the future.

5 *Confidentiality* – participants' data should not be disclosed to anyone or used for any purpose other than those agreed in advance.

6 *Anonymity* – participants should be referred to by numbers, not names, so that data cannot be traced back to them; this includes in the practical report. Confidentiality rather than anonymity is preferred in cases where participants might need to be followed up or checked on later.

7 *Inducements to take part* – participants should not be encouraged to participate through offers of financial gain or other forms of gratification that encourage or motivate them to take part against their better judgement.

8 *Observational research* – observations should only occur in environments where people would expect to be observed by strangers so that *violation of privacy* does not occur.

9 *Cost–benefit analysis* – only if the benefits of research, in terms of knowledge gained etc., outweigh the costs, in terms of possible harm to participants etc., should the research be undertaken. However, it could be argued that is biased against the welfare of the individual participant, as benefits are usually seen as superior through being perceived in terms of the usefulness of a study to society, while costs are perceived as being inferior in terms of harm to the individual.

If deception is unavoidable, there are measures that can be taken.

1  *Presumptive consent* – people of a similar nature are given full details of a study and asked if they would have been willing to participate. If so, it is presumed the real participants would not object.

2  *Prior general consent* – participants agree to be deceived, but without knowing how it will occur.

3  *Debriefing* – immediately a study finishes, participants should be given full details and the right to withdraw their data. This applies to all studies, not just those involving deception, and also helps to alleviate possible psychological harm, so that participants leave in the same state they entered.

---

### ■ STRENGTHEN YOUR LEARNING

1  Why should research be conducted in an ethical manner?

2  Explain what is meant by the following ethical issues:

   a  informed consent,

   b  deception,

   c  protection of participants,

   d  right to withdraw,

   e  confidentiality,

   f  anonymity,

   g  inducements to take part,

   h  observational research,

   i  cost–benefit analysis.

3  Explain what measures can be taken if deception is unavoidable in a study.

---

**Expert tip**

Students often get confused between the terms ethical issues/considerations and ethical implications. Ethical issues/considerations are the moral-based rules under which studies should be conducted, while ethical implications concern the consequences of conducting unethical studies.

# Reliability

Revised ☐

**Reliability** refers to the extent to which a test or measurement produces consistent results. To be reliable, if a study was repeated exactly, with the same method, design and procedure, then the same results should be obtained. Reliability can be improved by developing more consistent forms of measurement, using more clearly defined operational definitions and by improving inter-observer reliability (see 'Ways of assessing reliability').

## ■ Types of reliability

There are two main types of reliability:

1  **Internal reliability** concerns whether findings are consistent within themselves. For example, a measurement of height should measure the same distance between two metres and four metres, as between five metres and seven metres.

2  **External reliability** concerns whether findings are consistent over time. For example, an IQ test should produce the same level of intelligence for an individual on different occasions, as long as their level of intelligence remains the same.

## ■ Ways of assessing reliability

■  *The split-half method* – measures internal reliability by dividing a test in two and having the same participant do both halves. If the two halves of the test provide similar results, then the test is seen as having internal reliability.

■  *The test–retest method* – measures external reliability by giving the same test to the same participants on at least two occasions. If similar results are obtained, then external reliability is established.

■  *Inter-observer reliability* – measures whether different observers are viewing and rating behaviour similarly. This can be assessed by correlating the observers' scores, with a high correlation indicating they are observing and categorizing similarly. Inter-observer reliability can be improved by developing clearly defined and separate categories of behavioural criteria.

---

**Key terms**

**Reliability** – the extent to which a test or measurement produces consistent results.

**Internal reliability** – the extent to which results are consistent within themselves.

**External reliability** – the extent to which results are consistent over time.

## ■ The connection between reliability and validity

To be valid, results must first be reliable. However, results can be reliable without being valid. For example, if 1 + 1 was added up on several occasions and each time the answer given was 3, then the findings would be considered reliable (consistent), but not valid (accurate). However, if 1 + 1 is added up on several occasions and the answer given is always 2, then the results are considered to be both reliable and valid.

---

### ■ STRENGTHEN YOUR LEARNING

1  What is meant by reliability?
2  How can reliability be improved?
3  Outline the two main ways of improving reliability.
4  Outline ways of assessing reliability.
5  Explain the connection between reliability and validity.

---

**Expert tip**

Students often mistakenly think that reliable results are valid. This is not necessarily so; reliable results are consistent (the same repeatedly), but they could be consistently inaccurate and therefore not valid.

# Validity

**Revised** ☐

**Validity** concerns accuracy, the degree to which something measures what it claims to. Therefore, validity refers to how accurately a study measures what it claims to and the extent to which findings can be generalized beyond research settings as a consequence of a study's internal and external validity (see below). Validity can be improved by improving reliability and by improving internal and external validity.

Reliability and validity are important concepts in areas like the diagnosis of mental disorders (see 'Abnormal psychology', page 93). Reliability here concerns the extent to which clinicians diagnose a patient's abnormal condition consistently between different independent clinicians and over time by the same clinician. Validity here concerns the degree to which a patient's disorder has actually been diagnosed correctly.

## ■ Types of validity

There are two main types of validity:

1  **Internal validity** concerns whether findings are due to the manipulation of the IV or to the influence of confounding variables upon the DV. Internal validity can be improved by reducing investigator effects, minimizing demand characteristics and by use of standardized instructions and a random sample. The more a study is conducted under controlled conditions, the surer we can be that findings are due to the effect of the IV and not poor methodology.

2  **External validity** concerns the extent to which findings from a study have *ecological validity* (can be generalized to settings other than that under which the study was conducted), *population validity* (can be generalized to people other than those used in the study) and *temporal validity* (can be generalized over time). External validity is improved by carrying out studies in more naturalistic, real-world settings.

## ■ Ways of assessing validity

■ *Face validity* – involves 'eyeballing' items to assess the extent to which they look like what a test claims to measure.

■ *Concurrent validity* – assesses validity by correlating scores on a test with another test that is accepted as being valid.

■ *Predictive validity* – assesses validity by seeing how well a test predicts future behaviour, for instance, the extent to which school entrance tests accurately predict later exam results.

■ *Temporal validity* – evaluates to what extent research findings remain true over time.

---

**Key terms**

**Validity** – the extent to which results accurately measure what they are supposed to measure.

**Internal validity** – the extent to which results are due to the manipulation of the independent variable or to the influence of confounding variables upon the dependent variable.

**External validity** – the extent to which results can be generalized to other settings, other people and over time.

■ **STRENGTHEN YOUR LEARNING**

1 What is meant by validity?

2 Explain what is meant by reliability and validity when applied to mental disorders.

3 Explain what is meant by the following types of validity:

a internal validity,

b external validity,

including reference to ecological validity, population validity and temporal validity.

4 Outline ways of assessing validity.

**Expert tip**

Students often mistakenly believe that external and ecological validity are different types of validity. This is not so; ecological validity is merely a type of external validity (as are population validity and temporal validity).

# Data analysis

Revised ☐

## Quantitative and qualitative data

Revised ☐

**Quantitative data** is numerical, while **qualitative data** is non-numerical. Quantitative data tends to be objective, reliable and simple, while qualitative data tends to be subjective, less reliable and more detailed. Both forms of data can be combined to give deeper understanding.

Qualitative data gives insight into feelings and thoughts, but analysis can be affected by researcher bias. It can be converted into quantitative data through content and inductive content analysis.

Quantitative data is produced from experiments, observations, correlational studies and from structured interviews and closed questions in questionnaires. Qualitative data is produced from case studies and from unstructured interviews and open questions in questionnaires.

### ■ Meta-analysis

**Meta-analysis** involves combining findings from similar studies. This permits identification of trends and relationships not possible with individual studies. Meta-analyses are helpful when individual studies find contradictory or weak results, as they give a clearer, overall picture.

### ■ Content analysis

**Content analysis** (CA) is a method of turning qualitative data into quantitative data. Coding units are used to categorize the material being analysed, like the number of times positive words occur in a written description. Coding units can involve *words*, *themes*, *characters* and *time and space*.

### ■ Strengths

■ *Ease of application* – CA is easy to do, inexpensive and does not require interaction with participants.

■ *Complements other methods* – CA can be used to verify results using other research methods and is useful as a longitudinal tool to detect trends.

■ *Reliable* – CA is easy to replicate, meaning checking reliability is simple.

**Key terms**

**Quantitative data** – data that occurs in numerical form.

**Qualitative data** – data that occurs in non-numerical form.

**Meta-analysis** – a statistical technique of combining the findings of several similar studies to give a more typical overview.

**Content analysis** – a method of quantifying qualitative data through the use of coding units.

## ■ Weaknesses

- *Descriptive* – being purely descriptive, CA does not reveal underlying reasons for behaviour, attitudes, etc.

- *Flawed results* – as CA is limited to available material, observed trends may not reflect reality.

- *Lack of causality* – as CA is not performed under controlled conditions, it does not show causality.

## ■ Inductive content analysis

**Inductive content analysis** (ICA) identifies and analyses themes within qualitative data.

Identified themes become categories for analysis, with ICA performed by a six-stage process of coding:

1 *Familiarization with data* – inspecting data to become immersed in its content.

2 *Coding* – generating labels that identify features of the data important to answering the research question.

3 *Searching for themes* – labels and data are inspected to identify potential themes.

4 *Reviewing themes* – potential themes are checked against data to see if they explain it and fit the research aim. Themes are refined, which can involve splitting, combining or discarding them.

5 *Defining and naming themes* – each theme is analysed so that informative names can be given to them.

6 *Writing up* – information gained from the ICA is combined together.

## ■ Credibility

**Credibility** concerns the validity of qualitative findings. Triangulation and member-checking are used to assess credibility.

*Triangulation* involves multiple methods, sources of data, observers and theories to gain a full picture of research: *methods triangulation* uses different data collection methods to assess reliability of findings, *triangulation of sources* assesses different sources of data within the same research method, *analyst triangulation* uses other researchers to assess inter-rater reliability and *theoretical triangulation* assesses the 'fit' of findings to various theories.

*Member-checking* assesses the degree to which participants agree with conclusions drawn from data.

**Key terms**

**Inductive content (thematic) analysis** – a method of scrutinizing qualitative data that involves analysing text from a variety of media to identify patterns.

**Credibility** – the level of validity of qualitative data.

---

### ■ STRENGTHEN YOUR LEARNING

1 Explain the difference between quantitative and qualitative data.

2 Explain how qualitative data can be converted into quantitative data.

3 What type of research methods generate:
   a   quantitative data,
   b   qualitative data.

4 Explain what is meant by meta-analysis. What is the purpose of meta-analyses?

5 Explain what is meant by content analysis. How is a content analysis carried out (include reference to coding units in your answer)?

6 Explain strengths and weaknesses of content analyses.

7 What is inductive content analysis?

8 Outline the six-stage process of coding involved in ICA.

9 What is credibility?

10 Explain, including reference to member-checking and different types of triangulation, how credibility is assessed.

---

**Expert tip**

Students often confuse what is meant by credibility, triangulation and member-checking. Quite simply, triangulation and member-checking are ways of assessing credibility.

# Presentation of data

Revised

## ◼ Measures of central tendency

**Measures of central tendency** display the 'mid-point' values of sets of data.

The **mean** is calculated by totalling scores and dividing by the number of scores. For example:

$1 + 3 + 2 + 1 + 4 + 5 + 6 + 8 + 7 = 37 \div 9 = 4.1$

### ◼ Strengths of the mean

- The mean is the most accurate measure of central tendency as it uses all the scores in a set of data in its calculation.

### ◼ Weaknesses of the mean

- The mean can be skewed by extreme scores.

- The mean may not actually be one of the scores from a set of data.

The **median** is the central value of scores in rank order. For example:

For the set of scores 2, 3, 5, 7, 9, the median is 5.

With an odd number of scores, this is the middle number, while with an even number of scores it is the average of the two middle scores.

### ◼ Strengths of the median

- The median is not affected by extreme scores.

- The median is easier to calculate than the mean.

### ◼ Weaknesses of the median

- The median can be unrepresentative in a small set of data.

- The mean does not use all the scores and so is not as mathematically correct as the mean.

The **mode** is the most common value in a set of scores. For example:

For the set of scores 2, 7, 2, 5, 6, 7, 8, 7, the mode is 7.

### ◼ Strengths of the mode

- The mode is less affected by extreme scores than the mean.

- Unlike the mean, the mode is always a whole number.

### ◼ Weaknesses of the mode

- There can be more than one mode in a set of data.

- The mode does not use all the scores and so is not as mathematically correct as the mean.

## ◼ Measures of dispersion

**Measures of dispersion** are measures of variability in a set of data.

The **range** is calculated by subtracting the lowest from the highest value.

### ◼ Strengths of the range

- It is easy to calculate.

- It includes extreme values.

---

**Key terms**

**Measures of central tendency** – methods of estimating mid-point scores in a set of data.

**Mean** – the mid-point of the combined values of a set of data.

**Median** – the central score in a list of rank-ordered scores in a set of data.

---

**Key terms**

**Mode** – the most commonly occurring score in a set of data.

**Measures of dispersion** – measurements of the spread of scores within a set of data.

**The range** – the difference between the highest and lowest scores in a set of data.

## ■ Weaknesses of the range

- ■ It is distorted by extreme scores.
- ■ It does not indicate if data are clustered or spread evenly around the mean.

**Standard deviation** measures the variability (spread) of a set of scores from the mean.

## ■ Strengths of standard deviation

- ■ It is more sensitive than the range, as all values are included.
- ■ It allows the interpretation of individual values.

## ■ Weaknesses of standard deviation

- ■ It is more complex to calculate.
- ■ It is less meaningful if data are not normally distributed.

**Key term**
**Standard deviation** – a measure of the variability (spread) of a set of scores from the mean.

## ■ Tables

Raw data is not presented in tables; instead an appropriate summary of the data is shown, such as totals, means and ranges. Individual scores are not presented, as they are displayed in the raw data (given in the appendices). As with graphs, tables should be clearly labelled and titled.

Table showing male and female scores on a test of concentration

|  | Males | Females |
|---|---|---|
| *Total scores* | 160 | 132 |
| *Mean* | 8 | 6.6 |
| *Range* | 9 | 13 |
| *Number of participants* | 20 | 20 |

### ■ STRENGTHEN YOUR LEARNING

1 What are measures of central tendency?
2 How is the mean calculated?
3 Explain strengths and weaknesses of the mean.
4 How is the median calculated?
5 Explain strengths and weaknesses of the median.
6 How is the mode calculated?
7 Explain strengths and weaknesses of the mode.
8 What are measures of dispersion?
9 How is the range calculated?
10 Explain strengths and weaknesses of the range.
11 How is standard deviation calculated?
12 Explain strengths and weaknesses of standard deviation.

**Expert tip**
Students often get confused as to what the difference is between measures of central tendency and measures of dispersion. Quite simply, measures of central tendency concern averages, 'middle' numbers in a set of data, while measures of dispersion concern how widely distributed scores are in a set of data.

# Graphs

Revised

**Graphs** are a descriptive form of statistical analysis, where quantitative (numerical) data is displayed in a visual form, so that patterns, trends, etc. within results can be more easily perceived.

Graphs should be fully and clearly labelled on both the *x* and *y* axes and be appropriately titled, with presentation occurring best if the *y*-axis is three-quarters of the *x*-axis width. Only one graph should be used to display a set of

**Key term**
**Graphs** – easily understandable, pictorial representations of data.

data. Inappropriate scales should not be used, as these convey misleading, biased impressions. Different types of graphs exist for different forms of data.

**Bar charts** display data as separate, comparable categories – for example, findings from young and old participants. The columns of the bars should be the same width and separated by spaces to show that the variable on the *x*-axis (horizontal axis) is not continuous. Data is 'discrete', occurring, for example, as the mean scores of several groups. Percentages, totals and ratios can also be displayed.

> **Key term**
>
> **Bar charts** – pictorial display of data in the form of categories being compared.

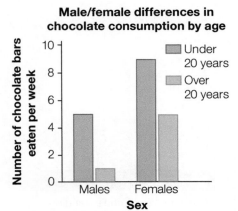

**Figure 8.1** An example of a bar chart displaying two values together

**Histograms** display continuous data, such as test scores, and these are displayed as they increase in value along the *x*-axis, without spaces between them to show their continuity. The frequency of the data is presented on the *y*-axis (vertical axis). The column width for each value on the *x*-axis is the same width per equal category interval so that the area of each column is proportional to the number of cases it represents on the histogram.

> **Key term**
>
> **Histograms** – pictorial display of continuous data.

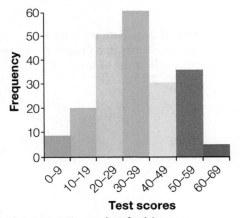

**Figure 8.2** Example of a histogram

**Frequency polygons** (line graphs) are similar to histograms in that the data presented on the *x*-axis is continuous. A frequency polygon is constructed by drawing a line from the mid-point top of each column in a histogram to allow two or more frequency distributions to be displayed on the same graph, thus allowing them to be directly compared with each other.

> **Key term**
>
> **Frequency polygons** – pictorial display of two or more sets of continuous data that allows comparison.

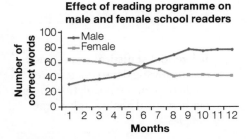

**Figure 8.3** Example of a frequency polygon

**Pie charts** are used to show the frequency of categories of data as percentages. The pie is split into sections, each one representing the frequency of a category. Each section is colour-coded, with an indication given as to what each section represents and its percentage score.

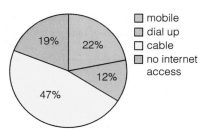

☐ mobile
☐ dial up
☐ cable
☐ no internet access

**Figure 8.4** Pie chart showing the different ways British people accessed the internet in 2010

> **Key term**
>
> **Pie charts** – pictorial display of the frequency of categories as percentages.

---

■ **STRENGTHEN YOUR LEARNING**

1  What is the purpose of a graph?
2  Explain the requirements of a graph.
3  Outline the following types of graph:
   a  bar charts,
   b  histograms,
   c  frequency polygons,
   d  pie charts.

---

> **Expert tip**
>
> A simple way of understanding graphs is to consider them as showing results from a study as a picture rather than as numbers in a table.

# Normal distribution

Revised ☐

**Normal distribution** occurs when data has an even amount of scores either side of the mean. For example, IQ scores (as a measure of intelligence) were assumed to be normally distributed, which means most people's IQ score would be on or around the mean of 100 IQ points, with decreasing amounts either side of the mean.

> **Key term**
>
> **Normal distribution** – data with an even distribution of scores either side of the mean.

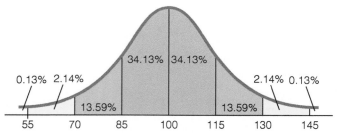

**Figure 8.5** Normal distribution of IQ scores

Normally distributed data is symmetrical – when it is plotted on a graph it forms a bell-shaped curve with as many scores below the mean as above.

There are several ways in which data can be checked to see if it is normally distributed:

■ *Examine visually* – inspect the data to see if scores are mainly around the mean.

■ *Calculate measure of central tendency* – work out the mean, median and mode to see if they are similar.

■ *Plot the frequency distribution* – put the data into a histogram to see if it forms a bell-shaped curve.

**Inferential statistical tests** require data to be from a normally distributed source in order for them to assess whether a significant difference has occurred.

> **Key term**
>
> **Inferential statistical tests** – ways of scrutinizing data, which makes predictions about populations from mathematical analysis taken from samples.

The statistical infrequency definition of abnormality (see page 87) uses normal distribution to define mental abnormality, with those falling outside normal distribution (two standard deviation points away from the mean) seen as abnormal.

## ■ Correlational data

**Key term**

**Correlational data** – data produced from correlational studies.

**Correlational data** (scores generated from correlational studies) is plotted on *scattergrams*, which show the degree to which two co-variables are related.

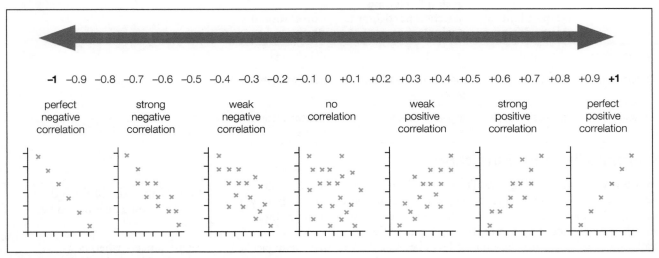

**Figure 8.6** Scattergrams and correlational strength

If a positive correlation is indicated, data will be plotted from the bottom left to top right of a scattergram, while if a negative correlation is indicated, data will be plotted from bottom right to top left of a scattergram. If no or very little correlation is indicated, data plotted will form no discernible pattern. Whether a correlation is *significant* (beyond the boundaries of chance) can be determined by subjecting the data to a *Spearman's rho* or *Pearson's product moment* statistical test (see page 241).

> ### ■ STRENGTHEN YOUR LEARNING
>
> 1  Explain what is meant by normal distribution.
> 2  Give another name for normal distribution.
> 3  Outline the ways in which data can be checked to see if it normally distributed.
> 4  How does the statistical infrequency definition of abnormality include the concept of normal distribution?
> 5  Explain how correlational data is plotted on a graph.
> 6  What statistical tests can be used to assess whether correlational data is significant or not?

**Expert tip**

A normal distribution curve is also sometimes referred to as a 'Gaussian curve', named after the mathematician Carl Gauss, who devised the concept.

# Statistical testing

Revised ☐

## Inferential testing

Revised ☐

Research produces data which is analysed by inferential statistical tests to see whether differences and relationships found between sets of data are significant (beyond the boundaries of chance) or not. Three criteria need to be considered when choosing an appropriate statistical test:

1  *What design has been used* – was an independent groups design, repeated measures design (including a matched pairs design) or a correlational design used?

**Key term**

**Inferential testing** – statistical procedures that make predictions about populations from mathematical analysis of data taken from samples.

2  *What type of outcome is being tested for* – is a difference or a relationship between two sets of data being sought?

3  *What level of measurement has been used* – was the data produced of nominal, ordinal or interval/ratio level?

## ◼ Choosing an appropriate statistical test

|  | Independent groups design | Repeated measures design (including matched participants design) | Correlational design |
|---|---|---|---|
| *Nominal data* | Chi-squared | Sign test | Chi-squared |
| *Ordinal data* | Mann-Whitney | Wilcoxon signed-matched ranks | Spearman's rho |
| *Interval/ratio* | Independent t-test | Repeated t-tests | Pearson product moment |

## ◼ Probability and significance

**Probability** involves deciding if results are significant, by producing a cut-off point that determines whether findings are beyond chance factors or not. Psychology uses a **significance** level of $p \leq 0.05$, giving a 95 per cent assurance of findings being beyond chance. This means that 5 per cent of the time that significant results are found (seemingly beyond the boundaries of chance), they are in fact not significant and are actually due to chance factors. This is seen as being an acceptable level of error. In some instances, like testing new drugs, a more stringent level is used where $p \leq 0.01$, entailing a 99 per cent certainty of findings being significant (this means there is only a 1 per cent chance of insignificant results that are actually explainable by chance factors being seen as significant and beyond the boundaries of chance).

## ◼ Types I and II errors

**Type I errors** occur when findings are accepted as significant, but are not, as the significance level was too low, while **Type II errors** occur when findings are accepted as insignificant, but are not, as the significance level was too high.

## ◼ Levels of data

◼ *Nominal data* – consists of frequencies, for example, how many days in a week were rainy or not. Nominal data is relatively uninformative, for instance, it would not tell us *how* rainy any particular day was.

◼ *Ordinal data* – involves putting data into rank order, for example, finishing places of runners in a race. This is not fully informative, as although we know who the better runners are, we do not know by how much they are better.

◼ *Interval/ratio data* – involves data with standardized measuring distances, such as time. This is the most informative type of data. *Interval data* has an arbitrary zero point, for instance, zero degrees temperature does not mean there is no temperature. *Ratio data* has an absolute zero point, for instance, someone with zero pounds in their bank account has no money.

## ◼ Interpretation of significance

Statistical analysis produces an *observed* value and this is compared to a *critical* value to see if it is significant or not. To do this, critical value tables need to be referenced, taking into account whether a hypothesis was one- or two-tailed, how many participants or participant pairs were used and what level of significance was used. The Mann-Whitney, Wilcoxon and sign tests require observed values to be equal to or less than a critical value to be significant. The Chi-squared, independent t-test, repeated t-test, Spearman's rho and Pearson product moment require an observed value to be equal to or greater than a critical value to be significant.

### Key terms

**Probability** – the likelihood of events being determined by chance.

**Significance** – whether a calculated result from a statistical test is beyond the boundaries of chance.

**Type I error** – when a difference/relationship found in a set of data is accepted as real (beyond the boundaries of chance) and is not.

**Type II error** – when a difference/relationship found in a set of data is rejected as real, but actually is beyond the boundaries of chance.

**Interpretation of significance** – comparison of observed values from statistical analysis to expected values in a critical value table to determine if a result is significant or not.

# Types of test

- *Sign test* – used when a difference is predicted between two sets of data, data is of at least nominal level and a RMD/MPD has been used.

- *Chi-squared* – used when a difference is predicted between two sets of data, data is of at least nominal level and an IGD has been used. Chi-squared can also be used as a test of *association* (relationship).

- *Mann-Whitney* – used when a difference is predicted between two sets of data, data is at least of ordinal level and an IGD has been used.

- *Wilcoxon signed-matched ranks* – used when a difference between two sets of data has been predicted, data is of at least ordinal level and a RMD/MPD has been used.

- *Independent (unrelated) t-test* – used when a difference is predicted between two sets of data, data is normally distributed and of interval/ratio level and an IGD has been used.

- *Repeated (related) t-test* – used when a difference is predicted between two sets of data, data is normally distributed and of interval/ratio level and a RMD/MPD has been used.

- *Spearman's rho* – used when a relationship (correlation) is predicted between two sets of data, data is of at least ordinal level and consists of pairs of scores from the same person or event.

- *Pearson product moment* – used when a relationship is predicted between two sets of data, data is normally distributed, of interval/ratio level and consists of pairs of scores from the same person or event.

---

## ■ STRENGTHEN YOUR LEARNING

1 Explain what is meant by inferential testing.
2 Outline the three criteria that need to be considered when selecting an appropriate statistical test.
3 Explain what is meant by:
   a probability,
   b significance.
4 Explain what is meant by:
   a Type I errors,
   b Type II errors.
5 Outline the following types of data:
   a nominal,
   b ordinal,
   c interval/ratio.
6 What is the difference between interval and ratio data?
7 Explain the purpose of interpretation of significance.
8 When using statistical tests, explain how significance is assessed.
9 Outline the different types of statistical tests used in psychological research.

---

### Expert tip

Students often mistakenly refer to statistical tests 'proving' a hypothesis to be true. This is not so. Due to the scientific concepts of probability and significance, we can say a result is probably true (beyond the boundaries of chance), but we can never say we have 100 per cent 'proof' that this is true. There is always, however small, a margin for doubt.

## EXAM-TYPE QUESTIONS

A researcher wanted to assess the effect of revision on students studying for the IB psychology examination. Twenty-four participants responded to a poster asking for people to take part. The participants were then assigned, without bias in selection, to two conditions. In the first condition, participants revised for two hours a day for the month before the exam, while in the second condition participants did no revision before sitting the exam. Participants were informed before the study started that they were under no obligation to take part and that they could leave at any time. No names were recorded; participants instead were referred to by number.

The researchers planned to publish their findings in a peer-reviewed journal.

The table below shows the number of marks out of 100 that each participant gained in the exam.

| Participant | Revision condition | Participant | No-revision condition |
|---|---|---|---|
| 1 | 75 | 7 | 52 |
| 2 | 52 | 8 | 67 |
| 3 | 92 | 9 | 32 |
| 4 | 78 | 10 | 52 |
| 5 | 66 | 11 | 32 |
| 6 | 78 | 12 | 52 |

The results were subjected to statistical testing and a significant difference was found.

1   a   Identify the research method used and outline two characteristics of the method. (3 marks)
    b   Describe the sampling method used in the study. (3 marks)
    c   Suggest an alternative or additional research method, giving one reason for your choice. (3 marks)
2   Describe the ethical considerations in reporting the results and explain additional ethical considerations that could be taken into account when applying the findings of the study. (6 marks)
3   Discuss the possibility of generalizing the results. (9 marks)

A team of researchers decided to assess the effect of anxiety on memory recall.

An opportunity sample of an equal number of male and female participants aged between 18 and 53 was recruited from a university common room and shown a tray containing 30 unrelated items for 30 seconds, after which time the tray was removed from sight.

Participants were placed in different states of anxiety, by being made to wear fake electrodes that they were told would give them electric shocks, ranging from 15 volts and going up in 15-volt increases to 150 volts for every item they failed to recall. One participant was told they would receive 15 volts, another 30 volts, another 45 volts and so on, up to a participant being told they would receive 150 volts. A total of ten participants were used.

Before the study began, participants were given full details of the study and signed an informed consent form. They were also given a debriefing afterwards to reduce the effect of their incurring any harm from taking part in the study.

It was found that, as the level of electric shock participants believed they would receive for failing to recall items went up, the number of items forgotten went down.

It was recommended that future research should take place to assess whether high levels of anxiety would produce a different effect on memory recall than very low anxiety.

4   a   Identify the research method used and outline two characteristics of the method. (3 marks)
    b   Describe the sampling method used in the study. (3 marks)
    c   Suggest an alternative or additional research method, giving one reason for your choice. (3 marks)
5   Describe the ethical considerations in reporting the results and explain additional ethical considerations that could be taken into account when applying the findings of the study. (6 marks)
6   Discuss the possibility of generalizing the results. (9 marks)

Researchers decided to conduct a study of a young girl, aged about seven years, who was found living with a troop of monkeys in an Ecuadorean forest. When discovered, she made noises like a monkey, but had no human language abilities. She preferred to walk on all fours and spent a lot of time climbing trees. She had an intense fear of humans and behaved very aggressively in their presence. She was fostered by a child-centred couple and gradually with lots of sensitive care came to trust people and develop human abilities. By the age of 21, she was normal in all respects, had an IQ of 110 and was studying to be a teacher at university.

Data was collected through interviews with her foster parents and interviews with the girl herself, when she developed language abilities, about her recall of her early life living with the monkeys.

Before the study began, informed consent was gained from her foster parents and care was taken to not identify the girl by name, referring to her instead in the findings by a fake name.

It was hoped that the results would be useful in devising strategies to help children overcome the negative effects of early life trauma so that they could develop normally.

7   a   Identify the research method used and outline two characteristics of the method.   (3 marks)

    b   Describe the sampling method used in the study.   (3 marks)

    c   Suggest an alternative or additional research method, giving one reason for your choice.   (3 marks)

8   Describe the ethical considerations in reporting the results and explain additional ethical considerations that could be taken into account when applying the findings of the study.   (6 marks)

9   Discuss the possibility of generalizing the results.   (9 marks)

# Answering exam questions

Paper 1, Section A consists of short-answer questions using AO1 and AO2 command terms.

| **Assessment objective 1 (AO1)** <br> **Knowledge and comprehension of specified content** | |
|---|---|
| These terms require students to demonstrate knowledge and understanding and learn and comprehend the meaning of information. | |
| Describe | Give a detailed account. |
| Identify | Provide an answer from a number of possibilities. |
| Outline | Give a brief account or summary. |

| **Assessment objective 2 (AO2)** <br> **Application and analysis of knowledge and understanding** | |
|---|---|
| These terms require students to use and analyse knowledge and understanding, explain actual situations, break down ideas into simpler parts and to see how the parts relate. | |
| Comment | Give a judgement based on a given statement or result of a calculation. |
| Explain | Give a detailed account, including reasons or causes. |
| Suggest | Propose a solution, hypothesis or other possible answer. |

Paper 1, Section B, and Paper 2 consist of answering essay questions. AO3 command terms are used in the essay questions.

| **Assessment objective 3 (AO3)** <br> **Synthesis and evaluation** | |
|---|---|
| These terms require students to make a judgement based on evidence and, when relevant, construct an argument or rearrange component ideas into a new whole and make judgements based on evidence or a set of criteria. | |
| Contrast | Give an account of the differences between two (or more) items or situations, referring to both (all) of them throughout. |
| Discuss | Offer a considered and balanced review that includes a range of arguments, factors or hypotheses. Opinions or conclusions should be presented clearly and supported by appropriate evidence. |
| Evaluate | Make an appraisal by weighing up the strengths and limitations. |
| To what extent | Consider the merits or otherwise of an argument or concept. Opinions and conclusions should be presented clearly and supported with appropriate evidence and sound argument. |

## Short-answer questions

Short-answer questions tend to be worth 9 marks, focus on one particular aspect of a topic and can require either *descriptive* or *evaluative* content. Such questions should take about 20 minutes to answer.

### ■ Example one

*Outline one study investigating neuroplasticity.*                    *(9 marks)*

## ■ Sample answer

One study investigating neuroplasticity was Danelli *et al.*'s (2013) case study of neurolinguistic architecture. The aim of this study was to document information concerning a boy, EB, with only one functioning brain hemisphere. Aged two, the boy had his left hemisphere removed to get rid of a tumour, which resulted in loss of language abilities (the language centre of the brain is found in the left hemisphere of 95 per cent of right-handed people, which EB was). From age two, EB underwent an intensive rehabilitation programme, though it wasn't until age five that improvements in his condition began to be seen, with complete recovery apparent at age eight. Tested at age 17 by comparing his language abilities to control participants of a similar age who hadn't suffered the loss of their left hemispheres, it seemed that EB's right hemisphere had compensated for the loss of his left hemisphere. Brain scans revealed little difference in processing of language between EB and the controls. EB did have minor issues with grammar processing and speed of oral response when naming objects, but in his early 20s further testing revealed that these issues had lessened. The study therefore seems to indicate that hemispheric lateralization can be compensated for by the other hemisphere, even if that hemisphere isn't usually used for certain functions.

### Guidance

The command term 'outline' means to briefly describe. This could be achieved by detailing the aims, procedure, findings and conclusions of a relevant study. It should be noted that there are no marks available for evaluation of the chosen study, so inclusion of strengths and weaknesses of the study would not gain credit.

## ■ Examiner comment

A relevant study has been selected and coherently outlined in terms of the type of method used, the aim of the study and an in-depth, accurate description of the procedure. The conclusions are expressed in terms of the results and are directed at neuroplasticity, which was the main requirement of the question.      9/9 marks

## ■ Example two

*Outline one or more techniques used to study the brain in relation to behaviour. (9 marks)*

## ■ Sample answer

Perhaps the earliest technique to study the brain in relation to behaviour would be the use of post-mortems, where the brains of dead people were inspected to assess function. For instance, Paul Broca (1861) dissected the brain of LeBorgne after his death to find a brain area associated with producing speech. More modern methods of study, such as brain scanning, are less invasive and can be used on live brains. MRI and the more dynamic fMRI generate a radioactive field over the brain to which hydrogen atoms then move in line to the field. This results in high-resolution images of the brain. fMRI scans additionally use information derived from the oxygenation of blood to produce moving pictures of activity. MRI scans only produce static images.

CAT scans are another method of providing still pictures of the brain, but through the use of X-rays. Participants are placed in a cylinder, which X-rays pass along, with photos taken as the cylinder rotates around the head. Merging these pictures allows the formation of a three-dimensional picture of the brain.

There are also PET scans, which like fMRI scans produce dynamic images of the brain. Radioactive glucose is introduced into the bloodstream and shows up in brain areas that are more active during different behavioural and cognitive tasks to help establish which specific brain areas are associated with specific functions.

### Guidance

The command term here again is 'outline', which means a brief description of techniques used to study the brain is required. It should be noted that if candidates choose to outline just one technique (which is allowed by the wording of the question) then more detail would be expected than if more than one technique was outlined (which is again allowed by the wording of the question). The greater the number of techniques outlined, the less detail would be required for each.

## ■ Examiner comment

A range of techniques are outlined here, each with a sufficient level of detail and accuracy to merit the awarding of full marks. Classifying scanning techniques into those that produce still and dynamic images especially shows good understanding of the techniques.      9/9 marks

## ■ Example three

*With reference to a study investigating neurotransmitters and their effects on behaviour, explain one strength and one limitation of a research method used in the study.* *(9 marks)*

## ■ Sample answer

Kirkpatrick *et al.* (2014) performed a study on the effects of MDMA and oxytocin on social and emotional processing.

A strength of the research method used, a laboratory experiment that incorporated an independent groups design, was that controlled conditions were used, allowing the establishment of causality (cause and effect relationships). The experimental conditions were kept the same for both testing groups, except for the expression of the independent variable, which was manipulated by the researcher. This was whether participants were given MDMA, nasal oxytocin or a placebo containing no MDMA or oxytocin. The difference in the measurement of the dependent variable, where participants given MDMA experienced feelings of euphoria and those receiving oxytocin experienced heightened sociability, while those given a placebo did not, can therefore be only attributable to the administration of MDMA and oxytocin. The control of conditions means that extraneous variables (variables other than the IV that could affect the DV) did not become confounding variables that affected the measurement of the DV, and thus did not make the findings invalid.

A limitation of the research method is that researcher bias may have occurred, invalidating the findings. Although participants did not know which condition they were in and so could not experience demand characteristics where they falsely experienced the feelings they felt they ought to, the researchers did know who had taken MDMA, oxytocin or a placebo. This means they could have interpreted participants' behaviour and answers in a biased way that matched their hypothesis that participants would be affected in certain ways by MDMA and oxytocin, but not by the placebo.

> ### Guidance
>
> The command term here is 'explain', which means to show an understanding of, in this case a relevant strength and weakness of a research method used in a relevant study. As the marks are awarded here purely for evaluation (in terms of the strength and weakness selected), no description of the study in terms of aim, procedure, results and conclusion would be required. To gain access to all the marks available would require a relevant strength and weakness to be identified and detailed sufficiently to show a deep understanding of why they are a strength and weakness.

## ■ Examiner comment

The candidate details both a strength and a limitation of a relevant research study and so gains access to all the available marks. Both the strength and limitation are accurate, coherently explained, with a depth of detail that displays good understanding of the points being made. **9/9 marks**

# Essay questions

Essay questions tend to be worth 22 marks and require both descriptive and evaluative content. Essay questions are marked by reference to three criteria:

1  Knowledge and understanding – *9 marks*
   - Relevant theories/explanations/models, etc. are apparent.
   - Accurate level of detail is apparent.
   - Insight and understanding are shown.
   - Appropriate psychological terminology is provided.

2  Critical thinking (application, analysis, synthesis, evaluation) – *9 marks*
   - Relevant evidence of critical thinking is provided.
   - Research evidence is used to provide evaluation.
   - Analysis in the forms of conclusions is generated.
   - Relevant issues and debates are explored.
   - Inclusion of practical applications and implications.
   - Discussion of ethical and/or methodological considerations.

3  Organization – *4 marks*
   - The requirements of the question are addressed.
   - Sequencing of ideas is logical.
   - Structure and organization are apparent.

Such questions should take about one hour in total to answer, with equal amounts of time (30 minutes each) dedicated to construction of descriptive and evaluative content.

## ■ Example

*Discuss biological explanations for anorexia nervosa.* (22 marks)

## ■ Answer construction

Probably the best way to construct an answer would be to first outline one biological explanation, such as the genetic explanation, and then to evaluate it and then repeat the process for one or more biological explanations. The outline could be constructed by describing how two or more biological explanations view the development of anorexia, such as the genetic explanation seeing the disorder as having an inherited component, neural explanations seeing the disorder as resulting from abnormally functioning brain mechanisms and the evolutionary explanation perceiving anorexia as having an adaptive survival value. Marks awarded would depend upon the accuracy, relevance and clarity of the descriptions and the degree of elaboration (detail) – for example, by detailing specific genes and brain areas associated with the disorder, such as the insula brain area, or by detailing specific evolutionary explanations, like the reproduction suppression hypothesis and the adaptive response to famine explanation.

The evaluation would probably centre on the degree of research support for the explanations. Bulik *et al.*'s (2006) Swedish twin study would be useful for evaluating the genetic explanation, as would Kortegaard *et al.*'s (2001) Danish twin study and Hakonarson *et al.*'s (2010) DNA study. For the neural explanation, Oberndorfer *et al.*'s (2013) fMRI scan study of brain areas associated with anorexia would be useful, as would Mayo-Smith *et al.*'s (1989) study of leptin levels in females and Nunn *et al.*'s (2012) study of the association between noradrenaline and anorexia. For evolutionary explanations, relevant research studies could include Frisch & Barbieri's (2002) study of body weight and menstruation, Ellison's (2003) study of disruption to energy levels and female reproductive ability, Arcelus *et al.*'s (2011) study that relates mortality rates due to anorexia to the adaptive value of the condition, as well as Rakison's (2002) study of the association between eating habits and attitudes towards sexual attention.

Additional evaluation could be formed from critical analysis of the model in general terms, such as abnormal biochemistry being possibly an effect rather than a cause of the disorder. Evaluation based on practical applications could focus on the degree of effectiveness of biological treatments, such as drug therapies.

Evaluative material focused on methodological and ethical criticisms, such as the problems of generalizing from female samples to male sufferers, would be most relevant if focused on the validity of the explanation being discussed.

Remember that the most effective evaluation is created from a number of evaluative points being woven together to form a sophisticated commentary, rather than being a series of unconnected evaluative points.

### Guidance

The command term 'discuss' means to both outline and evaluate – in this particular instance, explanations for anorexia. The wording of the question requires that at least two explanations are given; if more than two explanations are given, less detail would be expected. Explanations must be biological, although psychological explanations could be used as a form of comparison that illustrates strengths and weaknesses of biological explanations. Criterion A marks will be awarded for the relevance, accuracy and level of detail for the explanations provided. Criterion B marks could be gained by reference to the level of research support for the explanations provided, practical applications and implications of the explanations, comparison of explanations to highlight individual strengths and weaknesses, as well as discussion of relevant issues and debates and ethical and methodological considerations.